SECURITY IN DISTRIBUTED COMPUTING

Did You Lock the Door?

HEWLETT-PACKARD PROFESSIONAL BOOKS

Atchinson	Object-Oriented Test & Measurement Software Development in C++
Bruce, Dempsey	Security in Distributed Computing: Did You Lock the Door?
Blinn	Portable Shell Programming: An Extensive Collection of Bourne Shell Examples
Bloomers	Practical Planning for Network Growth
Caruso	Power Programming in HP Open View: Developing CMIS Applications
Cook	Building Enterprise Information Architectures
Costa	Planning and Designing High Speed Networks Using 100VG-AnyLAN, Second Edition
Crane	A Simplified Approach to Image Processing: Classical and Modern Techniques
Fernandez	Configuring the Common Desktop Environment
Fristrup	USENET: Netnews for Everyone
Fristrup	The Essential Web Surfer Survival Guide
Grady	Practical Software Metrics for Project Management and Process Improvement
Grosvenor, Ichiro, O'Brien	Mainframe Downsizing to Upsize Your Business: IT-Preneuring
Gunn	A Guide to NetWare$_®$ for UNIX$^®$
Helsel	Graphical Programming: A Tutorial for HP Vee
Helsel	Visual Programming with HP-VEE
Holman, Lund	Instant JavaScript
Kane	PA-RISC 2.0 Architecture
Knouse	Practical DCE Programming
Lee	The ISDN Consultant: A Stress-Free Guide to High Speed Communications
Lewis	The Art & Science of Smalltalk
Lund	Integrating UNIX$^®$ and PC Network Operating Systems
Madell	Disk and File Management Tasks on HP-UX
Madell, Parsons, Abegg	Developing and Localizing International Software
Malan, Letsinger, Coleman	Object-Oriented Development at Work: Fusion in the Real World
McFarland	X Windows on the World: Developing Internationalized Software with X, Motif$^®$, and CDE
McMinds/Whitty	Writing Your Own OSF/Motif Widgets
Phaal	LAN Traffic Management
Poniatowski	The HP-UX System Administrator's "How To" Book
Poniatowski	HP-UX 10.x System Administration "How To" Book
Poniatowski	Learning the HP-UX Operating System
Ryan	Distributed Object Technology: Concepts and Applications
Thomas	Cable Television Proof-of-Performance: A Practical Guide to Cable TV Compliance Measurements Using a Spectrum Analyzer
Weygant	Clusters for High Availability: A Primer of HP-UX Solutions
Witte	Electronic Test Instruments
Yawn, Stachnick, Sellars	The Legacy Continues: Using the HP 3000 with HP-UX and Windows NT

SECURITY IN DISTRIBUTED COMPUTING

Did You Lock the Door?

Glen Bruce

Rob Dempsey

To join a Prentice Hall PTR
internet mailing list, point to
http://www.prenhall.com/register

Prentice Hall PTR
Saddle River, NJ 07458
http://www.prenhall.com

Library of Congress Cataloging-in-Publication Data

Dempsey, Rob.
    Security in distributed computing: did you lock the door? / Rob
Dempsey, Glen Bruce
        p. cm.
    Includes bibliographical references and index.
    ISBN 0-13-182908-4
    1. Computer security. 2. Electronic data processing—Distributed
processing—Security measures. I. Bruce, Glen. II. Title.
QA76.9.A25D454 1997
005.8—dc20

                                                                96-33404
                                                                    CIP

Production Editor: *Kerry Reardon*
Acquisitions Editor: *Karen Gettman*
Cover Designer: *Design Source*
Cover Design Director: *Jerry Votta*
Manufacturing Manager: *Alexis R. Heydt*
Manager Hewlett-Packard Press: *Patricia Pekary*

 ©1997 Hewlett-Packard Company
Published by Prentice Hall PTR
Prentice-Hall, Inc.
A Simon & Schuster Company
Upper Saddle River, New Jersey 07458

The publisher offers discounts on this book when ordered in bulk quantities.
For more information contact:

Corporate Sales Department
Pentice Hall PTR
One Lake Street
Upper Saddle River, N.J. 07458
Phone: 800-382-3419
FAX: 201-236-7141
E-mail: corpsales@prenhall.com

Printed in the United States of America

10   9   8   7   6   5   4   3   2   1

ISBN 0-13-182908-4

Prentice-Hall International (UK) Limited, *London*
Prentice-Hall of Australia Pty. Limited, *Sydney*
Prentice-Hall Canada Inc., *Toronto*
Prentice-Hall Hispanoamericana, S.A., *Mexico*
Prentice-Hall of India Private Limited, *New Delhi*
Prentice-Hall of Japan, *Tokyo*
Simon & Schuster Asia Pte. Ltd., *Singapore*
Editora Prentice-Hall do Brasil, Ltda., *Rio de Janeiro*

CONTENTS

FOREWORD   xi

PREFACE   xiii

ACKNOWLEDGEMENTS   xix

INTRODUCTION   xxiii

PART I UNDERSTANDING THE PROBLEM   1

CHAPTER 1 COMPUTING SECURITY— A BUSINESS ISSUE   3

Business Drivers   10
Business Issues   14
Summary   16

CHAPTER 2 DISTRIBUTED SECURITY CHALLENGES   19

Stories   20
Security Issues   22
The Top Ten List   27
Conclusions   29

PART II FOUNDATIONS   31

CHAPTER 3 COMPUTING SECURITY BASICS   33

What is Security?   34
Trust—What Is It?   40
Trust—Why Do We Need IT?   43
Summary   44

CHAPTER 4 SECURITY ARCHITECTURE   45

Foundation   48
Trust   50
Control   54
Summary   57

CHAPTER 5 FOUNDATIONS   59

Principles   60
Security Policy Framework   62
Security Criteria   64
Summary   70

CHAPTER 6 SECURITY POLICY   71

Security Policy Framework   73
Example of a Policy   84
The Process of Creating Policies   86
Summary   89

PART III TECHNOLOGIES   91

CHAPTER 7 THE NETWORK   93

A Tale of Two Networks   94
Systems Network Architecture   96
Introducing TCP/IP   102
SNA versus TCP/IP Security   114
Conclusions   114

CHAPTER 8 NETWORK OPERATING SYSTEMS   117

About Network Operating Systems?   118
Issues Surrounding NOS Implementations   123
Conclusions   127

CHAPTER 9 CLIENT/SERVER AND MIDDLEWARE   **129**

Client/Server   131
Middleware   134
Enabling Technology   137
Distributed Objects   139
Things to Watch Out For   142
Summary   143

CHAPTER 10 UNIX SECURITY   **145**

Why has UNIX Such a Bad Reputation for Security?   146
UNIX Security   147
Typical Abuses   158
Conclusions   165

CHAPTER 11 MORE UNIX SECURITY   **167**

UNIX Network Services   169
A Burglar's Tools   184
Conclusions   186

CHAPTER 12 UNIX SOLUTIONS   **187**

Control Monitors   197
Conclusions   202

CHAPTER 13 WINDOWS NT SECURITY   **205**

Security Controls   210
Networking   216
Conclusions   218

CHAPTER 14 THE INTERNET   **219**

What is the Internet?   220
Internet Firewall   230
Conclusions   238

CHAPTER 15 CRYPTOGRAPHY   **239**

Private Key Encryption   241
Public Key Encryption   244
Encryption Issues   247
Digital Signature   251
Summary   253

CHAPTER 16 THE DCE ENVIRONMENT 255

What is DCE? 256
Concerns about DCE 264
Conclusions 264

CHAPTER 17 DCE SECURITY CONCEPTS 265

DCE Authentication 266
Authorization 274
Is DCE Bulletproof? 277
Conclusions 278

CHAPTER 18 DISTRIBUTED DATABASE 279

What is a RDBMS? 280
Different Models to Enable Applications 281
Issues Surrounding RDBMS 289
What is a Data Warehouse? 292
Conclusions 293

CHAPTER 19 ON-LINE TRANSACTION PROCESSING 295

What Is a Transaction? 296
Components of a Transaction Processing System 299
The Top Five List 311
Summary 312

PART IV SOLVING THE PROBLEM 315

CHAPTER 20 SECURE APPLICATIONS 317

Concepts 318
System Development Life Cycle 318
Summary 327

CHAPTER 21 IMPLEMENTATION EXAMPLES 329

Electronic Mail 330
Lotus Notes 338
What's Next 341
Summary 342

CHAPTER 22 SECURITY MANAGEMENT 343

System Management 345

Network Management 350
Conclusions 359

CHAPTER 23 DEVELOPING A SECURITY STRATEGY 361

A Security Strategy 362
The Security Strategy Roadmap 366
Conclusions 374

CHAPTER 24 AUDITING 375

What Is an Audit? 376
What Role Should Audit Play? 380
Sample Criteria for a UNIX Audit 382
The Basics of Computer Auditing 383
Expanding the Focus 384
Other Types of Audits 386
Conclusions 392

CHAPTER 25 THE FUTURE 393

APPENDIX A STRONG AUTHENTICATION 401

APPENDIX B SMART CARDS 407

APPENDIX C PERSONAL COMPUTER SECURITY 413

Viruses 414
Personal Computer Access Controls 415
How Far Should Security Be Extended? 416
Conclusions 417

APPENDIX D REMOTE ACCESS 419

GLOSSARY 423

REFERENCES 437

INDEX 443

FOREWORD

"You never fully appreciate something until it is gone." How many times have you either thought this or, even worse, been reminded by someone also of this simple fact of human nature? Unfortunately this expression usually only comes to mind after you have lost or had something stolen, that you now realize was treasured.

Imagine this. You have, at last, taken the plunge and have started your own business. you have been extremely successful in selling imported travel gadgets to an extremely loyal but small customer base. The hard work is just beginning to pay off, when you are taken by surprise by an extremely puzzling phone call you receive from your largest customer. H is calling to cancel all his existing orders. He is furious with the letter he has just received from your office, confirming that his orders are backlogged and so will not be delivered in time for the Christmas season. You try to explaining\ that this is not true and that you never sent such a letter but the damage is done. You rapidly check your computer system and find your customer information and order files have been deleted. The phone rings again. Different customer, same letter. In a matter of minutes, the trust that you have so carefully built up with your customers has evaporated. Your business livelihood is threatened. This story could be an example of an employee's mistake or business espionage. The result is the same; business and personal chaos.

Technology today offers us tremendously exciting opportunities. Like never before, we demand that both personal and business information is immediately accessible and available. Only when we realize we are dependent upon this information do we value it and it's security becomes important.

This book opens the door on computer security. Glen Bruce and Rob Dempsey have done an excellent job of educating the reader on the business and technology issues posed by our increasing need for information security. They also have provided pragmatic and in-depth recommendations on how to design and implement a security strategy. This is compelling reading for I.T. and business professionals who are facing the challenge of using information technology in a safe and simple way to conduct their business.

Reading this book does not guarantee a fail safe security implementation, but it will give you a foundation from which to move our own specific strategy forward. Of course, you can still choose to do nothing at all... but can you take the risk?

Glenn Osaka
General Manager, Professional Services Organization
Hewlett-Packard Corporation

PREFACE

The problem of safeguarding corporate computing from misuse is a perplexing one for many organizations. From the smallest personal business to the world's largest financial corporations, organizations have experienced assaults or security problems with their computing systems.

Computer security incidents, which have been widely reported by the press, have increased the general public's awareness of the existance of the problem. Management appreciation of the problem, and their commitment to address it, has never been higher. New commercial security solutions, offspring from the advanced technologies used in the defense industry, are available in the marketplace. Corporate expenditures on these technologies have been rapidly rising.

Most organizations have recognized that the problem exists, and have taken active measures to address it. But incidents and attacks continue to be reported, almost on a daily basis. Unfortunately, there is a strong feeling in the computing community that the problem is going to get a lot worse. Why, then, isn't the problem of computing security being solved?

The answer lies in the fact that computing security is a business problem with many complex aspects. It cannot be solved by technical solutions alone. In fact, uncoordinated expenditures on diverse technical solutions actually contribute to the problem. The purpose of this book is to make the reader aware of all aspects of the problem. It will guide you through the issues and the somewhat confusing array of potential solutions.

When you stop and think about it, there are a number of analogies one can draw between computer and home security. We lock our doors at home as a basic preventive measure. This action by itself does not make a break-in to our home impossible, but it certainly makes it more difficult. As with home security, locking the doors to computing assets is simply common sense.

There also needs to be balance in our approach to security. There is no point in spending money on a superb lock on the front door if the back door doesn't have a lock—neither does it make much sense to only lock one door!

Balance is likewise required in expenditures on security solutions. No one would spend $100,000 on home security to protect $5,000 worth of contents. This is especially true if the neighborhood hasn't experienced a break-in in the past five years. The cost of security must be appropriate to the expected loss and associated risk.

It is also common sense that we should focus on the most likely security exposures. Thieves do not usually carry ladders. Money should therefore be first spent on barring the lower level windows.

Unfortunately, you cannot simply buy total security. The best technology will be of little use if people are unaware of their responsibilities. If your children leave the door unlocked when you are away, whether or not you've used the strongest lock in the world is immaterial. Security cannot be viewed in isolation from the environment. The safety of our homes is directly related to the security of our neighborhoods. You cannot fully address one without addressing the other.

The movement to distributed, client-server technologies has dramatically changed the computing environment of many organizations. The complex systems that are present in mainframe environments have assured trust in their operation. Mainframe security solutions, such as those available from IBM and Computer Associates, have allowed strong, centralized controls to be enforced. The security of a distributed, client-server world, however, is much more complex. Unlike the mainframe, the controls and security functions are distributed across several platforms and are not usually under the control of any single processor. The challenge is to ensure that distributed controls are all working together for a common goal.

We will identify and explain the key issues in computer security today. These are issues that must be addressed if the overall business problem of computing security is to be solved. The key issues in computing security include the need to securely authenticate users and to authorize their actions. Networking has allowed the global computing community to communicate and interact as never before, but it has also exposed corporate networks and computing systems to access by outsiders. Employing technology in an effective manner to address computing security is another key issue.

Explaining the technology involved in computing security is a key focus of this book. The ins and outs of various security technologies will be explained. Our intent is not simply to discuss technology, but to provide an understanding of how technology can be used to solve key security issues.

One example of a key issue is how to trust the integrity of an authentication process when it is communicated over a network. Most network traffic, including the user identification and authentication password, is currently transmitted in clear text. By monitoring network traffic, it is possible to discover passwords and use them to compromise security.

The Kerberos model of trusted-third party authentication can be utilized to address the problem of maintaining the integrity of the authentication process. Named after Cerberus, the mythical three-headed dog that guarded that gates of Hades, the Kerberos model provides a method for authentication within heterogeneous technologies. It presupposes that the network is untrusted, and that any traffic sent over the network may be intercepted. Kerberos has been designed to counter this threat. We will examine this authentication model through its implementation in the Distributed Computing Environment (DCE) of the Open Software Foundation (OSF). Armed with an understanding of its strengths and weaknesses, the reader will be able to judge how effectively OSF/DCE solves distributed computing security problems.

On-line transaction processing (OLTP) has traditionally been delivered from large mainframe-based systems or specialized transaction processing systems. The "Big Iron" was needed to supply the networking capabilities, the central control with the raw horsepower required to push through transactions and maintain control over the shared database. The OLTP system processes transactions to collect or review the information of the business systems and post changes to the shared databases of the organization. The migration of these transactions to distributed servers and the desktop has made the provision of security, with the same protection and utility as the host-centric OLTP systems, difficult.. The challenges of system management and security must also be addressed for the promise of effective distributed OLTP systems to be realized.

There are two driving requirements to provide transaction processing systems on "open system" platforms. The first requirement is to provide a robust transaction processing environment on the nonmainframe platform while maintaining the same function and capabilities as the mainframe. The second is to provide a distributed processing capability to allow transactions to execute functions and access data across more than one operating platform. The Encina technology from Transarc was developed to address the transaction processing environment on a UNIX platform. The IBM transaction monitor, CICS, has been ported to the UNIX environment by both IBM and Hewlett-Packard. These transaction monitors, when coupled with the DCE components of OSF and enabled with Encina, provide distributed transaction processing capabilities. The implementation of these technologies to provide a trusted transaction environment, through DCE, will be explored.

We will also study the centralized management of the controls on distributed systems. Using advanced network and system management technologies, confirmation can be obtained that security controls have been established and remain in place. Network alerts may also be used to provide early indications of illicit activity. We will examine the use of dynamic alert techniques and provide suggestions for implementing various detection mechanisms.

The problem of computing security cannot be addressed by technology alone. We will spend a good deal of time discussing the people and organizational aspects. This will include a comprehensive review of the formulation of computing security policy, the areas it should cover, and how best to communicate the policy to users. The security policy outlines the decisions of the organization on security and provides the foundation upon which a security program can be based. Commitment by management to security awareness programs is required to realize the benefits of these important activities.

An architecture is a structured way of describing the functionality of the various components. It presents the relationship of complex components in a manner that makes it easy to understand. Computing security can also benefit from an architecture as a way to describe the components and how they interrelate. A security architecture includes elements which attempt to guarantee the confidentiality of information and ensure that all access to the computing resources is authorized and authenticated. The overall objective of the architecture is to allow trust to be placed in the distributed environment. We need to be able to trust all of the points, or have compensating controls, where users access the various systems rather than have the trust placed only where the information and tools are resident. The security architecture is comprised of a number of building blocks which together define the framework for a comprehensive solution. We will review an approach to a security architecture and outline how it can be used as a basis for the enterprise security solution.

Another nontechnical area that will be explored is the role of audit. An explanation of the purpose of a computing audit, why it is important, and how to best prepare for an audit review is covered. The interrelationship of the Audit Department with other corporate departments is examined, and suggestions are provided to make this relationship more effective.

One of the most important areas when dealing with the problem of computing security is the use of a structured methodology. A security strategy is a series of specific steps that an organization can take to raise the existing level of security within the organization from a base level to a more secure one. The strategy methodology will take an organization through an organized process of assessing where they are currently positioned with their computing environment, defining where they want to be, and planning the steps required to get them there. Using a defined methodology ensures that all the windows and doors have been locked. That planned new addition to the house will also include secure doors and windows while it is being built. The methodology has been successfully used to address the problem in a number of diverse organizations.

This book is for anyone interested in the area of computing security. System administrators and analysts will be able to understand how core technologies such as Kerberos and public and private key encryption work. Application developers and architects will benefit by understanding how the security components fit together and should be integrated into the system design. Security must be designed in and not added on.

For those given the responsibility for security management or audit of distributed computing applications, this book will provide insight into the core security issues in client-server computing. Senior managers, concerned with the safety of computing security, will be guided through a methodology to address the problem.

Computing security is a business issue as well as a technical one. It is a complex problem which will require a number of issues to be addressed. Sophisticated technologies are available to address various security problems; however, they must be used in a planned and coordinated manner to be effective. The development of a security strategy and architecture is required. This book will make you more aware of both the problems of computing security and their potential solutions. Hopefully, you will be able to avoid that "I wish I'd remembered to lock the door!" feeling before travelling too far on the road to distributed, client-server computing.

ACKNOWLEDGMENTS

Writing a book is lot like polishing a stone using simple tools. It's very time consuming and it takes an awful lot of polishing before the beauty of the stone can be seen. We were very fortunate in the creation of this work in that we had so many friends, relatives, and colleagues who helped, from the very beginning, in polishing this very rough stone.

First of all, we would like to thank our family members, who provided both support and objective criticism. To John Beveridge, Erika Dempsey, Peter (PaPete) Dempsey, Don Duffey, Gerald Duffey, Charlotte Holmlund— our thanks for so many long hours.

Many of our colleagues at Hewlett-Packard, and elsewhere, spent their precious free hours in helping us. To Debbie Caswell, Murray Clark, Investigator R.W. Davis of the Royal Canadian Mounted Police, Mike Devall, Sue Farmer, Ron Freund, Anne Hopkins, Rose Janjicek, Mike Jerbic, Ray Langdeau, Cricket Liu, Paul Lloyd, Ron McOuat, Justin Murray, Chuck Nyle, Jim Schindler, Bruce Spence, Jay Terrill, Ron Williams and Susan Zuk—we say a heartfelt thank you.

Many thanks also to Lonny Frydenlund and Dave Harris from IBM for their comments and information.

A special thanks is given to Murray Clark and Ken Rausch, who supported this activity from the very beginning.

FROM GLEN:

I would like to thank my sister, Donna Barclay, for her support and helpful comments. I would also like to thank my coauthor, Rob Dempsey, who originally proposed the idea to write this book during the last time a Canadian team won the World Series. Although we sometimes traveled on different paths, the collaboration and synergy have been a terrific experience.

FROM ROB:

I owe a special thanks to my girls—Charlotte, Erika, and Laura—for your patience and understanding the past two years. I'll start on the basement right away! I would also like to thank my good friend and coauthor, Glen Bruce, for his guidance, patience and understanding on this very difficult project. Been a pleasure!

The authors have endeavored to identify all trademarks of which they are aware by printing them in caps or initial caps.

CMDS is a trademark of the Science Applications International Corporation.

Encina is a trademark of the Transarc Corporation.

Ethernet is a registered trademark of the Xerox Corporation.

HP-UX is a registered trademark of the Hewlett-Packard Corporation.

Kerberos is a trademark of the Massachusetts Institute of Technology

LAN Manager, MS, WIN32, MS-DOS, Windows, and Windows NT are registered trademarks of Mircosoft Corp.

Netware is a registered trademark of the Novell, Inc.

Notes is a trademark of the Lotus Development Corporation.

AIX, CICS, MVS, OS/2, and SNA are trademarks of International Business Machines Corporation.

SAIC is a trademark of the Science Applications International Corporation.

Sun and NFS are registered trademarks of Sun Microsystems, Incorporated.

UNIX is a registered trademark of AT&T Bell Laboratories.

All the views expressed in this book are the authors, and should not be attributed to other Hewlett-Packard employees or to the Hewlett-Packard Corporation.

Some illustrations were created using clipart from the Visio 4.0 clipart gallery from the Visio Corporation.

The authors would like to thank Mr. Arens and Loebbecke for providing permssion to use their definition of the term "auditing."

INTRODUCTION

This book is intended to provide the reader with an appreciation for the challenge of obtaining security in distributed computing. It is intended to describe the overall problem and present some ideas about how it may be solved. We have purposefully focused on areas that will give the reader an appreciation of what it will take to meet the challenge, rather than providing an encyclopedia of computing security. For this reason, we have limited our examination to selected technology topics.

For example, the role of personal computers in the distributed systems has not been extensively examined. This is because personal computers running DOS and perhaps Windows have very few security mechanisms. The solution to this problem is to add third-party security software or hardware products to the personal computer. A discussion of the various vendor offerings would add little to our overall objective of describing the business challenge of security in distributed computing. We have focused our discussion on the problem facing distributed client systems, which include personal computers, instead of focusing on the personal computer itself.

For the same reason, we have spent little effort in describing solutions for remote access to networks and systems. While remote access adds to the challenge of security, there are a number of solutions available to address this particular problem in the marketplace. The discussion of these solutions will not significantly add to our examination of the key problem; How do I authenticate an individual over an untrusted network?

We expect that while many people may read the book cover to cover, quite a few may only be interested in selected sections of the book. We have used a roadmap diagram, shown below, to demonstrate where a particular chapter or section is located in the general flow of the book:

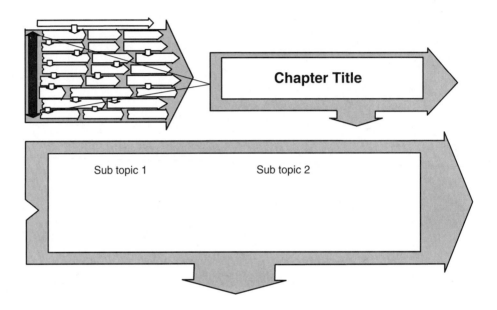

We hope the layout will assist both the casual, and more thorough, readers of the text.

PART I

UNDERSTANDING THE PROBLEM

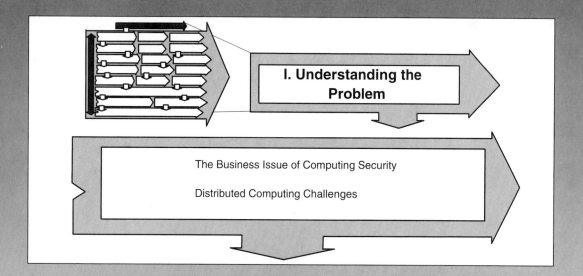

I. Understanding the Problem

The Business Issue of Computing Security

Distributed Computing Challenges

The first step in dealing with any problem is to recognize that the problem in fact exists. In the first two chapters of the book, we will try to gain an understanding of the drivers and issues involved in distributed computing security. You will see that computing security is a very complex problem. There are many facets to the problem, including technological aspects, uncertain management commitment, and a general lack of user awareness. As with the problem of quality, security in computing cannot be solved by expenditures on technology alone. In fact, acquiring too much technology can contribute to the problem. The problem is complex enough to demand a strategic approach.

There are also a number of similarities between the problems of home security and computing security. Doors are the natural entrances to a home, and therefore attract a good deal of attention. But they are not the only ways to gain illegal entry into a home. Windows, if unbarred, are likely to be used. Smash the window, open the latch and intruders are quickly inside! The best door locks in the world won't save your valuables if a window is left open. Just as in home security, security in distributed computing is more than *locking the front door.* It involves a number of elements, including policy, user awareness, attention to system administration, and the proper implementation of technology.

In the first chapter, we will explore the overall problem of computing security. We will focus our examination on the distributed computing environment and see how distributed computing adds to the overall complexity of the problem. We will examine the business drivers and issues that contribute to the problem. The second chapter will lead you through some interesting, and, we hope, informative, security incidents. We will also explore more specific security issues when dealing with a distributed environment. These early sections of the book will give you an understanding of the factors that contribute to the security challenge. In later chapters, we will examine factors to gain an understanding of how specific technologies and actions can be used to address the problem of security in distributed computing.

CHAPTER 1

COMPUTING SECURITY— A BUSINESS ISSUE

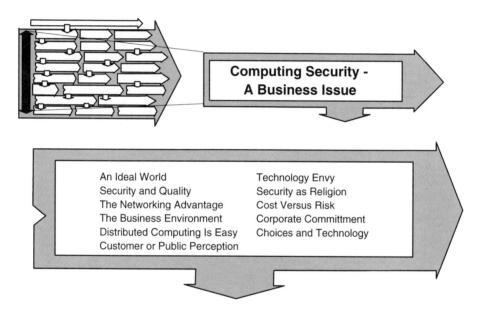

Computing Security - A Business Issue

An Ideal World

Security and Quality

The Networking Advantage

The Business Environment

Distributed Computing Is Easy

Customer or Public Perception

Technology Envy

Security as Religion

Cost Versus Risk

Corporate Committment

Choices and Technology

The total number of computer systems installed within any organization has been increasing at a phenomenal rate. The relative ease of installing and utilizing computer applications is a compelling reason for connecting computer systems together and distributing or sharing the work. These distributed systems allow you to take better advantage of the vast array of processing power now available. Will these systems keep your confidential data secret? Will all of the data be kept in synchronization? Do you put your faith into the results generated by these computing systems? Can you *trust* a distributed system to securely deliver everything you require?

There was a time when all of the data and the associated processing applications were available from a single location, most likely from within a single computer. Anyone could proudly point to a computer and say "There's where the magic happens." Protection of the system was fairly straightforward: either you put whatever security was needed around the system, or you put the system in an environment that was totally secure. In today's processing environment the magic can happen almost anywhere by using several levels of computers, each containing a portion of the data and applications. It is easy to lose track of where the protection is required, what is needed, and how to go about implementing it. It may not be obvious where the data or the processing application actually exists. It is much easier to secure money in a single bank vault than money distributed among a network of automated teller machines.

In many ways we now have more computer processing power in my home computer than a typical multimillion-dollar insurance company had to manage its entire business just a few short years ago. The power of the processors is continuing to increase while the unit cost for this processing power is decreasing. This rapid expansion of cheap, processing power has provided the capability to manipulate and process increasingly large amounts of data and provide immediate results. It makes sense to exploit inexpensive computing power that can be close at hand. With the rapid evolution of local area networks and other networking technology, this capability can be distributed and shared with many others. But, without adequate processes and controls, the distribution of data and processes may cause more problems than it is attempting to solve. In this chapter we will explore what a distributed computing system is and some of the drivers that are providing us with opportunities as well as problems.

An Ideal World

A computer is an extremely flexible tool that is capable of executing almost anything that you tell it to as long as it is done in a way the computer understands. What would the ideal computer system do for you? It would provide access to any data that was needed, and it would be in the format required. Any updates to this database would be available immediately. Any application could be executed wherever that application may be. The system would always be available and provide instant response. You could rely on the security and integrity of the data, and any updates to the data would always complete successfully. If there was a system problem and it became unavailable, the system would be restored almost immediately with all of the data reset to the point before the failure occurred when the system was again available. If all of the data and the applications you require are contained on your own computer, this wish list could be possible. If the data and/or the applications are distributed among two or more computers, attaining this ideal becomes much more complex.

WHY IS DISTRIBUTED COMPUTING LIKE A CAR?

Have you noticed what it takes to keep the family vehicle in tip-top shape today? Not so long ago you would take the car to the corner service station where they would work whatever magic was required to keep the car in running order. This included fixing flat tires, relining brakes, installing new batteries, rebuilding an engine, aligning the steering, changing the oil, or doing almost anything else that was required. Where are the corner service stations today? Now there are "lube shops" that specialize in changing your oil in under 10 minutes, tune-up places that make the engine hum, and muffler, brake, and shock specialists. There is a specialty shop to take care of almost every aspect of car maintenance. Today the corner service station only sells gas, lottery tickets, and soft drinks starting with "Big" something or other. The do-it-all corner station has all but disappeared.

You, as the owner of the car, are responsible for ensuring that all of the maintenance is completed when and where it is needed since this work can be distributed across several specialty service locations. When you buy a new car you are usually covered by a warranty and have a single point of contact with the dealer for service. You shouldn't have to worry about how your vehicle is running as long as the dealer is taking care of it. You trust that everything has been done to make sure the vehicle is functioning properly and that it will get you where you want to go. Using the dealer for continued service, however, tends to be expensive once the warranty period has expired. You may elect to follow a less expensive route and take the car to the specialty shops for maintenance. You now have the problem of tracking and managing all of the service requirements to be able to maintain your trust in the vehicle.

When you distribute your data and processing among more than one computer it begins to resemble this new reality of car maintenance. The single-vendor mainframe environment is similar to buying a new car from the dealer. All of the service and warranty work comes from a single place. If all of the components of the distributed system are also obtained from a single vendor it is again rather like buying a new car from a dealer. If the system components come from many different vendors, then it is rather like maintaining a vehicle using the specialized shops. It is up to you to ensure that all of the required components are present and working together.

Figure 1.1 indicates the perceived differences between some of the qualities of systems operating on a centralized or mainframe system and operating on distributed systems from a single supplier or more than one vendor. The lower cost of the installed technology base and greater flexibility in a distributed multivendor system may be a trade-off with the increased complexity and a decreasing ability to manage the distributed system. A distributed system from a single supplier is part way between the cost and flexibility of the fully distributed system and the relative lack of complexity of the centralized or mainframe system. In many cases this perception of a lower cost from the distributed systems may not be true when all process and management factors are accounted for.

Getting back to our car, the cost of maintaining it exclusively at the dealership may in fact be more expensive, but you don't have to worry about managing the maintenance timing or activities. If you shop around at the specialty repair shops for repairs you have more choice and can obtain competitive prices: but you may need to visit a lot of places to have all of the work completed. You may also elect to do everything yourself, an ambitious undertaking considering the increasing complexity of the automobile technology. If you are a skilled mechanic and build a highly customized vehicle, the chances are good that you will be the only one that can maintain and enhance it.

One of the most valuable innovations that has exploited the power of a personal computer has been the use of a spreadsheet program. You can sit

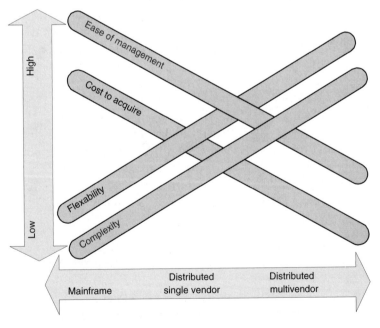

Figure 1.1 Mainframe versus distributed

down and draft your annual departmental budget in no time. These departmental budgets are gathered together to produce the division budget which is then merged with other departments' budgets to form the corporate budget. However, the data and the process for producing this corporate budget may be spread across several different computers and locations. What happens to this process when changes have to be made to the department budgets in order to meet a corporate objective? You are told to sharpen your pencils and revise your respective budgets and resubmit them for another draft.

Coordination mechanisms must be used to ensure all of the current budget information is being used for this next draft and that confidentiality is being preserved. The major effort to produce the corporate budget is the coordination of the data rather than the production of the data. If an integrated budgeting package or a distributed database is being used, this can be largely automated. If this process is not automated, there is probably a collection of very harried individuals trying to determine if the latest spreadsheet files have been included or if the correct diskettes have been used. You can trust the accuracy of the corporate budget if the data and the processes to produce it are well managed.

DISTRIBUTED COMPUTING—WHAT IS IT?

Distributed computing probably means many different things to many different people. To some, it means client/server; to others, it's cooperative processing; and to still others, it's using a distributed database. Further explanations and definitions may be required to ensure that everyone has a common view and understanding of a distributed computing system. When referencing a distributed computing system, every user should be able to see the same thing. It should be like looking at a car where everyone sees the same thing rather than fine art which can be open to interpretation. Almost everyone understands what a car usually looks like and what it is used for. Art can be open to a variety of interpretations. A typical computer processing application can be separated into components, each dealing with a different aspect of the process. In this case the assumption is that the computer process is initiated by a person with a keyboard or some other input device. Figure 1.2 represents the components of a typical computing process.

Each of these components may be a separate unit or grouped together as a processing unit and may communicate with the other components through a network connection. The separation and grouping of these components in various ways can be described using distributed computing models. Figure 1.3 illustrates some of the common groupings of these components. If the end-user interface, application, data management, and the data

End-user device	End-user interface	Application	Data management	Data

Figure 1.2 Process components

are all contained on a single processor, we have the usual host-centric processing model. You can alter this model by using the local intelligence of a personal computer (PC) to provide the end-user interface while using the application, data management and data supplied by the host. This model is called remote presentation.

If you move the application to the local PC and maintain the data on a host computer, you have what is usually referred to as client-server computing. If you split the application into components that are executed on both the host and the local PC, you have cooperative processing. If the local PC application also has a data manager that can request service from the host database, you have a distributed database. If all of the components are separated into various processors, we have a fully distributed system and most likely chaos unless significant management processes have also been implemented.

A system is defined as a set of different elements that are connected or related in order to perform a unique function that cannot be performed by the elements alone. A distributed computing system is composed of system elements which are then distributed across different processing platforms connected by a network. One required quality of a distributed computing system is transparency, which refers to the ability to make the system elements interact and operate the same way in a distributed environment as they would in a single-host environment. Transparency is required if the interaction between the various system components is to be the same if distributed across a number of hosts as in a single system.

WHAT'S THE DEAL WITH CLIENT/SERVER?

Client/server is one of those terms that seems to have captured the imagination of the information system (IS) industry but seems to vary in definition, depending on who is doing the defining. Definitions have ranged from a simple PC network connection to elaborate multilevel, multilocation application and data integration. In simplest form, a server is a manager of one or more resources, and a client is a user of the server's resources. It is also generally accepted that a client is a programmable workstation, although this is not a finite position. In simple terms, client/server can be thought of

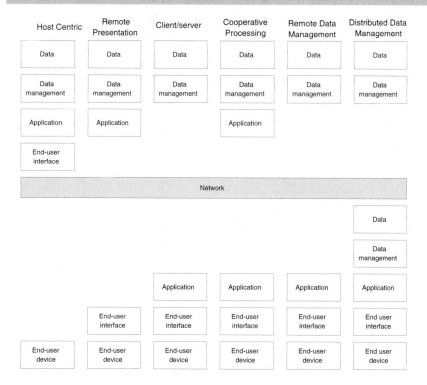

Figure 1.3 Distributed processing models

as an implementation of distributed computing where the application and the data reside on a server and the client provides the end-user interface. Unfortunately a simple definition usually means that the term client/server can be attached to almost any activity where more than one computer is involved. This is especially true when a client-server system is generally thought of as state of the art and is used as a selling feature. For the purpose of addressing security, client-server will be treated as an implementation of distributed computing. Items that may be specific to client/server implementations will be addressed in this book as required.

Security was a relatively simple matter in the large-scale processing systems when all of the processing was completed at a central computing center. All you had to do was build a moat around the computer with a single draw bridge. Everyone who entered could be identified and provided with the permission to do what needed to be done. Only one set of guards to recognize the people were needed. It was very apparent when unauthorized activity was about to take place. Now we have many computers linked with bridges. Do we have many moats? Who is responsible for maintaining the moats? How do we ensure all the moats are the same size and can do the same job?

SECURITY AND QUALITY

Security in the business systems of today is not only about the technical protection of information, but must be considered and included in every aspect of the automated business. Quality programs have lately become very popular for enabling corporations with the ability to improve their processes and products and thereby maintain or improve their position in the market. Widely recognized standards, such as the ISO 9000 series, have been implemented by many companies as a way of demonstrating their commitment to quality to their customers, and to the world at large. The successful corporate quality programs have resulted from a corporate commitment starting with the top executives.

We believe that computing security, like quality, must also be embraced by the corporation and included in all aspects of the business operation. Customers and corporations will be measuring their suppliers and other business relationships on their corporate commitment to, and implementation of, security standards. You would probably not use an automated teller machine (ATM) if you thought the security provided by that machine or network it is connected to was not as high as another ATM.

Security standards will be required to be able to compare the operation of one corporation with another. Appropriate standards will be demanded by the implementation of more intercorporate on-line transactions such as electronic data interchange and electronic commerce. The awarding of large business contracts is already sometimes dependent on the ability of an organization to deliver and operate a secure computing solution. You might have to prove how secure it is. The proper implementation of security can be a competitive advantage: the lack of adequate security is a competitive disadvantage.

BUSINESS DRIVERS

So what is really driving the need for security? One thing that has been very clear to us in our work is the fact that a secure computing environment is a business problem and not a technical one. There are plenty of technical solutions available, and even worse, plenty of standards upon which to base this technology. The problem is not deciding what technology to apply but what should you apply the technology to and how you should go about applying it. Too much technology and too many standards with too little planning, and too little management, is a recipe for security risks, or worse, disaster. Too little management can create holes and gaps in the distributed environment, leaving doors unlocked and windows open. Failure to address such a situation can cause increased risk and exposure and potential liability.

THE NETWORKING ADVANTAGE

One of the main business drivers is the impact of the computer network: the ability of computers to communicate. Almost all companies that have more than one computer also have some form of a computer network. As well, almost all of the difficult networking issues have been solved making it relatively easy to connect computers together. Networking technology is easy to implement and easy to use. The corporate network has been expanded to include business partners, customers, contracted relationships, and employees from home.

In some cases, the corporate network has even extended to direct competitors. Consider, for example, a network connection to an industry marketing board or to support a large project that may have multiple suppliers of similar components. You will want to be able to sleep at night knowing all of your corporate assets and intellectual property are protected from discovery or, worse, sabotage. Although the networking technology problem has largely been solved, the easy ability for machines to communicate introduces new challenges to the problem of maintaining security. You have to worry about the security capabilities of all of the other connected computers, not only your own.

THE BUSINESS ENVIRONMENT

In recent history the computing systems were used to automate the business processes developed and perfected by the company. These were really an electronic acceleration of the typical manual business processes. Another wave of processing arrived when people discovered how to access the wealth of data that was accumulating as a product of the automation. This type of access to the data was usually in conflict with the other automated processes. The knowledge of how the computing process worked and how to access the data was kept within the information technology (IT) department. Security was the responsibility of someone in IT and was fairly easy to implement. The business could still operate, perhaps in a somewhat crippled manner, if the computer systems were not available.

The current state of automated business processes is now quite different. Several major forces are converging to change the way computing technology supports the business. Many advances in technology allowed almost exponential increases in computing power to be installed for the same or less cost than previous systems. More and better automated tools are being used to support the business. Alternate ways of obtaining or presenting information, video, image, sound, voice capture, and so on, are changing the way computers support the business. The business decision making process has fundamentally changed, we hope for the better. The more we rely on the information that the systems generate and present, the more trust we need to have in that information.

A more compelling change has been the restructuring of the business processes itself which was brought on by economic necessity. It was not good enough to just automate the processes, they had to be rebuilt from the ground up, supported by computer technology. The computers ceased to be only a tool, they are now an integral and essential part of operating the business. The business functions are now dependent on the computers and you have to be able to trust them. Certain businesses will fail or be severely crippled if their computing systems are reliable and not available even for a short period of time.

This reengineering of the business has also brought about a fundamental change in the requirements of the users of the systems. The first wave of business automation allowed the computer systems to analyze data, construct reports and provide decision recommendations based on the input the system was given. The users provided the input and acted on the decision advice the system provided. The next wave of systems moved the input of the data out to the point where it was generated and was processed without human intervention. The banking systems lead the way on this wave.

We have now migrated to systems that support knowledge workers who have many applications at their disposal and the ability to access almost any data they might require to be effective in their job. The applications and data may be anywhere in the world to which they have access. The applications and data required to complete the tasks may not always be predictable. We have replaced the assembly line and need-to-know approach to data processing with highly knowledgeable users and the ability to access almost any computing resource and data that may be required. The mechanisms to protect the confidentiality of the information must also be able to keep up to this way of doing business.

DISTRIBUTED COMPUTING IS EASY

Another force at work is the ease with which distributed systems can be put together. For some reason a lot more care and attention seems to be put into something that is difficult to do and has uncertain outcomes rather than something that is easy and has predictable results. Security seems to be less of a concern if a distributed system is easy to implement. This same comparison holds true for the cost of computing. There seems to be a lot less concern if the distributed solutions are inexpensive. Almost anyone can obtain and implement a system that can participate in a distributed computing system, but the protection mechanisms must also be included and be able to keep up to this expanded use. Since distributed computing is easy you had better be able to trust it.

CUSTOMER OR PUBLIC PERCEPTION

When we withdraw money from an automated banking machine, or even more important deposit money, we need to be assured that security and confidentiality of that transaction is absolute. We trust that the transaction that we have just completed will be the only same transaction that is applied to our bank account and that no one else knows about the transaction. If a bank has been the victim of theft using the machines or involving our transactions somehow, we will quickly stop using those machines and possibly that bank. Not only must the security be stringent it must also be widely perceived as being effective. As more and more organizations use computing technology and networks to transact business between themselves or with their customers, the security under which this takes place must be perceived to be strong. Security can be used as a selling feature. Although it may not historically have been a large issue, a competitive advantage can be gained if your organization's computing environment is perceived as more secure than a competitor's.

TECHNOLOGY ENVY

Another driving force behind many new computer systems can be called technology envy. A lot of people involved in information processing have a tendency to want and, in some cases, develop a strong need for the latest and greatest technical advances. There is always a desire to have the latest technology and the fastest, most powerful systems. Information processing originally was used as a tool to apply to the automation of a business process. Subsequent generations of these automated systems have had a tendency to be implemented because of technical advances rather than a change in the business requirements. In many cases this resulted in a saving in the data processing hardware and software budget. However, it may not always result in an overall saving in the cost of operating the business. Technical obsolescence is now measured in months and not years.

Decisions and strategies for applying information processing technology are sometimes based on the latest popular technologies rather than business requirements. A well-written article that is strategically placed in the airline magazines can have a significant influence on the strategies of a company. Technology is often embraced because of a fear of being left behind. In fact, many companies have ended up distributing their computing without realizing that they were heading in that direction or understanding the business issues that may be involved. Security considerations tend to lag behind the desire for the latest and greatest technology.

BUSINESS ISSUES

The business drivers we have just mentioned outline the reasons that distributed computing is an important part of the business. There are, however, many important issues that accompany the distributed environment. This environment requires that more thought and planning go into the big picture. Where once we were able to protect assets with the simple implementation of technology we now need to provide the rules and the structure that all of these distributed elements can and must adopt.

SECURITY AS RELIGION

Sometimes the approach to security is based more on a religiouslike belief in the need for security than founded on defined requirements and principles. There may be two or more *religions* that are maintained in the distributed environment. It this happens, the approach to security in one distributed domain may be fundamentally different from the approach in another domain. This makes it very difficult to share applications and data across these domains if the doors around them require different keys. Too much security is almost as much a problem as not enough. If the security mechanisms become a burden on the productivity of the users, a lot of effort will be devoted to circumventing them.

There may be a difference of opinion or view of the world between the various levels of corporate management on the need for, or impact of, security. One level of management may be responsible for employee productivity and view stringent security mechanisms as getting in the way of completing the business tasks. A higher level of management will be responsible for the operation of the business and be held accountable for the protection of the intellectual property. There have been cases where company secrets have been stolen and sold to competitors who have then used this information to produce competitive products that damaged the business of the victim company.

Cost Versus Risk

One major challenge is to balance the cost of security solutions and controls against the risks these solutions are addressing. The cost of providing a secure solution should be in proportion to the value of the assets that the security mechanisms are protecting. This cost must also be balanced with the risk associated with any potential loss or compromise of the asset. Even if the assets are deemed to be valuable, it may not be cost effective to address all of the possible risks which can occur. It must then be a business decision to balance the cost providing security against the potential risks.

The risks are viewed in terms of criticality of the systems to the business, the disclosure of confidential information, or potential loss through fraud. An analysis of sensitivity to risk should also include considerations for the safety to both employees and customers. The bottom-line message is to fully understand what risks are present and what the impact of those risks are before solutions should be considered. The customers, however, demand that their assets be protected.

The nature of risk, along with the technology, will continue to change. The risk from external sources, once thought of as limited because of the existence of relatively few network connections, will increase. The ability and stated requirement of corporations to communicate, both interenterprise and intraenterprise, will continue to grow. In the future, electronic communication across a wide data highway to customers, other utilities, suppliers, and governments must be expected. This will also heighten the requirements for management controls within the organization, to prevent exposure not only to internal fraud but also to the possibly of external attacks.

Corporate Commitment

Previously, we drew a parallel between the corporate commitment to quality and the commitment to security. To be able to provide security in a distributed environment, there needs to be demonstrated leadership and vision for security which can be applied across all of the distributed areas. Any differences in the approach and implementation must be aligned across the enterprise against a common understanding. Many organizations implement security processes without providing the adequate foundations, including principles and policies, that will allow a security program to be effective. Security is a corporate problem and should be treated as such. A defined corporate strategy on security may be required.

Another important area of corporate commitment is in the education and awareness of the employees about security. The security of the corporate assets is only effective if people understand the importance of security and what their responsibilities are in order to keep the assets secure. This awareness must extend into all areas of the organization. The design and development of the systems must keep the security requirements in mind as much as the operation of the systems and the network. People will not pay much attention to security if they don't know that security is important to the organization and what they can do about it.

CHOICES AND TECHNOLOGY

Unfortunately there is no silver or magic wand to address all of the distributed security problems. There is no one right way or technical solution to solve the problem. Often there are conflicting goals, or levels of concern, about the relative importance of information and the associated risks involved across the distributed environment. Conflicts arise about what is or needs to be secure. There is always the trade-off between easy information access and security. Any decisions about security solutions can only take place once the whole picture is understood.

There is an overwhelming urge to jump to a technical solution to the security problems. This is further complicated by the many different security solutions available. As we mentioned before, distributed computing security is a business problem and not a technical one. It doesn't make much sense to look for a technical solution before you really understand what you want to protect and why you want to protect it. It is also very difficult to keep up with all of the distributed and security standards and what impact they may have on the organizations. Many of the standards are still evolving.

SUMMARY

There are many reasons why distributed computing is an important factor in our current automated systems. There are many considerations and issues that need to be addressed to ensure all of the information assets in this environment are protected. Is distributed computing security possible and is it worth the cost? The challenge of providing distributed system security is going to get worse before it gets any better. The benefits, however, can far outweigh the risk if the security requirements are properly dealt with. We will try to offer some help in understanding the issues and provide some advice on how to approach these problems.

In the following chapters we will try to explain the challenge in more detail and help you get started to address these challenges. Distributed system security is possible once you understand the problem and how you can organize to address it. In the next chapter we will continue with a review of more specific challenges presented by the distributed environment.

CHAPTER 2

DISTRIBUTED SECURITY CHALLENGES

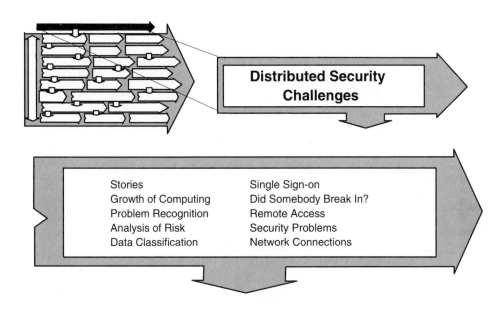

Distributed Security Challenges

Stories	Single Sign-on
Growth of Computing	Did Somebody Break In?
Problem Recognition	Remote Access
Analysis of Risk	Security Problems
Data Classification	Network Connections

Security in distributed computing is not an easy thing to attain. Like the pioneers who crossed the Great Plains to California and Oregon in 1849, there are plenty of dangers to be overcome. The Cimmarron and Oregon trails featured wide rivers and deserts that had to be crossed. Weather was a constant enemy, and the possibility of losing your way was ever present. But by using the experiences of others, the dangers became known and could be dealt with. The stories are quite diverse, and so are the security problems. No single solution or technology can address all the problems we may encounter.

STORIES

Our objective in this chapter is to relate the dangers and some of the problems that should be considered. Just like the old weathered plainsmen who guided the forty-niners across the great plains would, we'll start by telling a few stories ...

A CUCKOO'S EGG

In August 1986, Clifford Stoll, an astronomer turned computing system administrator at the University of California Lawrence Berkeley Labs, discovered a 75 cent discrepancy in the monthly computer billing records. Tracking this discrepancy led the researcher to uncover a determined group of German hackers who had infiltrated many government and military networks around the world. Using relatively unsophisticated techniques which preyed on weak security implementations, they were able to penetrate many computer sites. The hackers were eventually caught after many months of tracking their activities and attempting to get several different agencies interested in this problem. The entire story is told by Clifford Stoll in the book *The Cuckoo's Egg* [Stoll, 1989], which has become a popular primer for information on the topic of computer hackers.

A WORM ON THE NET

On November 2, 1988, thousands of VAX and UNIX systems connected to the Internet mysteriously began to crash. They had been invaded by a special type of computer virus called a worm. The worm launched process after process, quickly consuming the resources of the infected computer. The infected computers eventually crashed.

The worm also sought out new victims over the network. Taking advantage of little-known security holes in the operating system, it propagated itself rapidly across the entire Internet. The worm eventually caused many thousands of computers to slow to a crawl or be taken off of the network. Many people were shocked to discover the author of the worm was Robert T. Morris, the son of the National Security Agency's chief computer scientist. A university graduate student, Mr. Morris claimed that the worm was nothing more than a failed experiment to test computer security.

PHYSICAL SECURITY

In 1969, a student demonstration turned into property destruction as the computer complex at Sir George Williams University in Montreal was attacked. The computer complex was occupied, and computer printouts were strewn from windows into the streets below.

"It reminds me of the time," my grandfather said, "that our horse-drawn sled was surrounded by wolves on a frosty night in eastern Ontario. I jumped down in the middle of that wolf pack with my gun, but the darn thing wouldn't fire," he related with a sigh. "What happened," I asked with fear in my voice. "Well son, I died."

PASSWORD THEFTS

In February 1994 a major advisory was released by the Computer Emergency Response Team (CERT) at Carnegie Mellon University. The advisory warned of computer intruders who were using compromised systems to steal passwords on the Internet. It was reported that tens of thousands of passwords may have been stolen. The hackers used diagnostic software to intercept network traffic on systems to which they had gained access. This theft went unnoticed by the majority of the systems that were compromised.

ERRORS OF OMISSION

Many computer vendors deliver systems to customers which include diagnostic facilities supported by a separate user account. These accounts usually had common passwords, such as *support*. The documentation indicates that these passwords should be changed once the system has been correctly installed, but many are not changed. In the installations where the passwords are not changed, the users may fail to understand how quickly a bulletin board system can be used to spread this information, indicating that a door has been left open.

BUT NOTHING WAS TAKEN!

A manufacturer returned to the office after a long weekend to find that the office had been broken into. After a careful search it was determined that nothing was missing. Only later, when this company lost a major contract to a competitor, was it realized that the break-in had occurred to copy computer files loaded with information concerning the contract bid of the victim company. The theft of information may not be easily detected but can be very damaging.

GOTCHA

A software company nabbed illegal users of its product. The company offered free demonstration software of its new line of products. The demonstration software was loaded onto the customer's PC. Besides executing the demonstration, the software searched the hard disk for illegal copies of that company's software. This software company had been a popular target to pirate its software. If an illegal copy was found, the user was invited to print, fill out, and return a voucher for a free product handbook. Several hundred people completed and returned the voucher, and instead of a handbook, they received a letter from the company's lawyer demanding payment for the illegal software.

SECURITY ISSUES

The way to do business today is with the automated support of computers. We are doing a good job of automating our own companies processes and expect other companies processes to be automated sufficiently that we can do business with them without detracting from our automated system. The trust aspect of these relationships must be dealt with in order to maintain the effective interaction. The various relationships we now have with our customers, our suppliers, and our partners lead us into a trusting relationship with these entities. We must have a solid foundation for this trust. There are many issues to deal with in order to establish and maintain this trust. In this chapter we will explore some of those specific areas where trust is required.

GROWTH OF COMPUTING

In the previous chapter we mentioned that one of the business drivers that has promoted the implementation of distributed computing systems is the fact that it is now relatively easy to do. Other business issues have spurred the growth of distributed systems and, therefore, the need for security. What were once small departmental print servers have now grown to full function minidata centers. In most cases they are still being operated and protected as if they are still only print servers. In the world of corporate downsizing, the distributed computing systems in the operational departments are not generally staffed with information system professionals. There may be a need to centralize the administration of the security functions, but the tools to do this are still immature or not readily available. In general, the growing complexity and the number of systems make providing a secure environment difficult.

PROBLEM RECOGNITION

The growth in the number of systems also resulted by downsizing and spreading out of computing power into the various departments from the central data center. There was a mad dash to move applications from the mainframe to more *open* platforms. In many cases this meant replacing a single large machine with several computers. The challenge of dealing effectively with these multiple computers and locations, caught many organizations off-guard. In many cases, management failed to recognize the change in the responsibility for security and the challenge that this new distributed environment presented.

The recognition of the problem is admittedly more difficult in a distributed environment. On one hand, the assumption that security of the distributed platforms will be the same as on the mainframe does not necessarily hold true. On the other hand, the recognition of the "big picture," including all of the distributed platforms, may not be apparent. We need to look at the impact on the whole enterprise and not just the current neighborhood. There is also a need to recognize when we are dealing with strangers and when we are dealing with neighbors. Usually a communal trust is formed with neighbors, but we may question the requirement for strangers to visit.

Computer viruses are becoming a serious problem in many organizations. In fact, in a recent survey, over two-thirds of organizations reported that they had been impacted by a computer virus. These impacts have ranged from simple annoyance viruses to actual destruction of corporate data. Viruses can be introduced into the organization from many sources. Employees working at home with home computers, bringing software or shareware into the office, even licensed software distribution from vendors have been sources of viruses. The cost involved in cleaning a system from a virus attack is significant. The impact of this problem must be recognized, and care must be taken to maintain a "clean" environment. The proliferation of more and varied viruses will probably get worse before it gets better.

ANALYSIS OF RISK

Any protection of your valuables from threats involves some analysis of the risk involved. How far do you go to protect your valuables? Controls are put into place to reduce the risk, but these controls have a cost. The more security that is introduced, the more the cost of the controls rise and hopefully the cost of the expected losses decrease. An understanding of the risks, the value of what you are trying to protect, and the cost of the controls leads to the formation of a well-balanced security system. Unfortunately, in computer systems, the cost of the controls is usually much easier to determine than the risk or even the value of information involved.

A major problem with distributed processing is an unclear idea of what is valuable or where the valuables are located. The objective of a security system is to spend only as much on the security controls to offset the value of the expected losses if the controls were not present. The lack of any security problems does not indicate the lack of risk. Many organizations have focused on technology to solve a security problem before they understand what they are protecting, and from what risks this protection is avoiding. You can avoid risk by implementing controls, assigning risk to others, or assuming the risk yourself. The bottom line is to understand what you are protecting before you protect it.

DATA CLASSIFICATION

Do you know exactly what business information should be secret and what should not be? The separation of information into categories that have different requirements for confidentiality and availability is one of the main building blocks of a security system. Many organizations have not taken a great deal of time to determine how important various information is to the business. This may influence the security measures that are implemented or how security is applied. Without a classification system, restrictive secure mechanisms may be applied to everything, potentially limiting productivity, or very little security being applied and increasing the risk. We must try to understand what is important to the organization and why, before security measures are implemented. The security and availability of the data will determine what security measures should be required and how broadly these measures should be applied.

SINGLE SIGN-ON

The issue of single sign-on is by far the issue most commonly mentioned by our clients. We have been used to "logging on" to a computer system with a user ID and a password as a form of identification and authentication. If we need to access several systems in the course of a day, it may be necessary to logon to many different systems, each requiring a user ID and a password. In fact, the more complex the security system, the bigger the problem in remembering how to get through it to access the actual application. People will work around the problem or find alternatives that may introduce additional exposures.

Even the most conscientious person can unwittingly render the most robust security technology useless. Have you ever noticed the terminal or PC in the next office with several yellow sticky notes around it displaying the various logon sequences, system IDs, and passwords of the application so they won't be forgotten? Productivity can also suffer if the passwords are forgotten or confused, which can provoke several calls to the system administrator to reset the passwords. The challenge is how to provide the required security without requiring the user to jump through multiple hoops to access the distributed applications.

DID SOMEBODY BREAK IN?

One of the biggest headaches for a distributed system is detecting that a security problem has occurred. It is usually quite obvious when a burglar has visited your home. If your home is reasonably secure, there will be some evidence of forced entry; there may be signs of a hasty search for loot if drawers have been dumped or specific items are missing. Unfortunately it is not as easy to tell if someone has burgled your computer system. The target of such a burglary is your intellectual property, and the theft involved is simply to take a copy of it while the original remains intact. Evidence of an unauthorized entry would be available only if information is captured to audit, or if specific detection mechanisms are in place, having a video camera recording of the activities that took place in the house.

The majority of computer security systems deny access by at least locking the front door but may have trouble detecting if someone has slipped in through an open window. Many passwords and user IDs have been captured by mechanisms installed in a system or attached to the network without the knowledge of anyone responsible for the compromised system. It's similar to lack of security in cellular phone conversations. Anybody can be listening in on your conversations, and you have no way of knowing it is happening. The cellular phone security problem is understandable, but to assume your computer conversations are secure can be costly. Isn't it better to be sure?

REMOTE ACCESS

The availability of affordable personal computers and relatively high-speed communications has permitted many employees to have the ability to access the corporate computer systems from home. In some cases this may be a requirement of the type of job involved in order to support the system after normal working hours. This usually means the implementation of some form of facility that the employee can use to "dialup" the corporate system. Allowing this type of doorway into the network, however, also invites other nonemployees to try the locks of this door. There are many technical solutions that can be implemented to provide the required level of security and ensure that only authorized individuals gain access to the corporate network using such a door.

Remote access to the corporate network can also be a requirement for an employee "on the road" who requires access to the corporate database or electronic mail to enhance their ability to communicate and work effectively even when out of the office. Many security solutions rely on the fact that the origin of access is defined and predictable. In the case of the "road warrior" employee, this is not available, and other security solutions to prove identity will be required.

The requirement for remote access is not only a technical security problem but also a policy issue. An issue of expanding importance is the fact that access to the corporate network may also provide a doorway to other networks. This can become an issue, for example, if you or your child want access to the Internet from home through your corporate access point. A desire to access the Internet has prompted some employees, sometimes without the support or knowledge of management, to install a modem and software on the PC at the office to provide an easy access to the corporate network from home.

WHERE DO SECURITY PROBLEMS COME FROM?

One of the more interesting elements of reviewing the impact of security incidents is the understanding of where most of the problems come from. Most people, and the press would have us believe that the origin of security events and loss comes from evil hackers, but by far the largest number and impact of security-related events originate within the organization. More than half of all losses are caused by security problems, committed by current or former employees. Most of these problems stem from mistake, oversight, or disgruntled employees rather than malicious hackers, although the hacker is the one who gets most of the attention. Management has been slow to recognize this fact and secure the internal environment as well as the external one.

NETWORK CONNECTIONS

In the previous chapter we outlined that one of the compulsions for security was the availability and implementation of computer networking. We believe that the interconnection of networks will be one of the single most important factors for future successful business as well as one of the greatest potential security risks. Networks are being used to support access that were normally outside the organization. Work is being let to subcontractors. Corporations are establishing business ventures in partnership with each other. Processing is being performed by external companies. In some cases fierce competitors have connected their networks to a common third party or even to themselves.

This problem will continue to grow because of the global nature of these interconnection requirements. How do you provide security between different organizations if their computing systems are interlinked? What do you do to guarantee that all of those accessing your network and systems are authorized to do so? What common security base will you use and how will you manage it? What influence will you have on another organization's security practices? All of these factors will force security issues to be addressed and solved.

THE TOP TEN LIST

In our opinion, the following is a list of the top ten problems, in terms of trust and security, facing organizations who use distributed computing. They are not presented in any particular order of importance, however, we feel that they are all important.

1. Reaching the Right Balance. Computer security does not make anyone (vendors and consultants excepted) any money. It is a cost of doing business using computers. The need for security must be balanced with the other needs for effective system utilization. No commercial enterprise normally has all of the resources required to make their computing environment totally secure.

The risks to the enterprise must be balanced against the costs of protecting against those risks. Other requirements, such as ease of use and system performance, must also be weighed against the need for secure systems. As mentioned earlier, we don't want to implement a security system that cripples productivity. We also don't want to spend more money on security than the value of the things being protected.

2. Weak Authentication. Authentication is the basis of most security mechanisms. We need to make sure that people or systems are who they say they are. Current authentication methods place reliance on passwords or the network address for authentication. Passwords are usually transmitted over a LAN or network in clear-text and may easily be intercepted by anyone with access to the LAN or network. Network addresses can also be counterfeited. Stronger authentication, which prevents the discovery of clear-text passwords and does not place reliance on network addresses, is required.

3. Management Tools. One cardinal rule of data processing is, if it executes, manage it. For the distributed environment that uses multiple vendor products, there is a lack of comprehensive management tools. Centralized tools are required for common authentication, access control, audit, and detection. These tools will be required to support environments using a variety of products as well as across multiple technical environments.

4. The Internet. There is something big on the horizon. It's either brilliant sunshine or a dark, dark cloud depending on your point of view. The access to the Internet is now one of the most talked about and published topics. Internet access is either the greatest thing to happen since the printed page or the beginning of the end of civilization as we know it. Access to the multitude of information and contacts is truly remarkable.

Letting the world have access to your front door with a welcome mat and maybe even a key under the mat that you don't know about is unnerving to say the least. As you will find out later in this book, network access presents some security challenges and implications. Serious consideration must be given to the implications of a network connection to the Internet and precautions taken to ensure your security is not compromised.

5. Weakest Point on the Net. The weakest point on the corporate network will be the first place to experience an attack. Once a weak system has been overcome, it will be used as a base to compromise more critical systems and applications. Either accreditation to ensure all systems meet a defined standard and an audit of all systems are required to raise the general level of security on the enterprise, or the weak systems need to be isolated from the enterprise network. Your security is only as strong as the weakest link in the network.

6. Diverse Technologies. The problem is not that we have insufficient technology, it is rather the reverse, there is too much technology. A lack of established standards has prevented the acceptance of comprehensive solutions to solve the problem. There are either lots of different standards to deal with different aspects of security or multiple standards that deal with the same aspects of security. There is not all for one or one for all. There are many strong and efficient technologies available to address almost all of the security problems, but they are difficult to interact with each other and more difficult to manage.

7. Physical Access. If physical access to the computer system or networking devices are available to an unauthorized person, illicit access to the system can be gained. With the majority of computer incidents being attributed to employees, this is still a major issue to be addressed. Simple access to the disk in a networked PC is enough to provide easy access.

8. Inappropriate Policies and Procedures. Many organizations have either security policy and procedures rooted in the mainframe environment, or have no policy at all. With distributed computing, employees can be given responsibilities and access to information far greater than ever envisioned in the mainframe environment. A fresh look at the distributed computing environment is required with new policies and procedures implemented to address this changing environment.

9. Education. As with every aspect of computing today, advances in both criminal activity and security techniques are being made. It is not clear which is evolving faster. It is very difficult for the average system administrator to stay abreast of the changes or the threats. Many security holes are exploited simply because they were known by the hacker and unknown to the organization. Many of the current expert hackers know more about the intricacies of your hardware and software than anyone in your organization.

10. Failure to Plan. The movement to a distributed computing environment will cause many changes in the current security architecture. Perhaps the greatest mistake an enterprise can make is to fail to plan for the new environment, and allow that environment to be defined in reaction to the immediate needs of the computing community. The result of a lack of planning will be a "dogs breakfast" of conflicting controls and unmanageable solutions. Even worse, significant security doors can be left unlocked or wide open.

CONCLUSIONS

There is currently no single solution to the problem. The very nature of the operating and network systems that make interaction between these systems easy also presents exposure. The very things that help our work also cause us to be exposed. Security was less of a concern when it was difficult for computers to talk to one another. In the distributed environment one level of security for a system may not be good enough for another system. What happens when these are interconnected? In the large central systems, our protection was generally provided by technology and technical obscurity. In the current decentralized world we need a consistent set of laws and a common blueprint to provide the same level of protection and confidence.

Global commerce will create new demands for greater communication between organizations, linking more than ever our internal networks to other networks. The stories of attacks on computing systems are likely to increase. Organizations must act now to ensure they will not become a target themselves. Our next chapter will cover a few of the security basics, define some terminology, and prepare the ground for the construction of the security system needed to deal with these issues.

PART II

FOUNDATIONS

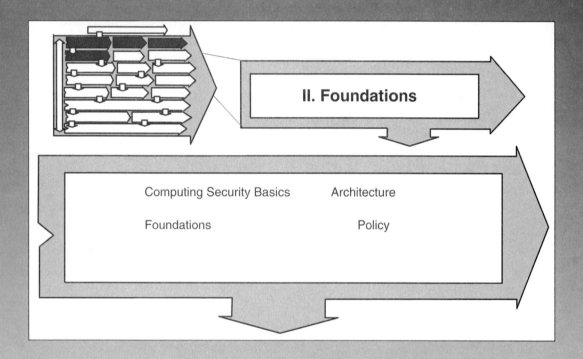

II. Foundations

Computing Security Basics   Architecture

Foundations   Policy

Solving a complex problem requires a proper foundation. There is simply no point in attempting to build a fine home on an inadequate foundation. Inevitably, cracks in the walls, uneven floors, and other problems will appear. Similarly, there is little point in investing time and resources to address the problem of computing security if the proper foundation has not been put in place.

In Chapter 3, we will review the basics of computing security. The intent is to introduce common concepts and terminology that will be used throughout the book. The following chapter will examine the foundations of computing security. It will examine the principles behind security and explain some of the different approaches to security used by organizations. Chapter 4 also introduces the topics of computing policy and guidelines. In Chapter 5, an architecture, or model, for security in the distributed computing environment will be introduced. There are two main reasons why organizations have a security architecture. First, it permits them to use a visual model to demonstrate the interrelationship of various security components, such as the relationship between authentication (e.g., Who are you?) and authorization (e.g., What are you allowed to do?). The second reason is to help align the security architecture with the overall computing architecture. Using a visual model helps to identify places where the architectures may need alignment. The final chapter in this section deals with the creation of computing security policy. Security policy addresses acceptable user conduct and management responsibilities. The policy should provide broad guidance and demonstrate senior management support for addressing the problem of computing security.

CHAPTER 3

COMPUTING SECURITY BASICS

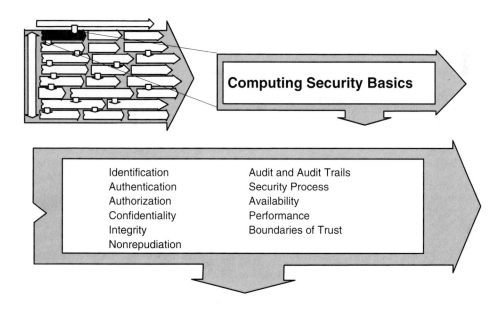

Computing Security Basics

Identification	Audit and Audit Trails
Authentication	Security Process
Authorization	Availability
Confidentiality	Performance
Integrity	Boundaries of Trust
Nonrepudiation	

With any discussion of computing security we require common terms and concepts to describe what is involved in a security system. One of the basic challenges to computing security is simply to identify who needs to do what in the computing system. We need to have a method of proving that the users of the system are who they say they are. When we are sure we know the identity of the person or entity requesting an action, we use this identity to decide whether or not they have the authority to do so. In this chapter we will review some of the definitions and concepts for the basic security components. The concept of trust is a very important one in the way we deal with our neighbors, friends, and the community. It is also a powerful concept when applied to a computing system. We will examine what is meant by trust in a computing sense and why it is important.

WHAT IS SECURITY?

The objective of any security system is the ability to keep a secret. This is as true for automated systems as much as it is for people. We will explore the requirements for having secrets and the methods and technologies that help us keep them. It is as important to keep the information secret when it is stored as well as when it is sent over a network. In most cases, information that is currently sent over a network has about the same security as a cellular telephone. With the right equipment and opportunity, anyone can listen in on what you have to say. There needs to be a method of making sure that the only one who hears what is being said is the person to whom you are saying it.

The X/OPEN definition of information technology security is: "IT security is the state of an IT system in which the risks of the IT system's applications because of the relevant threats are reduced to an acceptable level by taking appropriate measures. The purpose of IT security is to protect assets against threats" [XOPEN1]. X/OPEN is a not-for-profit consortium of member corporations dedicated to the advancement of open systems. Security is needed to protect assets, mostly in the form of data, from threats, to ensure the correctness of data and to help users *trust* the system. Security is comprised of the sum of integrity, authentication, access control or authorization, confidentiality, and nonrepudiation. All these topics need to be addressed.

IDENTIFICATION

Who are you? The most basic element of a security system is the ability to identify who the person is. We need to know if you are a friend or a foe before granting access to the system valuables. If there is a private party at a hotel ballroom, we may need formal invitations or a guest list to identify who is supposed to be attending the event. In a computer system, there needs to be some way of identifying an individual and checking the guest list, to allow us to know when an intruder is in our midst. We first have to know who it is before we have the ability to determine if they are who they say they are. A more important question perhaps may be what we use for identification. Is it an assigned name such as a user ID, a biometric trait such as a thumbprint or can we use a defined location for identification? The identification should also be unique. We should avoid the situation where someone is using the same identity at the same time as someone else.

AUTHENTICATION

Prove you are who you say you are. Once we have identified the requester, the next most important element in a computing security system is the ability to prove someone is who they say they are. Authentication is the proof of identity. This proof can be based on a wide variety of things. The most common way to authenticate someone is for them to know a secret only they should know. Using a secret password is the most common form of proving identity in a computer system. The security system requires you to prove you know the secret before allowing you to do anything. This is commonly referred to as first-function authentication, something you know.

An additional form of authentication is for a person to be in possession of something that only they can have. This could be in the form of a unique card, a disk, or a special token. This is commonly referred to as second-function authentication, something you have. An even stronger form of authentication is based on some physical trait or characteristic that only you possess. This could be a finger- or thumbprint, a retina scan, a voice print, or some other individual characteristic. This is referred to as biometric authentication or third-function authentication, something you are.

There are many different ways to authenticate and many support technologies available to apply to the specific requirements. The strength of the authentication required defines which type of function or technology should be implemented. A simple password may be useful for most people in an office. It is assumed that when these people have entered the office complex, they already have passed some form of security screening if only by the other employees. A second-function authentication, such as a security token, an electronic password generator, or other device, may be required to control access to individual floors within the office. A security token is also a popular way of providing remote dial-up access to a network. Third-function authentication is implemented in only the most secure environments.

An interesting addition to providing authentication is by using location as one of the required measures. The global positioning satellite (GPS) systems can provide us with an accurate location in the world within a few meters. We can use the position information from a GPS system as a parameter to generate a location signature. We can compare this location signature with one where we expect it to be from to determine its authenticity. A transaction between a bank in Canada and a bank in Brazil should be viewed with suspicion if it has been generated in Europe.

AUTHORIZATION

What are you allowed to do? Once we know, and can prove, that someone or something is who they say they are, we need to decide what they are allowed to do. Authorization depends on the success of our ability to identify and authenticate the user or the request. Authorization is the granting of rights to a user, program, or process. We use authorization to define what can be seen or used and where it can be dealt with. Access to system resources and services to users or processes, which have been authenticated, is selectively granted. These rights can be granted on many different levels depending on what level of authorization is required.

Authorization can be explicitly granted or explicitly denied. If we explicitly deny access, we will let anyone have access to information except for that information that we wish to remain confidential. When we explicitly grant access, we will not allow access to any information except when we specifically grant them access to it. This authorization can be defined as systemwide or, depending on the technology, limited to the specific data elements. We can also grant authorization based on the type of access. This type of access is generally considered to be read, write, create, update, delete, or execute.

CONFIDENTIALITY

Can you keep a secret? Another important element is the ability to keep a secret. Confidentiality is defined as the protection of information from unauthorized disclosure. There are generally two ways by which we can provide confidentiality. One way is to limit access to the information by restricting access to a limited number of individuals. We build a high, strong fence that blocks anyone from entering or even seeing what is going on. Only those with the proper authority and that have been strictly authenticated, are allowed into the area. The confidentiality of the information would be compromised if there were some way of circumventing the guards and sneaking into the area.

The other approach is to scramble the information using a special code known only to us. This is called encryption. We scramble or encrypt the information to hide it and unscramble or decrypt the information when we want to use it. Only the people who know the scrambling code or key and how to use it will be able to access the information. This is generally a better way of providing confidentiality than the big fence. Even if someone managed to scale the fence, the information on the inside would not make any sense. In order to be able to provide confidentiality, encryption is generally considered to be a required component in any security system. The ability of encryption to protect secrets is based on two factors. The first is the strength of the encryption algorithm. The second, and more important, is the ability to keep the secret codes safe.

INTEGRITY

Did you get the message I sent? Integrity is the quality that ensures that the message or data is safe and has not been altered. Integrity checks provide for the detection of unauthorized use or modification of the system, applications, data and network. One way of providing an integrity check is to attach a special indicator or message digest on the end of a message or piece of data before it is transmitted or stored. This message digest is the product of a hashing process that is executed against the contents of the message producing a much smaller data item. Any change to the message contents will produce a different message digest value. This digest may then be itself encrypted before the message is sent or stored.

This same process is executed at the other end of the message transmission or when the data is retrieved. If the calculated message digest matches the digest appended to the message, it has not been tampered with. If the digests do not agree then the message has been altered in some fashion since it was originally sent or stored. There are many ways of providing integrity.

NONREPUDIATION

You did so get my message! Nonrepudiation is the prevention of denial that a message has been sent or received or that an action was taken. It proves that a message has been sent and received. It ensures that the sender of the message can't deny having sent it or the receiver deny having received the message. Nonrepudiation is based on a unique signature or identification that proves who created the message or information and what happened to it. When nonrepudiation is present, we can prove that a person is connected to an action or event.

A colleague of ours told us a really good, true story that illustrates one requirement for nonrepudiation. A covert military operation using various listening devices was taking place deep in a jungle without the host country's permission. This operation was in place to monitor and listen to various communications within the country. The mundane quiet was suddenly broken by an emergency encoded message sent from headquarters. It was quickly decrypted and authenticated. The resulting coded command indicated in no uncertain terms to leave immediately and destroy the operation. The message contained a special authenticator to prove that this could only come from an authorized individual in headquarters, which was verified by a special process. The message could only have been sent by the person authorized to do so.

As a result of this command, everyone scrambled into the jungle while the "special red button was pushed," starting the destruction process. All of the equipment in the building was surrounded by explosives for just such an event. The evacuation and destruction order was executed and the building and contents were destroyed. For a few days the soldiers hid in the jungle awaiting rescue. It soon became evident that something was amiss, since no one came to pick them up.

The simple truth was that the message was sent to the wrong location. The operation that was required to be terminated wasn't, and this one, that didn't need to be terminated, was. This is a good illustration of the requirement for not only requiring nonrepudiation of origin but also nonrepudiation of delivery. The origin of the message was proved to be without dispute. If an acknowledgment of proof of delivery was required by headquarters, the order could have been recognized as having been sent to the wrong location and corrected.

AUDIT AND AUDIT TRAILS

Audit seems to be one of those necessary evils that usually shows up in a security system. An audit is described as a process by which a trustworthy, knowledgeable and independent individual accumulates and evaluates evidence for the purpose of reporting how the subject under review meets established criteria. The purpose of computer auditing is to review the conformance of the system or network that is under review against established security policy, guidelines, or industry standards. We need the ability to keep track and review everything that may be considered to be a security problem and everything that may lead to a security problem.

An audit trail is an organized list, usually kept by the time an event occurred. These events can be triggered by access to information, utilization of system resources, or interactions with security mechanisms. If we have been the target of an unauthorized intruder, we need to understand the impact of that security compromise by reviewing what information was accessed and if any improper use of the system was executed. A review of the audit trails will help with this understanding. A good security system will have robust audit facilities and audit trails.

SECURITY PROCESS

We can now put these security components to work. Figure 3.1 will illustrate where these components are used. We will assume that a personal computer, called the *client,* is the major entry point into the system. The need is to connect to another computer, called the *server,* in order to execute transactions. The client and the server are considered to be in one *domain.*

The user ID and password are submitted by the user at the client using a login request. This user ID and password should be kept confidential by encrypting them before they are sent to the server for authentication. The password is used by the server to authenticate the user. The passwords should always be stored in encrypted form on the server. The login request generates the authentication response if the user ID and password are valid. Subsequent transactions will be executed if the user is authorized to do so based on the users authenticated identity. The transaction messages can include integrity and nonrepudiation components in the form of appended message digests and digital signatures if they are required.

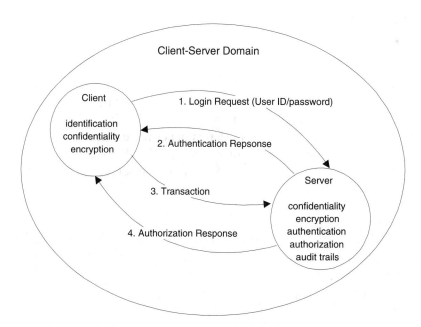

Figure 3.1 Login process

TRUST—WHAT IS IT?

Why should you trust your business processes to the system that is spread across more than one processor over which you may not have control? Unless all of the components that make up the system meet your required trust level, you will not use the system. This level of trust is established only if all of the required qualities are included in the system. The components and qualities that meet this required level may be quite different depending on your point of view and specific requirements. Different people may require different qualities from the same system components for different reasons.

The builder of a house wants the design of the house to be simple and relatively easy to build. The builder wants good quality materials to be used and quality tools to be available to make efficient use of his or her time and expertise. The finished house should be free of defects, and any changes that may be required should be easy and inexpensive to implement. The realtor wants to represent a house that has lots of features and is built by a reputable builder so that it is easy to sell. The buyer wants a home that is reliable, secure, and good value for the money. All of these requirements are different, but they must be satisfied by the same house. Trust is established when all of the specified qualities have been satisfied for each of the parties involved.

Trust can be defined as a confident reliance on the integrity, honesty, or justice of another. Trust refers to the ability of the application to perform actions with integrity, to keep confidential information private, and to perform its functions on a continuing basis. Those charged with the design, deployment, and management of computing systems must recognize and respond to the question: How can we maintain a high level of trust in a system which may be distributed and where the system and controls may be at a greater risk of violation? Once trust is lost, it takes a lot of work and convincing to be reestablished.

With any automated system, you will have an idea of what the system must provide to allow you to trust it. The model we use to explain the components of trust in a computing system is composed of three major sections: security, availability, and performance. Security is made up of the security building blocks—authentication, authorization, integrity, confidentiality, and nonrepudiation—we have just discussed. Availability depends on those facilities and qualities that ensure the system is always available for use. Acceptable performance is required to prevent frustration and a potential circumvention of controls. We will have greater confidence in obtaining a

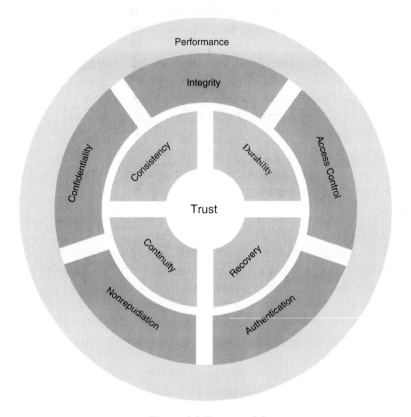

Figure 3.2 Trust model

trusted environment if all three of these factors are present and addressed to our satisfaction and before trust can be assured. Figure 3.2 illustrates the components and the qualities for the major sections of a trusted system.

AVAILABILITY

The second characteristic required for trust is availability. You need to be able to have faith that a transaction that you have entered will in fact be executed in a timely manner. There is a undocumented but acknowledged system frustration level. This level is a factor of how much the actual response time experienced is in relation to what you expected. If there is a wide variance or if it is erratic, the frustration level rises exponentially with this variance. If the system is not ready to be used when you need it, your work processes will be impacted. Even if the system does exactly what you need to meet your business requirements, it must be available *when* you need it and be able to complete the tasks within a reasonable time. Availability includes:

- *Continuity*—the ability to withstand a complete service interruption and invoke subsequent recovery in the event of the failure of physical components.

- *Durability*—the ability to withstand a partial or gradual degradation in service that would occur in the event of failure of some of the physical components of the distributed system.

- *Recovery*—the ability to recover from a complete service interruption with no additional manual effort.

- *Consistency*—the ability to always realize the same results given the same data and processing criteria. The distributed process must always be consistent.

PERFORMANCE

The third component of a trusted environment is performance. In order for a computing system to be accepted and utilized, it must perform the required functions as quickly as needed. However, if using the system impedes your work to an aggravating degree or the task is faster to accomplish manually, you are unlikely to use it. An example of this would be an authentication process that requires a password to be entered for several portions of the process or a query that uses several processors connected by a slow network connection. A system should not be frustrating to use. The design of a secure system and the associated security policy should take into account the practical trade-offs needed to deliver an appropriate, trusted system that performs well and at a cost in line with the value of the assets it is designed to protect.

BOUNDARIES OF TRUST

In any distributed computing environment, there is a need to define what are the boundaries of our trust. If we live in a high-rise apartment that has a locked entrance or a security guard in the lobby, we will assume that everyone who is in the building is authorized to do so. We grant them a certain degree of trust after having passed the first test, the front door. We also need to define what the boundaries of trust are in the distributed computing environment. Whenever we distribute information or intelligence, we want the places to which we distribute them to be secure. How far does the authorization span? When and where do we need to check the authentication and authorization again?

One of the problems already discussed deals with too many boundaries of trust. As a user, we want the boundary of trust to include everything with which we may need to interact in the course of our business. This means that we shouldn't have to log-on to several systems using different passwords. From a security viewpoint, we want the boundary to be vary narrow and only allow those with explicit authority access to the system and information. The boundary of trust must be wide enough to be able to promote productivity without introducing too many risks.

TRUST—WHY DO WE NEED IT?

When you use a single computer, it is relatively easy to detect if the system is operating as expected. If the system is not operating properly, there are a limited number of places to look for the problem. These are generally simple operations where information is obtained and possibly a file is updated. More sophisticated systems, where multiple files may be updated, require that mechanisms be put in place to deal with the odd occasion where an update fails and more than one file has to be reset to the point before the operation was initiated. Now imagine the complexity involved when the computer program execution and the file updates can occur across several individual computers in various locations. How can you trust the system to produce what you want, determine whether it was successful or not and return all processes to the same point as if the failure never happened? Trust is never having to question the state of the system or the data.

There are three things that currently inhibit the implementation of distributed computing systems: available network bandwidth, robust management systems, and complete distributed security systems. In order to be able to place any part of a computing process on a system in a location where it makes the most logical sense, we need sufficient network communication capacity to ensure that using the network does not cause a bottleneck. The availability of sufficient network bandwidth is very much a factor of cost and not technology. The required network bandwidth is available if you can justify the cost. The systems management area is one that is probably causing the most concern at the moment. The standard system management components are not yet available for all of the desired platforms or for the various ways that distributed systems can be implemented. The standards for security components are lagging also in the definition and implementation level that is required to match the capability of distributing the work. We have the ability to distribute the data and processes without the required robust ability to secure and manage them.

SUMMARY

Trust must be designed into a computing environment and not added later. A system is rarely purchased for trusted qualities unless that is the driving requirement of the system. A trusted distributed computing system requires quite a bit more than just adequate security mechanisms. There are numerous ways to design a distributed computing system. The components that will ensure a trusted system should be selected during system design. A trusted computing environment must contain security, availability, and performance components that meet your required level of trust.

When do you know that you can have complete trust in a system? Unfortunately trust does not have an absolute measurement index. Even if there was an index, the level to which a system is trusted may not be the same for any two that are implemented. You can never have too much trust but how much is enough? The performance and availability requirements for a banking or air traffic control system will probably be more stringent than for an inventory system. Banking transactions have a very high requirement to complete when started and be accurate. The availability and security requirements may vary according to the number of users of the system. If there are footprints in the snow behind your house, should you be concerned? If your house is next to a playground, you may not be as concerned as you might be if your house is at the end of a rural road. Now that we have established the basic concepts of trust and we have a definition for security, it's time we looked at how we can use these concepts in distributed computing. One of the challenges in addressing the problem of computing security is to develop some structure around these security components and begin to build a security architecture.

CHAPTER 4

AN ARCHITECTURE

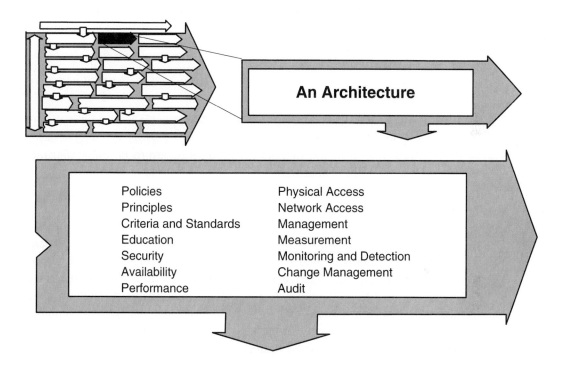

An Architecture

Policies	Physical Access
Principles	Network Access
Criteria and Standards	Management
Education	Measurement
Security	Monitoring and Detection
Availability	Change Management
Performance	Audit

Now that we have covered a few of the stories and outlined some of the issues, are you sure you still want to deal with a distributed environment? Let's start designing a secure environment now that we understand a little better what we are dealing with. We have defined what a distributed processing system is and have dealt with a few of the issues; it's time to start getting everything organized. We need to keep everything in view and make sure all of the required areas have been covered. In a centralized system, security can be mainly provided by the application of technology. It is much more difficult to manage the security components when they are scattered across multiple platforms and multiple locations. A blueprint dealing with security will give you a frame of reference to measure the security processes against the components of the distributed platforms. These required components are logically combined into a reference framework we refer to as the security architecture.

> All buildings that last for a long time are built on a solid foundation. We first need a blueprint for this foundation to make sure everything we need now and in the future will be supported. You can add to the foundation of the house after the first story has been completed, but it costs an awful lot more!

An architecture is defined as a vision that accomplishes the following;

- Provides a conceptual definition and structure of an undefined environment.
- Allows for the design of individual components within the environment.
- Specifies how the individual components are to be integrated into the overall environment.
- Ensures the completed environment meets the original established vision.

The goal of security is to reduce the enterprise's risk of financial and public image losses caused by intrusion, system misuse, privilege abuse, tampering, fraud, and service interruption. Protection must be provided against external threats (e.g., hackers, foreign adversaries, and the criminal element) and from internal abuse (e.g., unstable or unscrupulous employees). In addition, the security infrastructure must not prohibit the use of advanced information services in order to permit efficient and economic use of information technology. The goal of a security architecture is to produce a model that provides the required security components as well as a base for comparison of various mechanisms and approaches.

The security architecture incorporates elements to safeguard the confidentiality of information and ensure that all access to the computing resources is authorized and authenticated. Specific objectives of the architecture are to promote the integrity, consistency, and confidentiality of the distributed applications and information. The overall objective of the architecture is to allow trust to be placed in the distributed environment. This is achieved through mechanisms which provide authentication, access control or authorization, integrity, confidentiality, and nonrepudiation. All of these attributes must be present before security can be effective and complete. We need to be able to trust all of the points where users access the system rather than have the trust placed only where the information and tools are resident.

Is a security architecture essential? This is a question that is asked many times. The lack of a security architecture will not prevent a system from operating or be immediately compromised, but it can lead to vulnerabilities caused by mistake or oversight. For example, in a large organization that is made up of several business units, each with its own security mechanisms and supporting systems, it may not be easy or possible to securely access one system from another without each conforming to a common security architecture. Each system may have the required security, but the security systems may not be compatible with each other resulting in problems when access between the business units is required. This is highlighted if one business unit has higher security requirements than another.

A defined security architecture can be used to ensure the design of applications and systems will meet the required security objectives. The architecture will help guide decisions between systems and across platforms and ensure all of the systems meet a standard minimum level of security. It is much more difficult to apply a security architecture to systems that have already been designed or built. The security architecture is not dependent on the existence of a system architecture. A defined security architecture does not deal with technologies.

A usual component of an architecture is the definition of the critical success factors. A critical success factor is defined as the things that absolutely must go right in order to achieve the business objectives. A major critical success factor in the security architecture is not an identification of things that must be successfully changed but rather how to maintain the secure integrity of the business processes in the face of changes to those processes and structures.

> One of the ways to help understand the distributed environment is to put an architecture in place. This will provide a reference point you can use to make sense out of all of the parts and provide some consistency of the secure solution.

The security architecture is comprised of a number of building blocks which together define the framework for a comprehensive solution. Figure 4.1 represents the major components that should be considered in a security architecture. This model is one way of representing the major components

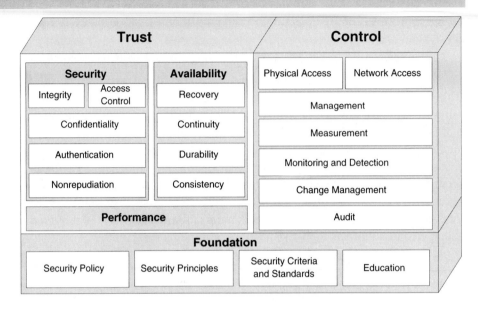

Figure 4.1 Security Architecture Model

of a security architecture and how they maybe positioned between each other. It is useful to help explain the components and how the components interrelate. Other models or representations may be valid but it is important that an architectural approach be used.

This model is divided into three major components, the *foundation, trust,* and *control.* The foundation is comprised of the overall security principles that are defined by the organization. It also includes the security policies which govern the implementation and use of the security mechanisms. It may also include the specific security criteria or standards if they have been selected. The trust layer defines the security, availability, and performance characteristics that will establish trust in a distributed system. The control layer outlines the mechanisms used to manage and control the required security components.

We will look at each of these major components in more detail.

FOUNDATION

The basic building block of a security architecture is the foundation. It is anchored by the definition of the corporate policies, principles, and perhaps a defined security criteria and selected standards. The establishment of a secure, distributed processing environment must be governed by clear, concise guiding statements, supported by management. These security policies provide a framework which is essential in the distributed environment to ensure the informational assets are secured with a governing policy. Another building block of the foundation is the security principles. The principles reflect the philosophy and style of the organization. The security criteria may specify an established security reference standard that has been chosen or is required. Specific security standards may also be selected or required as a base for the architecture. The components of the foundation will be explored in more detail in the next chapter.

POLICIES

The security policy can be described as a series of statements from senior management that articulate the goals and acceptable procedures of the organization. These statements will generally be unique to each individual organization. A security policy is essential in a distributed computing environment to ensure that all of the informational assets are protected by a governing set of acceptable actions. The policy will set direction, give broad guidance, and demonstrate management's support and commitment to a secure environment. The procedures of the organization define the implementation processes of the policy. A policy is the fabric which promotes the consistency of user actions and acceptable behavior.

The computing security policies must be complete and easy to understand. The objectives of security policies are to effectively manage risk, define employee accountability for the protection of information assets, establish a basis for a stable process environment, ensure compliance with applicable laws and regulations, and preserve management options in the event of asset misuse, loss, or unauthorized disclosure.

PRINCIPLES

The principles are statements, particular to the organization, that define what security means to the organization and how it will be implemented. The principles provide a fundamental base which guides the requirements and decisions concerning the security system components and technology. If the corporate principle states that users will be inherently trusted, the security policies and mechanisms will be implemented to explicitly deny access to unauthorized resources and implicitly grant access to all others. If users will inherently not be trusted, the security policy and mechanisms will be implemented to explicitly grant authorized access and deny all others. The principles define the philosophy of the organization to security. The policies translates this philosophy into laws that can be applied and followed.

CRITERIA AND STANDARDS

Security criteria and standards are an optional component of the foundation. A security criteria is a defined reference standard that can be applied to security components and technology. One of the most widely acknowledged reference standard is the Trusted Computer System Evaluation Criteria defined by the U.S. Department of Defense. This standard is used as a technology selection criteria in many government systems.

Security standards can also play an important role in establishing the foundation of the architecture. The selection of specific security standards may in fact be a requirement for systems that require interaction outside of the organization. The ability to use automated teller machines that have been interconnected requires that security standards be strictly applied and adhered to.

EDUCATION

One additional component of a solid foundation is an awareness and education program for everyone who will be affected by the security architecture. An awareness program will outline the value and commitment that the organization places on security. A formal education program should be developed and maintained to assist those who are responsible for the security mechanisms and processes. The security policies will not have an impact or be enforceable if the people do not know that the policies exist or what their individual responsibilities are. The education and awareness program must be considered as a required component of a security architecture.

TRUST

Trust in computing systems is defined as a composite of security, availability, and performance. All three components must be present and within acceptable bounds before trust can be established. Trust refers to the ability of a computer system to perform the processes with integrity, keep confidential information private, and perform the required functions on a continual basis. Trust can be difficult to establish across a distributed network where many factors and entities can influence the ability to obtain the required security, availability, and performance. Trust can be secured if the requirements for security, availability, and performance are satisfied.

SECURITY

The first building block of trust is security. This block contains all of the basic mechanisms that are needed to build a secure distributed environment. As we have seen in Chapter 3, the security building block is comprised of the components integrity, authorization, confidentiality, authentication, and nonrepudiation.

INTEGRITY

An integrity protection mechanism protects data from corruption (modification, loss, replay, reordering, or substitution), either by accident or deliberate tampering. An approach to integrity accepts that data may be accidentally or deliberately corrupted and mechanisms are put in place to ensure any corruption is detected and either corrected or flagged to be noticed. A number of methods are available to deal with integrity. Most methods involve the use of a control value that is compared to the data.

These methods can apply to data contained in a transmitted message or stored on disk. An agreed-upon set of data is processed with an algorithm and the result attached as an appendix to the message. The receiver of the message uses the same algorithm to reprocess the message to recreate the test data which is compared to the appendix. A match indicates that the message has not been altered. A more secure variation of this method involves adding some secret data to the message before computing the appendix and then removing the secret data before sending the message. The receiver applies the same secret data to the message before computing the appendix. In this way, the creation of the appendix is not totally dependent on data present in the message.

Another area that requires integrity is the operation of system applications. Mechanisms are required to control the development, modification and implementation of applications to ensure the integrity of the system in operation. We need to be sure that the distributed applications themselves have not been altered in an unauthorized way. The integrity of the applications should be governed by a security policy specifically dealing with this issue.

ACCESS CONTROL

The use of access controls provides a means of enforcing authorization to use system resources. Authorization, also called access control, is usually based upon an identification mechanism accompanied by an authentication mechanism. Access to resources is then granted if the identity is authenticated. In distributed computing, the two most common ways of determining authorization are by user ID accompanied by a validated password and authenticated system ID.

A single common solution for authorization is not likely included in all of the distributed systems. It is more likely that authorization will be based upon the nature and target of the request. Relational database technology provides authorization with access controls at the data record, element and view levels. The access control list (ACL) mechanism, such as implemented in the Distributed Computing Environment (DCE), provides a standards-based authorization mechanism for access to processes and data resources. The operating systems themselves also implement various types of access restrictions, based on system ID or user ID.

Authorization can be based on time dependency, data classification, role or function of the user, system address, type of transaction, and type of service requested. Authorization is also sometimes implemented at the function level within an application, using a user/function matrix approach. Administration of the authorization mechanisms is a major challenge in a distributed environment.

CONFIDENTIALITY

In computer systems, confidentiality refers to the ability of the system to keep confidential electronic information secret and protect it from unauthorized disclosure. The implementation of confidentiality ensures that information cannot be accessed by a user or process other than those that are authorized. The primary method for keeping information confidential is to alter the form of the data through encryption. The various networks that are available today do not, in themselves, allow a high degree of trust to be placed in their operation. The encryption of the data, at least all data used for authentication, should be considered mandatory to prevent unauthorized detection and tampering. While an obvious solution would be to encrypt all traffic, encryption is costly and relatively slow to perform. A balance is required between security needs, network and processing costs, and network performance.

AUTHENTICATION

Authentication is the method of uniquely identifying a user, machine or application and verifying this identity. It is the basis for authorization and a fundamental requirement for access control and audit. Authentication may be based on something you know (e.g., a password), something you have (e.g., an electronic ID card) or a combination of these approaches. Considerations for authentication include the choice of a unique authentication mechanism for every system/application or using a common authentication mechanism across multiple systems (single sign-on), authentication of both the client and server in a client/server environment, and the integrity of the authentication process (e.g., clear-text passwords).

NONREPUDIATION

Nonrepudiation is the characteristic that allows total confidence in the identification of the owner/creator of a resource. Nonrepudiation refers to the ability to prevent denial that a message has been sent or received or an action taken. Nonrepudiation is provided when there is a means of proving that the message or action could only have been produced by the sender. There are two distinct cases where nonrepudiation would apply. *Repudiation of origin* is a disagreement of who originated the data item, and *Repudiation of delivery* is a disagreement of whether the data was actually received. In electronic media, nonrepudiation is accomplished by the use of digital signatures.

AVAILABILITY

Availability is always required but not usually considered to be tightly aligned with security. Availability should be an important component of trust when referring to a security architecture. You will trust a system more if it is always available when you need it. The factors that determine availability are

- *Continuity*—the ability to withstand a complete service interruption and invoke subsequent recovery in the event of the failure of physical components.
- *Durability*—the ability to withstand a partial or gradual degradation that would occur in the event of failure of the physical components of the distributed system.
- *Recovery*—the ability to recover from a complete service interruption without manual intervention.
- *Consistency*—the ability to always realize the same results given the same data and processing criteria.

The implementation of a distributed system should take the availability factors into account. Availability may be impacted by an unauthorized attack on a system, designed to preoccupy the system with unproductive processing and denying legitimate users the productive use of the system. This is called a denial of service attack. Mechanisms should be put in place to support the availability requirements before a system can be classed as trusted.

PERFORMANCE

Performance is the third component of trust and is especially important in a distributed processing environment. A system that is distributed across more than one platform must be able to provide the results of a distributed process in the time desired by the user. You won't rely on or even use a system that will not respond within a tolerable timeframe. Any system that stands in the way of an effective job function, because of performance problems, will not be used. Overall performance can be impacted by the choices of security technology that are implemented and the depth to which the security mechanisms are utilized. For example, the encryption and decryption of data transactions will add a substantial percentage of overhead to processing time. You can't always trust a system if the responses never seem to come back. There will be a great urge to clear the screen and try again.

CONTROL

Now that we have established the policies and principles for a security architecture and the trust mechanisms, we need to think about how to manage them. The third area which contributes to security architecture contains the functions used to control the security mechanisms. These functions provide the management and measurement capability that is required to oversee the secure operation of the system. This is the area where the least number of controlling or guiding standards exist. The management and control of distributed security elements can present an administration and security challenge. Distributed security control and management processes must be implemented as a necessary component of an overall security architecture.

Required control mechanisms include

- *Physical access*—control of access to the actual computing and network devices.
- *Network access*—control of access to the network.
- *Management*—the control of the security mechanisms.
- *Measurement*—the impact of security mechanisms and potential detection of unusual events.
- *Monitoring and detection*—the ability to detect when a compromise situation is in effect.

- *Change management*-the management of changes to the security mechanisms.
- *Audit*-the trail of information available to track security events.

PHYSICAL ACCESS

Access to a computing or networking device is generally not very difficult for those wishing to compromise the system if additional stringent controls are not in place. In general, the access controls that come standard with the machines are not adequate or haven't been implemented to support the secure use of the equipment. Additional access security requirements can be implemented using an additional device (key, smart card, token) to physically secure a device or system access. These can be used to locally prove the individual should have access, or in the case of a challenge-response unit or smart card used to authenticate the user to the system. Higher security requirements that restrict access to a specific individual can be satisfied with the use of biometric devices such as fingerprint scanners, retina scanners, voice pattern, keystroke pattern, and signature verification devices.

NETWORK ACCESS

Network access controls provide the ability to limit access to the network to only those people or processes that are authorized to do so. Network access controls are easier to put in place when the entire network is within the management and control of the corporation. This trusted network, however, may not be totally secure. Access to the network may be gained by tapping a communication line and monitoring the traffic. A trusted network does not preclude other security mechanisms such as encryption. Additional controls must be put into place when the corporate network is connected to a public network or is interconnected with other networks.

MANAGEMENT

Distributed systems management is a complex problem involving a variety of resources to be managed, management tasks, and solution structures. A key challenge for system managers is the uniqueness of each distributed environment. Effective management is required in many layers of a distributed system including the operating system, network, access control mechanisms, key management, database management, middleware, and network operating systems. Management tools may span two or three of these areas, but it is very difficult to find tools that span all of them. The management functions of a number of these areas may also be centralized, but probably not integrated into a single management unit.

MEASUREMENT

Measurement facilities are used to analyze and report on the performance state of the components. The facilities for measurement are also often used to account for the usage of components. The use of measurement facilities is not often referenced in the control of the security elements, but they can be useful to detect unauthorized behavior outside the norm of expected behavior. Technologies are available that can perform an analysis of computing usage and flag any unexpected behaviors which might indicate a problem area.

MONITORING AND DETECTION

Another nagging problem that accompanies the implementation of a distributed security system is the requirement for monitoring the operation of the security system and detecting actual or potential security problems. There are two approaches to this problem. The implementation of passive monitoring will use a mechanism that can review all of the available information and produce a report on any weaknesses that were found. A dynamic monitoring system will actively exercise and probe the security system looking for weaknesses. A dynamic system is best if it is implemented with automated controls.

CHANGE MANAGEMENT

Another challenge in a distributed processing environment is the management and maintenance of the security components such as user and password lists, access control lists and encryption keys. These changes are required to be done in a secure environment to provide integrity of the security mechanisms. Processes and mechanisms for the implementation and coordination of change across the distributed environment are also an important requirement. The security of the administration functions for the distributed security environment must also be considered, because these may be manipulated to gain unauthorized access to a system.

AUDIT

Audit can be separated into two areas, each having a different focus and purpose. Every security architecture should include an independent and knowledgeable review of the control mechanisms. This will measure the security system as implemented against the standards and established criteria. The second area is the use of an audit trail to trace user actions and events and which can be used for reporting and control purposes and for reconstruction or investigation into an event. The placement and operation of audit functions may be influenced by performance and/or cost issues. An accreditation process will review the security mechanisms to provide assurance that they are in place and operating as expected. Accreditation should be performed to verify the operation of the security mechanisms after updates or changes are made.

SUMMARY

The security architecture will provide a reference point to compare the requirements and various security mechanisms of a distributed system. If all of the components that are listed in this chapter are addressed in the appropriate manner, you are well on your way to building a secure distributed environment. Now that we have a solid blueprint we can start to lay down the foundation for trust in the distributed environment.

In the next chapter, we will look at the key building blocks for security and trust. We will provide you with an understanding of what comprises a solid foundation and provide a common starting point for the many complex areas concerning security and trust in a distributed computing environment.

CHAPTER 5

THE FOUNDATION

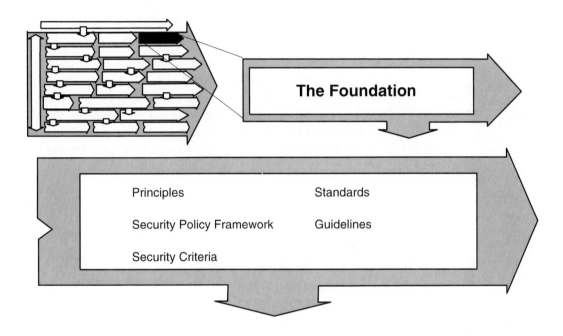

The Foundation

Principles   Standards

Security Policy Framework   Guidelines

Security Criteria

Now that we have taken a look at the big picture of the security architecture, it's time to start looking into the decisions that form the foundation of the architecture (Figure 5.1). The architecture determines what the house looks like and what qualities it will have. The foundation will determine the character of the house and establish its ability to support the desired structure when the construction is completed. The foundation should also be able to support future renovations and additions. In a security architecture, the foundation is made up of the statements and decisions that describe what type of secure environment is required and the qualities that this environment must have within the organization.

The first building block that we will look at in this chapter are the principles, the statements that describe the attitude and philosophy of the organization. We will next examine the security policies that are needed to govern the distributed environment. Many times you may see references to "C2" or "B1" security as a way of describing a level of security provided by a system. These levels are used to compare the security qualities of one system against a reference standard. We will look at what these levels are and what they mean as a base for security. There are a few standards dealing with computer security, specifically in the area of term definition and criteria. We will identify some of these as they relate to a security architecture. Awareness and education of the need for security and the responsibility that everyone has to maintain a secure environment rounds out the foundation. Once a sturdy foundation has been built, the rest of the security infrastructure rests safely on top.

In this chapter, we will describe the components of the foundation and how the foundation supports the other parts of the architecture. As mentioned before, the foundation of the security architecture is based on a collection of decisions or statements the organization has made or should make. These decisions and statements are then used as a reference to develop the details of the security architecture, the collection of policies and the identification of a security criteria. Some of the questions that should be answered by these decisions and statements are

- What does the organization need to protect?
- What is the security philosophy of the organization?
- What standards should be followed?
- Do the employees have access to all information?
- Who is responsible for security?

PRINCIPLES

The principles used for security are statements of values, operation, or belief of the corporation that in turn define or influence all of the elements of the security architecture. The collection of principles provides the security philosophy under which the security architecture and the security policies

Figure 5.1 Security architecture foundation

are developed. The security policies and procedures should in turn be founded on business principles, the statements of the corporate philosophy. The principles should be complete, and be simple to understand and carry out. Principles are statements of values, operation, or belief that drive all of the elements of the security framework. These principles can be thought of as rules by which the security policies and processes must follow. The following are examples of the type of statements that would be listed as principles for almost all organizations.

"Data is a corporate asset and must be managed with a corporate perspective."

"The organization will provide adequate security and business controls to safeguard data, given management's assessment of the risks involved."

"Data is the representation of discrete facts; information is an aggregation of data which is used for decision making."

"The corporation will provide adequate security and business controls to safeguard data, given management's assessment of the risks involved. These controls will define a minimum standard that should be used for all systems and provide a criteria against which systems are to be measured."

"The responsibilities and accountability of owners, providers, users of information, and other parties concerned with the security of information must be explicit."

"Owners, providers, users of information, and other parties must be able to readily gain appropriate knowledge of the existence and general extent of the policies, practices, and procedures for security."

"Security measures, practices, and procedures should not significantly reduce the productivity of authorized individuals using the resources of the corporation. These measures, practices, and procedures should be coordinated and integrated to create a coherent system of security."

"Security requirements vary depending upon the value and importance of particular information systems. Security practices and procedures will be appropriate to the value of the information systems and the degree of reliance placed upon them by the corporation. These policies should be proportionate in direct and indirect costs to the severity, probability, and extent of potential harm."

"Owners, providers, and users of information, and the management of the corporation, must act in a timely, coordinated manner to prevent, detect, and respond to breaches in security."

"The security of information must be reassessed periodically, considering changes in technology and business requirements."

"The security policies, standards, and procedures will be established to serve as a basis for management planning, control, and evaluation of information security activities."

There may be a few principles that are dependent on the specific philosophy and culture of the organization. An organization may inherently trust all of the employees or grant access on a strictly need-to-know basis. For example, a principle may be defined that indicates the organization specifically grants access to sensitive information and denies everything else or explicitly denies access to sensitive information and grants access to everything else. This principle will influence how security mechanisms will be implemented. The following are examples of the type of statements that may vary from one organization to another.

"The information security approaches should favor small and simple safeguards that provide the required level of security as opposed to large and complex ones."

"The employees of the corporation will be granted sufficient privilege to accomplish assigned tasks and are inherently trusted to use information resources in a responsible manner for the legitimate business purposes of the corporation."

"The security policies of the corporation will be centrally enforced in the distributed computing environment."

SECURITY POLICY FRAMEWORK

The establishment of a secure distributed processing environment must be based on clear, concise statements, supported by management. The security policies provide a framework which is essential in the distributed processing environment to ensure the corporate informational assets are secured with a governing policy. The security framework defines the policies that provide direction for the implementation and maintenance of security measures to protect the information assets of the organization. The framework is intended to provide guidance and outline responsibilities. It is not intended to be a definition of processes or procedures. The objectives of a security policy framework are to effectively manage risk, maintain employee accountability for the protection of information assets, establish a basis for a stable process environment, assure compliance with applicable laws and regulations, and preserve management options in the event of asset misuse, loss or unauthorized disclosure.

The security framework must be subject to an open process for continual development and update. There are many reasons to implement a security framework and the processes for framework management. The acquisition, merger, partnership or interface with other organizations may bring into question components of the security policy or criteria. The selected policies and criteria may not address all aspects of the environment as it evolves and will be subject to continued review and update.

The success of the security framework of policies can be measured by critical success factors. These are defined as the things that absolutely must be achieved for the policy framework to be successful. The critical success factors include senior management commitment and support for the security policies and criteria, user community awareness of the policies and criteria, keeping the policies and security criteria independent of technology, the readability and clarity of the policies, and the integration of the policies and security criteria into a security architecture.

Information and the resources used to access, process, and communicate information will be referred to as information assets. The security framework applies to all information assets and services which support business activities of the organization. Information assets include data, image, text, voice, video, any information processing equipment (e.g., mainframe, PC, printers), media (e.g., diskettes, tape), networks, supporting facilities, and information processing services.

Security policy provides the foundation of a security infrastructure. In the absence of formal policy, it may be difficult to hold users accountable for their actions. Policies will provide important guidance to assist with the increasing interconnection or merging among organizations. The policies and procedures are independent of technology. The policies and procedures of the organization must be applicable and be easily understood.

Policies usually exist for areas that include data classification, identification, authorization, authentication, and data custodianship. Policies can also provide direction on the relationships and responsibilities within the organization and between organizations. We will go into more detail on the topics to be considered and the policy development process. We are assuming that the security framework policies will not cover the conduct of the employees. These should be addressed by other standards of conduct or other business policies.

SECURITY CRITERIA

The definition of security criteria, along with the principles, forms the second major block of the foundation for a security architecture. The security criteria refer to the determination and definition of the required attributes of a secure environment. These attributes are grouped into classifications which provide a basis for product and process choices for the security components and mechanisms. The criteria form a reference standard against which an evaluation of the security components and features of technology and processes can be performed. This definition of the required collection of security functionality is independent of platform or vendors. Different classes of security will be appropriate to different industries or type of computing systems involved. The criteria will influence the choice of technology and products that are chosen to supply systems and services over all of the interconnected distributed platforms.

There are a few definitions of standard security criteria that are recognized as industry standards, although most of them are applicable to military systems. The U.S. Department of Defense, National Computer Security Center, has produced a number of books dealing with several different aspects of security. Each of these books is identified by a different color. The Trusted Computer System Evaluation Criteria (TCSEC) *Orange Book* provides a generally accepted framework that system vendors base the secure components of their products. The Trusted Network Interpretation (TNI) *Red Book* of the Trusted Computer System Evaluation Criteria provides an extension to the *Orange Book* with detailed guidance on how the *Orange Book* should be interpreted in a network environment. The *Red Book* also describes additional security services that are appropriate in a networked environment. A more commercially oriented security criteria has been defined by the European Computer Manufacturers Association (ECMA). The open systems organization, X/Open, has undertaken the initiative in defining a minimum set of operating system security features to be included in systems with an X/Open brand.

TRUSTED COMPUTER SYSTEM EVALUATION CRITERIA
(ORANGE BOOK)

A description and the requirements of security classes have been defined by the U.S. National Computer Security Center in a document called the *Orange Book*. This document can be used to evaluate commercial products and provide an overall rating or classification which is published in an evaluated products list. This list is used by various departments and agencies to compare the security capabilities and components between the various products. A decision on a specific security class for the organization will provide a base standard for the definition of requirements and the evaluation of security products and mechanisms.

The *Orange Book* classifications, as defined in the Trusted Computer System Evaluation Criteria, are tuned more toward military and government requirements for confidentiality of classified information but can also provide guidance for a general technology approach to security. Many operating systems will be marketed as "C2" certified or "C2" compliant. A system that is certified has been subjected to an official certification process whereas a compliant system includes all of the features defined by the class but has not been subjected to the certification process. In general, "C2" is considered to be the minimum classification that should be used as a goal for every system in the enterprise. Table 5.1 outlines the security classifications as defined in the *Orange Book*.

TABLE 5.1
ITSEC ORANGE BOOK SECURITY CRITERIA SPECIFICATIONS

Division	Description
None	Any system that fails to meet the requirements in division A, B, or C.
C1	**Discretionary Security Protection:** Systems incorporate some form of controls capable of limiting access on an individual basis. The user decides what protections to enforce, such as the UNIX file permissions.
C2	**Controlled Access Protection:** Systems in this class enforce more access control than C1 systems, making users individually accountable for their actions through logon procedures, auditing of events, and resource isolation.
B1	**Labeled Security Protection:** All the features required for class C2, plus an informal statement of the security policy model, data labeling, and mandatory access control over named subjects and objects must be present. The system enforces some form of protection that is not under your control.
B2	**Structured Protection:** All controls in B1 extended to all subjects and objects in the system. In addition, convert channels are addressed.
B3	**Security Domains:** Must satisfy the reference monitor requirements that it mediate all accesses of subjects to objects, be tamperproof, and be small enough to be subjected to tests and analysis.
A1	**Verified Design:** Functionally equivalent to B2 except the user must prove that the security model and/or the implementation is secure.
A+(2)	**Verified Implementation:** Extensive verification methodology, trusted design environment, and advanced testing process.

The "B"-level security classifications are used mostly for military systems although this level may also be applicable in some cases to financial systems. A class of "B1" would be a target for applications and data that are of a sensitive nature that require secure protection. A "B2" class implementation may be required for specific applications and data that require a high level of protection for all components on the host or server. The B1 level of security classification will provide mandatory access controls and labeling for exported information. The C2 level of security establishes a base for controlled access protection that provides guidance for choices across distributed platforms. An identified security criteria classification will establish a common base for security mechanisms that can be evaluated, selected, and implemented across the distributed platforms.

COMMERCIALLY ORIENTED FUNCTIONALITY CLASS

Another specification of security enforcing functions and definitions has been documented in the European Computer Manufacturers Association (ECMA) released Standard 205 called Commercially Oriented Functionality Class (COFC) for security evaluation. This standard is targeted primarily at the commercial marketplace and currently at multiuser stand-alone IT systems. The network and distributed computing considerations are under development.

The COFC standard is intended to define a widely accepted basic security functionality class for the commercial market. This standard is intended to differentiate itself from the *Orange Book* while contributing to the ongoing harmonization process with the TCSEC. The COFC standard is articulated in a manner consistent with the TCSEC. The COFC can also be used as a base for security terminology definitions.

X/OPEN BASELINE SECURITY SERVICES

X/Open is an organization that was founded in 1984 to coordinate requirements and standards for open system products. Products that conform to the standards defined by this body can apply for and utilize the X/Open brand. The X/Open organization has defined a distributed security framework which is used to guide the development of security technologies for open systems. The X/Open baseline security services (XBSS) specification defines the minimum set of security-related functions that must be provided by open systems as well as the default settings for the security related parameters for those systems. The XBSS specification is intended to be used as part of the X/Open branding procedure for branding the systems that support security. Many of the operating systems that are shipped from the vendors do not have the security features turned on. The system will operate without security until the features are turned on. The XBSS will provide a way for the vendors to obtain formal recognition for the security features included in their products.

STANDARDS

The selection of standards for security components and approaches also provides a few bricks for the foundation. As part of the foundation of the security architecture, we are looking for established standards that help with definitions and generic components of the architecture. We have not yet reached the point where it makes sense to determine the standards for technology. As mentioned previously, the security architecture should not be dependent on technology. The establishment of the policies, principles and security criteria will include technology standards when it is time to define a security solution based on the architecture. The following is a selection of standards that are available that may be useful in determing the security architecture.

PRINCIPLES

In the accounting world there is a collection of statements called the Generally Accepted Accounting Practices. These statements provide a base that can be used to compare the accounting practices of one organization with another. In a similar manner there has been work put into the definition of the Generally Accepted System Security Principles (GSSP) by the Information Systems Security Association and other interested organizations. A report was published in 1994 which provides definitions and recommended framework and outlines principles that should be addressed by information security professionals and by information processing products. The GSSP document outlines 17 principles that can provide guidance to the development of the security principles defined by an organization.

POLICY

There are no specific standards associated with the development of policy or procedures. The choices of policy topics and content are mostly unique to each organization. The "color books" of TCSEC of the U.S. Department of Defense, National Computer Security Center, can provide some guidance for policy standards.

- *Orange Book:* Trusted Computer System Evaluation Criteria
- *Red Book:* Trusted Network Interpretation
- *Green Book:* Password Management Guide

- *Blue Book:* Personal Computer Security Considerations
- *Brown Book:* Trusted DBMS Interpretation
- *Yellow Book:* Trusted Environment Interpretation

DEFINITIONS

The security architecture standard ISO/IEC 7498-2, Information Technology—Open Systems Interconnection—Basic Reference Model—Part 2: Security Architecture (also known as ITU-T Recommendation X.800), provides formal definitions for terms that are used in standards definition. This set of definitions should be used to establish a common frame of reference when defining and describing security components.

PHYSICAL SECURITY

The only standard currently in place is specified in the National Communication Security Instruction 5100A (NACSIM 5100A) for the U.S. government, called the Tempest standard. This standard addresses the situation where information can be obtained by electronic eavesdrop of the electrical emanations from computer equipment. Tempest refers to the technology that contains or suppresses signal emissions from electrical equipment and specifies the allowable limits of emissions from electronic equipment. Products built to the Tempest standard can only be exported outside of the United States with the appropriate export license from the Office of Munitions Control of the U.S. State Department. The Tempest standard documents (NACSIM 5100A and NACSI 5004) are themselves classified and only available on a need-to-know basis.

SECURITY MANAGEMENT

Version 2 of the SNMP standard includes RFC 1351: Administration Model; RFC 1352: Security Protocols; and RFC 1353: Definition of Managed Objects for Administration of SNMP Parties. These standards ensure the authentication and privacy of network management communication. Authentication ensures the appropriate origin of the message while privacy protects the messages from disclosure.

MONITORING AND DETECTION

The OSI standard, ISO/IEC 10164-7 (X.736), Security Alarm Reporting Function, lists 14 types of security alarms and their probable causes. A time domain violation, for example, would occur if an attempt were made to perform an operation outside of a scheduled time frame.

AUDIT

There are few standards dealing with the audit process and mechanisms. The DCE RFC 29.0 outlines implementation specifications for the design of an audit subsystem for DCE. There is an OSI standard, ISO/IEC 10164-8 (X.740), Security Audit Trail Function, that defines a audit trail record and the class of events that generates the record type.

AUTHENTICATION

Standards for authentication are addressed by the ISO with ISO/IEC 10181-2 (X.811), Authentication Framework, and ISO/IEC 9594-8 (X.509), Directory Authentication Framework. The X.811 standard explains the terminology which describes authentication principles and architectures, along with a high-level classification scheme for different authentication exchange mechanisms. The X.509 standard addresses X.500 directory authentication using passwords or public key cryptography.

ACCESS CONTROL

The ISO/IEC 10181-3 (X.812), Access Control, standard provides terminology and an architectural model for providing access control in a distributed environment.

CONFIDENTIALITY

The ISO/IEC 10181-5 (X.814), Confidentiality Framework, standard describes the terminology and mechanisms required to provide confidentiality. This standard is a component of the ISO Open System Interconnection—Basic Reference Model—Part 2: Security Architecture. The ISO/IEC 10181-6 (X.815), Integrity Framework, documents definitions and specifications required to provide integrity services.

NONREPUDIATION

The ISO/IEC 10181-4 (X.813), Nonrepudiation Framework, provides terminology and an architectural model for providing nonrepudiation in a distributed environment.

ACCREDITATION

The Guidelines for Computer Security Certification and Accreditation is a document available from the Federal Information Processing Standards Publications (FIPS PUBS #102). This document contains information about establishing a program for certification and accreditation of the security systems.

GUIDELINES

Guidelines are another important component of a comprehensive distributed security environment but are not considered to be part of the security architecture. Guidelines are the documented implementation processes and procedures that apply the principles, policies, and standards to specific areas. The principles, policies, and standards will be consistent across the defined scope of the architecture. The guidelines will provide detail on how these will be applied to specific platforms or technology. For example, a policy may define the purpose, scope, and conformance requirements for authorization across the distributed environment. Specific guidelines will then be defined to indicate how the authorization functions will be implemented on specific platforms. The guidelines function as the translation between the theoretical definitions of the security laws and rules defined by the policies and principles, and the actual mechanisms that are utilized. There may be different guidelines for implementation on platforms with a different technology base.

SUMMARY

Just like a house that will last generations, a well-constructed distributed security system should be built on a solid foundation. Some of the components of the foundations will vary from one organization to another. A well-thought-out foundation is more important in a distributed environment than a centralized one. The foundation is where decisions should be made on an organization's philosophy toward security. These decisions should not have to change when significant changes to the information technology systems are introduced. Any existing principles and policies, created for a centralized environment, should be reviewed for applicability to a distributed one. In the next chapter we will discuss how organizations can create the proper environment by providing guidance to employees through a formal computing policy.

CHAPTER 6

SECURITY POLICY

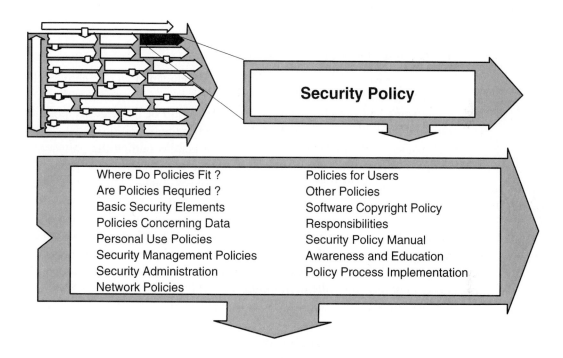

Security Policy

Where Do Policies Fit ?	Policies for Users
Are Policies Requried ?	Other Policies
Basic Security Elements	Software Copyright Policy
Policies Concerning Data	Responsibilities
Personal Use Policies	Security Policy Manual
Security Management Policies	Awareness and Education
Security Administration	Policy Process Implementation
Network Policies	

As we have outlined in the previous chapter, security policy is one of the most important components with which to build the foundation of a security architecture. Security policy is an area that usually gets some attention, especially when the auditors have their say. But a hastily implemented policy usually fails to cover all of the areas that are involved in a distributed environment and may not accomplish what it is intended to do. An organized approach is required to create a proper structure which will address the acceptable conduct, privileges and duties in a comprehensive policy. Such a structure will set direction, give broad guidance to the organization, and demonstrate senior management support, contributing to security-related actions.

A security policy is important in all computing environments to ensure that all corporate informational assets are secured, but is essential in a distributed environment. These assets may be distributed across many individual platforms and geographic areas. The policy protects not only confidentiality, but also the availability of information, the utilization of the information, the authenticity of the information presented, and the integrity of the information. A security policy is actually a collection of individual policies that address specific topics or areas of concern. These can be thought of as the security framework that we previously mentioned in Chapter 5.

WHERE DO SECURITY POLICIES FIT?

In Chapter 5 we outlined the need for a solid foundation which includes the corporate principles and security policies. Figure 6.1 indicates how the flow of decisions and directions leads to the definition of the security policies and guidelines. The corporate principles lead to the definition of the corporate business code of conduct. While the principles outline the philosophy of the corporation, the business code of conduct translates these principles into the expected manner in which the employees conduct themselves. If the principles indicate that the corporation will conduct its business in an ethical manner, the business code of conduct will outline how the employee is expected to accomplish this. The security policies will use the principles and the business code of conduct as a base with which to construct specific corporate policies dealing with security issues. These policies will, in turn, provide the input into the definition of the guidelines which define the way in which the security policies will be implemented.

ARE SECURITY POLICIES REQUIRED?

Strictly speaking, the lack of a security policy will not prevent a corporation from operating. The value of a policy may not be apparent to the corporation until a security incident occurs or situation develops. In many cases policies are put in place because of a specific problem or as a result of a periodic audit. The type and number of subjects where policies may be required will vary within each organization, especially by the type of business involved. The more the organization depends on its information systems to conduct business, the greater the need for robust policies. This is

Figure 6.1 Where policies fit

even more true if customers or business partners also rely on your information systems.

The absence of a security policy may in fact prevent an organization from taking an action even if an incident clearly contravenes the intent of the organization. Take, for example, the situation where an employee is making use of the organization's computing resources to operate a private business. This may be considered to be in conflict with the goals of the organization. However, any basis for recourse by the organization may require that a corporate policy be in place to indicate that this type of behavior is not tolerated. Otherwise, the employee may have legal recourse if disciplinary action is taken. The organization may, however, allow an individual to use the computing resources to support a nonprofit or charity organization such as a gymnastics club or local food bank. A policy in this case should identify what is and is not allowed and how these will be identified and authorized.

> Policies may be required to legally protect the corporation from the actions of an employee. Legal recourse to a security-related incident may not be possible if a governing policy does not define what is acceptable or unacceptable.

The Internet is an area that is getting a lot of attention and connection between organizations and is another very important reason to consider the adoption of specific security policies. If the organization provides a connection to the Internet, the employee can be recognized as representing the organization to the Internet world. This can be reflected in the email address or information postings. You would expect the employee to use the Internet for legitimate business purposes and be a responsible representative of the organization. It would probably not be acceptable if the employee used the Internet to access adult-oriented material or provide extreme views that are contrary to those of the organization. The drafting of an acceptable Internet use policy should address the expected use of the Internet for business purposes and acceptable behavior as an electronic representative of the organization.

SECURITY POLICY FRAMEWORK

The construction of the security policy is very much dependent on the individual organization and will vary considerably from one to another. Such a security policy framework has been used by several organizations. The same framework, however, may not be applicable to all organizations. It has been provided as one approach to security policies. The policies in a security framework are usually composed of standard sections which outline the policy and the reasons for implementing the policy. The policies should be kept short and to the point. They are intended to be distributed to all related business entities. They are not specific to any hardware platform, and are intended to be technology independent. Each policy should include

- *Policy statement*—A formal statement of the corporate policy. What does the organization require to be done or not done? The policy statement should be specific and to the point.
- *Purpose*—Why is the policy required? What problem is it solving? What are the components of the policy? Are there any definitions in the area that the policy covers?
- *Scope*—What are the boundaries of the application of the policy? How far does the policy extend?
- *Compliance with policy*—This section contains the specific components and the application of the policy. What is specifically required to comply with the policy? Are there any situations where deviation from the policy is allowed and if so what are the processes involved to authorize the deviation?
- *Penalties/Consequences*—What are the penalties and/or consequences of not complying with the policy? These may identify formal sanctions and/or specific consequences if the policy is violated.

The topics included in a policy framework will vary from one corporation to the next depending on the business environment, mode of operation, and management principles. Several topics are presented here for your consideration. This list is not meant to be exhaustive, but it identifies many areas where a specific policy may be required. The policy topics have been organized into groups, the first of which deals with policies that almost all organizations should address.

BASIC SECURITY ELEMENTS

There a few basic security elements found in any security framework. These basic components should be addressed by a policy or a group of policies to stipulate that the security component is required, what form the component takes, and how it will be used. This group of security policies identifies the base for the security mechanisms. These policies, or the security mechanisms that address these policies, are included in most security systems.

IDENTIFICATION

An individual user of data processing systems and data must be uniquely identified to provide individual accountability. A unique user identification code, called a user ID, is normally used to represent a user's identity to the system. A valid user ID, when verified by a password, provides authentication of a user's identity. The identification policy should detail the requirement for identification and outline how identification is accomplished. For example, the policy could identify that a unique user ID will be assigned to individuals and used for identification of that individual. This user ID will be used as an unique identifier and used for authorization, authentication, and auditing purposes.

AUTHENTICATION

The basis of any security system is to be able to know who or what is requesting the data processing operation. The verification of this identity is a fundamental requirement to allow access to data assets and systems. The identity can be authenticated when some form of unique item or trait accompanies the unique identification. A policy should state when authentication is required, what the authentication will be based on, and what type of authentication mechanism will be used. An authentication mechanism can be a unique user identification used with a secret password or something the user has, such as a smart card or a thumbprint.

AUTHORIZATION

Access to the computing resources of the corporation should only be granted to those individuals or connected hosts that have been granted permission by management. This permission is granted by authorization mechanisms which are used to allow, deny, or limit individuals or connected hosts access to the resource. The authorization is usually based on an authenticated identity. The policy will define the elements that will be used for authorization such as an authenticated user ID. The policy should also identify who establishes the authorization criteria, who grants the authority to access resources, and who manages the authorization processes.

PASSWORDS

The unique identification of a user or system and an accompanying password is generally all that is used to provide a basic level of security to protect system resources. Additional security protections may be required, such as a smart card, depending on the classification of the object data. A policy on passwords will deal with the handling of the passwords, the format, criteria to change passwords, and the requirement to keep them secret.

One of the key components of the password policy should be the requirement to keep your individual passwords secret and the consequences of failing to do so.

INFORMATION INTEGRITY

Information integrity is concerned with the reliability, accuracy, and management of the collected data that comprises the target information. The correct operation of systems and preservation of the integrity of the information are required for a business computing system to be reliable. Since information is an aggregation of data, the implementation of integrity features will help ensure all of the data is reliable and accurate. An example of integrity features would be the requirement to identify the originator of the information, or for the periodic execution of integrity checking utilities. A policy on information integrity will outline the need to implement integrity mechanisms, what they are, and how they are to be used. Data integrity is concerned with the availability and accuracy of the individual data elements. A policy concerning data integrity is described in the next section of this chapter.

POLICIES CONCERNING DATA

Other elements of a security framework revolve around the protection of the data. The secrets contained in the organization are the primary reasons for security precautions. An understanding and definition of the confidentiality requirements for the various data components will provide some answers about the type and depth of the security measures that are required to protect them. For example, an organization will define a policy concerning the publication of corporate documents and who may have access to them.

DATA CLASSIFICATION

One of the main anchors to a comprehensive security framework is the classification of the data. Information generated and maintained within the organization has varying degrees of sensitivity depending on the nature and the use of the data. All data should be classified by its nature and purpose in order to define the appropriate measures concerning the integrity, availability, and confidentiality of the information. A policy would identify the classes of data kept by the organization and what access, control, and management operations are required for each classification. For example, a policy would perhaps state that highly confidential data must be stored or transmitted only if it is encrypted.

DATA GUARDIAN (OWNERSHIP)

The data within an organization is a valuable corporate asset and must be protected. The assignment and management of asset protection is the responsibility of the data guardian. The term "data guardian" is used to differentiate it from data ownership. In most organizations the ownership of the data is not given to any individual but rather remains with the organization. The data guardian is responsible for the data asset without the requirement for assuming ownership. Within certain types of corporations this may be called the protection of intellectual property rights. A policy on data guardianship would outline the responsibilities of the data guardian and the relationship with the owner or custodian of the data.

DATA CUSTODIAN (MANAGEMENT)

Not only must the data be protected but it must also be managed. The responsibility for this management is given to a person identified as a data custodian. The data custodian is responsible for the reliability of data asset performance in accordance with the data guardian's specifications. The data custodian provides a trustee function for data management in relation to the data guardian. The data custodian has authorized possession of the asset and is responsible for following the data guardian's authorized or specified controls. The data custodian is responsible for managing the availability of the data and ensuring that the appropriate controls are in place and utilized, assuming the role of corporate representative responsible for the data, analysis of the risk of unauthorized disclosure, and the risk of destruction of the data and establishing appropriate data classification and authentication standards for data access and utilization.

DATA INTEGRITY

Data integrity is concerned with the accuracy and availability of the individual data elements. The data used to provide the corporate information must be accurate and available for use when required. This data must be protected from compromise or abuse, and include measures to ensure its accuracy and availability. The policy concerning data integrity may identify the requirement for secure data storage and mechanisms for backup of the data storage, the requirement for procedures and processes to preserve the accuracy of the data and to test the accuracy of the processes and procedures used to manipulate the data, the replication of data, and the privacy and integrity of the data. The policy on information integrity deals with the requirement for managing the integrity mechanisms.

PERSONAL USE POLICIES (GENERAL)

Access to computing has revolutionized the way that we perform our tasks in the office. You should consider policies concerning the use of computers by the employees or others associated with the corporation.

PERSONAL USE

Computing resources are put in place to service the requirements of the corporate business. Use of these resources for personal activities other than the execution of job responsibilities may be prohibited, except in cases where these activities are sanctioned by management. A policy will specify the acceptable personal use of corporate computing facilities, and the criteria and process for obtaining management permission where warranted.

USE OF INFORMATION SYSTEMS

The expanding use of technology for electronic mail and messages both internally and externally provides an expedient way to create and distribute information. The users of information technology systems must utilize the systems in a legal, responsible manner. The systems and network should not be used to generate or distribute material which is illegal or immoral or contravenes the principles of the corporation.

PRIVACY

The corporation holds personal and other data in trusteeship with which to manage and conduct business. The protection of the privacy of personal information is of utmost importance. Active steps must be taken by all employees to ensure privacy is maintained. The corporation may also be governed by protection of privacy legislation or statutes. A policy should outline the requirement for adherence to statutes or legislation if they govern the actions of the organization.

SECURITY MANAGEMENT POLICIES

The management of security mechanisms is another area where policy should anchor the actions and responsibilities of those involved. Security mechanisms will only be effective if they are subject to well-defined and comprehensive management policies.

MANAGEMENT RESPONSIBILITIES

The success of the security mechanisms, processes, and procedures is a management responsibility. This responsibility is generally given to all those individuals within the organization with management responsibilities. It is the responsibility of management to monitor and enforce adherence to the security structures by all of the individuals and system components within their direct control. A policy on management responsibilities will outline these responsibilities and the processes required for effective management.

RECORDS MANAGEMENT

A record of access to confidential information and alterations to important corporate data is essential to the provision of a comprehensive security framework. The records are used to provide audit trails of activity against data and systems. The policy may also specify the retention requirements of the information, and when dated confidential information is required to be removed or destroyed. Records may be required to be kept to satisfy regulations and legal requirements.

SECURITY ADMINISTRATION

Security administration is the focal point for the information security mechanisms within the enterprise. The area of security administration is responsible for making sure that all of the security measures and mechanisms are appropriately implemented, administered, monitored, and changed in response to the business conditions. This area is also responsible for coordinating security information and security incident investigations. Security administration is not responsible for policing the policies—that responsibility is outlined in the management responsibilities policy.

SEGREGATION OF DUTIES

The segregation of duties when dealing with security is an important principle. It is better to assign components of security and management related tasks to different individuals. If no one individual has total control over all of the security components, no one person can compromise the security systems. The segregation of duties is typically implemented among the positions dealing with systems development, system administration, security administration, and system operation. A policy will reinforce the principle of segregation of duties and outline how the principle will be implemented. An example of the segregation of duties is a bank that requires two employee signatures, the teller and a manager, on large transaction amounts.

RISK ASSESSMENT

Risk assessment is the process of identifying threats to an asset and specifying the controls that are necessary to secure that asset based on the value of the asset and the impact of its loss. A basic requirement of an effective security plan is to identify and classify all of the assets to be secured. A formal risk assessment program will help the planning and selection of protection measures used for an asset. Not all risks can be offset at a favorable cost; it is not only legitimate but prudent for management to accept certain levels of risk. Security and controls are not ends in themselves, and should always be justified by a business need to limit genuine exposure of the assets to unauthorized users.

COMPLIANCE MONITORING

Security is an important element in the operation and utilization of data processing systems. Policies, facilities, processes, and procedures are implemented to obtain the required security levels. There should be methods which can be implemented to monitor compliance with the security measures and policy. Noncompliance with the security measures may cause exposure and possible impact on the business processes.

DEVIATIONS TO POLICY

The policy has been established for the standardization of business controls across all platforms and applications. The policies and standards provided in the framework are to be used for direction and governance. Deviations from or noncompliance with the framework should be noted and dealt with as directed by the policy.

POLICIES FOR SYSTEMS

The computer systems of the organization are now an essential component of carrying on the business. Some businesses will cease to be viable or be subject to large losses if systems are not available for a significant amount of time. This significance can be measured in hours in some cases or in minutes if the business is driven by time dependent transactions such as the stock market trading floor.

SYSTEM ADMINISTRATION

The system administrator is responsible for maintaining a consistent and effective operating environment for the information processing systems. Stable and consistent operation of the systems will provide a productive environment. An unstable environment may be open to compromise.

SYSTEM CLASSIFICATION

The systems operated and maintained within the organization have varying degrees of importance depending on the nature and use of those

systems to support the business. All systems should be reviewed and classified according to their confidentiality and availability requirements in order
to apply the appropriate security and protection mechanisms and to include
key systems in disaster recovery and business continuity plans.

BUSINESS CONTINUITY

Reliance on information processing systems is an important aspect of
the business. The unavailability of data, components, or systems will have a
serious impact on business operation. The systems that are defined as critical to the operation of the business should be subject to a policy indicating
the requirement to have a business continuity plan in place.

NETWORK POLICIES

The network provides access to the computer systems and presents potential
vulnerability if not managed under strict security policies. The policies
should identify who can be granted access and under what conditions this
network access may be granted.

EXTERNAL NETWORK ACCESS

The interconnection of networks to further business interests is
becoming a standard and accepted mode of operation. Connection to the
Internet for information and business purposes is becoming a business
imperative for many organizations. Any connections of an organization's
network to an external network should be tightly controlled and subject to
stringent security measures. Without stringent security for network interconnection all computer assets may be subject to compromise.

REMOTE NETWORK ACCESS

Employees may request or require access to the systems from network
locations that are outside of the corporate network. This remote access may
be granted with the appropriate justification and if the required security
measures are in place. A second function authentication mechanism may be
required. These requests must not compromise the security of the systems,
network and data.

Third parties may request access to computing systems for contract
work or to conduct special projects such as the annual audit. These requests
should have the appropriate approval and be subject to stringent security
mechanisms such as specific location access, time of day limitations, or
other limitations. These requests must not compromise the security of the
systems, network and data.

PRIVACY OF COMMUNICATIONS

Electronic communications has become an integral part of doing business. Concern for the protection of the corporate intellectual property may prompt an organization to monitor electronic mail and telephone conversations. A privacy of communications policy will outline the position of the corporation on the privacy of phone conversations and electronic mail. The electronic communications may be subject to eavesdrop or review, depending on the corporate principles and culture and the level of concern for the protection of sensitive information or intellectual property. The policy should state if this potential for eavesdrop exists or not.

POLICIES FOR USERS

The system user must be aware of, understand, and be able to deal with the policies. Security policies are not of much value if they are unknown or not understood.

USER AWARENESS

A major component of the application of security mechanisms and components is the knowledge that they exist and the reason why they have been implemented. The organization must implement and maintain a user awareness program to ensure the policies are known and understood.

USER RESPONSIBILITIES

A user is an individual authorized to utilize information assets and services. Data users are individuals who have permission from the data guardians to access and use data. All users must be aware of the security features and policies and why they are in place. The user has a duty to act responsibly concerning the protection and use of the information assets and the computing services of the organization.

SOFTWARE POLICIES

The software of the corporation is the managing engine of the computer systems. It is the responsibility of the corporation to ensure that legal rights have been obtained for all of the software utilized. It is also the responsibility of the corporation to protect against the impact of software viruses.

SOFTWARE COPYRIGHT

Copyright laws protect the right of software manufacturers to create and distribute their software. Restrictions on use are included in manufacturers' licensing agreements, which accompany each software package. Most manufacturers allow users to copy software for a backup or working copy. However, licensing agreements typically specify that software may only be installed on one machine at a time. If copies of software are desired for other machines, users must obtain additional licenses or be a party to a site licensing agreement. If the organization is involved in the development of computer applications, obtaining the appropriate patents, trademarks, and copyrights is important for the protection of the company's interests.

VIRUS PROTECTION

A virus protection and detection process is required to be maintained in the operation of the IT systems. All external data and software introduced into the system must be first checked for the occurrence of any known viruses. Virus detection sweeps should be available and enacted on a regular basis. The responsibilities and processes required if a virus is found should be identified. Another approach to the virus problem is to prohibit any importation or use of personal software by the individual users.

OTHER POLICIES

There are several other areas where security policies should be considered.

APPLICATION DEVELOPMENT

Considerations for security should be addressed during all application design and development stages of a system development life cycle. The designers and developers of application systems should be aware of any security requirements depending on the system and data classifications involved. A policy may require a formal application system review for security before it is implemented.

EXTERNAL PROCESSING

External service organizations used for processing systems or off-premises processing done by employees should be protected by the equivalent secure environment and controls as the internal systems. You may not have direct control over the environment, which may introduce security concerns. Any external processing should only be conducted under the same or equivalent security processes as required internally. There should be a certification or review process to establish the security of the environment. This should be one of the requirements used for establishing the relationship.

PHYSICAL SECURITY

Physical access to areas containing data processing facilities should be restricted to those with a clear business need for access. A secure, protected environment is essential for efficient system operation. A policy of this kind would consider access and protection requirements for the computer assets, as well as storage and protection mechanisms for corporate data. Other considerations may include computer assets while in the possession of employees.

USE OF STANDARDS

The adoption of de jure or de facto standards is an important principle that will provide direction for information technology systems. A de jure standard is generally accepted to be one that is defined and managed by a government or industry standards body. A de facto standard is one that is broadly implemented by multiple vendor products but does not have a representative standards body for management. An example of a de jure standard would be the Open System Interconnection (OSI) standards managed by the International Standards Organization (ISO). An example of a de facto standard is the Network File System (NFS), adopted by almost all UNIX operating system vendors. The adoption of standards provides guidance for the selection, development and implementation of technologies. Standards will aid interoperability and portability of applications in a distributed computing environment.

FAX AND VOICEMAIL

Voicemail is typically a security weak point in the organization but a very important one. Policies should cover the protection of access passwords to voicemail systems under the same conditions as the computer system access. Policies on fax utilization should consider the classification of the data potentially involved in a transmission. The classification may prohibit the utilization of fax transmission or other fax specific security mechanisms utilized if warranted. The organization should require that the privacy of voicemail and fax be respected and protected and these forms of business communication be used in a secure manner.

EXAMPLE OF A POLICY

Consideration should be given to defining specific policies for each of the areas previously outlined. The preceding list was not meant to be exhaustive but will give you an indication of the major components when security policies should be considered. The following is an example of a policy concerning software copyright will give you an indication of topics that should be covered in a policy.

SOFTWARE COPYRIGHT POLICY

> The corporation requires that all users of software strictly adhere to the terms and conditions regarding copyright, as outlined in licensing agreements accompanying each individual software product.

PURPOSE

Copyright laws protect the right of software manufacturers to create and distribute their software. Restrictions on use are included in manufacturers' licensing agreements, which accompany each software package. Most manufacturers allow users to copy software as a backup or working copy. However, licensing agreements typically specify that software may only be installed on a specified number of machines at a time. If copies of software are desired for other machines, users must obtain additional licenses or a site licensing agreement.

Many seemingly innocent practices violate copyright laws. These include

- Copying software for testing purchases prior to purchase
- Making temporary copies to use until a purchased copy arrives
- Copying company software to use elsewhere
- Retaining evaluation or demo copies of software past the trial period

SCOPE

Knowledge of existing software copyright agreements is a prerequisite for use of all software. All employees are required to be knowledgeable of the licensing agreements in effect for software controlled by them.

COMPLIANCE WITH POLICY

Ignorance of the individual licensing agreement is not a valid excuse for noncompliance. To assure compliance with the terms and conditions regarding copyright, the user must

- Make copies only in accordance with terms and conditions set out in software licensing agreements.
- Follow the software licensing agreements relating to version and release upgrades.

- Obtain management approval prior to removing software for use at home.
- Have documented proof of purchase available at all times for all proprietary software used at the corporation.
- Remove proprietary software after completing demonstrations, evaluations or diagnostic testing. Proprietary software is software copyrighted by someone other than the corporation.
- Obtain management approval before installing or using personally owned software on the corporation computers.

PENALTIES/CONSEQUENCES

Practices which involve copying of software for purposes other than those outlined in licensing agreements are illegal and are strictly prohibited. **Users who knowingly or unknowingly violate copyright or licensing regulations may be personally liable.**

THE PROCESS OF CREATING POLICIES

Now that we have defined the framework of policies, we need to add some way of making sure these policies are known, documented, approved, updated, and managed. The framework of corporate security policies must be governed by an organized management process. This process will define the authority for establishing the process, how the requirements and creation of the policies is accomplished, the process for approving the policies, the mechanism for the enforcement of the policies, and the procedures and responsibility for the ongoing maintenance and management of the policies. A key responsibility of effective security policy management is the establishment of an awareness and education program to ensure that all of the people affected by the security policies are aware that they exist and what they say. The security framework should include the methodology for the definition and management of the policies contained within the framework.

RESPONSIBILITIES

There may be several individuals and groups responsible for the creation, implementation, enforcement, and management of the security policies. These responsibilities should be defined and documented as part of the security policy process. The construction, implementation and enforcement of the security policies should be supported by a sponsor with senior management responsibilities in the corporation. This sponsoring management should ultimately be responsible for the successful operation of the business to which the policies apply. This responsibility will include the ability to not only invoke remedies when security events occur but also have the authority to dictate changes to security policy when warranted.

A formal process for this review of policies will need to be established. The objective of the review is to examine the appropriateness of the policies and ensure the policy is consistent with the principles of the corporation, the business of the corporation and other defined policies. The approval of the policies should come from the sponsoring senior manager or other designated senior management. The more senior management is involved in the policy approval process, the greater the impact of the policies. The policy review and approval process should be planned and scheduled at regular intervals.

The enforcement of the security policies is typically the responsibility of anyone with a defined management responsibility, but senior management is ultimately responsible for the enforcement of the policies. This should not be the responsibility of the group responsible for the management of the security mechanisms. Behavior which is contrary to security policy should be determined by the usual management processes.

SECURITY POLICY MANUAL

The main focus of a security policy process is a security policy manual. This manual should contain the purpose or requirement for the security policy framework, the principles upon which the policies are based, the methodology used to develop the policies, how they are managed, and the specific policies contained in the framework. This manual should be available for reference by anyone governed by the policies. The policy manual should be reviewed on a regular basis and kept up to date as policies are changed or new ones adopted. Updates to the policy manual will be a product of the policy review and approval process. Updates should take place when policies have been formally approved, with all updates sent to holders of the manual. These updates should also be included in regular communication with all of the staff or users who are impacted by the policies.

AWARENESS AND EDUCATION

It is important to establish a comprehensive awareness and education program. Policies will have no impact if the people for whom they have been constructed do not know what they specify or if in fact that they exist. The security program cannot function effectively without an awareness by *all* employees of the policies and other organization rules. It is important that individuals clearly understand what assets they are responsible for, and what protection those assets are to receive.

A formal education program should be developed and made available for all staff and users, especially new staff and users. This education program should present an overview of the requirement for security and the importance and responsibility for everybody to know and understand the policies. The program should cover the main policies and indicate where detailed information on all of the policies can be obtained. Signed certification that the staff or users have read and understand the security policies is highly recommended. The education material must be kept current.

POLICY PROCESS IMPLEMENTATION

One way of initiating a policy process is with a workshop within the organization specifically dealing with security policies. For example, a selected group is invited to participate in a meeting with the specific objective of resolving the need and level of security required, the roles and responsibilities for security, and the process for implementing the policies. The participants in this meeting or workshop would be the decisions makers who are responsible for providing security as well as ultimately responsible if security breaches occur. The internal auditors should participate in this type of event. This type of workshop will provide a common understanding of the security problem and a forum for defining the plan required to address it.

It is very important to obtain the agreement, support and approval for the policies from the highest level of management possible in the organization. Security must be seen as a very important corporate requirement. Just like a commitment to quality, if the policies have a high level of management consensus, support, and approval, they will be viewed as important and will be followed. The management of the organization must be given the responsibility and authority for enforcing the policies.

Various organizational departments, such as internal and human resources, not necessarily associated with the information technology area should be involved in the security policy process. These areas can provide input into the requirements and content for specific policies. The Human Resource Department can advise on the penalties and consequences of not following the policies. Many human resource departments incoporate computing security awareness with their own employee orientation programs. Policies are to be included in any new employee familiarization material. Internal audit can review the policy and indicate any problem areas where policy is either required or needs to be altered.

SUMMARY

A framework of security policies is an important building block to a secure distributed computing environment. It provides direction for employees to follow the corporate standard and specifies consequences if they do not. It is intended to increase overall security by requiring conformance to accepted standards of behavior. But it is not sufficient just to create the policies. To implement the security framework successfully, users must be aware of the policies and understand their content to support the successful implementation of the security framework.

PART III

TECHNOLOGIES

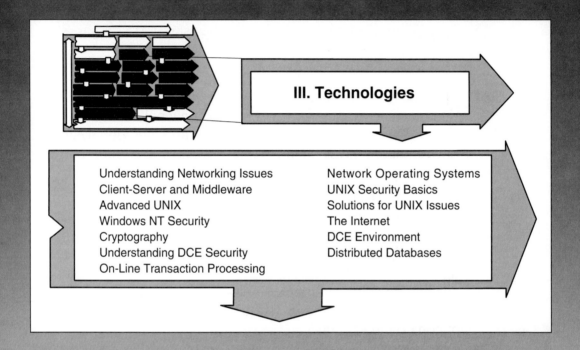

III. Technologies

Understanding Networking Issues
Client-Server and Middleware
Advanced UNIX
Windows NT Security
Cryptography
Understanding DCE Security
On-Line Transaction Processing

Network Operating Systems
UNIX Security Basics
Solutions for UNIX Issues
The Internet
DCE Environment
Distributed Databases

There has been a widespread movement, in recent years, to embrace distributed computing. Organizations, in which one rarely heard the mention of distributed systems and client-server technology a few years ago, have successfully deployed critical solutions based on this technology. Before the promise of client-server productivity can be realized, however, the issue of security and trust must be addressed. Our belief is that knowledge is fundamental to the solution of most problems. To explain why, we will introduce a concept called *footprints in the snow.*

Many of us live in the suburbs, and while crime is not unknown, we do not live in a fortress. We lock our windows and doors, and trust that a large dog will deter any wrongdoers. However, if you noticed footsteps in the snow to your bedroom windows, your awareness of security would be greatly increased. You would take active steps to detect the intruder. Footprints in the snow, mud on a carpet, and scratches on a door's lock can be clues to homeowners that they have cause for concern.

People who abuse computer systems also leave footprints in the snow. The problem is that the ordinary network or system administrator does not look at the snow in the backyard, and if they do, they might not know what the footprints to the bedroom window imply.

In our review of distributed computing technology, we will examine and explain the many electronic equivalents to a "footprint in the snow." We will review the weaknesses and vulnerabilities of the network, middleware, and the open systems environment as well as provide an overview of cryptography.

We will also examine the security aspects of Windows NT and an area in which many organizations have security concerns, the use of the Internet. The final chapters in this section will examine the Open Systems Foundation (OSF) middleware offerings to help solve some of the issues with distributed computing as well as discuss the use of security in transaction processing. In every chapter, we will examine both the challenge technology presents, and the solutions it offers, to the problem of computing security.

CHAPTER 7

THE NETWORK

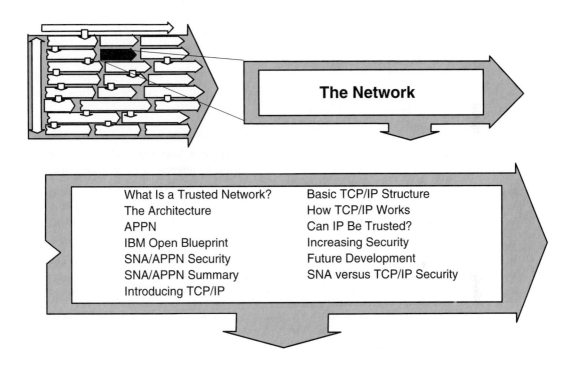

The Network

What Is a Trusted Network?   Basic TCP/IP Structure
The Architecture   How TCP/IP Works
APPN   Can IP Be Trusted?
IBM Open Blueprint   Increasing Security
SNA/APPN Security   Future Development
SNA/APPN Summary   SNA versus TCP/IP Security
Introducing TCP/IP

Networking has become the lifeblood of most computing environments. Security, which has traditionally been focused on the operating system and application, must expand its focus to include networking aspects. A focus on network security is warranted because networks play such an integral role in today's computing environment. Mechanisms must be put in place to allow the trusted operation of the network, including authentication, integrity, and authorization controls. The security of the operating system, application, and network cannot be divorced from one another. They all contribute to the overall level of trust in the computing environment. Deficiencies in one area must be compensated for in other areas. For example, if the network is exposed to monitoring of its traffic, the application can compensate by employing encryption for its own traffic.

93

In order to understand why networking control mechanisms are required, we will look at what makes a network trusted and, conversely, untrusted.

A TALE OF TWO NETWORKS

Let's look at the security features of two very different approaches to networking—SNA and TCP/IP. The System Network Architecture (SNA) was developed and introduced by IBM in the 1970s. It remains one of the most common networking architectures in use today. SNA has evolved into Advanced Peer-to-Peer Networking (APPN) to address the realities of distributed, peer-level networking.

The TCP/IP protocol has been around as long or longer than SNA but is a relative newcomer to the corporate networking scene. By far the most widely used networking protocol, it is used to interconnect millions of computers throughout the world. We will compare and contrast the architecture, the security controls, and issues in both the SNA and TCP/IP environments in this chapter. But first we will discuss trusted and untrusted networks.

One area of disagreement, between networking and security personnel, is a concept we call the open highway. Under the open highway concept of networking, all networked users are given full and complete access to any resource on the network. The network should not impose any restrictions on communication between network nodes. The concept is at odds, however, with the security concerns of many of our business clients. It makes for an interesting philosophical disagreement. The resolution to the debate usually involves balancing the need for communication with security. If the open highway concept dominates, then increased controls on key servers and applications are mandated.

WHAT IS A TRUSTED NETWORK?

A trusted or secure network is one which has sufficient security controls to prevent abuse of its operation. It has internal controls to ensure the integrity of the network. The internal controls provide protection, both against unauthorized access to the network and illicit monitoring of its traffic. One technique used to counter monitoring is the encryption of sensitive network traffic. Networks of this type are employed by governments, the military, and the defense industry.

An untrusted network is one in which access to the network is not authorized. It is possible for an attacker to attach to the network and to monitor and interpret traffic. Attackers may also insert their own traffic, counterfeiting it such that it appears to come from a legitimate source. Or they may simply disrupt the flow of traffic over the network.

Attaching to a network can be accomplished in a number of ways. An attacker might bring in a notebook computer with the appropriate interface, find a network connection (either in a spare office or by unplugging a legitimate workstation), and connect to the LAN. Having connected, they can instruct the notebook computer to capture network traffic onto its local disk drive. Since clients on an untrusted network typically communicate with each other without the use of encryption, it is easy to intercept and interpret traffic gathered in this manner. The other reason this is so easy is the widespread use of broadcast LAN technologies like Ethernet. Software is publicly available, for example, that is capable of watching for the word "login" and selectively copying the next hundred characters. The data gathered is almost certain to contain the account name and password of the user attempting to login. The attacker can then log in at a legitimate machine and begin accessing the resources owned by that user. Monitoring can be performed in a similar fashion by gaining access to a legitimate workstation.

Inserting traffic such that it appears to come from a legitimate source is also possible with this type of network, in either of the two monitoring scenarios presented above. Each computer on the network has at least one address which identifies the computer. It is easy for an attacker to generate network traffic which *spoofs* another machine into thinking that it came from a legitimate source, simply by using that machine's address.

The malicious disruption of network traffic can deny service to legitimate users. Anyone with access to a untrusted network has the ability to generate sufficient garbage traffic that the network will become inoperable. Figure 7.1 illustrates the security issues faced when using an untrusted network.

Next, we will examine how two very distinct approaches to networking—SNA and TCP/IP—address these issues.

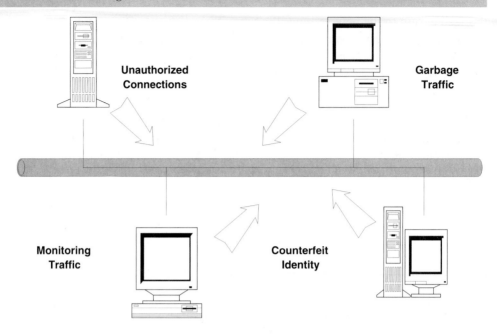

Figure 7.1 Issues facing an untrusted network

SYSTEMS NETWORK ARCHITECTURE

Systems Network Architecture (SNA) came on the scene from IBM in 1974 as the answer to large-scale computer networking. It was one of the first times that a comprehensive architecture was used to identify all of the components of networking and specifications for the attributes, qualities, and behaviors of the components. In 1985 additions were made to the architecture to permit lower-level peer-to-peer communications to take place. In 1992, IBM came out with the Open Blueprint, which describes a structure of the distributed system environment. The architecture has now migrated from a host-centered network to a distributed peer-centered network.

The architecture utilizes the concept of a session. When two network nodes establish contact with one another, and agree on the rules under which they will communicate, they are said to have established a session. Many sessions can be active between two network nodes. The architecture is also based on the concept of subareas around which the network is defined. There is a subarea number for each mainframe computer and communication controller in an SNA network.

The architecture was originally established as a hierarchical network, managed by the Virtual Telecommunications Access Method (VTAM). VTAM was the application that controlled the network operating on an IBM mainframe computer. Nothing on the network happened without VTAM knowing or worrying about it. VTAM knows all and sees all. The Subsystem Control Point (SSCP) is the *master of the universe* for the SNA network. The SSCP controls all of the network activity from initializing the network to helping to establish the sessions.

THE ARCHITECTURE

SNA is based on a seven-layer model similar to the OSI model. The layers start with the physical layer, which defines how the network nodes are connected (the wiring specifications, etc.). The data link layer contains the transmission protocols between network nodes that sends the data to the physical layer for transmission. The network or path control layer provides the routing mechanisms and administers predefined network routes. The transport or transmission control layer regulates the rate at which one network node can transmit messages to another network node. Encryption and decryption can take place in this mode if the proper options are enabled. The session or data flow control layer regulates the delivery of the messages to the end users. The presentation layer manages the data streams that flow between the network nodes. This may involve compression or translation. The application layer manages the interface with the applications on the network.

A lot of the communication under SNA uses a connection-oriented transport, the Synchronous Data Link Control (SDLC) protocol. SDLC is a bit-oriented protocol that organizes information into well-defined units known as frames. A bit-oriented protocol transmits data as a stream of bits instead of bytes. This type of protocol can use a specific stream of bits as control codes instead of the reserved characters that are used in a byte-oriented protocol. Network routing follows fixed paths that are set up at network initialization time or when specific routing components are activated. Traffic control is managed by the class of service specified. Data traffic for multiple network sessions can share a network route. Transmission priority will be given based on the class of service. Since SDLC is a frame-based protocol, print streams and on-line transactions can share the same line without an impact to the on-line service. The SDLC protocol provides transmission integrity to ensure all of the message frames are transmitted and assembled in the correct order.

Within the architecture are definitions called nodes which are categorized into either subarea nodes or peripheral nodes. There are several types of nodes that are used to describe the different network characteristics and qualities that each may have. The root for all network activity is the type 5 node, which resides on a host computer. The next node in the chain is the type 4 node or the communications controller. This is the hardware unit where all of the network communication lines are attached. The communications controller is loaded with a program called the network control program (NCP), which defines the configuration of the connected network and manages the communication lines. A lot of the lower-level network activity is off-loaded from the mainframe to the communications controller. Both the type 5 node and the type 4 node are defined as subarea nodes. Figure 7.2 illustrates the relationship between the nodes in the architecture hierarchy.

At the end of a communications line sits the type 2 node or cluster controller. This is the box that sits in the wiring closet or on the floor where all of the miles of coaxial cable lead. Attached to the cluster controller are the network access terminals. These can be a variety of terminals, PCs, and printers. So where is the type 3 node? It seemed like a good idea at one time, but the specification was scrapped before the architecture was published.

An item called the network accessible unit (NAU) is another base component of the architecture. The NAU is the item that implements the upper four layers, the transaction services, presentation services, data flow control, and transmission control of the architecture. The NAU can be defined as the entity that communicates while the lower three layers of the architecture define how the NAU communicates. There are three different kinds of NAU, the physical unit (PU), which activates and manages links; the logical unit (LU), which defines the types or characteristics of the SNA functions that are supported; and the control point (CP), which manages the network resources within a domain. We have already talked about the SSCP, which controls the network resources from a type 5 node.

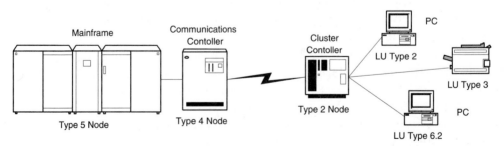

Figure 7.2 SNA network

The architecture also contains definitions for logical units (LU). LU type 1 is used for printers and remote job entry stations; LU type 2 is used for the 3270 type terminal; and LU type 3 is used for a 3270 class of printer. LU type 4 is used for more intelligent forms of printers. LU type 6.2 came later as an extension to the architecture to specify application program to program communication or APPC. In the SNA terms you can think of the PU as hardware that controls a device and the LU as the device the PU controls.

Another of the foundations of the architecture is the concept of a session. A session is a logical connection between two NAUs in the network. The physical connection between two NAUs is defined as a route for the session. A session is similar in concept to logging onto an application. Once you log on to an application, you have established the rules about how you will communicate with the application. Once a session is established between two NAUs, the rules for communicate between them have been established.

APPLICATION PROGRAM-TO-PROGRAM COMMUNICATIONS

An addition to the architecture is a specification to provide Application Program-to-Program Communication (APPC) across networked computers. APPC was developed to support distributed processing between two intelligent end points. It defines a full array of services to applications including synchronization options, process activation, confirmation options, and error management. APPC is based on the LU 6.2 specification, which has been included in a large variety of OEM and third-party products to allow application-based communications with IBM-based networked applications. APPC is the communication vehicle for distributed transaction processing in the CICS OLTP products and is the main vehicle for supporting interprocess communication in the SNA world.

An advancement called the Common Programming Interface for Communications (CPI-C) allowed APPC applications to be easily developed using a common interface to the underlying LU 6.2 structures. This common interface also allowed applications to be moved from one type of platform to another with a minimum of change. When a pair of transaction programs uses APPC, a session is established between two type 6.2 logical units called a conversation. This conversation represents a logical connection between these two programs. APPC is a mechanism to implement true distributed processing on a transaction level between two network connected applications.

ADVANCED PEER-TO-PEER NETWORKING

Another extension to the architecture was introduced in 1986 with the addition of Advanced Peer-to-Peer Networking (APPN). This was originally introduced for IBM's minicomputer market to provide internetworking between computers without the need for a mainframe. A new type of physical unit was introduced, PU type 2.1, to allow peer-to-peer networking instead of requiring the hierarchical approach. APPN is designed to handle transaction processing between host applications and distributed platforms in sustained batch type or conversational communications. You no longer needed a type 5 node to operate a network. This was a major innovation to a peer connected network from the former hierarchical architecture specification.

A further evolution of APPN came in 1993 with the introduction of High Performance Routing (HPR). The basic change with HPR is to provide high-speed routing between intermediate nodes at a lower level than the previous APPN level. HPR is comprised of the two main components, Rapid Transport Protocol (RTP) and Automatic Network Routing (ANR). The protocol supports the transmission of data at very high speeds. Automatic Network Routing is a high-speed source routing protocol that carries the entire routing information in the network header of the data packet. HPR is positioned to exploit switched network technologies such as Frame Relay or Asynchronous Transfer Mode (ATM).

APPN has two types of defined devices: APPN end nodes and APPN network nodes. The end nodes are computers with their operating systems, applications, and peripherals. The network nodes are the intermediate routing nodes that move traffic between the end nodes. Many platforms can operate as either end nodes or network nodes. APPN supports a variety of network protocols and topologies. The APPN network addresses are alphanumeric and can include up to 10,000 nodes in an APPN subnode. The network nodes can automatically learn the details of ports, links, and resources through the automatic registration feature. APPN is the new network structure that could replace SNA. Several people think that it already has.

IBM OPEN BLUEPRINT

A major stake was put into the ground by IBM in 1994 with the definition of the Open Blueprint. This is a description of several resource management services upon which distributed applications can be built that will operate in a distributed, heterogeneous environment. The basic approach to the blueprint is to allow a network of operating systems to operate as a single networked operating system. As with other blueprints, the IBM Open Blueprint organizes the various resource managers into layers of services.

The base layer represents the physical network. The network services layer contains the various networking protocols such as SNA/APPN, TCP/IP, OSI, NETBIOS, and IPX along with the Common Transport Semantics. The Distributed Systems Services layer contains communication services, Object Management Services, and Distribution Services. These services are designed to provide the mechanisms between the distributed application and the resource managers. The Applications and Application Enabling Services provide the suite of resource managers to deal with topics such as Presentation Services, Data Access Services, System Management Services, Local Operating System Services, and Development Tools.

The Open Blueprint is not really a finite specification of products or standards as much as it is a framework that is useful to illustrate the relationships between the key functions and standards in a distributed computing environment. IBM has acknowledged that there are various different technologies and standards that have a place in the distributed world, and there will likely be many more. The blueprint is a way of organizing these technologies and standards into a framework as a way of explaining their relationship to one another.

SNA/APPN SECURITY

In a hierarchical network implemented with SNA, security is easy to deal with. Foreign devices cannot be added to the network. Tight security control was provided on the host by specific security packages such as Resource Access Control Facility (RACF) from IBM and Access Control Facility 2 (ACF2) from Computer Associates. Many of the vulnerabilities that a peer network contains, such as TCP/IP, are avoided when a central point controls the network. Network transmission integrity is provided by the protocols such as SDLC and RTP. The implementation of the protocol includes transmission error checking and correcting facilities. High availability of the network traffic is provided by the dynamic routing and recovery capabilities between subarea nodes.

Data security can be provided at the logical unit level for session-level cryptography, logical unit-to-logical unit verification, and end-user verification. The encryption at the session level can be mandatory, all data is encrypted, or only selected data fields will be encrypted. The Data Encryption Standard (DES) encryption protocol is used for both session-level encryption and LU-to-LU verification. Logical unit-to-logical unit verification is based on a password supplied by the LU during session activation. End-user verification is used to authenticate an end user by using a password. This password is verified by a type 6.2 conversation during the allocation of the conversation.

APPN and APPC can then provide security services at both the session and conversation level. A user-supplied password is checked by APPN before a session is established between two end nodes. Applications themselves must also supply a correct password in order to establish a conversation with the user. APPN/APPC security can be provided at the network level. Most other security mechanisms rely on application-level security.

SNA/APPN SUMMARY

The main drawback to SNA is the fact that it is a proprietary architecture to IBM. It works well with IBM hardware and software and with other entities that interface with the IBM network. SNA was not really established to interoperate within a heterogeneous environment. The architecture has gone thorough several transformations. There is an existing debate over the peer network model that APPN represents and the hierarchical model of SNA. The refinement of APPN has placed IBM back into the mainstream distributed environment. APPN will be attractive to existing SNA shops in their efforts to accommodate other distributed systems.

The Open Blueprint outlines IBM's commitment to the open, distributed environment. The blueprint is late in coming but is very complete and perhaps somewhat ambitious. It represents the new IBM as wanting and willing to operate with everyone else in the open, distributed market. The success of this blueprint will depend on IBM's commitment to products and services to carry thorough with the blueprint. This blueprint will be influenced by the evolution of other standards, especially in the TCP/IP arena.

INTRODUCING TCP/IP

TCP/IP was developed by the U.S. Department of Defense as a project of DARPA, the Defense Advanced Research Project Agency (now called ARPA). It was intended to provide redundancy in networking by using packet switching technology. The intent was to create a networking protocol which would remain functional even if a section of network was lost. The protocol would allow multiple routes to be determined and used to a single destination. If a route were lost, the protocol would support the automatic rerouting of traffic. The first large-scale deployment of TCP/IP was the ARPANET, which is a predecessor of the current Internet.

IP, TCP, AND UDP

TCP/IP is the term used by many people to generically describe a number of different protocols used on the Internet, including IP, TCP, UDP, ARP, and ICMP. The Internet Protocol (IP) is the lower level of the first three protocols. It provides the foundation on top of which the TCP and UDP blocks of information, commonly called *packets,* travel. An IP packet contains both a source and destination address, as well as other packet integrity information and data. At the IP level, there is no control over the sequencing of the packet flow (i.e., a packet sent later may arrive first). It is the job of higher-level protocols or applications to properly gather and assemble blocks of packets.

The Transport Control Protocol (TCP) exists on top of the IP protocol and provides sequencing and integrity controls. It uses sequence numbers to ensure packets are assembled in the correct order and resends lost packets. There is, of course, overhead associated with TCP because of these integrity controls.

An alternative method of transmission is provided by the User Datagram Protocol (UDP). UDP has limited integrity checking and sequencing controls. If a packet is lost or arrives out of order, that's just too bad. The application, however, is free to deal with packet ordering and retransmission. Some need one and not the other, so UDP is a good starting point. UDP is generally used for messaging and challenge/response applications which do not require integrity checks or sequencing controls. Most people are surprised to discover that the Network File System (NFS), used by many UNIX systems to share disc resources, is based on UDP (although it can also run over TCP). NFS has been constructed with knowledge of the limitations of UDP and has additional controls to ensure the integrity of the data transport.

The Address Resolution Protocol (ARP) is a method of translating two different types of addresses. For example, ARP can translate the higher-level IP address to the Ethernet (or link-level) address. Other types of LANs, such as FDDI, use other mechanisms such as SNAP. In a way, ARP is more a part of Ethernet than IP. The Ethernet address is a lower-level address used by hardware devices (e.g., LAN card and a bridge). ARP essentially provides a mapping of IP addresses to hardware addresses. Alternate protocols, such as RARP or BOOTP, provide a reverse mapping of hardware addresses to IP addresses.

A comparison may be made between TCP and UDP, and courier and postal services. UDP is similar to the exchange of postcards using a postal service, while TCP is like using a courier service. When you send a number of packages, using either the postal service or a courier, there is no real guarantee that the parcels will reach their destination. It is possible for one, or all, of the parcels to be lost regardless of the method chosen. But, generally, 99 times out of 100, they will arrive! If a mailed parcel does not arrive, the recipient will have no knowledge that it is missing (unless you've told them to expect 3 parcels and only 2 arrived). Even if you know one is lost, there is simply no method to track it.

TCP is similar to using a courier service. The letters are placed in a single package, assigned a control number, and the number of items in the package recorded. The recipient is informed of the delivery and knows how many packages to expect. Understandably, this service costs more than using the postal service!

The Simple Network Management Protocol (SNMP) is a higher level protocol. It uses both TCP/IP and UDP/IP to communicate between local SNMP agents and an SNMP manager. SNMP is used to provide a wide variety of networked management services. A local system or device will contain a Management Information Base (MIB), which contains information maintained by the local SNMP agent. The SNMP manager will query, or can update, these variables using the SNMP protocol.

The Internet Control Message Protocol (ICMP) is used by an IP network to monitor and control the flow of traffic on the network. It's used, for example, by the *ping* service, which determines whether or not a remote destination can be reached. It is also used to provide routing information and as a messaging transport.

Basic TCP/IP Structure

Communication with TCP/IP occurs over five distinct levels, each with its own responsibilities. They are the application, transport, network, link, and physical levels. It is the application level that interfaces with the client, be it an application program, an operating system utility, or a TCP/IP networking service. The latter includes terminal sessions, file transfer and print services. The transport level is used to ensure the integrity of transmitted data and to provide for the movement of traffic. Sequencing and reorganizing of data packets takes place in this level. The network level is responsible for routing packets through the network. It essentially provides an air traffic control function, ensuring packets can find their destination. However, the network level has none of the authority of a federally regulated air traffic control system. The link level is tasked with ensuring the correct transport of data between network nodes. It should be noted that TCP/IP is supported over various communication links, including Ethernet, Token Ring, and serial lines. The physical level is comprised of hardware devices which support, but are not part of, TCP/IP. It includes the cabling and network devices such as hubs, bridges, and routers.

The primary communication unit is the packet. Packets come in various formats and sizes, based upon a number of factors including the protocol used. Figure 7.3 illustrates the type of information contained in the IP level protocol and the TCP and UDP transports.

How TCP/IP Works

To understand how TCP/IP works, we'll look at what goes on behind the scenes with a simple *telnet* session. Telnet is a TCP/IP service that allows users to have an interactive terminal session with a server. If a user wanted to start a telnet session from his machine *my.own.box.com* to the server *where.am.i.com,* he would type

```
telnet where.am.i.com
```

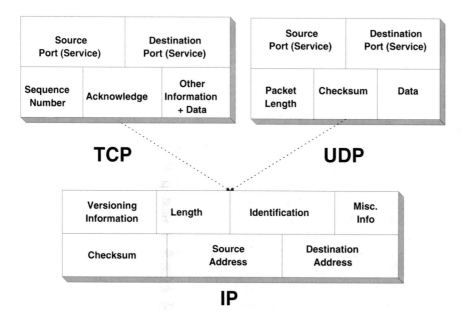

Figure 7.3 Conceptual view of IP, TCP, and UDP

The server's name is *where,* and it is located in a domain called *sub-org.i.com.* The *com* designation indicates a company (others include *gov* for government or *edu* for educational institution). The *i* is corporate designation (e.g., *hp* for Hewlett-Packard), and the *suborg* is the subentity (e.g., research). The server, if found, will respond by asking for a valid user ID and the associated password. Once both are entered, the terminal session may begin. This seems pretty straightforward, but behind the scenes a number of things are happening. Figure 7.4 shows many of the operations that must occur before the terminal session can begin.

Let's now look at how this connection is made. First, we do not want to send a six character request for a service called telnet. It is more efficient, both in terms of space and because an ASCII string comparison is slower than a numeric comparison, if we can reference telnet by a 2-byte number. In TCP/IP parlance, this number is called a *port number.* The port number for telnet is 23, and as 23 is commonly used for telnet, it is termed a *well-known port.* TCP/IP actually uses both destination and source port numbers, which allows conversations between clients and servers to use unused ports. Depending on the TCP/IP service, the port that the server uses to answer the client may be determined only at connection time. This can cause complications if we wish to block traffic for these services based on port number, because we cannot determine exactly what port the server may use for a response.

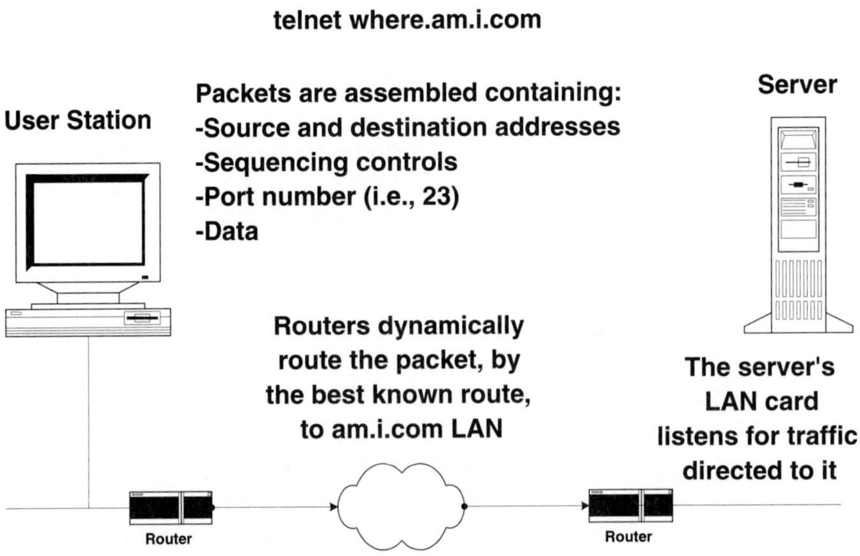

telnet where.am.i.com

User Station

Packets are assembled containing:
-Source and destination addresses
-Sequencing controls
-Port number (i.e., 23)
-Data

Server

**Routers dynamically
route the packet, by
the best known route,
to am.i.com LAN**

**The server's
LAN card
listens for traffic
directed to it**

Router   Router

Figure 7.4 An example of how TCP/IP works

Port numbers are not the only things that need to be translated. The name of the server where.am.i.com must be translated into a 32-bit IP destination address. The machine name my.own.box.com is also translated into a source IP address. An IP address is assigned by the system administrator, but there is no guarantee that it is unique to the organization, let alone the world at large. These addresses should be unique to every machine, but TCP/IP has no method of ensuring that they are. There are, however, central authorities (NIC and InterNIC) that register Internet addresses and domain names that are visible outside of an organization. Within an individual organization, it is common for a central authority (e.g., the network group) to issue and control the use of IP addresses. But the point must be made that there is no enforcement of addressing; it is under the direct control of the local system administrator.

IP addresses for known machines may be stored on the local system. But it is more common to use an IP lookup service to translate the machine name into an IP address. Methods of doing this include the Domain Name System (DNS) or the Network Information Service (NIS).

Another translation is required because IP addresses are not used at the link level. A separate address, called a *link-level address,* is used. Link-level addresses are provided by the vendor of the LAN card. While these addresses should be unique to each card, they can also be changed. Both UNIX and DOS systems allow the system administrator to modify the link-level address. A special facility is used to translate the IP addresses to the link-level address. For Ethernet networks, the Address Resolution Protocol is used to perform this translation.

After the packet is properly formatted, it is transmitted over the LAN connection by the LAN card. Its actual route to the server may vary, because TCP/IP networks constantly discover and use new routes to remote networks. If the local router does not know the direct route to the am.i.com subnetwork, it will forward the packet to a default router. Routers never guess the next destination. They either have an explicit route to the destination network or a default route for "everything else." This default router may, in turn, pass the packet on to another router. If no route can be found in an acceptable time, the error "network unreachable" will be returned to the user. The destination server constantly listens on its LAN card, and when the telnet packet addressed to it passes by, the LAN card receives it. The packet is examined, and the request for service is responded to by sending a packet to initiate the login sequence. A returning packet might or might not follow the route of the initial request. Both machines will exchange packets containing the login request, user ID, password prompt, and actual password. It is important to realize that all the data that is exchanged, including the user ID and password, is stored in the data field in human readable form.

CAN THE INTERNET PROTOCOL BE TRUSTED?

There are a number of ways to circumvent security on those operating systems and applications that use the TCP/IP and UDP/IP protocols. In the absence of compensating controls (such as packet encryption), these protocols are vulnerable to the following types of abuses:

- Packet monitoring
- Leakage
- Counterfeit addressing (spoofing)
- Sequencing attacks
- Routing attacks
- Denial of service
- Diagnostic addresses

PACKET MONITORING

The TCP/IP protocol does not prevent any client on the LAN, who has the ability to trap packets, from doing so. Software is publicly available, or provided by vendors as diagnostic software, to capture and analyze network traffic. Contents of data packets may be examined and modified.

It is easy to capture most passwords using these tools, as they are often transmitted in clear-text. Some operating systems and middleware services, such as Windows NT and Kerberos, do protect user passwords using their own encryption services. But even if the password is encrypted, it may be possible for an attacker to recognize a packet as belonging to a login procedure. The password packet may be copied, the source address modified, and the packet forwarded to a server in a replay attack.

LEAKAGE

Leakage occurs when a network device mistakenly provides information, such as network addresses or services, it was supposed to keep hidden to an untrusted network. The most common reasons for leaks include improper setup of the network device and inadvertently exposing a network when reconfiguring access lists on a network device. The access control lists on most routers are rather tricky to configure. More than one network administrator has been shocked to discover that a protected network has been wide open to attack through a simple configuration error!

COUNTERFEIT ADDRESSING

Many TCP/IP services, including the Berkeley "r" commands, NFS, and X Window, authorize clients based upon a network identity. This type of authorization generally involves the use of access control lists, which authorize clients based on their machine name or IP address. The problem is that source addresses, as well as anything else about a packet, can be changed. There have been a number of recent attacks recorded where this weakness has been exploited.

A question that comes to mind is "If the source address is faked, how does the attacker receive any information from the attack?" The answer is that the attacker, in many cases, will employ techniques that do not require a response. For example, an attack that mails the password file to the attacker does not require a valid source address or the receipt of any reply packets, but only a valid email address.

The technique is not limited to software services, but has also been used against networking devices such as routers. Acting as filters on firewall configurations, routers have been fooled into allowing entry to the internal network of illicit packets from the outside. The router encounters a packet with a source address from the internal network. Assuming the packet must be outside the internal network by mistake, the router allows it to pass to the internal network. The problem is especially evident when three or more LAN cards are used in a single router, and one of the cards is used to connect to an external network. The router, which must pass internal traffic as well as filter external traffic, might be fooled into passing counterfeit traffic.

The problem of routers with multiple LAN cards has been compared to an international airport that does not segregate passengers arriving from domestic and foreign destinations. It would be very difficult to determine which passengers were arriving from abroad and should clear customs from the domestic travelers who do not. Routers that can filter incoming packets can largely overcome these problems.

SEQUENCING ATTACKS

Random numbers are used by some TCP/IP services to determine where they are in the communication and, in some instances, the authentication process. After connection establishment, the client and server share a common TCP/IP sequence numbers. There are two numbers used: one tells the client which frame to expect from the server, the other tells the server which frame to expect from the client. The client, when a subsequent request is made to the server, will provide the shared sequence number as proof of the communication sequence. The problem is that in some implementations, the sequence number is not random and can be guessed or calculated. This allows the attacker to bypass normal authentication by submitting packets that fool the server into thinking that authentication has already occurred.

For example, it is possible for an attacker to construct a request to a UNIX system supporting the Berkeley *host equivalency* services that will convince the server that the client can be trusted even though no authentication has occurred. The UNIX X Window and Network File System services, as well as the Novell Netware LOGIN authentication, have also been compromised by this type of attack. While this is arguably not a TCP/IP network problem, and belongs to the application service that uses the scheme, it remains a problem associated with use of TCP/IP.

ROUTING ATTACKS

TCP/IP networks continually discover new routes to networks with which they wish to communicate. Routers pass information about foreign networks and suggest new routes to these networks whenever appropriate. Routing information accepted from an untrusted source should be treated with suspicion. This is especially true in the case of routing information for the internal network.

> An analogy we can make is that of the farm boy who asks about the best way to get home from town. He would be awfully suspicious of a suggested route that involved a trip through a deserted downtown alley (especially if it were suggested he bring his wallet!).

DENIAL OF SERVICE ATTACKS

A denial of service attack is simply a malicious attempt to prevent others from obtaining use of a service. This may include creating a large number of mail messages to a specific address that will eventually result in disk space problems. Or it may involve generating a sufficient quantity of garbage LAN traffic as to make it unusable.

DIAGNOSTIC ATTACKS

A special address is associated with most TCP/IP machines. The address is used to provide local diagnostic support of the LAN card. Many network services also use the loopback address when running stand-alone. For example, a DNS resolver might use the loopback address to communicate with a name server running on the same host. It's commonly set to 127.0.0.1 and is called the *loopback address.* Because it is known to exist on many machines, it has been manipulated in the past by attackers. Essentially, any communication over the network to the loopback address should be considered invalid. Any packets directed to the loopback address should be disregarded by routers and bridges.

INCREASING SECURITY IN AN IP NETWORK

One solution to solving the problem of security in an untrusted network is the encryption of sensitive network traffic. Unfortunately, the encryption of network traffic is not without price. Encryption is expensive, both in terms of the cost of encrypting devices and performance.

The most commonly used technique to enhance security in an IP network is to divide the network into subnetworks. Routers and bridges may be used to segment the network into sections (or subnetworks). Traffic can be filtered between the interconnected networks, with most traffic being kept within the local workgroup. Routers and bridges limit traffic, not destined to the outside, to the local workgroup. The implementation of subnetwork controls dissuades widespread monitoring of network traffic because the amount of traffic that can be monitored from a single node is limited.

Figure 7.5 shows how additional security can be implemented in a TCP/IP network.

Hubs may be configured to prevent unauthorized access to the LAN by only allowing access to predefined hardware addresses. Alerts may also be forwarded by the hub to networking operations software if new devices are detected. Secure routers might also be employed which can encrypt, and thus protect, traffic between them. These routers can be used to ensure the integrity and privacy of traffic over an exposed connection, such as between two buildings or a remote subnetwork. Other methods might include building a challenge-response authentication, especially if one is concerned about IP spoofing through an Internet firewall. We will examine the use of firewalls and other Internet security techniques in Chapter 14.

Most importantly, the design of a network with security in mind makes it possible to erect boundaries of trust between trusted and untrusted sections of the network. Routers and bridges provide the ability to filter unauthorized traffic from untrusted sections of the network. Not only may traffic from untrusted networks be filtered, but it is also common to filter based upon the type of service (i.e., port number). For example, all X Window traffic may be prevented if it originates from outside the local workgroup.

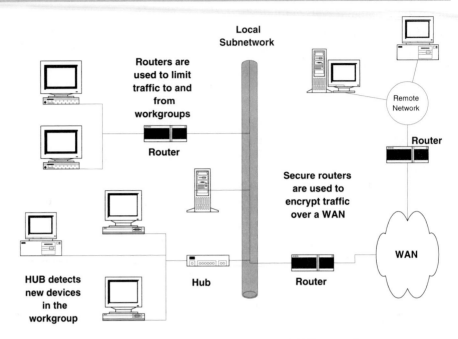

Figure 7.5 Increasing security in a TCP/IP network

There are other advantages to subnetworking, such as the ability to create autonomous administrative domains. IP addresses can be assigned within a range of subnet addresses to a local workgroup. For example, a software development group could be given a particular range of addresses. Software development groups, because of their need for high-level privileges and the instability of the environment, usually have less than stringent security controls. A trusted subnetwork approach can be taken to allow a full range of activity within the development workgroup, but isolates it from the internal network. This prevents the rather lax security, evident in many development environments, from being exploited.

> The good news is that increased network performance and security are not mutually exclusive objectives. Solutions and techniques used to accomplish one objective may also be used for the second. The use of subnetworks makes sense from a network perspective. Most network traffic is subject to the old phone company Pareto principle or "80/20" rule, which states that roughly 80 percent of communication is local and 20 percent outside of your area. If the same rule may be applied to network traffic, then limiting traffic to the local subnetwork whenever possible is a desirable action. It will result in increased performance on the rest of the network.

The downside to constructing trusted subnetworks is that the routers must allow some traffic to pass—why be connected at all if this is not the case? But filters are applied to IP addresses that may be counterfeited. Filtering schemes are somewhat difficult to implement. Loopholes may be left open that can be exploited. The administration of trusted subnetworks also requires a great deal of effort. Sophisticated network management tools are likely required in support of this activity. As well, using a trusted sub-network approach does not deter attacks from inside their boundaries. Traffic that passes from inside the trusted subnetwork to the untrusted inter-network is still exposed.

In spite of these limitations, many organizations have successfully segregated their networks into trusted subnetworks. It depends on the current use of networked computing, and the culture of the enterprise, to say whether or not this is an appropriate solution.

FUTURE DEVELOPMENTS

A major problem is now facing the TCP/IP world. It is simply running out of available IP addresses, due to the enormous popularity of the protocol on the Internet. A working group, called IPng for IP Next Generation, has been created to examine the problem and propose a solution. The solution has been termed IP Version 6 (IPv6). It proposes, among many other things, that Internet addresses be expanded from the current 32 bits to 128 bits. This will greatly increase the number of allowable addresses. One problem, however, is that IPng has been asked to solve a number of other issues. This has added to the complexity and delayed the release date of IPv6. Network security is also to be addressed by IPv6. In particular, methods to authenticate the source of a packet and to provide for the encryption of its contents have been proposed.

The Internet Protocol Security group (IPSEC) is reviewing a number of security enhancements including authentication controls, encryption, checksums and access control features. It is expected that the architecture will feature public key encryption techniques. It will be composed of a key management and security encapsulation protocol. The key management protocol will generate encryption keys and authenticate the sender of the transmission. Security encapsulation will protect the traffic and is expected to offer various levels of encryption. The technical standards have been documented in the Internet RFCs 1825 through 1829.

SNA VERSUS TCP/IP SECURITY

These two approaches to networking are fundamentally different. SNA authorizes all connections to the network, while TCP/IP connections are unauthorized. SNA is hierarchical in design, while TCP/IP is peer to peer. SNA use fixed paths, while TCP/IP uses dynamic routing. The performance of an SNA is largely predictable and can be managed. The distributed architecture of TCP/IP results in wildly varying network response times depending on network traffic. TCP/IP, however, is available on a very wide range of platforms and is very easy to set up and communicate with other computers. Moreover, the largest computer network in the world—the Internet—is TCP/IP-based. While the hierarchical SNA does authorize all connections to an SNA network, this does not imply that the security of an SNA network cannot be comprised. Using an SNA protocol analyzer, SNA traffic may be intercepted and examined. As with TCP/IP, passwords flow in human-readable form on an SNA network. SNA does not offer data encryption or protection services as part of the transport.

In general, the security capabilities of the SNA/APPN architecture are not as open to compromise as is TCP/IP. APPN was built to handle high-end, mission-critical, distributed applications. TCP/IP was invented to handle wide area communications between researchers in autonomous administrative domains. While SNA has a significant established base, TCP/IP has a vastly more significant "market share" in the computing world and is growing at a very rapid rate. The market penetration and growth of APPN is unclear at this time.

The TCP/IP environment will need to be provided with additional security features if it is to considered with the same degree of trust as the SNA networking environment. It is unclear at this time whether the necessary security controls will be built into the protocol, or designed into services and applications using the protocol. It is also possible that a hybrid approach will be used.

CONCLUSIONS

Until mechanisms are available to provide protection against eavesdropping and other intrusions, we will have two choices. Either we can accept the risk and wait for improvements to the existing protocol, or we can use compensating controls to diminish it. The compensating controls may include a number of approaches, such as dividing the network into trusted subnetworks. The use of encrypting network devices, such as secure routers, to connect portions of the network over an untrusted carrier can also be employed. As well, the use of secure middleware, such as OSF/DCE, which presumes the network is untrusted and provides a number of additional controls against intruders, can be considered. We will examine OSF/DCE and its security mechanisms in Chapters 16 and 17. Finally, the replacement of the current operating system authentication and access control mechanisms with commercial access control solutions can considered. We will examine these solutions in later chapters.

CHAPTER 8

NETWORK OPERATING SYSTEMS

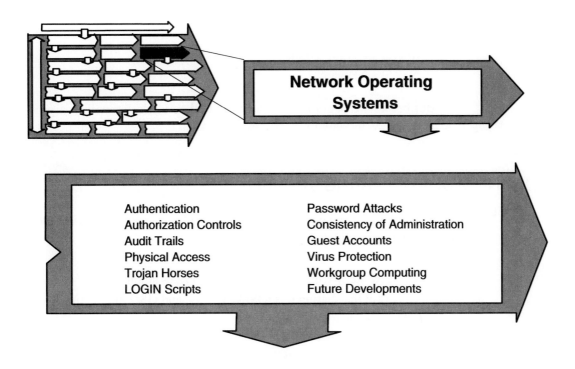

Authentication	Password Attacks
Authorization Controls	Consistency of Administration
Audit Trails	Guest Accounts
Physical Access	Virus Protection
Trojan Horses	Workgroup Computing
LOGIN Scripts	Future Developments

Network operating systems, such as Novell's Netware and Banyan's Vines, have become a common element of most organizations computing environments. To arrive at an actual definition for a network operating system is a difficult task. After all, isn't almost every operating system capable of interacting on a network? We are going to define a network operating system (or NOS), not in relation to where they are today, but rather from where they have come from. Network operating systems arose from the need to provide resource sharing, primarily disk and print services, to users on a local area network (LAN). The focus of this type of computing was the local workgroup. The definition does not hold much water these days. The focus has changed from the workgroup to the enterprise, as many advanced features have been added to the traditional NOS products. The distinctions between a NOS and other traditional operating systems with

117

strong networking capabilities (such as UNIX and Windows NT) are rapidly falling away.

We will examine the use of network operating systems, along with their benefits, and the security issues related to their use. Rather than look at specific implementations, we will review things common to all. We will base our review on four of the most prevalent network operating systems:

- Banyan's Vines
- IBM's LAN Server
- Microsoft's LAN Manager
- Novell's Netware

But before we begin to understand how they work, we will first provide an overview of network operating systems.

ABOUT NETWORK OPERATING SYSTEMS?

While a NOS environment is capable of providing many advanced functions, its primary use is

- To allow the sharing of file and print services among users.
- To permit the sharing of DOS, Windows, and OS/2 applications and data.
- To act as "front ends" to allow fast and efficient access to larger data stores of information.
- To facilitate the sharing of information within a workgroup.

We'll look at how NOSs typically perform the security functions of authentication, authorization, and audit. We will also briefly look at the use of control monitors and centralized security management solutions, which enhance the security and integrity of the environment. Last, we'll look at the major security issues facing the NOS environment and review expected future developments.

AUTHENTICATION

While network operating systems can use a number of different methods, the use of logon IDs and associated passwords is common in authenticating users. Users log onto the LAN by running a program which allows entry of an account name (e.g., logon ID) and password. The user ID and password are verified by a server. Most of NOS implementations store the user password in encrypted form on the server. Many NOS systems still transfer passwords in clear-text over the LAN between client and server. But some have implemented authentication mechanisms that protect against the discovery of the password.

Novell's Netware, for example, uses a one-way authentication scheme to authenticate the users. The LOGIN program requests that the server generate a special key (called the login key) on behalf of the user at login. Login keys are used once and only once, and they are invalid after use. The user then enters their password, which is used along with the login key to create a second key. The second key is forwarded to the server. The Novell server repeats the process that the user has just performed and compares the key it has generated with that forwarded by the user LOGIN program. A match authenticates the user! Figure 8.1 shows the Netware authentication methods.

The advantages of this approach are that the passwords cannot be detected over the LAN. Replay attacks are also prevented because the first login key is random and is never reused. As well, the password is not stored on the client nor is it transmitted in clear-text. The network operating systems also provide for the enforcement of password policy. Typical controls include the requirement for all users to have a password. Password aging

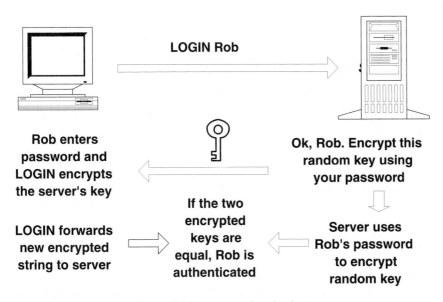

LOGIN Rob

Rob enters password and LOGIN encrypts the server's key

Ok, Rob. Encrypt this random key using your password

If the two encrypted keys are equal, Rob is authenticated

LOGIN forwards new encrypted string to server

Server uses Rob's password to encrypt random key

Figure 8.1 Netware authentication

may also be implemented, which forces the user to change their password on a regular basis. Some NOS implementations, such as LAN Manager, also permit the administrator to set a minimum number of days that the password must be active. The user cannot reset their password within this time frame. Other password related controls commonly found on most NOS systems include the enforcement of a minimum length for all passwords. The reuse of passwords may also be prevented. This is accomplished by the NOS keeping a list of previously used passwords. The user may not change their password to any password in the list. The lists are usually limited in size, and are typically set to hold the last five passwords.

AUTHORIZATION CONTROLS

Network operating systems provide controls and limits in three distinct ways: by the use of privileges, through file access permissions, and by event access controls. Privileges are special levels of authority that are assigned to individual users. For example, the OPERATOR authority may give a user the ability to manage printing services and perform backups. While their names vary from implementation to implementation, basic administrative and support functions available are common to each NOS. These basic functions are shown in Table 8.1.

Network operating systems authorize user access to files and directories through the use of permissions. Permissions limit the users and type of

TABLE 8.1
TYPICAL NOS PRIVILEGES

Privilege	Description
SUPERVISOR	Can perform user management, reconfiguration of the server and manage access controls.
OPERATOR	Manages print services and backup/restore operations.
DELEGATED PRIVILEGES	Most NOS implementations allow the authority of the SUPERVISOR to be fully or partially delegated to other users. These are generally assigned to an individual user.
USER	An ordinary user which conveys no special privileges.
GUEST	A common user ID used by individuals who are not given their own account on the system.

access based upon the user ID or group membership. Typical access permissions include those shown in Table 8.2.

The networking operating systems employ additional access controls based upon a number of events. These controls include

- Time of day controls which disable access after working hours.
- The automatic logoff of the user after hours.
- Logoff of the user after a period of inactivity.
- The disabling of the user account after a number (usually three) of failed login attempts.
- Concurrent sessions may be limited (usually to one).

Some vendors offer relatively unique access controls. Novell Netware, for example, can require the login to occur from a predefined LAN address. Banyan Vines has the ability to force the login from a particular operating system, such as OS/2 or DOS/Windows.

Novell has also been encouraging third parties to create security solutions for the Netware environment using Netware Loadable Modules (NLMs). NLMs allow for the extension of special privileges to ordinary users, and can be used for a variety of purposes including security. As an example, the NetSqueeze+Encryption NLM from LAN Support Group, Inc., will permit a user to automatically encrypt/decrypt sensitive files. NLMs may be protected by passwords.

TABLE 8.2
TYPICAL NOS ACCESS PERMISSIONS

Permission	Description
READ	Has the ability to open and read a file, or list the contents of a directory.
WRITE	Can change the contents of a file or directory.
CREATE	Can create new files or directories.
DELETE	Can remove a file or directory.
EXECUTE	The file may be run as a program.
CHANGE	The user may change permissions on the object.
ARCHIVE	The user can create a special reference to the table, called a foreign key.

AUDIT TRAILS

As with most things in the NOS environment, audit trails have a similar purpose but are implemented differently by each vendor. The basic types of activities recorded in audit trails, which are common to most vendors, include

- The recording of logon/logoff activity by user
- Changes to permissions concerning a resource
- Changes to user privileges and status
- The success or failure of a request to access resources, including login requests

Most audit trails are not enabled by default. Some of the NOS environments, including LAN Manager, allow tailoring of the audit trail to limit the amount of audit data created. Access to selected resources or by a selected user may be specifically logged. As well, failed access attempts (usually logins), may be audited to detect password guessing attempts.

There are a number of problems with the current implementations of audit trails. The audit trails are kept on the local system and can therefore be comprised by a user with sufficient privileges. A user who gains SUPERVISOR privileges can either erase their audit records or destroy the entire audit trail. As well, the format and structure of the audit trails differ from vendor to vendor. This makes consolidation and centralized reporting difficult. Alerts, if available, are forwarded to the system console which may not be regularly accessed by the network administrator. It may take some time for the network administrator to view the alert, if it is not overwritten by subsequent messages.

NOS SECURITY SOLUTIONS

Third-party solutions are available from various vendors to increase the overall security of the NOS environment. These solutions provide control monitoring and centralized security management functions. Control monitors are a special class of security tools which check for weaknesses in the NOS security structure. Typical checks include weak or nonexistent passwords, inactive accounts, and excessive user access rights

The Frye Utilities for Netware, for example, perform a number of checks at login, including nonexistent passwords and poorly chosen passwords. Accounts which have not been accessed in a predefined number of days are reported, as are users who have been given supervisory privileges.

Vendors have also developed a number of solutions that provide enhanced access controls and audit features. An example is the Net/Assure family of products from Centel Federal System, Inc. Net/Assure provides system access control, encryption, data access, and system integrity services to supplement native Novell security controls.

ISSUES SURROUNDING NOS IMPLEMENTATIONS

We'll now look at a number of problems surrounding the use of network operating systems. The issues are basically divided by the type of attack that can occur. We will begin by looking at the problem of limiting physical access to a NOS server.

PHYSICAL ACCESS

Most computers, including NOS servers, can be compromised using physical access to the computer's system console. Even if passwords are used to protect the system console, the system may be rebooted using a specially formatted floppy disk. Once rebooted, use of a common diagnostic tool, such as Norton Utilities, can easily betray the servers' secrets. It is therefore important to safeguard servers in locked facilities. Additional security can be obtained by implementing DOS or OS/2 access control solutions, either in software or via hardware. We have even witnessed administrators who have stripped the screws on their servers to deter tampering. This can make hardware maintenance an interesting exercise to say the least!

TROJAN HORSES

One the most common attacks on a NOS environment involves an attack on the personal computer client. By inserting a bogus login program or using a terminate and stay resident (TSR) program to capture keystrokes, passwords may be captured and later reused. If the client has not implemented strong access controls on the personal computer, these methods are very difficult to prevent and detect. Examples of personal computer access control solutions include the Menu Works solution from PC Dynamics, Inc., and PC-DACS from Mergent International, Inc. Both products provide for user ID and password controls and provide the ability to limit access to files and directories.

LOGIN SCRIPTS

Another potential vulnerability is the set of commands or programs which automatically attaches the user to the network. Access to these scripts can allow a hacker to capture passwords, and sometimes even bypass security mechanisms altogether. A popular computer magazine once demonstrated a program which would allow a hacker to bypass the Novell LOGIN program. It did so by fooling the server into believing it was dealing with a previously authenticated user.

PASSWORD ATTACKS

Attacks involving guessed passwords are used to gain unauthorized access to a NOS server. A hacker will use a program that attempts to logon to an account by supplying every word in a dictionary as the account password. A variant of this type of attack involves overt attempts to gain access to accounts that have no passwords. The most common method of deterring these types of attacks is to trap failed logins in an audit trail and to alert the system administrator.

CONSISTENCY OF ADMINISTRATION

Probably the most common problem related to us by our clients is with NOS administration. While some network administrators are very knowledgeable and diligent in their duties, there is a lack of consistency in fulfilling this duty in many organizations. Too many LAN administrators are poorly trained and overworked, which can result in weak security controls. Common complaints arising from the inconsistent application of controls include the use of default Supervisor passwords and the existence of active user accounts long after the user has left the organization.

A solution to this complaint may be provided by the recent "enterprisewide" releases offered by some NOS vendors. The Netware 4.1 release, for example, has many advanced features for enterprise computing. These include the Netware Directory Service (NDS), the Time Synchronization Service (TSS), and the central administration tool (NWADMIN). Banyan Vines has long offered replication of services as well as centralized directory services.

A common directory service can be used to impose naming and directory standards, while the TSS will give a common definition of time. The centralized administration function should allow greater conformance to standards and policy because a smaller number of administrators will be responsible for their implementation. Policy and standards may be enforced for an entire domain of network servers rather than on a server-by-server basis.

GUEST ACCOUNTS

Guest accounts are commonly used to give access to NOS resources to temporary employees or contractors. A GUEST account allows users, who may not have an individual account on the server, access to a limited number of resources on the server. They have the benefit of allowing casual access to the server, without having to involve the server administrator. Guest accounts are implemented in a number of different ways. Netware, for example, supports the use of a GUEST account. LAN Manager uses a PUBLIC share which basically allows anyone access to a specific directory and subdirectories.

Many problems are associated with the use of a GUEST account. They can be used to house illicit or improper items, such as pirated software or pornography. Many GUEST accounts have no passwords associated with them, which make them vulnerable to abuse.

Most users do not understand that placing an object in a GUEST account makes it accessible to all network users, not just their intended audience. Many organizations allow contractors and consultants access to their internal LANs. A commonly heard complaint is that information placed in a PUBLIC directory has inadvertently been made available to nonemployees.

VIRUS PROTECTION

The protection of servers against viruses should be a greater concern than individual personal computers. Unfortunately, we have witnessed a number of organizations that have invested in personal computer software, but failed to address the server. Viruses on a server should be taken very seriously because servers are accessed by many more users than a single personal computer. This increases the likelihood of a server coming in contact with a virus, simply because they are accessed by a larger number of people. They are also a central point for the spread of infection, capable of infecting many more users. The loss of work and disruptions in combating a "server" virus is much greater than on a single workstation. All users who have contacted the server should check their individual workstations for problems.

The use of virus protection software is a necessary precaution for all users of personal computers. It is simply common sense that virus protection be used on servers as well. There are some points about using virus protection software on servers that should be considered. Not all vendors of virus protection software support server versions of their products. The software should be able to detect the existence of masked viruses. For example, compressed files should be examined for viruses. The virus software should be capable of forwarding alerts to the network administrator. The virus protection software should be active when the server is booted from a floppy drive.

All viruses require the execution of code for the infection to take place. One simple way to lessen the probability of virus outbreak on a server is to deny write privileges to users on all directories that house programs. Of course, it is also a good idea to enforce the running of virus protection software on client machines through a login script. As well, execute permission to files on other users directories should be limited. And don't forget to regularly update the virus protection software!

WORKGROUP COMPUTING

A big advantage of using a personal computer is the productivity that you can attain developing documents and sharing work processes. This productivity can disappear, however, if you are part of a team and must coordinate the work in progress. A flurry of diskette trading can lead to uncertainty over who has the latest copy of the report or which is the current spreadsheet. Software solutions to this problem have been proposed to bring some order to this chaos and allow a group of individuals to work together. This class of software is referred to as groupware. Some would argue that email, for example, is an implementation of groupware.

Groupware refers to a class of computer software that allows groups of people, usually with a common business relationship, possibly in diverse locations, to work as a team using shared resources. These solutions can encompass a number of business activities including email, time management and planning, data management, and document development and management. The higher the level of integration of the groupware services and the span that those services can reach, the more productive groupware can be.

Groupware implementations also offer rather robust security controls, which include the use of public key encryption. We will look more closely at the subject of groupware, with a particular focus on Lotus Notes, in later chapters.

FUTURE DEVELOPMENTS

Many of the NOS vendors either use, or have plans to incorporate, the TCP/IP network protocol. While the use of the protocol will allow easier communication with the outside world, this will come with increased exposures and tests of the strength of the NOS controls. It is expected that this development will increase the number of security breaches involving NOSs.

A positive development by some vendors is the movement to incorporate the Distributed Computing Environment (DCE) from the Open Software Foundation into their product offerings. For example, Novell has announced support for OSF/DCE, which will allow other operating environments, including OS/2 and UNIX to share authentication services with the Netware environment. IBM has also announced DCE support for the OS/2 LAN Server offering.

CONCLUSIONS

The future should bring a convergence of the network operating systems and open systems operating systems. With this convergence, new issues will arise, but these should be offset by stronger administration, access controls, and audit capabilities. Already, authentication and access control solutions have been introduced which allow common security administration for the two environments. It is expected that this activity will continue, with many more integrated solutions available in the next few years.

We will continue our examination of networking in the next chapter, when we review the world of client/server. We will also examine the *glue,* or *middleware,* that binds applications and services together.

CHAPTER 9

CLIENT/SERVER AND MIDDLEWARE

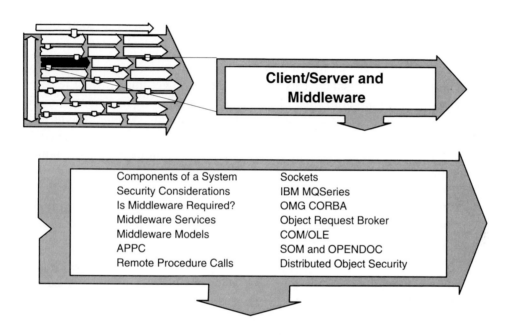

Client/Server and Middleware

Components of a System	Sockets
Security Considerations	IBM MQSeries
Is Middleware Required?	OMG CORBA
Middleware Services	Object Request Broker
Middleware Models	COM/OLE
APPC	SOM and OPENDOC
Remote Procedure Calls	Distributed Object Security

In the previous chapter we looked at network operating systems and the trust elements they bring to a distributed environment. In this chapter we will explore another level of distributing the work, the mystery (or misery) of client-server computing. A client-server system is not actually a mystery in concept but can be very mysterious in its implementation. We will try to outline the enabling components of client/server and explore some of the trust considerations. There are many different approaches and technologies available to provide client-server computing. Although we can't cover all of these, it is important to understand the concepts and to know where the strengths and vulnerabilities may exist.

It is important to understand the concepts and building blocks involved in advanced client-server systems to be able to apply the appropriate security mechanisms. In the first chapter we talked about the different distributed processing models. In this chapter we will concentrate on the client/server and cooperative processing models. Remember that these models involve the execution of some form of application program logic on both the client and the server. We will introduce the *logical unit of work* (LUW) as a way of describing how to define and partition the work that needs to be done. We will also review the two-phase commit process for keeping the database updates intact. A two-phase commit is essential when the database can be updated by multiple users. Middleware is a name given to software that provide services to make it easier to distribute and manage the work of the system. We will look at some of these middleware approaches and technologies. Finally, we will take a look at some of the enabling technologies that are available to help distribute the work.

Client-server computing is now assumed to be a standard way of putting systems together. This approach began to get this growing level of attention with the utilization of personal computers, the implementation of LANs, and the sophistication of the network operating systems. The growth of client-server computing seems to be evolving from two ends of the computing spectrum. The bottom up pressure comes from the increasing power of the PCs and the need to share this PC-generated data in a controlled manner. The top-down pressure comes from the need to exploit the relatively inexpensive processing power of the PCs while limiting the cost of expensive central processing. In both cases we need to manage the data and exploit the computing power at hand.

When PCs were implemented in organizations that also used mainframe computing, it quickly became apparent that the majority of output from one computing system actually became input to another. A lot of data was being reentered into spreadsheet programs taken from paper reports generated by a mainframe-based system. An improvement was developed to transfer a copy of the file from the mainframe to the PC and avoid the reentry of the data but still required several manipulations to be useful on the PC. Better yet was to have the PC program interface directly with the mainframe system and get the current data when it was needed. This integration, however, often required programming gymnastics to obtain and translate the data.

COMPONENTS OF A SYSTEM

When we closely examine a computer system, we find that it can be broken down into simple components. The first important piece is the data or information. There has been a debate about the definition of what data is and what information is. For the purpose of this book we can think of data as the specific items that are manipulated and stored in a computer system and information as the representation of the data that makes sense to you. In very simple terms when using a computer system, you either want to look at information, or manipulate data into new forms of information that you can look at. One of the key things you need to know about the data is where it is and who needs to deal with it.

The more data that we have available in a computer readable format, the more information we can generate, which in turn can make for better and more timely decisions. The more processing power we put with easy access to the user, the greater our ability to access and analyze the data. This access however, can also cause a lot of difficulty with maintaining the integrity of the data if these processes include modification to the data from multiple locations. We need sophisticated software to help manage the access and maintain the integrity of the data. We also need to be able to keep track of who is accessing and changing the data to ensure they are in fact who they say they are and are authorized to do.

CLIENT/SERVER

Definitions of client/server vary widely depending on the specific problem that is being addressed or what a particular software vendor has to offer. It has been described in such specific terms as a close programmatic coupling of distributed intelligence across multiple platforms or as general as anytime you use a PC to communicate with an application over a network. A very common use of the term client-server computing is used to describe the situation where the PC supports a graphical user interface used to access applications on a network connected server. We will keep the definition of client/server in as simple terms as possible for the purpose of this book.

A client is a process that requests services from a server. A server is a process that services the requests from the client. Client/server describes the approach to segmenting a computing system into client portions and servers portions.

LOGICAL UNIT OF WORK

An important concept in a distributed computing system is the logical *unit of work* or LUW. This logical unit of work is a collection of processes that must be coordinated and executed to completion. If there is a failure in any portion of the coordinated processes, all of the processing must be set back to the point before the logical unit of work was initiated. The LUW must be either complete in its entirety, or if the process is unsuccessful, be reset as if it never happened. The completion of a LUW is usually marked with a sync point or a commit to indicate everything is at a consistent state.

Figure 9.1 represents a process that contains two individual logical units of work. The action of reading files A and B and then updating file A can be considered to be one logical unit of work, while the action of reading and updating file C can be considered to be another one. Each logical unit of work represents a completion of a task and the synchronizing of the data in a consistent state. We can find LUWs that have been defined and are executed without our knowledge. All LUWs may not always include the requirement for a commit or sync point. Even an Internet browser such as Netscape contains program logic that can be considered to be a logical unit of work.

TWO-PHASE COMMIT

The two-phase commit protocol is important anytime database updates are involved in the distributed system. An important problem to overcome when distributing work over multiple processes is to ensure that either all of the work completes successfully or the data involved is returned to a point as if the work never occurred. The method for managing this requirement is the two-phase commit. This is especially important if the logical unit of work is spread between two independent processes.

Figure 9.2 illustrates the two-phase commit process. When a database update is requested from process A, a notification is sent to process B, the

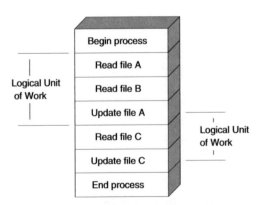

Figure 9.1 Logical unit of work example

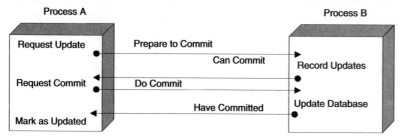

Figure 9.2 Two-phase commit

manager of the data, to prepare for an update. A positive acknowledgment of can commit by process B will cause process A to issue a commit request. Once process B acknowledges with a committed message, the logical unit of work is considered complete. If either process A or process B cannot complete their logical unit of work, the update process is aborted. This protocol is very important when the success of a logical unit of work is split between several processes.

COOPERATIVE PROCESSING

Before client-server computing became popular, the term cooperative processing was coined to describe the ability of an application function to be split between two or more processes, and still be executed as if it was a single application. Cooperative processing is used to describe the ability to spread the processing of a single logical unit of work over two or more processes, and have that unit of work completed in a timely and coordinated fashion. The processes are usually executed on separate processors, although that is not a requirement. An early implementation of cooperative processing came from IBM with their implementation of Application Program-to-Program Communication (APPC) facilities.

The definition of cooperative processing is purposely narrow to depend on distributing a single logical unit of work across individual processes as opposed to a more simple client-server relationship. To qualify as a cooperative process, the following conditions must be met:

- There must be more than one application function (program) involved in executing a single logical unit of work.
- The cooperating process must have programmable intelligence.
- Participating processors must use this programmable intelligence in the execution of the logical unit of work.

The processing between the cooperative components may be asynchronous or synchronous, and the control orientation may be master-slave or peer-to-peer between the cooperative programs until the end of a logical unit of work is reached. At a commit point at the conclusion of a LUW, the work must be either permanently applied to data or backed out across all of the involved systems. Cooperative processing is a specific form of the more general client-server computing where close integration of the application execution is required.

CLIENT-SERVER SECURITY CONSIDERATIONS

One of the most important elements in a client-server relationship is the mutual authentication of the client to the server and vice versa. The client must provide proof of identity to the server as well as the server proving that it is the correct one to the client. The ability to provide confidentiality using encryption for communication between the client and the server is required for any identification and authentication details and may be desired for other confidential data. The client-server relationship can take advantage of a third-party security such as that provided by Kerberos. This mechanism will provide mutual authentication and network confidentiality between the client and the server. Details of Kerberos are provided in Chapter 17. Secure storage for confidential data such as encryption keys is also required on both sides of the client-server relationship. Another major requirement is for the implementation of robust audit features across the client-server relationship.

MIDDLEWARE

Middleware sounds like one of those computereeze terms that you keep hearing but can't quite figure out what it means. There is a little-known language rule that allows you to stick "ware" on the end of anything and all of a sudden you can describe a new class of products. Middleware describes all that stuff that happens when you execute programs that use two or more computers that you don't want to understand. It is sometimes referred to as the magic glue that allows you to stick together applications and data from various locations. Middleware is really a collection of software services that can provide an easier way of implementing client-server applications instead of coding all of the required distributed services yourself. It can provide a common interface and selection of services when various different platforms are used. Advanced middleware can provide services that shield the applications from knowing specifically where the other applications or data are located. These will be addressed later in this chapter.

> Middleware is a layer of software that provides a common interface and translation between the application, the data and the operating system.

Is Middleware Required?

The simple answer to this question is no, it's not specifically required. However, if some form of middleware is not used, you will be faced with coding all of the services required for coordination, communication, and recovery between the intelligent processes yourself. Recovery in the event of a failure is where robust middleware is of most value. There can be many places in a distributed system where failure can occur. The appropriate middleware can help manage recovery in the event of a failure of a part of the system without placing that additional burden on the application. There is some debate about the requirement for the application to be aware of and involved in the recovery processes when failure is encountered. The middleware ranges from completely shielding the application from any knowledge of its distribution to providing the specific application interfaces and processes that can be used for managing distribution. The application may be required to know when failures occur with the middleware providing the procedural interfaces to be invoked by the application. The requirement for the application to be aware of how it is distributed is mainly a function of its need to control its execution with dynamic decisions applied with programmed logic against situations.

Middleware Services

There are several services that middleware can provide to enable the successful division of processing across the distributed environment. The following list indicates some of these services. This is not meant to be an exhaustive list, but it will give you an indication of the type of services middleware typically provides. Some middleware implementations will contain a richer selection of services while others may provide only basic services.

- **Directory**—keeps track of the location and characteristics of network resources such as files, servers and applications. The directory is based on a name that is independent from the physical location to enable the locations to change.
- **Security**—provides authorization, authentication and auditing services for both registered system and users and to protect network resources from unauthorized use.

- **Management**—includes such services as problem, operation, configuration, change, and performance management across the distributed environment.
- **Application programming interface (API)**—provides a consistent interface that applications can implement to invoke the middleware services. The APIs may be available on many different platforms to provide consistency across the heterogeneous nature of the distributed environment.
- **Time**—required to be coordinated between the network resources to be able to schedule services and coordinate activities.

MIDDLEWARE MODELS

There are many middleware approaches and technologies available for the client to interact with the server. The middleware mechanisms generally will fall into one of the models outlined in Figure 9.3. Middleware following the conversational model will provide facilities for simple communication between the client and the server. The client will ask the server to do something and wait for a reply. This type of interaction is similar to a telephone conversation and can be referred to as request/response. In some network protocols definitions this can also be referred to as connection oriented, implying that a network connection is required between the client and the server for the conversation to take place. In this case the application will detect any failure and assumes the burden for recovery.

The remote procedure call model provides a program call-return mechanism that can be directed to servers anywhere in a network. Figure 9.3 shows the similarity between the RPC and the conversational model. This call-return model is similar to those used to execute subroutines in an application. Again the application will be aware of any failure of the RPC requests and will be required to take action. This model is synchronous, dependent on the coordinated execution of the client and the server.

The messaging model uses message queues to communicate the required tasks between the client and the server. The client and server will look at these message queues to see if any messages have been placed in them and act upon those messages. The messaging model allows the implementation of message-driven processing rather than the transaction-driven processing we have been used to. The message-driven model is useful for implementing workflow processing or any coordinated processing that does not require a persistent relationship with the other processes. This model is referred to as asynchronous: the execution of the client and the server is not dependent on each other. In some network protocols this can be referred to

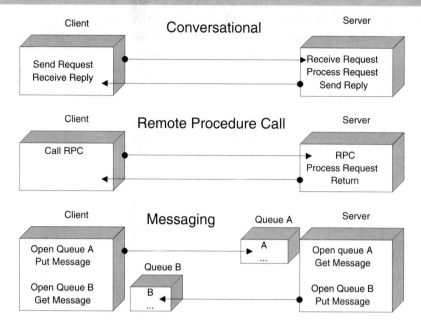

Figure 9.3 Middleware models

as a connectionless model where a specific connection between the client and the server is not required.

ENABLING TECHNOLOGY

There are many approaches and solutions which qualify as middleware that provide interprocess communication and execution. These technologies tend to fall into one of the middleware models we have previously examined. We have outlined a few of the technologies here to illustrate the different approaches, but we will not attempt to list all of the technologies and implementations available. This is a fast-moving area, so you would be well advised to keep tuned into developments in this area.

APPLICATION PROGRAM-TO-PROGRAM COMMUNICATION (APPC)

One of the first off the mark in the distributed processing environment was Application Program-to-Program Communication (APPC) from IBM. This is a structure provided to allow direct synchronous communication between two application programs. APPC defines the required interprocess communication protocol under IBM's System Network Architecture (SNA). The implementation of APPC is accomplished using the SNA peer-to-peer protocol logical unit (LU) type 6.2. LU 6.2 is a de facto standard that allows applications on different processing nodes to establish a communication session and then send and receive conversational messages between the applications. A full two-phase commit can be provided using APPC. Several software vendors have developed LU 6.2 capabilities and included them in applications and services to provide this distributed interoperability. Some of the first implementations of client-server computing used APPC.

REMOTE PROCEDURE CALL

The use of a remote procedure call (RPC) is another method of providing interprocess communication over the distributed environment. A client can interact with a server by issuing an RPC that requests the server to do something. The client will be suspended until a response is received from the server. The RPC mechanism is often used to provide security services across a distributed system.

The secure RPC mechanism that is provided by Sun Microsystems provides a set of system calls using the Data Encryption Standard (DES) encryption algorithm to pass confidential data over a LAN. Secure RPC uses an encrypted Network Information Services (NIS) server to store the user's secret key. A primary advantage of secure RPC is that it can be easily integrated with Sun's low-level RPC. This makes the conversion of existing applications that have been based on the common ONC RPC to a more secure environment easy.

The RPC mechanism included in the Distributed Computing Environment (DCE) for the Open Software Foundation (OSF) also provides a set of calls which allow for interprocess communication. Authentication is based on the Kerberos trusted third-party ticket-granting model from MIT. Kerberos provides for independent verification of both the client and the server and will provide a more robust controls environment, because of its tight coupling with the distributed file system (DFS). Authorization of access to applications can be provided once authentication has taken place. As well, the distributed file system, and its access controls, are tightly aligned with the RPC mechanism. We will look more closely at DCE and the implementation of the RPC mechanism in Chapters 16 and 17.

SOCKETS

The Berkeley Inter-Process Communication (IPC) mechanism (also called sockets) provides a set of system calls which allow for interprocess communication. The client process creates a socket and requests a connection to the server. The server listens on a predefined service number (called a port) for the request. Once the server process accepts the client request, full-duplex communication may occur between the two sockets on the client and the server. The socket mechanism is available on most UNIX implementations. Sockets provide the current de facto standard for network applications on TCP/IP networks. This mechanism is most suited to the conversational model. Comprehensive authentication and authorization controls are not available with sockets.

IBM MQSERIES

IBM provides technology that follows the messaging middleware model. The IBM MQSeries products provide queue-based interface and management services across the IBM platforms as well as other platforms. Applications using the MQSeries technology interact with the distributed components using queues. This technology, is comprised of a message queue interface (MQI) and a message queue manager (MQM) function. The MQI provides the interface to the applications and shields the developers from the network connections and protocols. The MQM provides name and address resolution, routing of messages, administration of MQM resources, and participation in synchronization points. Messaging provides for an indirect style of communication and the capability for asynchronous processing. The queuing mechanisms support assured delivery of the messages, recoverability, and sync point services. Commercial implementations using the MQSeries have been developed to support workflow computing.

DISTRIBUTED OBJECTS

Object-oriented systems are very involved in the distribution of processing. Distributed object processing systems are currently very complex; however, supporting software is evolving quickly. One of the key elements in a distributed object system is the implementation of a mechanism to manage the distribution and destination of the objects. A secure relationship must be maintained between the objects even when the navigation path of the distributed objects may not be predictable.

OMG CORBA

The Object Management Group (OMG) is a consortium of over 100 vendors that exists as a standards body to address interoperability and portability issues for object-oriented technology. The OMG is establishing a standard for building distributed object networks and defining how they communicate with one another. The mechanism that allows objects to communicate with each other is through the object request broker (ORB). The ORB is used to instantiate objects, provide communications between objects, and invoke methods on behalf of objects. The OMG is responsible for a specification called the Common ORB Architecture (CORBA), which defines the ORB, the object services, the common facilities, and the application objects. This specification provides the Interface Definition Language (IDL) and the APIs that enable client-server object interaction. The version 2.0 of the CORBA specification specifies how ORBs from different vendors can interoperate.

OBJECT REQUEST BROKER

The sharing of objects in a distributed environment is accomplished with the use of an object request broker (ORB). The ORB provides the connection services to communicate with, activate, or store server objects. The application objects components are specific to end-user applications. These could include spreadsheet - and word processor - type applications. The Common Facilities components define the way in which the objects are managed. Components such as task management, systems management, and the user interface would fall under this section. The object services extend the capabilities of the ORB. These extensions include items such as naming, transactions, and concurrence control. Time and security services are also included in this area. The ORB provides the middleware that establishes the relationships between the objects and the client/server. An example of the ORB architecture used by the Common Object Request Broker Architecture (CORBA) from the Object Management Group (OMG) is illustrated in Figure 9.4.

COM/OLE

The Common Object Model (COM) is the object request broker developed by Digital and Microsoft to support the object linking and embedding (OLE) environment. Objects can be implemented in a variety of languages, both traditional and object-oriented. The COM model is similar to CORBA and also uses an Interface Definition Language for the object interfaces and separates the object interface from its implementation. The COM distribution model is based on the DCE RPC. The object linking and embedding technology integrates multiple applications and data types within a

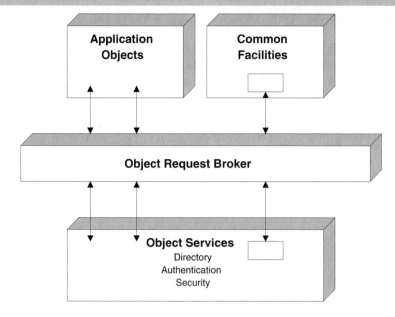

Figure 9.4 Common ORB architecture

Windows-based system. OLE supports over 350 COM-based application program interface calls and can communicate across a network using OLE facilities specifically provided for a network implementation. The COM/OLE implementation of distributed objects is in competition with the OMG CORBA model but remains proprietary to DEC and Microsoft.

SOM AND OPENDOC

IBM's entry into distributed objects is based on its System Object Model (SOM) and a component software architecture called OpenDoc. OpenDoc addresses a compound document specification, developed by CI Labs, which was formed under the direction of IBM, Apple, Novell, Oracle, Taligent, and others. A compound document can contain components made up of many things including text, graphics, image, sound, animation, and even movies. OpenDoc defines how all of these components parts will interface and interact to form a complete document. SOM is IBM's implementation of CORBA compliant object services and provides the local and remote interoperability of the OpenDoc components. SOM is one implementation of a CORBA object request broker and can be compared to COM while OpenDoc can be compared to OLE.

DISTRIBUTED OBJECT SECURITY CONSIDERATIONS

The use of distributed object technology presents additional challenges for security. Distributed objects have all of the security problems found in the usual client-server environment as well as additional unique issues. The main challenges have more to do with the difference between object-oriented technology and the more traditional approach. The interaction and interrelationship between objects is fundamentally different from the interaction between traditional application and data relationships. Objects don't themselves posses an inherent concept of a user. This can be a cause for concern since the main anchor of a distributed security system is the use of an authenticated identity. Either additional elements are required to map this requirement into the distributed objects or a higher level of trust is required along with an accompanying higher level of risk.

The relationship between objects may not always be clearly defined or in fact well understood. Encapsulation hides the details of implementation of the object from the programmer or the user. The objects can act as both the client and the server depending on the specific invocation of the object. It may not always be clear or predictable where trust is placed in the objects or for whom. The advantage of introducing new or changed object components without altering other components also introduces more risk. If the trust mechanisms are not carried forward and executed as a component of the navigation through the objects then trust must be abdicated to the execution environment within which all of the objects reside. It is like having a bus full of people arrive at a series of security checkpoints. Either the entire bus is considered to be authorized allowed to proceed or each of the people on the bus will be checked before the bus can proceed.

THINGS TO WATCH OUT FOR

The area of client/server unfortunately is currently a moving target. The good news is that it is still evolving, and we can look forward to richer and easier implementations. In the meantime there are perhaps a few things that you should consider when determining how you are going to approach client/server and the enabling middleware.

Middleware will continue to have a bright future especially in the area of object-oriented systems. Object-oriented systems have had a significant impact on information technology and will continue to evolve. The standards battle, however, has yet to be completed, a typical battle of *right* and *might*. The OMG with the CORBA specification would seem to be a popular approach with broad vendor support. Many would consider this to be the *right* standard, supported by many different vendors through a separate organization, the OMG. The COM solution would be the *might* approach with Microsoft promoting it through its operating systems and other proprietary products. Other contenders are also entering the field. The only sure thing to predict is that distributed objects will certainly be a part of future system developments.

The secure RPC mechanism is available on many systems in the UNIX marketplace. For a single application, secure RPC will provide adequate authentication and authorization controls. However, secure RPC is not well suited to distributing multiple applications over a distributed environment. Secure RPC does not lend itself to the management and control of multiple applications, as its enforcement is solely based on user password controls. The primary advantages to the OSF/RPC over secure RPC is that it provides integrated authorization and authentication controls through a security server and Distributed File System.

SUMMARY

In this chapter, we have reviewed some of the considerations and implementation approaches for client/server systems. The specific security issues and implications will be covered in the following chapters. The considerations for security must be taken into account when comparing the different types of middleware models and the technology based on those models. The requirements for identification, authorization, authentication, and confidentiality don't change with the differing technologies and approaches. Any design of a client/server system should adhere to a defined security architecture to ensure all of the required security mechanisms are in place. It's an old saying but it's true—your security is only as strong as the weakest link. It doesn't matter if you have the strongest doors and the best locks if that window to the basement at the back of the house is left wide open.

CHAPTER 10

UNIX SECURITY

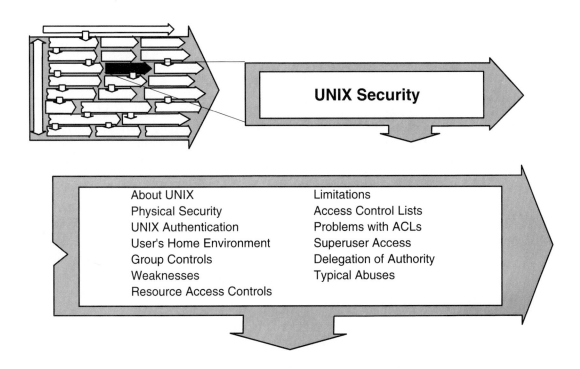

UNIX Security

About UNIX	Limitations
Physical Security	Access Control Lists
UNIX Authentication	Problems with ACLs
User's Home Environment	Superuser Access
Group Controls	Delegation of Authority
Weaknesses	Typical Abuses
Resource Access Controls	

There has been a widespread movement, in recent years, to embrace the technologies of open systems. The open systems operating system environment of choice for most organizations today is UNIX, which has become the defacto standard for engineering workstations, databases, and midrange computing. Organizations in which one rarely heard even the mention of open systems a few years ago, have successfully deployed solutions based on this technology. Because of the common operating environment, software vendors can easily port their products to open systems. This has resulted in greater choice and competitive prices for the consumer. Before the promise of open systems can be realized, however, the issue of security and trust must be addressed.

Many of us live in the suburbs, and while crime is not unknown, we do not live in a fortress. We lock our windows and doors and trust that a large dog will deter any wrongdoers. However, if you noticed footsteps in the snow to your bedroom windows, your awareness of security would be greatly increased. You would take active steps to detect the intruder. Footprints in the snow, mud on a carpet, and scratches on a door's lock are clues to homeowners that they have a security problem.

People who abuse computer systems also leave footprints in the snow. The problem is that the ordinary system administrator does not look at the snow in the backyard, and if they do, they don't know what the footprints to the bedroom window imply.

> UNIX systems can be made as secure as any other comparable operating system. However, it does require a higher degree of knowledge and effort to make this happen. For this reason, we will examine the security issues of UNIX in greater detail than with some of the other technologies.

In our review of UNIX, we will examine and explain the many electronic equivalents to "a footprint in the snow." We will review the weaknesses and vulnerabilities of the open systems environment. Once knowledge has been gained on the problem areas, solutions can be introduced and explored. One of our mainframe colleagues insists that UNIX is inherently insecure, joking that the term "UNIX security" can be found in the dictionary as an example of an oxymoron. While certainly not the security nightmare that some people think, UNIX does pose a number of challenges to those wishing to place trust in it. To deal with these challenges, we need to understand the basic UNIX controls. We must also identify problems that may occur and the fundamental issues that must be addressed. We will save our discussion of potential solutions for a following chapter.

WHY HAS UNIX SUCH A BAD REPUTATION FOR SECURITY?

Whenever I introduce the topic of UNIX security, I usually start with a discussion of the 1964 Volkswagen Beetle automobile. I'm certainly no mechanic, but even the mechanically challenged could understand and work on the 1964 Beetle. Everything was accessible, easy to change, and even I could find the fuel pump! With a screwdriver, duct tape, and some wire the average teenager could coax a few more miles from the Beetle. The basic mechanics of the Beetle were very well known by a wide number of people. If I couldn't fix something, one of my friends likely could.

On the other hand, when I look under the hood of my new Ford Taurus, its engine is sufficiently complex to deter any "hands-on" involvement on my part. The fuel injected engines of today can be likened to proprietary operating systems, such as those found in the minicomputer and mainframe environments. The internals of the security mechanisms have not been subject to detailed inspection. Source code of operating systems has been rigidly controlled in proprietary environments. But most important, in the case of mainframe systems, the centralized nature of the operating system has lent itself to strong controls over its resources.

Many people have grown up using UNIX, and as a result their knowledge of its internals is very high. With versions of source code available to the general public, people have been able to tinker with the mechanisms and learn its secrets. Some of the worst security abuses in UNIX are a result of knowledge of its internal mechanisms. Flaws have been discovered and used to abuse security.

However, the reality is that most abuses in UNIX occur because of the inappropriate application of the standard available controls. Knowledge has always been a key to the effective application of security, but it takes on even greater importance in the UNIX environment. Our objective in this chapter, and the next, is to give you a basic understanding of the UNIX security mechanisms. We'll "open the hood, poke around, and see what's there."

UNIX SECURITY

UNIX has been around for quite some time. Originally offered as a software development environment in the late 1960s, it gained popularity throughout academia in the 1970s. Commercial use of the UNIX operating system became increasingly more common in the 1980s. In recent years, UNIX has gained in popularity as the server component for client-server technologies. One reason for its popularity is the openness of the environment, which has led to a proliferation of software and hardware solutions. UNIX has also provided a cost-effective platform to operate database applications and rapidly develop applications. A final reason for popularity of UNIX lies in its strong networking capabilities. UNIX machines can communicate with one another using a wide variety of protocols and services.

It is important to understand that while UNIX may be configured with a strong web of controls, UNIX is not generally installed with these controls activated by default. The environment requires proactive measures be taken by the system administrator. Another fact of life is that as much effort must be placed on the review of the security controls, as on examination of the results of these controls. Unlike the mainframe environment with its centralized control of all processes, the functionality of an established control in a distributed environment must not be taken for granted. UNIX controls tend to "deteriorate" over time, and a key component of any security review must be the examination of existing controls. Controls may "deteriorate" as new software is added, for example, which may change the control structure. Files and directories may be introduced with lax permissions, or existing permissions may be altered.

PHYSICAL SECURITY

UNIX systems, like most other computers, provide little protection against an intruder who can physically access the machine. UNIX machines allow for a selection of alternative "boot" devices at startup. Intruders may also attach their own disk, tape, or CD-ROM to a hardware controller. By manipulating the appropriate bootstrap loader, they can easily boot from the device and gain access to the machine.

Many UNIX systems have a "back door" key called single-user mode. Single-user mode is a method of entering a UNIX system to perform maintenance. UNIX assumes that anyone who knows the method and has physical access to the system is to be considered a valid system administrator. One frightening aspect of single-user mode, from a security point of view, is that it bypasses all authentication and logs you in as the most powerful UNIX user, the superuser! You do not have to know the superuser password, you only have to have physical access to the system console and know how to use the back door key. Some UNIX systems, such as the AIX and HP-UX families, offer security controls for the bootup sequence. Under HP-UX 10.0, for example, optional controls have been introduced which when they are activated require a password be supplied when interrupting the bootup sequence.

But even if the illicit bootup issue is resolved, any computer that stores information on a disk is subject to physical attack by anyone who is able to remove the disk drive. Today, unlike in the not-so-distant past, disk drives can easily be taken to another computer, examined, and the controls or data modified on the disk. Having modified the configuration information on the drives, and returning them, the intruder can obtain system administration privileges. Backup media can also be compromised, yielding interesting information to a system violator, if it can be physically accessed. With a copy of your backup media, your password file can be retrieved and subjected to the password cracking techniques we will discuss later.

UNIX AUTHENTICATION

We now are going to examine how UNIX authenticates users and the very heart of UNIX security, the */etc/passwd* database. The authentication of users logging onto a UNIX system is most commonly performed by verifying the user's password. Passwords are normally stored in an ASCII file, called *passwd,* and placed in the */etc* directory in their encrypted form. When a user logs on to a UNIX system, she supplies both an account name (called a user name) and a password. The user name (or account) is compared to values in the */etc/passwd* file. If an entry is found, the password is encrypted and the output string is compared with the encrypted password in the */etc/passwd* database. If both encrypted values match, the user is considered to be authentic. UNIX uses a modified (and rather weak) version of the DES encryption algorithm.

An example of */etc/passwd* files is shown in Table 10.1.

Each record (i.e., line) in the */etc/passwd* file is termed an account in UNIX. The term is used interchangeably by UNIX people with user name. The first field in the record is the user name. They are also called accounts, which is perhaps a more accurate term as accounts do not always reflect a human being. The accounts *bin* and *adm,* for example, are used to manage administrative files and directories. User names are used by UNIX to look up your password and assign the corresponding user ID. The format of the user name is irrelevant and is left up to the system administrator. A convention may be imposed such as assigning user accounts as a combination of first initial and the first seven characters of the last name. The important thing to note is that after login, UNIX could care less about your user name. It's the user ID number that counts.

TABLE 10.1
AN EXAMPLE OF THE */ETC/PASSWD* DATABASE

Account Name	Encrypted Password	User ID	Group ID	Misc. Information	Home Directory	Login Program
root	8t6yrgbJJrg2d	0	0	,,,	/	/bin/sh
bin	*	2	0	,,,	/	/bin/sh
rdempsey	dJgrt2743ssdr	204	2	Rob D., 242-3387	/home/rdemps	/bin/csh
gbruce	tr56geJPhe34	0	204	Glen B., 242-7825	/home/grbuce	/bin/csh

The second field in the */etc/passwd* file is the account password. By default, the password field can be seen by any user in its encrypted format. If the password field contains a null value (i.e., is empty), then there is no password associated with the account. It is extremely important that all accounts be password protected. Suffice it to say that if an individual can gain access to an unprotected account, the task of gaining control over the system is made much easier. The attacker can then use this account to launch attacks on other systems on the network. If an "*" appears in the password field, the account is deemed inactive and cannot be logged onto by any user.

Password aging allows a system administrator to force users to change their passwords at predefined intervals. A standard UNIX feature, it is based on the premise that changing passwords on a regular basis will prevent their discovery. Password aging is accomplished by adding a "," followed by a password aging character (which signifies the number of weeks the password is valid) after the encrypted password string.

The third field is the *user ID number* that is associated with the user name. The ability to access resources is based on the User ID number. The user name only indirectly grants access through its relationship to the user ID number. By convention, user IDs on HP-UX systems start at 200, and are assigned sequentially. There is nothing special about the numbering; 201 is not necessarily any more powerful than 226. An important exception to this rule is the superuser, who is traditionally assigned the user name of "root." The superuser is any user whose effective user ID (more on this later) is 0. In our example, both gbruce and root are superusers. The account name has nothing to do with the power, it is the number 0 that determines that these users are superusers. We will examine the superuser later in this chapter.

The fourth field displayed in the */etc/passwd* file is the default group. UNIX grants access rights based on your group ID number. By default, you are assigned to the group whose group ID number is in your */etc/passwd* account entry. In our case, both *rdempsey* and *gbruce* are assigned to the group with a group ID of 110 and whose group name is *users*. Again, it is the group ID number that is questioned to define access rights. The group name only indirectly defines access rights through its relationship to the group ID number.

The fifth field in the database is called the GECOS field. It can be used to optionally provide information about an account. It's generally recommended that the default be left in this field (three commas is the default). Information about users, such as a phone number, in the GECOS field is thought to present a security exposure. An intruder could use the user's phone number, for example, to determine whether or not users are on vacation or otherwise unable to detect activity in their accounts.

USER'S HOME ENVIRONMENT

The sixth and seventh fields in the password file define the user's HOME environment. The sixth field determines the user's primary directory (referred to as the HOME directory). HOME directories are used to hold personal files, UNIX mail, and startup scripts. Startup scripts are ASCII text programs (like .bat files in DOS) which are automatically executed when the user logs on. While nothing prevents users from sharing a common HOME directory and these startup scripts, it is recommended that each user be assigned a private, secure HOME directory. If unlimited access is granted to the user's home environment, an intruder can place modified startup scripts in this directory and change file permissions, learn a password, and so on. The *.profile, .login, .kshrc,* and *.cshrc* startup scripts are automatically executed when a user performs a logon. They should never be readable or write-enabled for use by other users. If an intruder can enter commands in a user's startup scripts, those commands would be automatically executed at login by the user. This would effectively allow the intruder to issue commands as if they were the valid user.

The last field defines the startup shell or program. It contains a program name, (in our case */bin/ksh,* which is a UNIX command interpreter and programming language) that will be automatically invoked after a successful login. Most ordinary users are automatically placed into an application or presented with a menu of selected applications.

GROUP CONTROLS

UNIX will assign a user to a current group at login time based on the group ID number in the */etc/passwd* database. The group name and membership are determined by the corresponding entry in the */etc/group* file. The layout of the */etc/group* file is shown in Table 10.2.

As with user ID numbers, access to resources is granted based on group ID number. The group name is only a convenient method of referring to the group ID number. As with user ID, it is the number and not the name that counts. Groups may have passwords associated with them, but this feature is rarely used and usually disabled by having an "*" placed in the group password field. On some versions of UNIX, a user is automatically an active member of all groups to which they assigned. In other versions, the

TABLE 10.2
AN EXAMPLE OF THE */ETC/GROUP* DATABASE

Group Name	Group Password	Group ID	Group Members
root	*	0	root
other	*	1	root, sys
bin	*	2	bin
users	*	20	gbruce,rdempsey,grants
admin	*	21	gbruce,rdempsey

user is normally only a member of one group at one time. Versions of UNIX that do not support an automatic group membership may allow this feature to be configured by the system administrator. This provides a user with active group membership in every group without requiring the user to overtly change their active group.

Membership in system administration groups would allow an ordinary user access to system resources which normally would require high-level privileges (e.g., superuser privileges). System groups, such as *bin, adm,* and *sys* should have limited membership and never include ordinary users.

In the mainframe world, it is very common to superimpose a departmental structure on groups, because multiple group membership was difficult to implement. In UNIX, the reverse is true. It is relatively easy to set up additional groups (called special interest groups), but administration tends to become difficult if controls are not put in place to limit their growth. An excessive number of groups causes additional administrative effort in managing membership and reporting resource access privileges. In general, it is recommended that the number of special interest groups be kept to a minimum.

WEAKNESSES IN UNIX AUTHENTICATION

The first weakness in the */etc/passwd* and */etc/group* implementation is that they are just ordinary files, protected from tampering by the standard UNIX access controls. If a user could gain write access to either file, they could modify the contents of each file. Using their favorite editor, they could erase the superuser's password or add themselves to a privileged group. If they could obtain write access to the directory */etc,* they could overlay their version of the password or group databases and provide their own password files.

The fact that the encrypted password string is readable is also a weakness. The method to discover a password using the encrypted password string is called "cracking the password." We will examine how "cracking" works later in the chapter, when we look at typical abuses of the UNIX operating system.

UNIX does not enforce consistency between the */etc/passwd* and the */etc/group* databases. There is no guarantee that a group ID referenced in the password file actually exists in the group database. Fortunately, most UNIX systems provide standard utilities to check the integrity of the group database. Another issue to be addressed is the synchronization of the user and group IDs among networked UNIX systems. For example, if the user *gbruce,* whose user ID is 204 on system A, accesses a networked resource owned by *rdempsey* whose user ID is also 204, *gbruce* could gain access to the resource. The synchronization of user IDs, group IDs, and other values is a significant problem across a distributed UNIX environment. We will explore this problem, and possible solutions, in Chapter 16.

We've mentioned that UNIX will grant access to resources based on your user ID and group ID. Let's examine how authorization works in UNIX.

RESOURCE ACCESS CONTROLS

UNIX systems protect system resources, such as files and hardware devices, through a three-level permission access control model. Every resource is owned by a user ID (called the owner) and is assigned by default to the owner's group. Those requesting access to a resource are divided into three categories: the owner of the resource, members of the group to which the resource belongs, and all others. Ownership of a resource may be transferred to another UNIX account, and group membership may be reassigned to another group. If a user is a current member of the group to which the resource belongs, access to the resource is permitted.

The types of access rights that may be given to the categories of requesters (i.e., owners, group members and others) are *read, write* and *execute.* These three types of access have very specific meanings depending on whether the resource is a file or directory, as shown in Table 10.3.

If you have *read* access to a file, you may open the file and examine its contents. With *write* access, you are allowed to change the contents of the file. *Execute* permission allows the file (either ASCII text or a binary program) to be executed. ASCII text files with the execute permission are termed script programs. They are roughly equivalent to DOS .bat files and can include standard UNIX commands or programs.

TABLE 10.3
FILE AND DIRECTORY PERMISSIONS

Type of Resource	Permission	Description
File	r READ	Can open and read contents.
	w WRITE	Can modify contents of file.
	x EXECUTE	Can run the file as a script program.
Directory	r READ	Can list file names in directory.
	w WRITE	Can add or remove files.
	x EXECUTE	Can list details of files.
		Can cd to directory.

Read access to a directory allows you to list the names of files and subdirectories contained in the directory. *Write* access to a directory allows you to change the contents of the directory, to delete files, and to copy new files into the directory. *Execute* permission allows the user to obtain information about the files and subdirectories contained in the directory. It also allows the user to move to that directory and have it as the current working directory.

It is very important to note that it is the combination of both file and directory permissions that provide security. One is useless without the other. To prevent someone from modifying a file, you must limit their *write* access to both the file *and* the file's parent directory. With *write* access to the directory, they can replace the original file with their own version of the file.

LIMITATIONS IN AUTHORIZATION

There are a number of limitations and weaknesses in the standard UNIX resource permission model. It does not permit the definition of different access rights for individual groups or users. Also, the number of access types (*read, write,* and *execute*) is too limited. Additional access types, such as *create, modify,* and *delete,* need to be included to strengthen the current access control model. The access list mechanism is also insufficient (*owners, group members,* and *others*). It forces a system administrator to create a number of special interest groups. This is particularly frustrating when they need to define access for a single user. Another undesirable aspect is that the operating system files and binaries (including the operating system itself) are protected by the same permission model. There are too many directories and files (hundreds of directories and thousands of files are typical) to protect using this architecture. A case could be made for the incorporation of optional inheritance in the security authorization. The idea would be to selectively (at the discretion of the system administrator) force the inheritance of the parent directory's authorizations by a child resource.

The UNIX resource permission model is discretionary because the owner of a file may do anything with it. The file permissions could be adjusted so that even the owner cannot read a file, or, at the other extreme, anyone could read and modify a file. The owner of the resource may also give the resource away by changing the ownership to another user. Once given away, the original owner has no control over the permissions associated with that resource. We will see later that weaknesses in the control structure for operating system files and directories can be easily abused. Essentially, every directory and file which houses system binaries, startup scripts, and data must be adequately protected. With so many directories and files to protect, trying to manually scan a file system for problems is impossible. The system administrator must use an automated tool to ensure that the controls that are initially set up continue to remain functional and effective. We will be examining the use of controls management software in Chapters 12 and 22.

ACCESS CONTROL LISTS

A common complaint with standard UNIX permissions is that they do not allow for selective access. If access is required by a select group of users, and the users are not already identified within a unique group, a special interest group must be created for these users. But more important, the standard UNIX access control model does not allow for access rights to be independently defined for individual groups or users. It only supports access rights for one group of users. Aside from the owner of the resource, all users not in the group are generically classed as *others*.

Some UNIX systems provide a resource security mechanism called access control lists (ACLs) to address this problem. ACLs offer a greater degree of selectivity than standard UNIX permissions by allowing the owner of a resource to set access rights for individual users or groups. An ACL consists of a set of entries, associated with a file, to specify permissions. The entries are referenced by a pointer in the file's *inode* record. Each entry specifies, for one user ID and group ID combination, a set of read, write, and execute permissions. Multiple entries are allowed for each file, and wildcarding is permitted. Users may also be specifically excluded from file access, even though their group is allowed access. The standard UNIX permissions are automatically mapped to ACL entries whenever a file is created.

Problems with ACLs

ACLs must be implemented uniquely for each resource. This causes the administration of ACLs to be complex and time consuming because there is no automatic mechanism to update ACLs when new files or directories are added. Hereditary controls, which would pass ACL values to child subdirectories and files, would allow ACLs to be implemented at a selected level of the inverted directory tree. All new subdirectories and files would inherit the parent ACL by default. Most UNIX file transfer utilities, such as cpio, tar, and shar do not recognize the existence of ACLs. Any file transferred using a utility which does not support ACLs will lose its ACL entries. This causes further administration concerns as ACLs must be constantly reviewed to ensure they are still in effect. Furthermore, backup software may not support the use of ACLs. If the backup solution does not support ACLs, a restoration from backup will cause the current ACL to be lost. Transferring files with ACL entries over the network can cause the loss of the entry. UNIX vendors have not been consistent in their implementation of ACLs. For example, the command to list ACLs is *lsacl* on HP-UX systems and *aclget* on IBM's AIX systems.

Superuser Access

In design of the UNIX environment, the decision was made to give one class of user, called the superuser, absolute control over system administration activities. The superuser (any account whose user ID is 0) has access to all system administration and security functions on the local computer. The idea was that system administration would be limited to one individual who would perform all the system administration functions, from spooling to the addition of users.

> One of the problems with having a pitbull to protect your home is that you really have to trust that dog. You are still in charge of the house and might truly believe he won't harm you, but there is always the possibility that he'll turn on you and you'll be bitten. You could restrict his guard duties to the basement, but you've got to be sure that none of the kids will open the basement door and let him upstairs.

A scan of our */etc/passwd* example in Table 10.1 shows that the user accounts *root* and *gbruce* have a User ID of 0. It is highly recommended that use of the superuser be strictly limited. The superuser may access any resource, regardless of the security and controls that have been applied. Superusers may remove any or all access controls, violate security policies such as minimum password length, view and change any file, read anyone's mail, and remove passwords. In fact, there are actually very few activities that the local superuser cannot perform. It's only common sense that knowledge of the superuser password should be limited to a few individuals. Those individuals entrusted with the superuser password should not use superuser access for normal activities, such as reading mail. There are a number of traps (which we'll see later) that can be set to trip up the unwary superuser. Superusers are less likely to fall prey to these traps if their powers are used sparingly.

DELEGATION OF AUTHORITY

The idea behind the superuser was to provide for central and singular administration of the UNIX system. Back when systems had few users, and performed only limited functions, this was not an important consideration. While the single system administrator idea made a lot of sense when a system had ten or so users, it is hardly workable for larger systems. We may wish an operator to perform spooling, but we certainly don't want the operator to become a superuser. Unfortunately, the basic design of UNIX requires superuser authority to perform the most basic of system administration tasks. The central issue is how we ensure that those given superuser authority will not abuse the privilege? If superuser privilege is to be delegated, steps must be taken to ensure that the privilege is not abused and additional superuser privileges are not illicitly assumed.

UNIX allows users to change identities using the *switch user (su)* command. They must provide the password of the account (i.e., user), if it exists, with whom they wish to change identity. UNIX will create an *effective user ID (EUID)* if they are successful. Effective group membership may also be changed (for example, using the *newgrp* command in HP-UX). The problem with *su* is once a user changes identities to a new account, they assume all of the access privileges of that account. This is not a delegation of authority, but rather an abdication of authority.

UNIX uses a very special type of group, called a privileged group, to allow access to a special set of system calls. In a later chapter, we will examine how commercial solutions may be used to solve the delegation of authority problem.

TYPICAL ABUSES

We have examined the basic security structures of the UNIX operating system. We've looked at various controls, including file and directory structures, and seen how they protect important data. In the next part of the chapter, we will present issues and review additional problems areas.

GUEST ACCOUNTS

The compromise of a UNIX system is made considerably easier if legitimate access to any account, regardless of the level of authority the account gives, can be obtained. Many systems extend "guest privileges" to nonauthenticated users, thereby unintentionally allowing easy points of access to hackers. Guest privileges may be extended through accounts with no passwords, or accounts with obvious passwords such as *guest* or *support.* Unsecured guest accounts provide "unlocked windows" into the UNIX operating environment. Furthermore, such *guest* accounts prevent proper auditing because the individual user cannot be identified.

SPOOFS

One of the earliest methods of breaking into a computer system involved the use of a Trojan horse program to steal passwords. An intruder replaces the normal login program with one that both performs the login function *and* records passwords. The passwords are either kept in a secret location or mailed to the intruder. Spoofs are executing programs that imitate the actions of valid programs. A spoof executes on the local system and is a form of a Trojan horse attack. The difference between a spoof and a Trojan horse is that a Trojan horse is a nonactive program which requires its execution to perform its illicit functions. A spoof is a live program, which presents a false command line or screen to the user. A common form of spoofing is to present the user with a phony login screen. The screen will appear normal in every way, but will actually be executing a rogue program rather than being under the control of the operating system. After entering the account name, the user will be prompted for a password. Once entered, the password will be stored or mailed to the hacker. The spoof will then display an error message, such as "invalid login," that suggests the user has mistyped the password. The valid login program will be initiated, and the user will be prompted again for the account name. Normal login for the user will then follow, and the spoof will then be removed from the system. The user will naturally assume they have miskeyed the password. Spoofs of this nature, if properly performed, are very difficult to detect. Any indication of a spoof must be treated as a significant security threat. Networked spoofs are counterfeit programs which pose as valid clients or service providers. They will be discussed further in the next chapter which deals with UNIX networking services.

PASSWORD GUESSING

Password guessing is an old student technique of attempting to login by guessing the password of an account. Passwords such as *thor, support,* and *dilbert* are entered with the hope that eventually a match will be made. A number of failed logins, occurring over a short period of time, might be a "footprint in the snow." While it may indicate little more than a poor typist, it could also indicate an attempt to guess passwords. UNIX does not provide, as a standard feature, the ability to disable accounts after a successive number of invalid login attempts. It does, however, give the system administrator the ability to log the invalid attempts in the */etc/btmp* log file.

Software can easily be developed to monitor this file and notify the system administrator of password guessing attempts on a given account. Some administrators automatically disable the affected accounts, but this may expose the administrator to a malicious attack. If an intruder provides invalid passwords (perhaps on purpose) to the superuser account, automatic disabling of the account would prevent the superuser from accessing the system.

> Password guessing has generally fallen out of favor as a hacking technique in the UNIX environment because it is easy to detect and alternative methods have become available. It is interesting to note, however, that password guessing is being employed by hackers as a technique against Windows NT and voicemail systems. A recent security bulletin from the Royal Canadian Mounted Police reports "a program called VMB hacker which can be used to automatically dialup voice mail phone lines and try different passwords located in a file constructed by the hacker." [RCMP]

PASSWORD CRACKING

A far greater threat to UNIX security revolves around a known weakness in the standard UNIX authentication mechanism. The technique is called *password cracking*. To understand how password cracking works, we first must examine how the password encryption mechanism works. When you create the password, the first eight characters of the password you give are combined with a time stamp called the "salt." Both the password and salt are used as input to the encryption process. The salt is used to further scramble the password. The output is an encrypted string containing both the salt and the encrypted password. The encrypted string is stored in the */etc/passwd* file, with the first two positions of the encrypted string used to store the salt. When you login, both the entered password and the associated salt for the account you've typed are passed to the UNIX encryption mechanism. If the encrypted string in the password files and the output of the UNIX encryption mechanism match, the password entered has been verified and you are allowed to login.

Unfortunately, hackers are well aware of how the password mechanism works and use it to their advantage. While the encryption algorithm itself has thus far resisted widespread decryption, the standard UNIX password database is subject to attacks using a password cracker. Hackers long ago realized that if they could pass dictionary terms to the encryption algorithm, they too could compare the encrypted output to the encrypted password string. If a sufficiently large number of words were used, there would be a high probability of a match with at least one password. Later, algorithms were introduced that manipulated the dictionary terms used and greatly increased the probability of a successful match. Figure 10.1 demonstrates how a password cracker works.

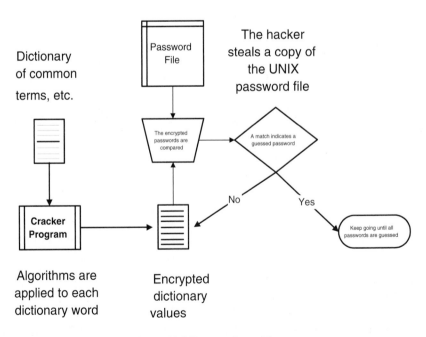

Figure 10.1 Password cracking

Generally, the */etc/passwd* database is only modifiable by the superuser, but it is normally readable by every UNIX user. Because the password file is readable, it can be copied and examined. The encrypted passwords can then be compared to the encrypted values of a user-defined dictionary, and a match indicates the password has been broken. The user dictionary will contain common words, slang, names, and so on. Algorithms may also be invoked to test case sensitivity, plus insert or append special characters and numerics.

Strong passwords will resist a password cracking attempt. Strong passwords are at least six characters long, containing combinations of upper- and lowercase, special characters, and numerics. For example, a strong password is F>Ru2n0. It should be noted that UNIX encrypts only the first eight characters of the password. Also, while minimum password lengths are typically enforced for endusers, the superuser is not subject to these restrictions.

Password-cracking tools have been demonstrated to UNIX system administrators and security personnel in order to show the effectiveness of this technique. Even with a limited dictionary of less than 10,000 words, our experience has shown that it is common to crack about 10% of the accounts on a normal UNIX password file in less than 10 minutes! An analysis of password security by Daniel V. Klein of Carnegie Mellon University tested the strength of a large number of passwords: "The results were quite dramatic, as a significant percentage of the passwords were discovered using password cracking techniques." It's important to realize that by using dictionaries with millions of words and more complex rules executed over a period of days, the number of discovered passwords can be much higher.

The best prevention against password cracking is to hide the */etc/passwd* database from the ordinary user. This will ensure the defeat of password crackers because the encrypted password strings cannot be copied. The C2 security implementation, which we will describe in Chapter 12, provides this capability.

HOME ENVIRONMENTS

All users that directly accesses a UNIX system are provided with a default directory into which they are placed when they initially login. This directory is sometimes called the HOME directory because the variable $HOME stores the directory PATH or location. The directory may be common to other users or unique to the individual user. It is wise to assign the user HOME environment uniquely to users and not share them between users. This is because the HOME directory normally stores a number of scripts which are automatically executed when the user logs in. If the directory or the login scripts are not protected, they could be modified to automatically execute commands under the false authority of the user. Read access to a HOME directory by others is also discouraged, as user mail and other personal information may be stored in this directory.

Obviously, an important corollary to the principle that a user's environment should be protected is that the superuser's environment must be absolutely protected. Modifications to the superuser login scripts would be automatically executed, and would probably be unnoticeable, by the superuser at login. Any additions to these scripts would be executed with full superuser authority. A variation on this form of attack is to sow a minefield. The intruder recognizes that startup processes are automatically run on behalf of a user, not only at login time. If a startup script can be modified, any statements in it will be executed under the full authority of the user.

An example of a mine can be seen with the *vi* editor. When the *vi* editor is invoked, a startup script, called *.exrc*, is searched for. If found in the current working directory, the script will be automatically executed. If an intruder places a modified *.exrc* in a number of directories (they will generally have write access to */tmp* and */usr/tmp* to name a few), the mine will silently explode the first time the superuser executes the *vi* command from one of these directories.

Users are normally set up with a number of default settings in their HOME environment. These settings include a number of variable settings which must be carefully implemented. A common mistake is to improperly implement the PATH variable. This variable sets the directories which will be searched for executables when a command is issued. If the value "." is included in the PATH, the current directory will be searched. The problem is obvious if one remembers that UNIX commands are just programs, and are located in selected directories. The *who* command, for example, is the binary file named *who* located in the */bin* directory. The PATH variable tells the operating system to look in the */bin* directory for the binary file named *who*. If a "." is the first directory in the PATH, the current working directory will be searched in advance of the /bin directory. The problem is that if a hacker can place a modified script or binary in the current working directory named *who*, it will be executed rather than the actual command because it is located before the */bin* entry in the PATH variable.

TROJAN HORSES IN SYSTEM DIRECTORIES AND FILES

The UNIX operating system includes hundreds of directories and thousands of files. Vendor and application software add further complexity to the environment. The system startup scripts, ASCII data files, binary executables, and libraries (all of which comprise the operating system) are viewable by the ordinary user. Very little of its functionality is actually kept in the operating system itself, but it is stored in ordinary files. UNIX commands are merely the names of these files. UNIX safeguards these assets using the standard UNIX file permission scheme, which relies upon the combination of file and directory permissions to enforce access control to UNIX operating system resources. If an operating system resource can be compromised, the entire system is subject to abuse. With the average UNIX system having hundreds of directories and thousands of files to protect, it should be obvious that an automated tool is the only solution to adequately ensure that access control is maintained.

STARTUP FILES

UNIX uses a series of interdependent startup scripts to boot the system. The master startup script, usually called */etc/rc,* invokes a number of other related scripts. The scripts are automatically executed at system start-up time and use high-level privileges. All commands in the scripts are automatically executed with the same authority as the superuser. It is imperative that both the directories used for startup, especially the */etc* directory and its files, be protected from modification. Any modifications to these scripts should be treated with the utmost suspicion.

DELEGATION OF AUTHORITY THROUGH SET USER ID PROGRAMS

Normally, programs in UNIX run under the authority of the user who invokes the program. Set user ID (SUID) programs are a special type of program, which execute under the authority of the owner of the program. SUID programs may be either binary programs or shell scripts (which are a set of ASCII commands). They have a special permission bit (called the SUID bit) turned on. SUID programs can be a security concern because an SUID program will execute as the owner of the file, rather than the actual user. Weaknesses in SUID programs may be exploited to obtain unauthorized privileges.

Root SUID are programs owned by the superuser and will execute under the authority of the superuser. Therefore, they are very dangerous, and must be rigidly controlled. If a user running a root SUID program can issue commands which modify files, they do so as the superuser. This is especially troubling if the user can escape from the program and obtain a UNIX shell prompt.

If a user can obtain the superuser password for a very short period, they can use the following sequence to create a dangerous SUID shell program:

```
$su

password: <Enter the root password>

#

#cp /bin/ksh .anytime_I_want_to_be_root

#chmod 4555 .anytime_I_want_to_be_root

#exit

$
```

Why is this dangerous? It is because the */bin/ksh* program is a UNIX shell or command interpreter, which provides the UNIX prompt and allows you to enter UNIX commands. The shell will normally run under the user's authority, and extends no special authority. However, the shell was copied by the superuser in our example and is therefore now owned by the superuser. If the SUID permission bit is enabled using the *chmod* command (e.g., *chmod 4555*), the shell would run as the owner of the resource—that is, root! Every time the new ".anytime" script is executed, it will run as the superuser. The user does not need to provide the superuser password ever again!

A UNIX operating system (and sometimes its applications) will contain a number of SUID programs. The occurrence of these standard SUID programs is not considered abnormal, but the presence of a new SUID program can be an indication of a system violation.

DEVICE FILE SECURITY

Device files, which are also called special files, are used by the UNIX operating system to communicate with its hardware subsystems. These subsystems include disk, tape, network devices (e.g., LAN cards) and memory. It is important to realize that device files can bypass normal UNIX, network, and database security controls. With access to a disk device file, a user can examine the contents of a UNIX file or database irrespective of the UNIX or database controls. With access to a memory device file, a user could change the effective user ID of the process and grant illicit superuser authority. On some UNIX systems, widespread misuse of the LAN card was made possible due to lax security permissions on the LAN device file called */dev/nit*. This incident was described in the advisory from the Computer Emergency Response Team (CERT) at Carnegie Mellon University of January 1994. Because they can provide the ability to bypass normal controls, device files must be rigidly secured and new device files examined carefully.

UNIX SCHEDULERS

UNIX includes two batch schedulers, *at* and *cron*. Both schedulers essentially operate in the same manner, but *cron* is the more commonly used of the two. Essentially, users can create batch schedules and submit them to the scheduler. The submission process copies the schedules to a secure directory. The scheduler examines the contents of these directories on a regular basis and invokes the batch job at the requested time. While various other problems have surfaced in the past, especially with the *at* scheduler, there are essentially two issues to be addressed.

The first issue concerns the security of the directory used for scheduling. Jobs submitted to the scheduler are run under the authority of the user who submitted the job. If the job schedule of the superuser can be modified, an unauthorized entry to the schedule will execute with full superuser authority.

The second issue involves the security of the actual batch job itself. If these jobs (which are just scripts of normal UNIX statements) can be modified, illicit statements in the job will be executed with full authority of the user. It is therefore imperative that the batch jobs initiated by the scheduler be properly secured using restrictive file permissions. The permissions should be set such that they do not allow unauthorized access to either the scheduled script or any programs it executes.

BACKUPS

The security of backup tapes is an important issue. Most backup tapes, unless the media is encrypted, are fairly easy to read. With access to copies of the system files, access to the system is highly likely if not guaranteed. The password file (even the hidden password file) can be retrieved, and can be subjected to intensive password-cracking techniques. It is very important to physically secure and account for backup tapes. Poorly secured backup media presents an open door to your system.

CONCLUSIONS

There are indeed many things that must be done to properly secure UNIX systems. It is important to set up a control structure properly in the beginning and to regularly monitor the controls. It is equally important, however, to actively examine the system under your responsibility for "footprints in the snow." All indications of hacker activity should be rigorously investigated. We will continue our examination of UNIX in the next chapter. We will look at one of its strongest features and biggest problem areas: networking.

CHAPTER 11

MORE UNIX SECURITY

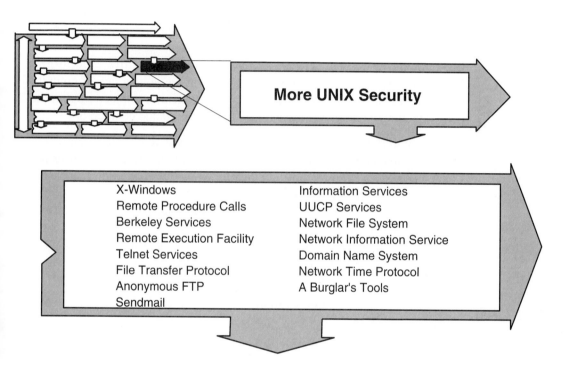

More UNIX Security

X-Windows	Information Services
Remote Procedure Calls	UUCP Services
Berkeley Services	Network File System
Remote Execution Facility	Network Information Service
Telnet Services	Domain Name System
File Transfer Protocol	Network Time Protocol
Anonymous FTP	A Burglar's Tools
Sendmail	

We will continue our examination of the UNIX operating system in this chapter. We will begin with a review of a popular UNIX user interface, the X-Windows system. But the primary focus of the chapter will be on UNIX networking services. The ability to communicate with other systems, through a wide variety of services, is one of the strongest features of a UNIX system. From a security viewpoint, it also represents the largest area of concern.

Many of the networking services that we will examine in this chapter are not specifically UNIX services. For example, the telnet service can be found on a number of computing platforms, including Windows, OS/2, and Windows NT. We have included these networking services in this chapter, not because they are exclusive to UNIX, but because they either originated or are commonly associated with UNIX environments.

As with the previous chapter, our intent is to review issues and problems. Solutions to the issues raised will be examined in the next chapter. We will conclude the chapter with a discussion of some signals indicating that you may have a security problem.

X-WINDOWS

The de facto standard for windowing, in the UNIX world, is the X-Windows System (X) developed by MIT. X is a marvelous tool to support user interaction. Its easy-to-use features provide excellent capabilities for the sharing of information and images among remote computers. Unfortunately, the architecture of X is rooted in the golden age of computing, when security was not an issue. For those wishing to place trust in the X architecture, a number of issues must be examined and countered.

An unfortunate flaw in the architecture of X is that X does not recognize that some actions may be privileged. Once authenticated, any user has full, unrestricted access to all the capabilities of the X-Windows manager. After access is granted to the X-Windows manager, requests are honored regardless of their impact on other users. A user attached to X may destroy windows they do not own. They may take over control of the mouse and keyboard of another user (including the superuser) and in very short order compromise the security of the X server. The only prevention for unauthorized activity is through the X-Windows access control mechanism.

Access control to the X-Windows server is performed by a program called *xhost,* and an associated set of control files typically named */etc/Xn.hosts.* Access control is based on the host name or the associated network address of the client. While host name- or network addressed-based access may have some validity in a single-user workstation environment, it does not flow to the multiuser environment. A multiuser environment requires access control that can recognize an individual user.

To address the issue of user-based access control, MIT developed an alternative mechanism with the wonderful name of the "Magic Cookie." The MIT Magic Cookie (introduced on the X11R4 release) uses a shared secret key to allow for the authentication of individual users. The key (really a computer generated string value) is stored in the file *.Xauthority,* which is located in the HOME directory of the user. If the *.Xauthority* file can be copied, the Magic Cookie may be stolen and fraudulently used. The Magic Cookie is also visible on the LAN and may be detected using packet sniffing techniques.

An additional access control mechanism, termed XDM-AUTHO-RIZATION-1, was introduced in the X11R5 release of X-Windows. It uses DES encryption to safeguard user keys over the LAN. Unfortunately for the global community, DES is subject to U.S. State Department export restrictions, so the use of XDM-AUTHORIZATION-1 outside of the United States is limited.

Any X user may weaken the authentication process by overriding the authentication policy and allow access to all clients. This is because X lacks the concept of privileged users and grants all authenticated users full access to the X server. While solutions exist for the problem of weak authentication mechanisms (XDM-AUTHORIZATION, Kerberos, or public key technologies), the architecture of X has prohibited a comprehensive response to the problem of administering access controls.

One of three approaches to the problem of X-Windows security is possible. The first is to live with the exposure, and this is certainly the most common response today. The second is to employ filtering, by using filtering software or a hardware router, to limit the X-Windows clients to specific network addresses. The third approach is to deploy a commercial product offering a more secure version of X-Windows. The access control mechanism must be reviewed continually to confirm its continued existence and functionality. Changes to access control policy, such as finding universal access to the X-Windows display manager, must be treated with the highest suspicion.

UNIX NETWORK SERVICES

UNIX servers may provide a wide range of networking services. These services include terminal connections, file transfer, disk and print sharing services, remote execution of local commands, and interprogram communication. Clients are free to request any of these services from a server. The servers have the ability to decide which networking services they will implement and, in some cases, which clients they will communicate with. It is important to recognize that each UNIX networking service introduces some form of security exposure. Only those services that are actually required should be enabled, but unfortunately most versions of UNIX are shipped to customers with a large number of the networking services enabled by default. We will explain how standard UNIX networking services work, and then review the major networking services which include the ARPA, Berkeley, and UUCP families.

How Standard UNIX Network Services Work

UNIX systems employ a special background process, called the *inetd daemon,* to invoke network services as they are required. The inetd daemon is invoked when traffic destined for your machine is intercepted by the LAN interface. There are two major categories of UNIX networking services: well-known services and remote procedure calls.

Services that are widely used are usually identified by a special number, called port numbers. The port number, not the service name, is included in the packet sent to the server by the client. For example, the usual port number for the telnet service is 23. A server, when it receives a packet addressed to it, will look up the requested service in the */etc/services* file using the port number. If it is located, the server will then launch the daemon process found in the */etc/inetd.conf* database to talk to the client. If the lookup fails, a communication error will be returned to the client. A notable exception to this rule of thumb is the Network File System (NFS), which uses remote procedure calls for communication.

Figure 11.1 provides a simplified overview of how UNIX networking services clients and servers communicate.

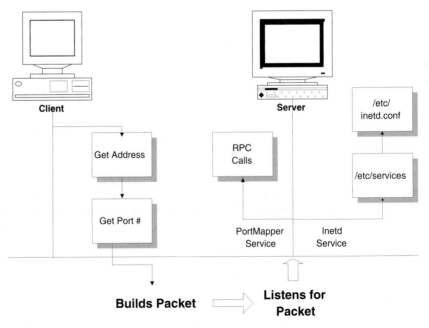

Figure 11.1 Overview of UNIX networking

REMOTE PROCEDURE CALLS

Remote procedure call (RPC) is a method used for client-server communication. A programmer will create an interface, which defines the location of subroutines in the server program and assigns a special program number for the required server. Generally, these server programs do not use a well-known port, but use the services of a special program, called the portmapper, to communicate with the client. The portmapper registers the server when the server starts and negotiates a port number with the server. The client will then contact the portmapper to determine which port number to use, and the client will make contact with the server using the port number returned by the portmapper.

Some RPC mechanisms can be fooled into thinking they are talking to an authenticated user. UNIX networking services keep track of where they are in the process of client-server authentication by the use of sequence numbers. Some intruders may use a technique, called a sequencing attack, which circumvents the authentication process by presenting a contrived sequence number to the server. In this case, the server will assume the user has already been authenticated. Many UNIX services, including NFS, have been attacked in this manner.

BERKELEY SERVICES

The Berkeley Services (which include the commands *rsh, remsh, rlogin,* and *rcp*) are used to perform remote command execution, remote login, and file copy. The primary problem with the Berkeley Services is that they allow host equivalency. Host equivalency is a concept based on the idea that if a user or process has been authenticated on one trusted computer (host), then there is no reason to reauthenticate the user on a second computer. This assumes the second computer *trusts* the initial computer, and therefore extends equivalency of authentication to the first system. Figure 11.2 provides an overview of host equivalency in UNIX.

The primary motive behind the development of host equivalency facilities was that of convenience. Host equivalency makes it easier to perform tasks on multiple computers without having to be authenticated on each individual computer. The obvious problem with host equivalency is if one host can be compromised by a security attack, all systems that extend host equivalency to that system may also be easily compromised. The exploitation of host equivalency was one method used by the Internet worm attack of 1988 to circumvent security.

Host equivalency is extended through use of *.rhost, .netrc* and */etc/hosts.equiv* files. It should be noted that in its least restrictive form,

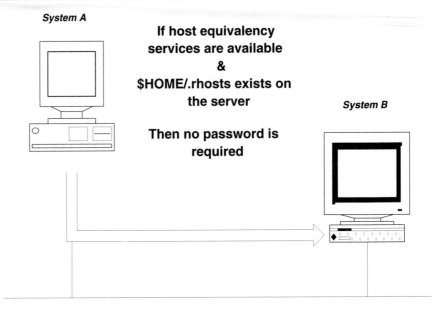

System A

If host equivalency
services are available
&
$HOME/.rhosts exists on
the server

System B

Then no password is
required

Figure 11.2 An overview of UNIX host equivalency

which is the default, host equivalency may be extended by ordinary users to other systems. A user who creates a file titled *.rhost* in his HOME directory will extend host equivalency for himself when accessing this computer from other systems. The user does not require the intervention of the system administrator. A more restrictive form of host equivalency may be enabled by the system administrator to counter this problem. By reconfiguration of the host equivalency services, host equivalency may be revoked from the ordinary user and forced through the */etc/hosts.equiv* file. This file is not normally modifiable by ordinary users.

While host equivalency must be discouraged, it should be recognized that situations will exist where equivalency between hosts is a functional requirement. Some distributed backup solutions, for example, require the client's root account to extend host equivalency to the central backup server. Unless compelling reasons exist for the use of Berkeley networking services, it is recommended that they be disabled. The existence of all *.rhost* files should also be carefully examined and questioned. They may be a "footprint in the snow" for possible violations and indirectly point to the compromise of other systems.

REMOTE EXECUTION FACILITY

The Remote Execution Facility (REX) is used to provide the remote execution of commands on a server. This function is similar to the Berkeley *remsh* (or *rsh*) facility. A special feature of REX also allows the automatic attachment of your local HOME environment to the server using NFS. REX also transfers local user settings, in the form of environment variables, to the server. Figure 11.3 provides an overview of REX.

REX has very serious implications in terms of trust. The default implementation of REX allows virtually every user access to the server, based solely on user ID number. The exception to this rule is the superuser, who is prohibited from using REX. There is no authentication of the requesting client's machine in this scheme. Any user with his own workstation may assume any user ID he desires. Even if the number of systems is limited, the user ID number is relatively easy to manipulate on the client system.

A further security complication lies with the ability of REX to attach the users local environment (i.e., their disk) to the server. While high-level authority on the server is normally required to attach a foreign disk system, a REX user can manipulate the method used to attach a local disk and actually attach a foreign disk system to the server.

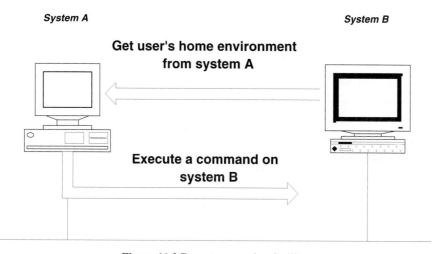

Figure 11.3 Remote execution facility

TELNET SERVICES

The telnet service is used to provide remote (e.g., LAN) terminal access. A successful telnet login will usually present the user with a shell prompt, but may be configured to provide an application or database menu. UNIX servers authenticate telnet users in the standard manner using the standard */etc/passwd* file, as described in the previous chapter. The telnet service does not provide for encryption over the LAN and exposes any user of telnet to packet sniffing attacks. A user who uses telnet to become the superuser will expose the superuser password, which is transmitted in clear text, to anyone listening on the LAN.

For this reason, many system administrators limit telnet access, by the superuser, to the directly connected system console. The system console does not communicate over the LAN, and is therefore not subject to password sniffing attacks. On most UNIX systems, a file called */etc/securetty* may to used to limit superuser telnet access (and rlogin as well) through the system console.

FILE TRANSFER PROTOCOL

File Transfer Protocol, or FTP as it is commonly known, is used to transfer files between systems. In the standard implementation of FTP, a user must have a valid UNIX account on the server. FTPs are authenticated using the standard UNIX password mechanism. A peculiar feature of FTP is that it requires a password be supplied prior to a connection being granted. Null passwords are not permitted, even for the superuser. Once connected, the user may copy any file to which they have read access, including the */etc/passwd* file. The user may also create a new file, or replace an existing file, in any directory which they have write access capability.

As with telnet, passwords sent over the LAN using FTP are in cleartext form and are not encrypted. As such, they are subject to password-sniffing attacks. For this reason, system administrators usually limit FTP usage to accounts that do not have high-level privileges. The file */etc/ftpusers* can be used to accomplish this. All accounts that are listed in the */etc/ftpusers* file are prohibited from incoming connection to the local system by FTP. Outgoing FTP sessions are not affected by this control.

FTP also permits the use of host equivalency through a file titled *.netrc*. If this file is placed in the user's HOME directory, and contains the name of the incoming system, the user will not be required to produce a password. The use of *.netrc*, as with all forms of untrusted host equivalency, is discouraged.

TRIVIAL FILE TRANSFER PROTOCOL

Trivial FTP (TFTP) is a simplified version of FTP that permits the copying of files without authentication. TFTP is primarily used in the X-Windows server environment to download fonts and other information to X-terminals. The TFTP service normally reserves access to selected directories, but older versions of TFTP did allow unrestricted access to the entire system. It should be noted that some routers use this as a delivery mechanism for software configurations. The reliability of this method is very suspect. In general, if TFTP is not required for specific functions, it should be disabled.

ANONYMOUS FTP

A more secure form of FTP (compared to TFTP), called anonymous FTP, is widely used on the Internet for public distribution of software to untrusted clients. Anonymous FTP uses the *chroot* system call to disguise the user's view of the file system. From a user's viewpoint, the anonymous FTP directory is the highest-level directory on the system. The user cannot change directories to higher or lateral directories, nor can they see directories or files on these levels. The operating system files and binaries are protected because the anonymous FTP user cannot see or access them! Figure 11.4 provides an overview of anonymous FTP.

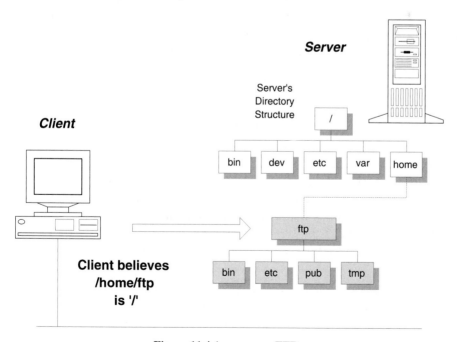

Figure 11.4 Anonymous FTP

To set up this service, authentication files and programs must be placed in the anonymous FTP directory. Files and programs placed here must be protected from modification by outsiders. Also, authentication files should not reflect the real system environment. Woe is the novice system administrator who blindly copies the */etc/passwd* file to the anonymous FTP directory. It will be quickly copied and cracked! But if properly implemented, an anonymous FTP implementation can be very difficult to compromise.

SENDMAIL

The UNIX sendmail program, which is responsible for UNIX mail services, is a highly complex program. Because of the complexity of the program, and its accompanying configuration file *sendmail.cf,* the sendmail program has long been a target of intruders. It is highly recommended that UNIX mail be disabled unless specifically required. (The disabling of the sendmail daemon will not affect mail within the system, only mail from the network). The application of all recent vendor sendmail security patches is strongly recommended if UNIX mail is enabled.

> If you received a handwritten invitation from Boris Yeltsin and Mother Teresa to meet for cappuccino after work, you'd immediately question your colleagues. The same skepticism should accompany every piece of electronic mail. It is just not secure. The identity of the sender may be easily forged. The document may be intercepted by anyone with postmaster capability along the route to the destination and altered. Mail is generally stored in either a common mail directory - or the user's HOME directory. If security is weak on either, the user's mail may be read.

A second problem is the UNIX mail process itself. The master file, and its accompanying binary, are very complex. One look at the *sendmail.cf* configuration file is enough to deter many system administrators. Because of its complexity, sendmail has been the target of numerous attacks, including the Internet Worm and recent HP/IBM/SUN advisories. One of the earliest techniques involved the manipulating of the sendmail program to obtain a copy of the UNIX password file. Recent advisories have indicated that manipulating sendmail is still possible and continues to be a popular activity for hackers. Another consideration is that clandestine executables or scripts may be delivered as part of the normal mail message. If not prevented, the effect may be analogous to receiving a letter bomb!

INFORMATIONAL SERVICES

UNIX informational services, such as finger services and *rwho,* provide information to unauthenticated outsiders. These services were created for debugging and system administration purposes, but can be used by attackers to receive valuable information about your system. The *finger* command can be used to find out information about a user account on a remote system. The rwho command can be used to see who is logged on to a foreign system. It could, for example, be used to check if the system administrator is logged on. The attacker will return later, if they are. It is recommended that all services of this nature be disabled.

UUCP SERVICES

UUCP (UNIX-to-UNIX Copy or UNIX-to-UNIX Communications Protocol—take your pick) is a software subsystem used to transfer files and execute commands on remote systems. UUCP also provides a subset of UNIX commands to the user. UUCP can be used over serial, modem or X.25 networks. Older versions of UUCP had limited security capabilities and are subject to attacks involving the sequencing of its operation. An improved version of UUCP, called HoneyDanBer (HDB), provided increased security. HDB has controls to deter sequencing attacks.

The directory structure of UUCP must be carefully implemented, and its control files properly secured. The */usr/lib/uucp/Systems* file, for example, contains passwords for remote UUCP systems. It could lead to the compromise of these systems if improperly secured. While UUCP was the defacto standard for UNIX communication in the 1980s, its usage is diminishing due to the growing popularity of serial-based TCP/IP services using the SLIP or PPP protocol. If UUCP is not used, it should be disabled.

NETWORK FILE SYSTEM

The network file system (NFS) allows disk and CD-ROM file systems to be shared over the network. Figure 11.5 provides an overview of NFS.

NFS allows a local client system to transparently attach the resources of other systems to their local directory tree. NFS eliminates the requirement for explicit file transfers by incorporation of remote file systems into the local directory tree. Once the client is attached to the server, access to files and directories on the server is totally transparent to a user. NFS usage is not limited to UNIX. DOS and other operating systems are also supported.

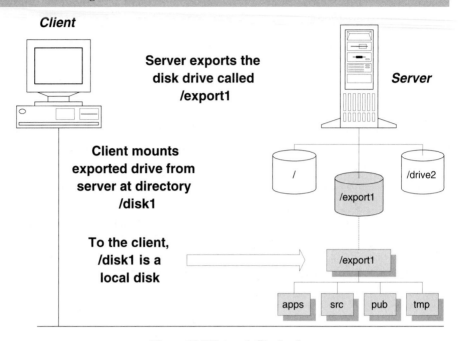

Figure 11.5 Network file sharing

Networked machines may be either servers, clients, or both. An NFS server provides file sharing to client systems. A client is any node that accesses an NFS network service. NFS servers are normally UNIX machines (but MVS, OS/2, and others are supported), while clients may be UNIX, OS/2, or DOS based. Servers are passive in that they wait for clients to request services. They also require that *state* be maintained by the client. In other words, it is the responsibility of the client to maintain where they are in the communication process. While this has the advantage of making a client somewhat immune to the reboot of a server, it does create concerns in terms of security. As mentioned earlier, if the client can concoct a fictitious representation of the current "state," the NFS server may believe them and allow unauthorized access to directories and files.

There are five questions that should be addressed surrounding the use of NFS:

1. What system resources should be exported, and to whom should they be exported?
2. Should the superuser access privileges be extended to the client system?

3. As a client, what types of files should I allow into my system?
4. How can I trust the integrity of files that are downloaded from an NFS server?
5. How strongly can one trust the authentication and authorization mechanisms of NFS?

We will examine the implacations of these questions in the following paragraphs.

NFS servers specify the disk resources which are made available to clients. The safest approach is to export only those resources and capabilities absolutely required by the client systems. An export of the entire directory tree of the server system would expose system binaries to tampering and provide access to the server's password file. Only a limited subsection of the server's directory tree should be exported. Whenever possible, the server should use the "read-only" flag on the exported file system. This prevents client systems from modifying the exported disk drive.

An NFS server has the option of universally exporting file systems. This would effectively "authorize" any system on the network access to the exported file system. Generally speaking, this is a very unsafe practice. In most cases, the NFS server should directly and succinctly specify its client systems. A possible exception to this situation is if the file system is exported as "read-only."

NFS servers use an access control mechanism based on the name of the client. There exists the potential for a rogue machine to masquerade as an authorized client or server by changing its system name and IP address. NFS has no inherent controls against a counterfeit client or server. The counterfeit or clandestine client or server could assume the identity of a valid machine and bypass the access control mechanism of NFS.

A second issue concerning authentication is that the NFS server and the client implicitly trust each other's user IDs. Many operating system commands and files are owned by an account called *bin*. If a user on the client can obtain a privileged user ID, such as the user ID of the account *bin* (normally user ID number 2), access would be granted by the server to operating system binaries. Essentially, the server should always be skeptical of the user ID of the client, and never place any reliance upon its authenticity. Whenever possible, the server should export read-only file systems or limit the directories and files available for export.

NFS has the capability of extending equivalency to the superuser on the client system. This is obviously a security concern, even if you explicitly trust the superuser on the client systems. A violation of any client would lead to the compromise of the server (unless the file system is exported as "read-only." Superuser equivalency can be extended by use of the optional "-root=" export parameter. If superuser equivalency is not extended, the superuser on the client system is assigned a token user ID (e.g., a user ID number of -2).

For the client system, the primary issue in terms of trust is to prevent the importation of security headaches from the server. Device files from the server can create security problems by allowing a user on the server access to the client's devices. As we have seen, SUID programs, especially *root* SUID programs, can be a security concern. If users can create a shell from a *root* SUID program, they will become superuser. NFS has the ability to disallow the device files and SUID programs from the server, and it is wise to implement this option on the client.

As mentioned previously, an NFS server is stateless because the state is retained by the client. The client retains a NFS *file handle,* which maintains the client's access rights to the NFS server. The weakness in this approach is that the server does not authenticate a request from a client, but trusts that the composition of the file handle indicates that the client can be trusted. In early versions of NFS, it was fairly easy to guess the composition of the file handle, and to present the server with a request using a counterfeit file handle.

A counterfeit NFS server may be able to intercept NFS client requests for files and respond faster than the valid server. Since the client has no way of validating either the source of the file or its integrity, imposters can download any file they want. This is especially dangerous if the requested files are executables.

NETWORK INFORMATION SERVICE

UNIX systems require a number of databases to implement system administration and networking. The files */etc/passwd* and */etc/group* are used for user authentication and authorization. The */etc/hosts* or an equivalent method is used to map system names to Internet Protocol (IP) values. In the absence of a centralized repository, *every* database and value would have to be maintained locally on *each* machine. Maintaining consistency of the databases across the network is a time-consuming administration task. The potential for the individual database values to become unsynchronized is very high. There are obvious problems if the *user rdempsey* is assigned user ID number 209 on system A, and the user *gbruce* is assigned the same user

ID number on system B. When these systems interact over the network, who is the user with user ID 209? The answer is that both users are! Any network service which uses user IDs will not be able to differentiate between the users *gbruce* and *rdempsey*. Figure 11.6 provides an overview of the NIS maps.

Network Information Service (NIS) is a distributed lookup service that is used to provide consistent database values to networked clients. Formerly called Yellow Pages (until a copyright infringement action was initiated by British Telecommunications), NIS is widely used to solve the problem of synchronizing system administration database values. NIS allows a single NIS master server (one per NIS domain) to propagate its database values in tables (called maps) to secondary NIS slave servers. Slave servers are used to provide redundancy in the event of a failure in the NIS master server. NIS clients attach (bind) themselves to slave servers to obtain the desired database values. There are no limits to the number or composition of the databases to which they may be mapped (as long as they are ASCII flat files). Customized NIS maps may be created by the NIS administrator.

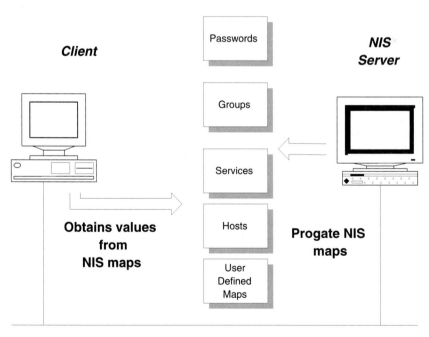

Figure 11.6 NIS overview

TABLE 11.1
Standard NIS Services

NIS Map	UNIX Database	Purpose
password	/etc/password	Authenticates and assigns the user Id.
group	/etc/group *	Stores group ID number and names.
hosts	/etc/hosts	Maps host name to IP address.
netgroup	/etc/netgroup	Assigns users to NIS groups.
/etc/rpc	/etc/rpc	Provides definition of known RPC services.
protocol	/etc/protocol	Provides definition of networking protocols.
services	/etc/services	Defines well-known networking services and assigned ports.

The standard databases exported by NIS are listed in Table 11.1.

NIS also provides for a local lookup service. This is used as an alternative to providing a full view of an exported map. To fully illustrate, if NIS has been implemented and a plus sign ("+") occurs before the user ID in the local */etc/passwd* file, the login procedure will resolve the user ID, password, and user ID number against the NIS password map rather than the local */etc/passwd* file. This has the effect of logically overlaying the NIS master password map over the local */etc/passwd* file.

But to protect certain accounts, NIS allows for the local resolution of selected NIS queries. Only those accounts in the */etc/passwd* database that contain a "+" in the first column will be resolved from an NIS server. All other accounts will use the local */etc/passwd* file. The advantage of this architecture is that it provides the ability to maintain accounts having high-level privileges, such as the superuser and database administrator, on a local basis. The superuser may (must!) then have a password unique to each machine, even though the NIS password map is used for ordinary users. NIS also provides for the use of a global "catchall" value. If the catchall value is implemented, any account that does not exist in the local */etc/passwd* file will be resolved against the NIS server. The catchall is implemented by adding an entry of the form "+:0:::::::::" to the local */etc/passwd* file. If the account is valid and the proper password is provided, the user will be allowed to login to the system, even though no local account exists on the systems. Some versions of UNIX will complain if the HOME directory does not exist.

NIS netgroups are a logical grouping of users or machines. They provide more of a system administration tool (e.g., convenience) than an actual enhancement to security. Netgroups are used to group users by a common netgroup name rather than requiring an entry for each individual user in the database. Netgroups can be used to restrict the individual's view of an NIS map. It must be noted, however, that the implementation of netgroups have been demonstrated to have no effect on the PC-NFS NISCAT command, which provides a personal computer user with the complete NIS maps.

NIS provides commands which can list an NIS map. These maps can provide information to individuals wishing to breach security. In particular, the *ypcat* command (which is called NISCAT on PC versions of NFS) can be used to obtain a copy of the password database. Although all passwords are encrypted, they are susceptible to the password-cracking techniques described in the previous chapter. Standard NIS does not provide support for the C2 hidden password file.

While the use of NIS will solve some problems for the system administrator (notably, the synchronization of passwords and user ID values), it also raises concerns about the ability to trust its mechanisms. NIS could expose an organization to increased vulnerability from password abuses. If an NIS propagated password becomes known, the individual would have access to a larger number of systems than if decentralized password maintenance was used. The problem is especially acute if a system administration or superuser account is exported via an NIS map, and subsequently becomes known to others. They would then have access to all machines within the NIS domain.

NIS allows the NIS master server to be replicated in systems termed slave masters. Clients may elect to bind directly to a NIS slave master, or to connect to the first slave master that responds to the bind request. The former method exposes the client to a single point of failure which defeats the purpose of using a slave master. Most clients elect to bind to the first available slave master. There is no authentication of the slave server by the client. If a rogue slave server is introduced to the network, the login controls for every NIS account will be suspect. Careful implementation of the master and slave-master systems is a necessity. If the NIS master can be compromised, passwords will be subject to modification.

A final consideration in the use of NIS, from the client's viewpoint, is that NIS is usually configured to provide the most liberal networking definition required by every system in the NIS domain. NIS will provide a central definition of the services, RPCs, and protocols used by the UNIX system. The networking services allowed by the NIS administrator may be too liberal for the local system administrator who may wish to impose a more stringent level of networking controls.

Many of the problems we have identified in NIS, such as the authentication of slave servers and support for the hidden password file, are solved by an improved version of NIS called NIS+. NIS+ uses the secure RPC mechanism to authenticate access to NIS and to authorize user actions. Unfortunately, secure RPC and NIS+ are not available on all versions of UNIX.

DOMAIN NAME SYSTEM

In the TCP/IP world, system names are mapped to a special address called the Internet Protocol (IP). UNIX systems may resolve this mapping in different manners, including using a local */etc/hosts* file and the Network Information Service (NIS). A third method is to use the domain name system (DNS). This protocol is also referred to by its Berkeley name, Bind. There are a number of concerns, in terms of trust, in the use of DNS. These include the impersonation of DNS servers, the corruption of selected portions of the naming tree, and revealing information about an internal network that DNS provides.

NETWORK TIME PROTOCOL

The Network Time Protocol (NTP) is widely used to provide a consistent notion of time among distributed computers for an entire organization. NTP allows client systems to synchronize time (both time of day and the movement of seconds) from a number of sources. For redundancy purposes, secondary servers are utilized which are updated from the primary server. Clients obtain time by constantly being sent the correct value of time (polling) or by making intermittent inquiries to the server by remote procedure calls.

Client systems rely on a precise and accurate definition of time for many purposes. These include the creation of accurate audit trails, for access control and the synchronization of multisystem transactions. Most attacks on a time service provider are usually a malicious denial of service. But more sophisticated attacks may use the disruption of accurate time to assist in corrupting an audit trail or to overcome time-sensitive security controls.

A BURGLAR'S TOOLS

It is important to note that your system may not be the target of an intrusion, but merely a stepping stone for subsequent attacks. The intruder may only be using your system as a safe house, having no desire to wreak havoc on your system initially. If the intruders are obvious in their activities, the local administrator will implement countermeasures and take the fun out of their game. Under these circumstances, the primary objective of the intruder is secrecy. Hackers normally do not want to be discovered. They will usually take elaborate steps to prevent the system administrator from discovering their activities. They will tend not to perform activities that will draw attention to themselves.

Disk storage may be required to store tools and associated contraband, and these items must be hidden from the inquisitive eyes of the system administrator. Directories might be created using spaces or special characters which are difficult to detect using a listing of the file system. File names of tools will be changed from the original name to something less noticeable. Logfiles and data will be archived and compressed. Encryption is widely employed as additional security should the hidden directory be discovered by a concerned administrator. If encryption utilities are not present on the system, they will be transferred and hidden. This is especially common outside of the United States, where the operating system does not generally contain the DES data encryption utilities. Disk mount points, which are local directories to which external file systems are attached, may be used to hide things. Files stored under the mount points cannot be detected when the external file system is mounted, but are readily available when the file system is unmounted. Log files which record the intruder's activities, such as *wtmp, syslog,* or the shell history log files, can be altered or erased.

Every burglar has special needs. Tools such as shims, crowbars, and lock picks to assist them in illicit entry are required. Safe houses are needed to store these tools and their loot. Hackers have the same basic needs. They require automated tools to check for weaknesses. They require the ability to store data (i.e., logfiles) for subsequent examination. They also require safe places were they can store their tools and data.

An intruder's toolset may include a wide variety of things. Scripts to automatically check the general security of UNIX systems are commonplace. SUID programs and device files, password crackers, favorite compilers, network sniffers, and debuggers are also tools of the trade. They may also be interested in trapping information. Logfiles of network traffic are created and scanned for passwords and other interesting information. Password files are copied and listings of remote procedure call (RPC) services are studied. The presence of files containing listings of passwords, server information, or logs of network activity may be an indication of illicit activity.

Device files are used as intermediaries between the operating system and the user. Discovering that the system has been configured to record all network traffic (called promiscuous mode) might indicate packet-sniffing attacks. The existence of device files, especially memory or LAN device files, with improper permissions or outside of the normal /dev directory would be another indication of illicit activity.

CONCLUSIONS

UNIX systems generally are shipped with a wide variety of networking services enabled. Each service introduces complexity into the controls environment. If a service is not required, it should be disabled. UNIX networking services also provide a wide variety of authentication and access control mechanisms, including universal access and host equivalency. But the greatest limitation lies in the TCP/IP transport mechanisms. With the ability of an intruder to view or tamper with the packets, new methods are required to encrypt and secure the transport mechanisms.

We have now reviewed some advanced topics in UNIX, including the UNIX networking services, and seen the security risks they pose. The next chapter will focus on the solutions available to address these issues.

CHAPTER 12

UNIX SOLUTIONS

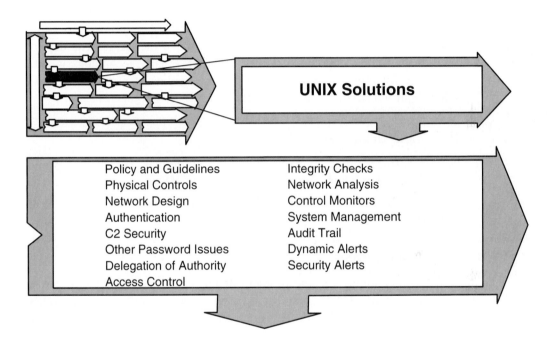

UNIX Solutions

Policy and Guidelines	Integrity Checks
Physical Controls	Network Analysis
Network Design	Control Monitors
Authentication	System Management
C2 Security	Audit Trail
Other Password Issues	Dynamic Alerts
Delegation of Authority	Security Alerts
Access Control	

In the previous two chapters, we have examined in detail some issues facing those who wish to place trust in the UNIX environment. Solutions to these issues do exist, and we will examine some of the solutions that may be employed in this chapter. Before we begin our discussion, a few points should be made about the use of security tools and utilities.

We will be examining the use of various contributed and commercial software solutions in this chapter. Most of these solutions do have software licensing and copyrights associated with their use. They should not be thought of as being free. The reader should take special care when using a contributed software solution to ensure they are not violating a provision of its use.

The first point is that while a particular solution may not be perfect, even the most rudimentary solution to the problem is infinitely better than none at all. The fact that a solution is not perfect should not be used as an excuse for doing nothing. The second point is that the weakest system on your network is the one most likely to be compromised. It can be used as a base to facilitate the compromise of more important systems. It is therefore wise to employ solutions on a widespread, rather than selective, basis in order to raise the general security level of the entire organization. The third point is that those who wish to compromise your systems will use automated tools—you should therefore use an automated response. No single source of technology exists that can address all of the issues. The deployment of multiple technologies will be required. Finally, technology is not a substitute for human intelligence, and even if solutions are found, knowledge about the environment is still required.

POLICY AND GUIDELINES

A well-defined policy, and accompanying guidelines, provide the proper foundation upon which solutions may be built. If policy and guidelines do not exist for the UNIX environment, it is highly recommended that one be developed.

PHYSICAL CONTROLS

The obvious solution to the problem of physical security is to, whenever possible, locate UNIX machines in physically secure environments. Sensitive data should only be stored on computers which have physical security, unless strong compensating controls exist. Most people can easily understand that a computer database server, costing hundreds of thousands of dollars, should be secured. Whenever possible, computer systems should be placed in an accessed controlled environment, such as a special computer room. Those machines containing sensitive data or requiring a high degree of trust must be relocated to physically secure environments. Less obvious, but equally important, are backup media and networking devices such as routers or bridges. Backup media and archives should be physically separated from the computing system to prevent the loss of both the computing system and backup media in the event of a disaster.

Vendors have also recognized the need for improved controls over the computer bootup process. Hewlett-Packard provides, for example, support for password control of the bootup process. Other vendors have also applied similar approaches to the problem. While total reliance can not be placed on internal controls, this will certainly be an improvement over past implementations.

NETWORK DESIGN

In Chapter 7, we explored the use of various design techniques for building security into a network. For example, we reviewed the use of trusted sub-networks, isolated by routers or bridges, to prevent unauthorized traffic from accessing the subnetwork. UNIX networking services can also take advantage of a trusted subnetwork.

For example, a UNIX development workgroup using X-Windows could be isolated from the corporate internetwork using a router. X-Windows traffic is generally local to the workgroup, as the need to exchange information using X-Windows is most common between cowork-ers. There is usually a performance advantage to localize X-Windows traf-fic, rather than have this traffic on the general network. In many cases all X-Windows traffic can be isolated to the local workgroup. If this is the case, security and trust may be enhanced by disabling X-Windows traffic outside of the workgroup. This would deter both unauthorized access and spoofing of the X-Windows server.

AUTHENTICATION

The UNIX operating system uses passwords and other methods such as a network address to authenticate users. Conventional wisdom dictates that certain characteristics are desirable in passwords to ensure trust in the pass-word mechanism. The password characteristics, and motives behind them, are listed in Table 12.1.

Contributed software, such as CrackLib, may be used to prevent the use of easily guessed passwords. Many versions of UNIX also support the enforcement of a password policy, which can dictate acceptable characteris-tics. System-generated passwords, which are very difficult to guess and resist cracking attempts, are also widely supported. But forcing users to

TABLE 12.1
PASSWORD CHARACTERISTICS AND MOTIVES

Characteristic	Motive
Unpredictable	Common terms are easy to guess. Minimum Length and varied composition. Password is difficult to crack.
Changed Regularly	Password is less likely to become well known; if compromised, the window of exposure is limited.
Unique	Compromise of a password on one system will not lead to the compromise of other systems.

adopt difficult to remember passwords will only induce the users to write it down. We regularly notice passwords recorded on "sticky notes" attached to computer screens or hastily scribbled on calendars. These have been used by coworkers to gain access to their computing accounts.

The use of isolated databases, network servers and distinct operating systems and hardware platforms requires separate authentication techniques. This separation, in turn, forces an individual to remember, and maintain, multiple passwords for different applications, databases, and LAN services. If password aging is used, and is uncoordinated, a user has no choice but to use identical passwords or record each individual password. But most important, these seemingly conventional recommendations on passwords do not address the major threats to the confidentiality of passwords. These include password guessing, password cracking, and the use of clear-text passwords over a network. We will examine solutions for the first two problems now, but reserve the examination of solutions for the last problem to Chapter 17 and Appendix B.

A solution to the problem of password guessing is to alert the system administrator when it occurs. When failed passwords are detected by UNIX, they are recorded in a local audit trail. The audit trail could be examined, and if a successive number of failed passwords discovered, an alert produced. The use of audit trails and dynamic alerts are discussed in both this and in following chapters.

Password crackers are very, very effective. As we have seen, password crackers use the encrypted, but readable, password string as input to a password cracking algorithm. The string is tested against the encrypted output string of a dictionary of terms. We have performed password cracking against a dictionary of over 2.5 million terms. Password crackers use a number of rules or algorithms. They can test for case sensitivity and insert numeric or special characters into the dictionary terms. They are extremely effective at discovering passwords. While the preventive use of a password cracker is an option, and contributed software is available to detect easily guessed passwords, the obvious solution to password cracking is to hide the encrypted password strings.

C2 Security

C2 UNIX systems offer improvements to the authentication and audit capabilities of the standard UNIX operating system under the generic title of C2 trusted system. A C2 trusted system is designed to meet the C2 level of security as defined by the *Orange Book* issued by the U.S. Department of

Defense (DOD). Unfortunately, C2 has been promoted as a panacea for the issue of trust and security in UNIX systems. It must be recognized that the implementation of C2 solves relatively few of the issues that must be addressed. This does not imply that the implementation of C2 is a bad idea (it's a very good one), but it will not solve the issue of security on its own.

The implementation of a C2 trusted system essentially provides two benefits. The password file is hidden from ordinary users, which deters password cracking. As well, auditing of operating system calls is enabled. An ordinary user is prevented from reading the encrypted password string. C2 security requires that all encrypted password strings be hidden. The encrypted passwords are stored in a file in a secured directory (readable only by the superuser), which is commonly known as the shadow password file. The original password file is modified to reflect the existence of the new password file, but retains most of the user based information. Most utilities (but not all) will support the use of the shadow password file.

C2 also allows for a better definition of the audit trail produced by the UNIX operating system. Selected groups of users and system calls may be combined to create the audit trail. For example, auditing may be limited to security-related system calls for ordinary users, and all activity of the superuser. The audit trails are stored in a secured directory which cannot be accessed by ordinary users.

The proliferation of distributed systems has also highlighted the need for the use of common authentication, which can be used on a wide number of systems and situations. Users simply do not want to be forced to remember a myriad of passwords. The solution is to use a single sign-on technology, such as the Kerberos security model adopted by OSF/DCE, which will be introduced in later chapters.

OTHER PASSWORD ISSUES

We have previously reviewed the issues of password cracking and guessing. Another issue organizations are grappling with is whether or not a password shared between a user and a server is in fact a security risk. The password, even if encrypted, may be captured on its way to the server and replayed. Many organizations are examining alternative approaches to shared password authentication in response to this threat. These approaches include the use of one-time passwords and strong authentication techniques, which are reviewed in the appendices.

Solutions to the issues identified are summarized in Table 12.2.

TABLE 12.2
PASSWORD ISSUES AND SOLUTIONS

Issues	Solutions
Guessing	System-generated passwords
	Alerts when guessing is detected
Cracking	Shadow password file (C2)
Single sign-on	Kerberos or one-time passwords
Clear-text passwords	Kerberos or one-time passwords

DELEGATION OF AUTHORITY

The execution of UNIX system administration tasks requires the use of high-level superuser privileges. How do we securely delegate the authority and power of the superuser without allowing the individual to become the superuser? Fortunately, both contributed, vendor-supplied and independent commercial solutions to this problem exist.

Contributed software, such as the *sudo* program, may be used to control superuser access. This software allows the superuser to delegate high-level authority to those individuals who require the use of superuser privileges. It allows the system administrator to set up tables of commands and programs that may be run with high-level privileges. A problem with sudo, like all SUID programs, is that if you can escape from a sudo-controlled program and enter a UNIX shell, you will do so as the superuser.

Vendor-supplied system management software, such as the System Administration Manager (SAM) from Hewlett-Packard, may provide a solution for local delegation of authority. SAM is used to perform a variety of tasks, including user management, resource configuration, and the administration of networking services. SAM has in the past required superuser authority to execute, but a feature of the HP-UX 10.0 release is the delegation of administration tasks.

A commercial product offering secure delegation of superuser powers is PowerBroker from Freedman, Sharp & Associates of Calgary, Canada. PowerBroker provides a networked solution to the problem and includes the ability of capturing superuser activity in a central audit trail. Memco Software Inc.'s Security for Open Systems (SeOS) software for UNIX provides an alternative approach to limiting superuser powers. SeOS combines operating system-level interception of security-sensitive events with an access rule-based database. The software provides an active access control mechanism that identifies who has access to a system and user activities once the user has logged in. SeOS is implemented as part of the UNIX OS without changing a single binary file or rebuilding the kernel. Although usually minimal, the interception of system calls may result in a performance degradation for the system. Proper analysis is required to analyse the overall effect.

Many of the centralized system management tools available on the market today, including backup and spooling solutions, also provide sophisticated solutions for the secure delegation of superuser authority.

ACCESS CONTROL

Access control refers to the ability of the operating system to limit the access to the resources under its controls to authorized users or process. Access control is usually based on one or more of the methods shown in Figure 12.1.

The standard method of enforcing access control in UNIX is through the use of file and directory permissions. As we have seen before, the combination of user and group IDs is used to confer, or deny, access rights to resources. UNIX may also be configured to restrict access to selected devices or networking services. For example, the */etc/securetty* file on certain UNIX systems may be used to force login from the system console. The */etc/ftpusers* file may be used to deny FTP usage to selected users. This is most commonly used to prevent the superuser from using FTP. The Washington University of St. Louis, Missouri, has made available the contributed FTP daemon (WU-FTPD) which can be used to enhance the security of FTP. These enhancements include the ability to set up a *chroot* envi-

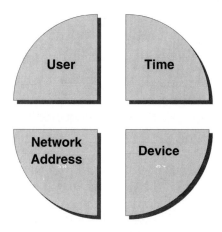

Figure 12.1 Access control methods

ronment, similar to that used by anonymous FTP, for individual users. Stronger access controls are also provided.

Access control by system name or network IP address is also common. Access to resources offered by NFS, for example, is controlled by system name and IP address. The HP-UX operating system supports the access control of network services through the */usr/adm/inetd.sec* configuration file. Acting as a software router, filtering schemes may be established that will allow selective access by type of service. For example, telnet access may be limited to selected addresses and FTP usage denied to all but those in the workgroup subnet.

Access controls based on time are also common. Typical controls based on time limit access to normal working hours and provide for screen locking after periods of inactivity. Contributed software is also available from the Internet to assist in access control. The Drawbridge software from Texas A&M University provides strong filtering capabilities. Wietse Venema of the Netherlands has also contributed TCP wrappers, which may be used to extend filtering access controls to a number of UNIX networking services.

INTEGRITY CHECKS

The hardware, operating system, and applications, when implemented with integrity, combine to form a computing environment termed the trusted computing base (TCB). We will further examine this concept in Chapter 20. Obviously, if unauthorized changes can be made to the components of the TCB, it will cease to be trusted. We have seen that the computing base may contain hundreds of directories and thousands of files and programs. How can we ensure the integrity of so many resources?

The first step is to properly secure the base through strong controls and to check that the controls (file and directory permissions) are still in place. An important second step involves the use of integrity checkers.

Integrity checkers are based on the following idea. After the operating system and application programs have been installed, a snapshot of the trusted computing base is taken. The snapshot creates a database of selected characteristics about the elements of the TCB. At a later date, the current characteristics of the current computing base are compared against the stored characteristics. Unauthorized modifications to the computing base constitute a "footprint in the snow" as they may be an indication of a time-bomb or Trojan horse program. Any unexplained changes to the TCB should be regarded with suspicion. Figure 12.2 shows how an external CD-ROM can be used to verify the integrity of operating system binaries.

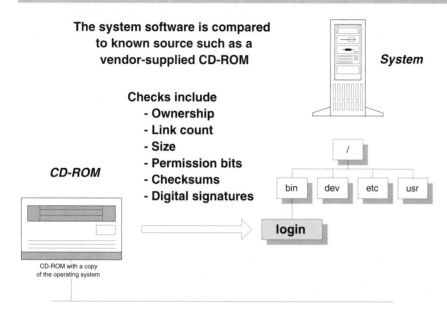

Figure 12.2 Integrity checks

It must be recognized that the use of integrity checking has a number of constraints. A computing base is not static, but is under a relatively constant state of change. Software fixes (e.g., patches), new versions of applications and operating system upgrades can change the characteristics of the TCB. An integrity checker is only valuable as long as the database that stores the characteristics of the computing base can be trusted. If this database is stored on a LAN-based system, its data might be modified by an attacker to reflect the unauthorized changes made to the computing base. A safer approach is to store the TCB in removable media or use a vendor-supplied CD-ROM.

An integrity checker is effective only if it can protect its own database. The characteristics stored by the integrity checker typically include the ownership, group membership, access rights (permission bits), creation dates, file size and a checksum. One type of checksum common on UNIX systems is the cyclic redundancy check (CRC). You should not place complete trust in identical CRC checksums because they are based on characteristics of the file. Hackers have used sophisticated techniques to mimic the characteristics of the original file and generate a fictitious, but identical, checksum.

A much more secure method involves the use of sophisticated cryptographic techniques to generate a digital signature for the resource (i.e., a file). They use the actual data from the file as input to the algorithm, so that any changes (however small) to the contents of the input data (e.g., binary code modifications) will be detected. The MD5 checksum has been suggested by RSA Data Security, Inc., in Internet RFC 1321 as a standard for data authentication. The digital signature produced by MD5 is generally thought of as immune from forgery. We will examine the entire area of cryptography, including digital signatures, in Chapter 15.

Discipline must be exercised to ensure that the integrity checker's database is updated when authorized changes, such as patches or versions upgrades, are made to the computing base. Integrity checks are provided as part of other security tools (e.g., control monitors) or as stand-alone tools. A very popular tool for performing integrity checks is Tripwire.

TRIPWIRE

Tripwire is a contributed software product developed by Gene Kim and Gene Spafford at Purdue University. The goals of Tripwire are essentially to detect unauthorized changes to the computing base. Tripwire is supplied as source code and has been ported to many different environments. It has optional support for use of the MD5 checksum which provides a strong capability in the detection of forged programs.

NETWORK ANALYSIS OF VULNERABILITIES

A special class of control monitors, commonly known as network analysis tools, may be used to provide an assessment of the vulnerability of UNIX network services to abuse. This class of tool provides a network, as opposed to system, centric view of the environment. They test the strength and ability of UNIX network services against a known set of vulnerabilities. Typical checks include attempts to gain control over the X-Windows manager and probes against the UNIX sendmail service. Other activities include attempts to steal password files, checks for host equivalency, and illicit use of FTP.

A contributed software tool by the name of *SATAN* (Security Administrators Tool for Auditing Networking), developed by Dan Farmer and Weitse Venema, was released to the Internet community on April 5, 1995. It uses a combination of shell programs, PERL scripts, and binary code to test for several known vulnerabilities. SATAN also has an easy to use GUI interface, similar to those used by many Internet WEB browsers. The introduction of SATAN has caused a great deal of controversy. While SATAN is focused only on known vulnerabilities, there is a widespread concern that tools of this nature promote hacking because of their ease-of-use features.

CONTROL MONITORS

The use of monitoring software allows for regular, positive confirmation of the existence and proper functionality of the UNIX controls. The primary role of the tools is to ensure that the "doors and windows" of the UNIX system are properly locked. They essentially run batch jobs, on a regular or ad hoc basis, which will sweep through the client file systems looking for weak file and directory permissions, write-enabled system binaries, irregularities in networking services, and so on. Reports are generated warning security or system administrators of failures to conform to standards and other violations. Figure 12.3 provides an overview of how control monitors work.

Equally important as the ability to detect conformance problems is the ability of these tools to detect "footprints in the snow." Unauthorized changes to security mechanisms are a definite indication that a system has been compromised. Control monitors have the ability to detect known vulnerabilities in UNIX systems and, therefore, act as an alarm system.

An important feature to look for in this class of products is their ability to allow for the use of templates. Templates allow the conformance to acceptable standards on the client system to be uniquely specified. Without the use of templates, control monitors tend to become verbose in their reporting of security problems. The important footprints in the snow may be overlooked, stepped on, or trampled beyond recognition. The idea is to tai-

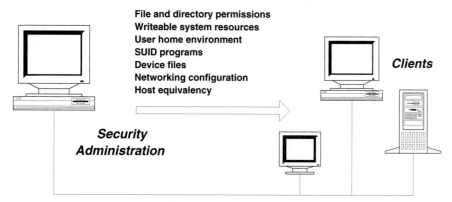

The central monitoring station performs checks on clients across the network for

File and directory permissions
Writeable system resources
User home environment
SUID programs
Device files
Networking configuration
Host equivalency

Clients

Security Administration

Figure 12.3 Control monitors

lor the information that is reported so that only significant security events, in relation to the client system, are reported. The checks made by controls monitors include

- Ownership of the password and group databases
- Permissions on the password and group databases
- A password for every account or the account will be disabled
- User and group ID consistency
- The proper setting of $PATH and $UMASK variables
- User home environment directories and files whose permissions are deemed lax
- Files which extend host equivalency
- Operating system directories and files which are write enabled by others
- Reports of all SETUID and SETGID programs
- Reports of all write enabled device files
- All failed access attempts (logon, privileged access, or resource access)
- If UUCP has been enabled, the */usr/lib/uucp/Systems* and */usr/lib/uucp/Permissions* files must exist and be secured, as well as the */usr/spool/uucpublic* directory
- Reports of all NFS global and Superuser enabled exports
- All NFS mounts which allow SUID and device files to be imported

This list presents a few of the weaknesses in controls that may occur and is by no means comprehensive. Control monitors fall into three classes: contributed software, vendor-supplied products, and commercial products.

CONTRIBUTED CONTROL MONITORS

One of the most widely used control monitors is the Computer Oracle and Password System (COPS). COPS is a collection of contributed (free) software developed by Dan Farmer and Eugene H. Spafford. It performs general checks for security weaknesses on UNIX systems. The software includes checks for bad permissions on various files and directories, as well as SUID/SGID checks. Source code is available, and COPS has been ported to almost every UNIX environment. COPS does not currently have a GUI interface, and is invoked by a command line shell program. Reports may be directed to a printer or mailed to the system administrator. Because COPS is essentially a free package, support for COPS is the responsibility of the local system administrator.

The contributed TAMU Tiger security toolset, from Texas A&M University, also provides a wide variety of security checks. These checks include tests of key binaries against various cryptographic checksums. TAMU also checks for the proper application of security patches and for known security exposures.

VENDOR-SUPPLIED PRODUCTS

Many hardware vendors provide control monitoring utilities as part of their system management toolsets. These monitors are usually supported by the hardware vendor's support organization. They also will generally do a better job at detecting weaknesses peculiar to the hardware platform. The downside is that they cannot usually be ported to other UNIX implementations.

COMMERCIAL CONTROL MONITORS

Several vendors also provide commercial UNIX control monitoring products which provide advantages over the noncommercial offerings. They have the ability to address mixed UNIX environments (e.g., AIX, SUN/OS, Solaris, and HP-UX). The software generally allows one system to act as a security master, monitoring systems over a security domain. It also promotes conformance to customer policy (e.g., password length checks). Reports can be produced using a template, which can eliminate invalid or inappropriate warnings. Commercial UNIX control monitoring offerings usually have an easy to use GUI interface. Another important feature is that the security checks are made for the specific computing environment. Security-related reports can be easily customized. Finally, software support is available.

Commercial control monitoring solutions include AuditorPlus from BrainTree Technology, and Intruder Alert from Axent Technologies. System management solution providers, such as Computer Associates, also include control monitoring functionality with their software offerings.

COMMERCIAL ACCESS CONTROL SOLUTIONS

This class of solutions supplements the local system controls through its own authentication, authorization, and integrity control mechanisms. The solutions differ from system management tools in that security is their primary focus. They do not typically provide for other system administration functions. Commercial products in this category of solutions include Armor from Los Altos Technologies, Inc.; BoKs from Dynamic Software AB of Stockholm, Sweden; and OmniGuard from Axent Technologies, Inc. These types of solutions are available for UNIX, Novell Netware, Windows NT, and other environments. They typically offer the following advantages:

- Centralized administration
- Password policy enforcement
- Filtering by network access
- Time-based access controls
- System-generated passwords
- Concurrent access restrictions
- Device specific access
- Password strength checks
- Self-auditing mechanisms
- Centralized audit trail

This class of solution also provides for the central management of many security functions. Armor, for example, can act as single source of user authentication for up to hundreds of UNIX workstations. Improved password management and auditing are common features. Both BoKs and OmniGuard, for example, enforce the requirement for strong passwords through the use of password composition rules and password aging.

System Management

Commercial system management solutions are also available for the distributed UNIX environment. These solutions provide a comprehensive approach to the problems of distributed system management, which include backup and recovery, job scheduling, and user management. Many security-related functions, including control monitoring and integrity checks, are also provided by system management solutions. Commercial system management solutions include CA Unicenter from Computer Associates, Hewlett-Packard's Openview Systems Management, SystemView from IBM, Omni-Guard ESM from Axtent Technologies, and the Tivoli Management Environment from Tivoli Systems. We will discuss both access control and system management solutions further in Chapter 22.

Audit Trail

UNIX does not use a single, comprehensive audit trail to record system activity. The operating system records audit data in a number of places, each using different formats and reporting techniques. Different locations and names are given to these individual audit trails. They are also not standard across the various UNIX platforms. Table 12.3 summarizes the major audit trails available in the HP-UX operating system.

TABLE 12.3
UNIX AUDIT TRAILS

Audit Trail	Nature of the Audit Trail
.history & .sh_history	User command line entries
/var/adm/wtmp	Successful logins
/var/adm/btmp	Failed logins
/var/adm/syslog/*	Network connection log files
/.secure/etc/auditlogX (C2)	Operating system calls
/var/adm/acct	User activity
/var/adm/sulog	Change to user ID

Commercial access control and system management solutions typically provide for a centralized audit trail and superior reporting capabilities.

DYNAMIC ALERTS

Many companies in North America provide electronic motion detectors for home use. These detectors will detect intruders, sound an alarm, and even dial the local police station. The existence of a sticker indicating their presence in a home is enough to deter many criminals. By combining the needs of network management and security, a similar capability can be extended to UNIX systems. Network management systems are primarily used for the management of complex networks of computers. They are capable of recording and processing alerts, even to the point of paging personnel. Their use can be extended to the area of security. We will examine the use of dynamic alerts in Chapter 22.

SECURITY ALERTS

The Computer Emergency Response Team (CERT) at Carnegie Mellon University and the Computer Incident Advisory Capability (CIAC) of the U.S. Department of Energy track known vulnerabilities to various operating systems. They provide security alerts and bulletins when security exposures become known. Advisories are forwarded to the security community describing security incidents and recommended courses of action.

TABLE 12.4
SOURCES FOR SECURITY ADVISORIES, BULLETINS, AND SUPPORT

Vendor	Email Address
CERT	cert@cert.org
CIAC	ciac-listproc@llnl.gov
Cray Research	support@cray.com
Hewlett-Packard	security-alert@hp.com
IBM	services@austin.ibm.com
Next	ask_next@next.com
Santa Cruz Operation	security-alert@sco.com
Silicon Graphics	security-alert@sgi.com
Sun MicroSystems	security-alert@sun.com/var/adm/wtmp

Several computing vendors also provide public notification of security advisories. Table 12.4 is a partial list of email sources for security advisories, bulletins, and support.

HP SECURITY BULLETINS
HP Security Bulletins may be subscribed to by sending an email message entitled *security_info* to *support@support.mayfield.hp.com*. To retrieve the index of all HP Security Bulletins, send a message titled *security_info_list* to *support@support.mayfield.hp.com* or access the Hewlett-Packard corporate web page at *www.hp.com*. For security concerns, send email to *security-alert@hp.com*.

CONCLUSIONS

There are solutions to the problem of security in the UNIX environment. Both contributed and commercial solutions are available which provide advanced utilities for authentication, access control, integrity checks, and monitoring of the controls environment.

Our discussion of the basic UNIX control structures, the issues surrounding their implementation, and the networking features has provided an understanding of security in the UNIX environment. There are three key points concerning security in UNIX.

The first point is that there are indeed a number of methods to compromise the integrity of a UNIX system. Knowledge of how UNIX works is important to properly implement security. Both security and system administrators must obtain a sufficient level of understanding of how UNIX works, remain current in their knowledge, and obtain the latest information on security exposures. It must also be recognized that it is impossible, due to the complexity of the environment, to manually check for weaknesses in the controls. The use of an automated tool to perform security checks is mandatory.

The second point, as important as the first, is that total reliance must never be placed in the continued functionality of the controls environment. It must be recognized that controls, when they are distributed, tend to deteriorate over time. Changes to application programs, updates to the operating system, or the actions of a new system administrator may affect the continued functionality of a given control It is imperative that those responsible for a UNIX system, or any computer system for that matter, actively examine the existing controls and look for weaknesses in the control structure.

The third point is the need to actively examine the UNIX environment for evidence of security breaches. But if controls are correctly implemented initially, and reviewed on a regular basis, why can we not simply rely on these controls? The reason is that, unlike the mainframe environment, controls in the distributed environment are generally enforced by the local administrator. Because there is no central authority, distributed controls can be weakened or circumvented over a period of time.

These points form the basis for our later discussions on the use of centralized security management solutions, and the role of audit in distributed computing. But the very foundations of open systems need bolstering before we can fully trust the environment. Additional requirements and areas of concern include

- The need for a single sign-on technology usable by a wide number of applications
- The mutual, secure authentication of client and server, and the need to protect data (including passwords) traffic over an untrusted transport
- The need for a centralized security administration of authentication and authorization privileges

The Distributed Computing Environment from OSF is intended to provide a strong foundation for open systems computing. We will examine the middleware offerings from OSF in a later chapter. But, first, we examine how a relatively new operating system, Windows NT, addresses the issue of computing security.

CHAPTER 13

WINDOWS NT
SECURITY

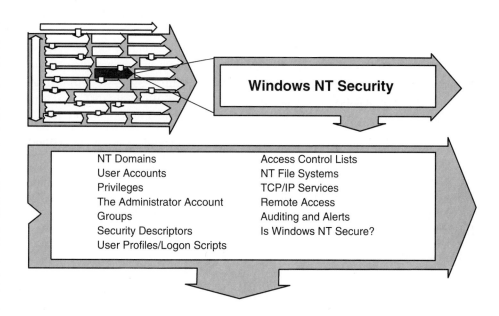

Windows NT Security

NT Domains	Access Control Lists
User Accounts	NT File Systems
Privileges	TCP/IP Services
The Administrator Account	Remote Access
Groups	Auditing and Alerts
Security Descriptors	Is Windows NT Secure?
User Profiles/Logon Scripts	

First introduced to the marketplace in 1993, the Windows NT operating system from Microsoft has steadily gained in popularity as a platform to deploy client-server applications. Based on a 32-bit architecture, Windows NT offers many advanced features, including multitasking, high availability, and resource sharing. It features an easy-to-use administration utility and provides support for many industry standard networking services. Windows NT also incorporates the Dynamic Host Configuration Program (DHCP) that allows network addresses to be dynamically assigned to clients. It has also proved popular as a platform for Microsoft's SQL server database engine.

From a security perspective, the Windows NT environment has incorporated many advanced security features over older operating systems, including UNIX. These features include the protection of passwords over the network, the ability to delegate administrative privileges, and a global approach to security management. Windows NT has recently received the C2 certification from the U.S. Department of Defense's National Computer Security Center. Microsoft has also published a collection of application programming interfaces (APIs) for a number of Windows NT functions, including security. These APIs allow both third party and customized applications to be incorporated into the Windows NT environment.

Windows NT includes both a client and server version. While both are roughly equivalent in features, the client version has a rather limited capacity when compared to the server version. For example, the remote access server now supports up to 256 simultaneous connections while the client only supports one connection. While the core functionality of the controls offered in both versions are equivalent, global security management functions are not supported on the client system. For this reason, we will primarily focus our discussion on the server version of Windows NT operating system.

As with previous chapters, our intent is to provide a good understanding of the security mechanisms used by Windows NT. Once an understanding is gained, we will discuss the prominent security issues and concerns. Let's begin with a review of the global nature of Windows NT security. We will start by examining the concept of a Windows NT domain.

NT DOMAINS

Windows NT security provides the ability to manage both user accounts and groups, as well as the ability to enforce security policy from a central viewpoint. Windows NT machines, both clients and servers, may be consolidated for administrative purposes within a single grouping called a *domain.* Machines within a domain can share a common user account database termed a global account domain. This provides users with a common user ID regardless of which machine in the domain they have logged onto. Users may also be assigned to groups which are defined for the entire domain.

Unlike the usual UNIX environment, security standards can be dictated to all systems within the domain. One machine is defined as the primary control system for the domain. From this system, a common security policy can be created and enforced for the entire domain. Access to this system is usually, but not always, limited to the domain administrator. Backup machines for domain control may also be designated to provide redundancy in case the primary domain is unavailable.

Windows NT also supports the concept of a trusted domain. This concept allows users that have been authenticated by their own primary domain access to services in another domain, providing the second domain trusts the primary. The domain security administrator of the secondary domain must have agreed to extend trust to the users' domains for this to occur. Windows NT can also extend support for a user who does not have an actual account in the secondary domain. Called pass-through validation, it allows a user casual selected access to foreign domains without requiring any administrative intervention. It is important to realize that access to a domain does not necessarily provide access to any resources. A local system administrator has complete control over what resources will be granted to users from either the local, or foreign, domains. An overview of the Windows NT domain model is shown in Figure 13.1.

There are two primary advantages in the use of the domain model. The first is that security standards, such as password aging, minimum password lengths, and account lockouts after a period of inactivity, may be enforced for all machines in the domain. Security weaknesses due to inconsistent local system administration are eliminated because the security policies of the organization are centrally enforced. This increases the overall security of the domain. But more important, domains provide a single point of reference for

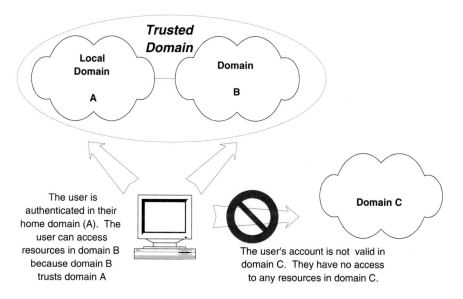

Figure 13.1 The Windows NT domain model

a user. An employee who is on a leave of absence or has been terminated may have their access privileges revoked in one centrally administered location. All access to Windows NT resources, unless they know a GUEST account, are denied to the user when their account has been terminated.

Another important aspect of the domain model is that nonemployees, including partners and contractors, can be easily identified. When a nonemployee is added to a domain, he or she can be assigned to a global group which identifies the special status. Local administrators can specifically accept or deny access to sensitive or confidential information based on the nonemployee group designation.

As mentioned previously, Windows NT allows the domain administrator to set and enforce standards for users in the domain. These standards are mostly directed at the user's account. They include the ability to require password aging and a minimum length for passwords. Corporate standards for password length and composition may also be enforced. Users may also be disconnected after a specified period of inactivity or a prescribed number of failed login attempts.

USER ACCOUNTS

Windows NT users are normally assigned their own accounts by a security administrator. User accounts may be defined either on a local or domain basis. Local accounts are validated only by the local system, whereas domain accounts are validated by the domain security service. Account information is stored in a security account database, which is managed by the security account manager (SAM) function. SAM can either exist on a local machine or be networked to provide security information for an entire domain. Domain versions of SAM may be replicated on a number of servers to provide redundancy.

Both Windows NT client and server systems also support the use of a GUEST account. This account is used to provide access to casual users who login using GUEST as an account name. GUEST accounts are enabled by default on Windows NT clients, but the reverse is true for Windows NT servers. If enabled, the GUEST account should be protected by a password. A smart administrator will regularly review the access rights to this account and ensure they are as restrictive as possible.

PRIVILEGES

Privileges are a set of rights that allow a user, or group member, to perform specific actions. Privileges may be directly assigned by the administrator to a user or inherited because of membership in a defined group. They are examined whenever the user wishes to access an object. These privileges include the right to access the Windows NT machine over a network, to perform a backup and manage the auditing system. Table 13.1 shows a few of the possible privileges that may be assigned to a user or group.

Table 13.1 provides only a small sample of the actual privileges available in Windows NT. There are actually quite a few of them. The important thing to realize is that the Windows NT security mechanism decides whether or not to allow a user to perform an action based upon two factors. These are the privileges the user possesses and the access controls on the object they wish to access. Even though users have been given the privilege to access a Windows NT server over the network, they may be denied access to any or all of its resources. Privileges may also be defined for the administration of the entire Windows NT domain. These global privileges are usually associated with a domain user manager.

THE ADMINISTRATOR ACCOUNT

Somewhat analogous to the UNIX superuser, the administrator in Windows NT has complete control of the Windows NT system. A notable difference between the two is that the Windows NT administrator has been granted power because they have been assigned the complete set of users rights. This power would be diminished if these rights are removed and assigned to other users. Without using third-party products or making operating system modifications, this is simply not possible in the UNIX world.

GROUPS

As is common with the other operating systems we have examined, Windows NT supports the use of groups. Access rights and privileges can

TABLE 13.1
SAMPLE LIST OF NT PRIVILEGES

Privilege	Description
SE_SYSTEMTIME_NAME	Reset the system clock.
SE_RESTORE_NAME	Retrieve files from a backup.
SE_DEBUG_NAME	Perform system debugging.
SE_SHUTDOWN_PRIVILEGE	Shutdown and reboot the system.
SE_TAKE_OWNERSHIP	Transfer the ownership of objects.

be assigned to multiple users using a composite entity called a group. Windows NT has a number of predefined, or default, groups for both the local machine and domain, such as the administrator, guest, and user groups. The system administrator can create and maintain new groups as they see fit. They may be created based on department structure, job function, or any other desired reason to link users together. The primary reason for creating groups is to simplify administration. From a security perspective, users that are assigned to the group inherit the rights and privileges associated with the group.

Windows NT supports two types of groups, local and global. A local group is only active on the local system and cannot be assigned privileges on another NT system. It can, however, contain user accounts defined by the domain or groups that have been defined globally. A global group is available for the entire Windows NT domain (or other trusted domains) composed of users. A global group cannot contain either local groups or other global groups. The important distinction between local and global groups is that membership in a local group is only useful on a local system, while membership in a global group may be give access rights on many different systems. As with the use of groups in other operating systems, it is important to control and monitor both group access privileges and membership.

SECURITY DESCRIPTORS

Windows NT allows access controls to be placed on a wide variety of system and domain resources. The types of resources which may be protected include files, directories, printers, programs, and network connections. Resource security is implemented by assigning special security information in a data structure, called a security descriptor, which is associated with the resource or object. Security descriptors contain the owner's name and associated group name for the object. They also hold lists of who can access the object, how it may be accessed, as well as auditing requirements for the object. The lists of users and groups, with their associated access permissions, are called access control lists (ACLs).

SECURITY CONTROLS

Users who successfully log on to a Windows NT environment receive an access token. It is this access token, and not the user ID, that is queried before access to an object is granted. The access token contains three key items-a user ID, the groups to which the user belongs, and the privileges that the user has been granted. Every program or process that a user runs is given a copy of the access token.

Users are authenticated and subsequently obtain access tokens, by logging in using a combination of user ID (i.e., account name) and associated password. A user ID is used to identify a user account. It may be up to 20 characters in length, but is not case sensitive. The user IDs *glenbruce* and *GLENBRUCE* are the same in a Windows NT environment. Passwords can be up to 14 characters in length, and unlike user IDs, are case sensitive. This anomaly has produced some frustration in users, including the author. The login process itself is protected by forcing the user to enter the ALT+CONTROL+DELETE keys, which if used outside of the login program, will cause a Windows workstation to enter a reboot screen. It is felt that this approach will prevent Trojan horse programs, but there has been some discussion that a DOS-based Trojan horse program could circumvent this control.

Figure 13.2 provides an overview of the Windows NT authentication and authorization mechanisms.

A security subsystem which runs on the local computer, called the local security authority, or LSA, is responsible for identifying the user, creating access tokens and maintaining audit trails. It is the LSA that is invoked by the login process. The LSA then contacts the security registry

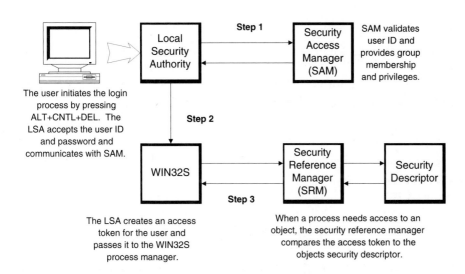

Figure 13.2 Authentication and authorization

(i.e., SAM), and SAM verifies the user's account and password. SAM also provides information about the user's group memberships and special privileges to the LSA. Once SAM has confirmed the identity of the user, the LSA creates a limited-life access token for the user. Essentially, the access token is valid for only as long as the user has a session, which may be automatically terminated due to inactivity or time restrictions. All communication between SAM and the LSA are encrypted using keys that are shared by the LSA and SAM.

The access token is then passed to the Win32S subsystem that monitors and controls the Windows NT processes. Win32S will then begin an initial process for the user. The Windows program manager is started, which displays the initial icons and desktop to the user. Every subsequent process initiated by the user will have the access token associated with it. The access token, and not the account name (i.e., user ID), is examined whenever a request to an object is made. Access tokens are examined by a second security function, the security reference monitor (SRM), to determine if access to Windows NT resources should be granted. The access token is compared to the security descriptor associated with the object. If the requirements requested by the security descriptor are met, access to the object will be granted.

There are several advantages to the approach for authentication and authorization used by Windows NT. First, passwords are not transmitted in clear-text and cannot be directly viewed on the LAN because they are encrypted. Second, there is a strong connection between the authentication and authorization process. Because access to an object requires an access token, an intruder cannot simply issue a system call using a false user ID. Access tokens also increase security by allowing the user's privileges to be examined as well as their identity.

User Profiles/Logon Scripts

The desktop environment for a user may be defined in a file called a user profile. User profiles are used to set up default printers and display common screen layouts and colors. A most important security aspect of their use is that they can prevent users from changing the environment. They can also be used to assign users to default HOME directories, which can then be used to protect files that are created or to limit the programs and information to which they have access.

Users profiles may be assigned either to individual users or groups. An important limitation of user profiles is that they only work for Windows NT clients and cannot be used on either Windows 95 or Windows for

WorkGroup clients. Logon scripts, which are batch files and automatically run after a user is logged on, are also supported. Although not as comprehensive as a user profile, the scripts can be used by all Windows clients. A logon script can be used to initiate further security checks, control the environmental settings, or initiate network connections to other machines.

ACCESS CONTROL LISTS

Windows NT uses access control lists to limit the access of users to resources. Used primarily in cooperation with the Windows NT file system, ACLs limit the ability of a user of a resource to access, maintain, or delete the resource. An access control list is actually composed of a number of entries, called access control entries, or ACEs. Each ACE contains information on how the object can be used by the particular requester and what auditing should occur. For a file, an ACE may grant read and write privileges to a particular user. A second ACE could be created to permit only read access for a group of users, and so forth. The rights granted by an ACE entry are also referred to as an access mask. The types of access which are controlled will vary depending upon the type of object controlled by the ACL. Typical access rights for files, which may be assigned to either users or groups, are shown in Table 13.2.

For NTFS directories, separate access control rights are used. These are described in Table 13.3.

TABLE 13.2
ACCESS CONTROL RIGHTS FOR FILES

Access Right	Description
READ	Performs user management, reconfigures the server, and manages access controls.
WRITE	Allows the user to modify the contents of the file.
DELETE	Allows the user to delete the file. On an NTFS file system, the file cannot be recovered using a disk utility.
CHANGE PERMISSION	Allows the user possessing this access right to change the permissions on the file.
EXECUTE	Executes the file as long as it is a program.
TAKE OWNERSHIP	Changes the ownership of a file to another user.
FULL OWNERSHIP	The user possesses all of the above access rights.

TABLE 13.3
ACCESS CONTROL RIGHTS FOR DIRECTORIES

Access Right	Description
NO ACCESS	User is not permitted to access the directory in any way.
LIST	Files or subdirectories contained in this directory can be listed.
ADD	User can create files or new subdirectories.
READ	User can display information about the file or directory.
ADD & READ	User can create new directories, display who owns the directory and its associated access rights.
CHANGE	Directory may be deleted.
FULL CONTROL	User possesses all of the above access rights.

The access rights for files and directories, when used in combination, allow the administrator to define a very restrictive set of access rights. In comparison to the UNIX file and directory permissions described in the previous chapter, a Windows NT implementation offers some important advantages. First of all, many UNIX systems do not support flexible ACLs and can assign file or directory permissions only by the categories of user, group, and others. The permissions used by UNIX to protect files and directories are also limited to READ, WRITE, and EXECUTE. For those UNIX systems that do support the use of ACLs on directories, they are not typically inheritable and cannot be passed down to subdirectories. Most significantly, UNIX can only apply these permissions to files and directories and does not support the use of controls on access rights on the wide range of system resources that Windows NT does. The net effect is that UNIX resource access controls are less comprehensive, provide less granularity, and are more difficult to administer than those of Windows NT.

NT FILE SYSTEMS

Microsoft created a new file system, call the NT File System (NTFS), for Windows NT. NTFS was created to overcome several problems in the traditional file systems used by Microsoft. The ability to recover from system or power failures, without incurring corrupt or damaged disk drives, was added to NTFS. NTFS has advanced features that ensure the consistency and recoverability of its data. As well, support for large files and disks were added. Support for data redundancy and an improved indexing scheme to find files quickly were also implemented. But perhaps the most important improvement over the traditional file systems used by Microsoft is the security of NTFS.

NTFS uses an approach which is roughly similar to UNIX to protect its files and directories. Every object, either a file or directory, in an NTFS file system has security information associated with it. The information is held in what is termed a security descriptor. Every request to access an object in NTFS is subjected to a security test. The user (or program) must present a security access token, which verifies that they are valid users. The identity of the user, along with the privileges held in the access token, are compared to the access permissions in the security descriptor. If the authority shown in the access token is compatible with the requirements of the security descriptor, access to the object is granted. If not, the user's request to access the object will fail.

The NTFS file system has several advantages, in terms of security, over the traditional UNIX file systems. First, as mentioned in the previous section on access control lists, Windows NT supports a wider number of access permissions. This allows the system administrator to employ more stringent security access settings for NTFS objects than UNIX can support. UNIX supports the traditional RWX (read, write, and execute) which are applied to users, group members to which the file belongs, and all others. Windows NT defines seven permissions and multiple access control lists. Another advantage is that auditing has been designed into the base functionality of NTFS. But the most important advantage is that NTFS evaluates user requests based on an access token, rather than the user ID. It is relatively easy in UNIX to counterfeit a user ID (we've provided a few examples in the UNIX chapters) and then issue unauthorized requests to the file system. The access tokens used by Windows NT are more difficult to counterfeit. They also contain additional security information, such as user privileges, which allow better decisions to be made on whether or not access should be granted.

It is a requirement for C2 security that deleted objects cannot be made available for reuse. The same concept holds for the use of memory. When a process finishes in memory, the area is cleansed and cannot be examined by another user. The Windows NTFS file system cannot undelete, as you can under the DOS file system, a deleted file.

Although NTFS does support an advanced security model, Windows NT systems do have a few Achilles heels. Windows NT systems may elect to support a number of different file systems, including the traditional file allocation table (FAT) file system used by MS-DOS systems. The FAT file system has relatively little security. The FAT or other types of file systems used by a Windows NT system will generally not support the NTFS security features we have described. Data or information held by these file systems can be easily compromised.

NETWORKING

TCP/IP SERVICES

Windows NT provides support for a number of the TCP/IP networking services common in the UNIX, Novell Netware, and Internet environments. These include support for communication, print, and management (i.e., SNMP) protocols and the traditional UNIX communication services, including telnet and FTP. In addition, support is provided for the Internet gopher, Domain Name Service, and World Wide Web services. The security concerns surrounding the use of these services are described in Chapters 11 and 14. A very important concern is the fact that most TCP/IP services send passwords in clear-text. The important thing to recognize is that this concern, and others, are still valid in the Windows NT environment when TCP/IP services are used.

REMOTE ACCESS

Windows NT provides support for remote users who wish to connect to the Windows NT environment. The remote access service (RAS) supports a number of different remote connections, including modem access over telephone lines and X.25 access. The Serial Line Internet Protocol (SLIP) and Point-to-Point Protocol (PPP) protocols are support for modem access. Once the RAS server authenticates the user, they may be allowed full access to Windows NT services, as if they had connected over the LAN. A RAS connection may use a number of LAN protocols, including TCP/IP, IPX, and NETBEUI.

Built-in security mechanisms are a strong feature of the RAS service. As with many features of the Windows NT operating system, RAS supports a number of options, and it is up to the system administrator to select the one most appropriate to their computing environment. Authentication of the user can be provided using the PPP Challenge Handshake Authentication Protocol (CHAP) or Password Authentication Protocol (PAP). While both protocols protect passwords and do not send them in clear text over the wire, CHAP, which uses a strong authentication mechanism, is preferred. It should be noted that CHAP is a PPP mechanism and is not supported on SLIP. It can be used with either DES or MD5 encryption.

After RAS receives the user ID and password, they are authenticated by the Windows NT security service in the normal manner. Even if the client is not known to the local domain, they may also login if they are a member of a trusted domain. A rather nice feature of RAS is that the security administrator can determine the range of activity for a RAS user. The administrator can decide whether or not the individual RAS user should be given access to the complete Windows NT domain or be restricted to those services provided by the local RAS server. A dialback control, which requires RAS to interrupt the authentication process, disconnect the user and dial them back at a predefined telephone number, is also supported. Data encryption of all traffic is also supported. Using RSA's RC4 data encryption algorithm, RAS can communicate in a secure manner (i.e., the traffic is encrypted) with a client possessing RC4 capability (e.g., Windows NT client).

Microsoft has also provided a number of application programming interfaces (APIs), which allow the incorporation of third-party products into RAS. For example, the one-time password SecureID product from Security Dynamics can be integrated into RAS. The C2-style audit functions of the Windows NT operating system have been extended to RAS. The success or failure of a number of events, including connections, disconnections due to authentication failures or inactivity, and protocol failures, can be audited. It is up to the RAS administrator to define the appropriate level of auditing.

AUDITING AND ALERTS

The Windows NT operating system provides support for the C2 level of auditing, as defined by U.S. Department of Defense *Orange Book*. C2 provides for audit trails, which log the success or failure of a number of events. These events may include the logon or logoff of users, file or resource access, changes to the security environment, or security policy changes. A number of audit trails are maintained on a Windows NT system, and include events related to operating system activity, changes to the security environment, and application-related information. An important consideration is that like most audit trails, Windows NT audit trails exist on the local system. If the permissions protecting the audit trails are lax or an individual can obtain ADMINISTRATOR privileges, local audit trails can be tampered with and their integrity compromised.

SUPPORT FOR OTHER SECURITY MECHANISMS

Windows NT does provide a number of application programming interfaces which will allow customized applications and third-party products to be integrated into the environment. However, the APIs are proprietary and are not based upon industry standards. Windows NT provides limited, but not full, support for the OSF/DCE environment. While the remote procedure calls provided by Microsoft are compliant with OSF specifications, they have not been created directly from the OSF specifications. As well, Windows NT does not support the full range of DCE services. DCE services are described in Chapters 16 and 17.

IS WINDOWS NT SECURE ?

Microsoft has had the ability, in its design of the security features of Windows NT, to understand the security problems and issues faced by many older operating systems. By understanding these issues, Microsoft been able to address a good number of them in the design of Windows NT. This being said, a poorly implemented Windows NT server is just as vulnerable as any other type of server. The use of unsecured GUEST accounts, improper access privileges and lax access control permissions will result in a vulnerable computer system. Third parties have recognized this problem and are offering solutions. For example, the Kane Security Analyst from Intrusion Detection, Inc., can analyze and report on the overall security of a Windows NT system. Password guessing and Trojan horse attacks are still real threats in a Windows NT environment. TCP/IP services on Windows NT, including telnet and FTP, are just as vulnerable to password-snooping attacks as on any other platform.

CONCLUSIONS

The Windows NT environment has been specifically designed to counter many of the security issues prevalent in other computer platforms, particularly UNIX. It is rated at the C2 security level, although many other computing environments either achieve or comply with this standard. An important factor in the overall security of Windows NT is that the actual source code for the operating system is strictly protected by Microsoft. But it is to be expected that this will not prevent interested individuals from discovering flaws or bugs and exploiting them. While Microsoft has addressed some standards, Windows NT certainly does not address all of them. One problem is the proprietary nature of Windows NT controls. A key question about Windows NT is whether or not emerging security standards can be easily incorporated into the product. If they can, Windows NT should be able to retain its claim as a secure and open computing platform. If not, Windows NT may become yet another isolated operating system complicating, rather than helping to address, the challenge of security in distributed computing.

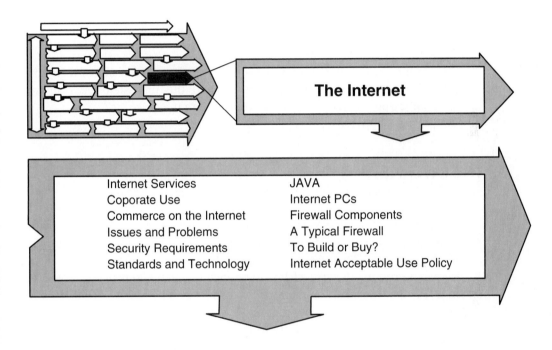

CHAPTER 14

THE INTERNET

The Internet

Internet Services
Coporate Use
Commerce on the Internet
Issues and Problems
Security Requirements
Standards and Technology

JAVA
Internet PCs
Firewall Components
A Typical Firewall
To Build or Buy?
Internet Acceptable Use Policy

The Internet is, in many ways, similar to a wild frontier. It is generally a lawless land that is governed mostly by peer pressure. Since there are no laws and no law keepers, the opportunity for security exposures is very large. The mass of available information and enthusiasm for getting connected makes a compelling argument for getting wired. Specific security concerns must be dealt with when any connection to an untrusted network, like the Internet, is implemented.

Most organizations either have, or have plans for, a connection to the Internet. It has been reported that over 20 to 30 million people currently have access to the Internet, although the estimates vary widely. It has become the world's commercial conduit, and unfortunately, a focal point for unauthorized entry into computer systems and networks. There are many interesting questions for organizations to answer in their use of the Internet.

How can an organization best control access between the corporate internal networks and the Internet? What sort of corporate information should be allowed to flow to the Internet? Are business partners, customers, or the general public to be allowed access to applications and systems on the internal network? If so, what limitations should be placed on their access? The central question is how an organization can make effective business use of the Internet. While this question has many aspects, a key item that must be addressed is security.

In this chapter we will review some of the business issues of using the Internet, explain the specific hazards of using this untrusted network, and offer some approaches you can take to deal with them.

WHAT IS THE INTERNET?

We had better start out by explaining what the Internet is and review some of the terms and technologies involved. The Internet was not originally intended to be the prevailing worldwide network it has become. It got its start early in 1969 by the U.S. Department of Defense when it commissioned the Advanced Research Projects Agency (ARPA) to provide research into network protocols. In 1973, the Transmission Control Protocol/Internet Protocol (TCP/IP) was proposed as a standard networking protocol for computer communication. The popularity of TCP/IP rose sharply in 1983 when the version of UNIX released by the University of California at Berkeley included this network protocol along with the operating system. Since many of the computers used by ARPA in its network used UNIX, TCP/IP became the de facto standard.

The U.S. National Science Foundation (NSF) began its involvement in the network in 1986 and provided funding for faster connections between supercomputing centers. This established a high-speed backbone for the network. The Internet began evolving into a shared network connecting universities, research centers, and corporations. By 1995, the Internet had rapidly grown into a network of millions of machines and tens of millions of users. The control of the Internet has been handed over to private interests. The Internet has grown from a small government-funded research project into a worldwide computer communications network. The interest and growth in the Internet have been unstoppable.

The term Internet is used to describe the common network communications and is actually made up of various services using the TCP/IP protocols. The TCP/IP network protocol is actually a collection of various protocols used for different purposes. Some of the qualities of TCP/IP made it very attractive for military use. TCP/IP is based on a dynamic packet-routing protocol. Major segments of a large TCP/IP network can suffer deterioration or be disabled without destroying the capability of the network nodes that are still operating to communicate. In Chapter 7 we have seen how easy it is to establish communications using the TCP/IP protocols. Security was never an important design consideration in this TCP/IP-based network used mainly for academic research. The very fact that this networking capability is pervasive and powerful is also its Achilles heel.

INTERNET SERVICES

The Internet is known mostly for the services that make use of the network. By far the best known service, the World Wide Web (WWW) is also one of the more recent ones. The WWW technology was developed in 1989 as a way of organizing technical documentation that was spread over several computers. The documents are linked using Hypertext Markup Language (HTML) as a way of providing pointers in one document to other documents. The development of HTML-based browser software enabled people to access and display this documentation by referencing these pointers. The information in HTML-based documents can be referenced by many paths following the embedded links. Advances in the browser software brought graphics, sound, and even animation to the user. Most recent commercial entries to the Internet began with making information available using WWW technology. An initial business Internet presence is the establishment of a WWW page of publicly available corporate information in HTML documents.

Documents are obtained with the use of the Hypertext Transfer Protocol (HTTP). HTTP is the protocol that is required for transferring information between the Web page and the browser. It uses uniform resource locators (URLs) to navigate through HTML documents. The URL defines a unique address that refers to a specific document, image, or other Web resource. An HTML document can have URLs embedded in the document that in turn point to other HTML documents. HTML defines the format of the links and HTTP defines how to retrieve the native Web documents from the Web servers.

Think of the URL as an index card indicating where a book is located in a library. We can use this card to locate the physical location of a (HTML) document. What if more index cards were contained inside the book which pointed to the location of additional, related information? This additional information may be in the form of another book, a photograph, or a recorded tape. We can follow the URLs to obtain this information instead of always going back to the main library index. What if this information is scattered among several different libraries in different cities? HTTP allows us to follow this trail of information no matter where it is located and presents it to us in an understandable format.

Other popular services using the Internet include the File Transfer Protocol (FTP), the Domain Name System (DNS), and the electronic mail facilities. FTP is a protocol used to transfer files from one host computer to another. The current WWW browsers also support FTP services. DNS allows clients to determine, or resolve, the IP address of a server they wish to contact using only the Internet name of the server. Electronic mail is another common service available on the Internet. It has become commonplace to print business cards that include an electronic mail address, available through the Internet, as well as the usual business address, phone, and fax numbers. There are several other network services that are available on the Internet, more than we can adequately deal with here.

For further information, we highly recommend two very popular books on the management of Internet services by Cricket Liu: Liu, Peek, Jones, Buus, and Nye [1994] and Liu and Albitz [1992].

CORPORATE USE

The Internet has become a very interesting and attractive medium to corporations for providing and accessing information. The availability of the World Wide Web for providing information has opened the flood gates for organizations investigating how they can take advantage of it. This is being fueled by an enthusiastic press and the availability of technical products and services to support use of the Internet. There are two fundamental questions that corporations should ask concerning the use of the Internet. How can the corporation utilize the Internet to its business advantage? How can the corporation make money using the Internet? The second question does not always follow the first one. Although the Internet presents an attractive prospect for business growth, it also presents new challenges, opportunities, and considerations.

One of the main advantages of the Internet is the ability to access a vast amount of on-line information. It can provide types of interactive information that are unavailable elsewhere. A business can take advantage of this to offer a diverse array of information on their products and services. This can include text, graphics, sound recording, and even video. One of the current challenges is to understand to whom you are providing this information. You cannot always know who is accessing the information that you provide or how they use it.

The Internet represents a *many-to-many* and *any-to-any* relationship between the providers and users of information and services. It is often described as providing A4 service: access, anytime, anywhere, to anybody. In a lot of ways the decisions of how the Internet is used are being made by the user community. The users are dictating what the providers will do or how information will be provided. For example, the business will conform to the capabilities of the Web browser rather than dictating how people will access the information.

The business use of the Internet can be segmented into categories depending on the type of relationship the organization has or wants to have with the users. These categories describe the relationship between the information provider and the intended audience. The type of information or application that is provided to the user and how it is presented differs depending on the desired relationship. A fundamental question to answer with an Internet relationship is whether there is a requirement to individually identify the person accessing the information.

CORPORATE INFORMATION

The first category describes the typical first use of the Internet by most organizations. The organization presents information about the company, and its products and services, using a WWW server. This type of use may include access to general company information, office locations, official corporate information such as annual or quarterly reports, and product descriptions and availability information. This information can be provided more quickly and much less expensively on the Internet than by traditional printing and distribution. In-depth product technical information can be provided at a more detailed level than may be provided in product brochures. A corporate Web page can also be used to provide related industry information and links to other Internet locations which may be of value to the user. There may in fact be some issues to consider before publishing certain types of financial data on the Internet. For example, issuing a financial prospectus on-line may break laws in certain countries.

CORPORATION TO NEW CUSTOMERS

Some corporations have extended their Internet presence to providing catalogs of products as well as the ability to submit orders for those products over the Internet. The business relationship has now been expanded to identified individuals, and not necessarily existing customers of the organization. On-line catalogs and product ordering is popular for clothing stores, bookstores, or other traditional mail-order operations. The availability of the catalog to the public increases the distribution outside of the companys' current mailing lists. One of the requirements to be effective in this type of business operation is to have a distribution network established to deal with these network collected orders. Again there may be issues to consider such as taxation and export controls when conducting business on the Internet.

Another popular area is the ability to provide customer support. Several companies offer specific customer support services for their products. This support service can be automated to a large degree. Software is available that can provide automatic support information in response to customer questions. Additional uses of the Internet in this area include software availability and distribution. Several computer hardware and software companies provide software such as device drivers or patches and updates over the Internet.

CORPORATION TO EXISTING CUSTOMERS

This type of Internet relationship is extended to existing customers of the corporation. The Internet can provide an alternate access method to the corporate systems for existing customers. This access can be extended to personal financial accounts and transaction execution. Several banks are providing access to customer account information, and a few have provided the ability to issue banking transactions to their customers. Another example would be the ability of obtaining time-dependent information specific to a customer. For example, a courier company can supply a customer with the ability of tracking the progress of the delivery of their packages.

CORPORATION TO CORPORATION

The Internet is being used as the communication mechanism to support corporate-to-corporate communication for such things as joint partnership projects or to support industry organizations. Many organizations maintain Web sites for information related to their work. Standards bodies such as the Object Management Group (OMG) use the WWW to provide documentation of the published standards, the schedule of the standards progress, and the minutes of meetings. This information is provided for use by participants in the standards bodies or other interested people.

The Internet has also been used to support joint development work of selected technologies, even among traditional competitors. For example, a large-scale development project may require the participation of several subcontractors who each supply material or components. The Internet can be used to share project information and provide a message communication path. The use of the Internet to exchange commerce documents using electronic data interchange (EDI) is another interesting application.

INTERNAL COMPANY "INTRANET"

A corporation can take advantage of the Internet technology without committing to an external connection to the Internet. The Intranet is the term used to describe the internal use of Internet technology. Many companies have established the Internet WWW technology as a standard way of presenting and maintaining internal information for use by their employees. Examples of this use includes access to daily companywide news, internal telephone directories, human resource information including benefit programs and job postings, specifically designed internal support applications, technical information, internal software availability and distribution, departmental communications (internal Web pages), and links to other division- or department-specific home pages. One of the major advantages to this approach is the relatively low cost of providing and accessing the information as opposed to using traditional paper documentation.

COMMERCE ON THE INTERNET

A natural extension to the business use of the Internet is to include commercial transactions on this untrusted network. This is a very exciting prospect but is also a large security concern. When we are talking about commerce on the network, we are generally referring to the transmission of financial or financial-related transactions. The commercial applications require that the two parties involved be able to authenticate each other and transact business confidentially. A more important security element of these commercial transactions is perhaps nonrepudiation. We need to have confidence that these transactions are real and valid. In essence, the security of the client relationship when using Web browsers and other Internet services must be similar to that of dealing with an automated teller machine or other banking mechanism.

When using the Internet to carry transactions using the established payment methods such as the use of credit or debit cards, there are generally five parties that need to be involved: the issuer of the credit/debit card, the merchant who sells the goods, the customer who buys the goods, the acquirer of the transaction (e.g., the bank the merchant uses), and some way of securing the transaction with the use of a security authority. The growing interest in these types of transactions promotes the need for a way of providing proof of identity and confidentiality from an Internet service available for just such a need. The availability of a common security authority will help promote commercial transactions on the Internet.

ISSUES AND PROBLEMS

The security problems with the Internet often get a lot of publicity when computer hackers use the Internet to illegally access systems. A computer hacker, Kevin Mitnick, also known as "Condor," was arrested in North Carolina in February 1995. It has been alleged that he illegally used cellular phone systems to gain access to the Internet and provide the opportunity for his illegal entry of many computer systems. He was caught with assistance from a noted computer security researcher, Tsutomu Shimomura. Using his knowledge and specialized tools, Mr. Shimomura assisted authorities in tracking down the Condor. The Condor had allegedly accessed Mr. Shimomura's own system and stole valuable information. The researcher responded by monitoring the Condor's activities, and with the assistance of telephone technicians, and working with the FBI, they were able to track him to a particular apartment. One of the most interesting aspects of the Internet is that there is no central authority that owns, manages, controls, or polices it. This is often one of the most misunderstood aspects of the Internet. When problems or security situations arise, the question, "why doesn't someone do something?" is often raised. While the Computer Emergency Response Team (CERT) and Forum of Incident Response and Security Teams (FIRST) organizations are available to Internet users when security incidents arise, there is no one authority that you can turn to. This lack of a central control or management authority presents some additional challenges which many businesses are unaccustomed.

The links to and the availability of the WWW pages are fragile. If they become unavailable, there is nowhere to turn. Change management is nonexistent. WWW links and pages can appear or disappear without warning. There is no guaranty that messages sent using the Internet will be delivered. Unless specific mechanisms have been implemented to provide an acknowledgment, there is no way of knowing if a message was delivered successfully or not.

SECURITY REQUIREMENTS

Connecting your network to the Internet is much like holding an open house at your place when you are not home. You may invite anybody in to appreciate the art on the walls in the living room or browse the books in the study. You may lock the doors to other rooms in the house to prevent entry during the open house. You may even give selected people keys to the locked rooms. How will you know if someone picked one of the door locks, entered the room, took a look around, and then locked the door again? How can you verify that only the people with keys entered the locked rooms.

Unless you had a guest book, you won't know who came to the open house. I'm sure if you ever hold an open house you will put strict controls in place to ensure the security of your residence.

The usual requirements for security including authentication, confidentiality, and authorization are present when using the Internet but with a few new wrinkles. The need for authentication, confidentiality, and nonrepudiation becomes more important when using an untrusted network. Security is required at both the content and the transport level of the network messages. The Internet can be like a dark alley where you don't know who (if anybody) is lurking in the shadows. You don't know who can see what you have sent over the net if the message or data is not protected with a confidentiality mechanism such as encryption.

Another concern about using the Internet is that people or things may not be who or what they appear. In Chapter 7, we examined how easy it is to manipulate TCP/IP packet information. In particular, the ability to modify packet addresses, in an attack called spoofing, was described. Spoofing has been used to invade secure systems by the ability to impersonate a system the target system trusts. The identity of people sending mail can be spoofed as well as the locations from which the mail seems to originate. Without strict authentication and nonrepudiation, you may not be able to prove the authenticity of information or the identity of individuals.

The use of digital signatures to verify an identity and preserve the integrity of messages is one way to solve this problem. A standard way of administering and verifying these signatures is required. It doesn't do you much good if you are not familiar with someone's signature to know if it is authentic or not. The use of common certification authorities is required to provide authentication of the signatures. The use of certification authorities is described in more detail in the next chapter on cryptography.

One of the obvious security requirements is to be able to protect your internal network from unauthorized intrusion when you connect to the Internet. The second section in this chapter on firewalls will give you an idea of how to proceed. There are a lot of benefits to be able to provide access to the Internet for your employees or open the corporate network to clients, customers, business partners, and contractors. You may want to allow access to specific information or applications or to specific individuals.

STANDARDS AND TECHNOLOGY

As often happens, one of the side effects of rapid interest and growth in the application of a new technical base is that a great number of conflicting standards will be created. Because of the size and growth of the Internet, a clear winner in the standards arena can have a dramatic impact and be a fantastic opportunity. A lot of development and positioning is taking place to offer the solution to all of the security problems. As a result, several different standards are being promoted. It remains to be seen which one will be the universally accepted standard.

Secure HTTP (S-HTTP) is an extension to the HTTP protocol to provide authentication and encryption facilities at the setup of a session. S-HTTP actually supports a variety of security options for the clients and the servers. The client and the server negotiate which encryption mechanism will be used to secure the messages. This method will provide end-to-end security and is very useful to secure transactions but it is limited to the HTTP protocol.

The secure sockets layer (SSL) provides server authentication, data encryption, and message integrity at the transport layer. One advantage of SSL is the ability to secure several Internet services, not just HTTP. The SSL protocol establishes a secure session at the beginning of a TCP/IP connection. The use of S-HTTP and SSL is not mutually exclusive. Many Internet transactions scenarios utilize both SSL and S-HTTP. Secure IP (IPv6) is a specification for extensions to the IP protocol that includes additional security functions. The Internet will be making a transition from version 4 of the IP protocol to version 6. This version includes two security mechanisms: an authentication header and the encapsulating security payload (ESP) protocol. The authentication header holds computed authentication information based on the message. The integrity of the message can be verified using this information. The ESP protocol provides the ability to encrypt some or all of the message. The secure IP protocol will greatly improve the security capabilities at the network protocol layer.

Additional security protocols are being developed and promoted to address the specific problem of transmitting financial transactions on the Internet. There is understandably a great reluctance to provide a credit card number over the Internet. It looks as if some of the standards battle is solved with the support of the secure electronic transaction (SET) protocol by the two major credit cards, Visa and MasterCard. One of the considerations in choosing a financial transaction protocol is who is supporting it. The banks with their current credit and debit processing systems coupled with the existing transaction capture and support systems are in a strong position to define which way Internet financial transactions will proceed.

JAVA

The Java technology from Sun Microsystems, Inc., has, a least in concept, some very interesting considerations in a distributed environment. Java is the name given to an object-oriented programming language, modeled on C++, that was developed by Sun to use with network devices and commercial appliances. The original objective was to provide program execution in a portable, highly distributed, heterogeneous environment. Java is an interpreted language, which means that the same code can be executed on a wide variety of platforms. A Java program is first compiled into transportable code called *bytecode* creating a small application called the Java Applet. The *bytecode,* or applet, can then be sent to the target platform, interpreted, and executed by local Java interpreter. Using this interpreted approach, the same Java program will be able to execute in the same way on any platform that contains a Java interpreter.

The excitement about Java comes from its ability to download and execute programs using the Internet network. This is perhaps a scary prospect when considering the security implications. Many people might be nervous about code that is loaded and executed on your machine from somewhere else in the network. Java includes several security features to protect the integrity of the applet and the environment it is executed in. The applet itself is verified by the Java interpreter to detect any potential problems during execution. The applet cannot create new processes. Additional checks ensure that the Java applet does not access files except in the manner in which it is allowed. An applet can only establish network connections with its originating host.

All of these measures however, do not guarantee safety from security breaches. There are a lot of people with plenty of time on their hands who enjoy looking for security holes. The approach that Java has taken seems to limit this potential although some security flaws have been found in the early reference implementation. This points out that it's difficult, if not impossible, to get it right all at once. The development of security mechanisms in the interpreter like Java is an iterative process.

INTERNET PCs

Another recent development concerning the Internet has been the announcement of the inexpensive Internet PC by several major computer vendors. The concept is to provide an inexpensive and limited-function device for the sole purpose of interacting with the Internet. The machine would consist of a processor, a limited-function operating system, functions to support graphics and network access, and a capability to execute Java applets. Almost all of the processing functions that would be required when using the machine will be downloaded from the network. The machine would execute small applets one at a time and only the ones needed at any one time.

One reason this approach is attractive is the expected low cost to support this type of network access. The cost and complexity of supporting a network of distributed, full-function PCs is growing when machine upgrades are required to support new application software and operating systems and the education of the users to use them. The distribution and change management of software on a large network of PCs is also a major cause of problems and expense. The limited function and low cost of the Internet PC is thought to be one way of reducing the cost of the overall systems and avoiding change and upgrade problems. This is more interesting to large corporations that are actively pursuing the implementation of a corporate Intranet.

INTERNET FIREWALL

A firewall, in firefighting terms, is a wall of brush that has been constructed to stop the spread of a fire. A network firewall performs the same basic function by attempting to isolate and prevent security problems. The objective is to protect trusted networks from those that cannot be trusted. All traffic between the two networks is forced to pass through the firewall, where it can be analyzed. Unauthorized traffic can be automatically rejected, and even traffic between authorized network locations can be examined for problems. Not only incoming traffic, but also outgoing traffic, may be subject to control. Firewalls may also ensure that information about the trusted network, an address list for example, which may be useful to an attacker, is not disclosed to the untrusted network. By far the most common use of firewalls is to protect trusted internal networks from problems when connecting to the Internet.

Our discussion on firewalls will provide an overview of the basic concepts, issues and terminology of firewalls and Internet services. For a more in-depth examination of this interesting area, we refer the reader to two excellent works on firewalls—Cheswick [Cheswick & Bellovin, 1994] and Chapman [Chapman, 1995].

FIREWALL COMPONENTS

When an organization states that it has a firewall, this can mean a number of things. A firewall is a concept rather than a specific model or product. Firewalls can be constructed, or purchased, in various shapes and sizes. They may be composed of a single networking device, such as a router. Or they may have many devices, including routers and computers, all performing the function of a firewall. We will examine, a little later in this chapter, an architecture that we have deemed a typical firewall. Keep in mind that this is a conceptual look at a typical firewall. It is simply easier to illustrate how a firewall works by separating the functions into discrete components. However, all of the components of this *typical* firewall could be combined in a single black box solution. Let's begin our review of firewalls by examining the components of a firewall, beginning with a filtering router.

FILTERING ROUTER

As we saw in Chapter 7, routers can be used to filter TCP/IP network traffic. They do so based upon two primary factors, the network addresses in the packet and, indirectly using a port number, the type of application referenced. The destination port number typically suggests the application involved, but it's a mistake from a security perspective to equate port with application. Filters may be applied to packets based on both the source and destination network addresses. The type of application requested, as defined by the source and destination port numbers, may also be filtered. The type of protocol (e.g., TCP and UDP) is also a candidate for filtering. Filtering allows the firewall administrator to control the type of packets that pass through the filtering device (which is in most cases a router) to and from the trusted and untrusted networks. Packet filters are usually enabled through access control lists, which define a combination of addresses, ports, and protocols that are to be allowed or denied.

There are limitations in the use of filtering. While a router can limit traffic based on packet header information, it cannot apply any intelligence to the content of the packet information in its decision. For example, a router configured to allow mail to pass will not be able to detect a time bomb within the mail. Second, router access control lists can be somewhat cryptic in their configuration. It is easy for an inexperienced or careless firewall administrator to make a mistake that will inadvertently allow an unauthorized service through the firewall. A final security consideration is that routers should not be configured to provide unnecessary information about the internal network nor accept information about the internal network (e.g., internal routing information) from the Internet. Finally, many TCP/IP-based services open communication on a known port but designate the use of higher numbered ports for later communication. The port numbers are not always predictable, and therefore a range of port numbers must be left open when filtering rules are applied. Stateful packet filtering is a feature of some firewalls that essentially allow a higher port number to be open for the duration of the communication to the client session. When the communication is finished, the higher level port is closed.

SCREENED SUBNET

The system of trenches used on the Western Front in World War I was designed to provide a concept called *defense in-depth.* A series of three trenches was designed, the idea being that the forward forces could fall back to the secondary and reserve trenches if the first trench was breached by the enemy. Trenches were also designed in a zig-zag fashion. Even if the enemy breached a particular portion of a trench, they could not command the entire length of the trench. The first set of trenches provided a perimeter defense of the interior of the front lines.

A screened subnet acts as a *perimeter defense system* between the Internet and the internal network. It further shields the internal network from the Internet. The use of this special subnetwork also allows a special class of computers, which are called bastion hosts, to be introduced. Traffic between these hosts and the internal and external networks can be controlled by routers. Not only can routers limit the nature of the network traffic, but they can force both incoming and outgoing traffic through special computer systems on the screened subnetwork called bastion hosts.

BASTION HOST

A bastion host (a bastion is the projecting, outer part of a fortress from which the defenders could command many different approaches) is any computer system that directly interacts with the untrusted network. Because it will be a primary point of attack for an intruder, it is important that a bastion host be rigidly secured. Bastion hosts are used to collect valid incoming traffic and forward it to appropriate locations on the internal network. In the reverse manner, a bastion host acts as a single collection point for internal traffic destined for the Internet. A bastion host may also be able to accommodate the need for some TCP/IP services to communicate on unknown port numbers by selectively opening the required port for a period of time. They can also provide access, for internal users, to applications or TCP/IP network services on a proxy basis, which allows additional controls to be placed on these applications.

DUAL HOMED HOST

Many computer systems have the ability to use more than one network card. These systems are termed *dual homed hosts* and are capable of moving traffic between the interfaces. In an Internet firewall implementation, one interface is commonly connected to the internal network, and a second is connected to the Internet. The trick is to not automatically pass traffic between the two networks, but rather to force all communication through the dual homed host. A system on the internal network must communicate with an external Internet system, and vice versa, through the dual homed host. No direct communication can occur and all communication may be monitored. On the downside, a dual homed host is more difficult to set up and administer than other types of solutions.

PROXY SERVICE

A proxy, in human terms, is someone who is authorized to act on your behalf. For example, a proxy can be assigned to cast a vote on behalf of a shareholder at a corporation's annual general meeting. Similarly, a firewall proxy service performs actions on behalf of a user who wishes to obtain Internet resources. Proxy service providers are somewhat transparent to the user, who is unaware that an intermediate is acting on their behalf when they access Internet services.

There are two primary advantages to using proxy servers. First, users do not need to login into, or have accounts on, a bastion host. This allows the bastion host to be kept as lean and simple as possible. From a security viewpoint, keeping things as simple as possible is always a good principle. Second, the use of a proxy server allows audit trails of user activity to be kept. One use of an audit trail on a proxy server may be to detect employees who have accessed inappropriate Internet sites, such as those that provide pornography or hate literature. Many proxies also transparently "launder" internal IP addresses, hiding your internal address space behind the address of the bastion host.

Proxy servers are available for many common Internet services, including telnet, FTP, and HTTP. However, there are disadvantages to using proxy services. While most common Internet services have proxy versions available, a particular service you may wish to use may not. Finding support for a particular protocol, for example, SNMP, may also be a problem. In general, however, the use of proxies whenever possible is recommended. We will now examine two different approaches to implementing proxy services—circuit relay and application gateway-based proxies.

CIRCUIT RELAY

A circuit relay is a type of proxy service, usually residing on a bastion host, that acts upon requests from clients and, if valid, forwards the requests to appropriate servers on the Internet. With circuit relays, special software must reside on the client. They usually require special software to be installed and configured on the client. A commonly used package of circuit relay services is SOCKS, which was developed by David and Michelle Koblas. Circuit relays may apply controls on both the source and destination of a request, but do not examine the nature or substance of a request. For example, a user's request to use the transfer utility FTP from their workstation to an Internet server can be controlled. But the files that are transmitted using FTP are not examined. A user may be transferring unauthorized material, but a circuit relay proxy has no method of controlling this activity. To apply intelligent controls based on the content of the communication, an application gateway proxy is required.

APPLICATION GATEWAY

An application gateway proxy has not only the ability to control connections, but can examine the very nature of the connection. Application gateways pass a user's request to an actual application service, where decision criteria can be applied by the application to the request. A rather uncommon, but needed, use of this type of proxy involves control of electronic mail. Mail messages may contain Trojan horse programs, viruses, or other unwanted material. Although the technology to perform this role is still being refined, an application gateway proxy can intercept all mail messages. The messages can be opened and the contents examined for illicit material. Application gateways also permit a much finer granularity in the use of audit trails. An FTP connection, if implemented through an application gateway, could log every keystroke of a user's connection.

A TYPICAL FIREWALL

Now let's look at a *typical* architecture for firewalls (remembering there is really no such thing as a typical firewall). The architecture involves the use of a pair of routers and two computer systems. One of the routers, called the external router, connects to the Internet using a wide area network (WAN) interface. The second router controls the connection to the internal network. On a screened subnetwork, connected to both routers, are a couple of systems. The first, called the dual-homed bastion host, is used to filter and process incoming network traffic. The second host is used to perform selected Internet services such as electronic mail, NTP, and DNS.

Figure 14.1 shows the architecture of our typical firewall.

The external router provides the initial connection to the Internet. It is used to filter all unauthorized traffic between the bastion hosts and the Internet. All incoming traffic is directed for processing on the bastion host, and all out-going external traffic must also flow from the bastion host. The internal router limits both the nature and origin of traffic from inside the internal network. It only forwards traffic destined to the bastion host or Internet service host, and only allows inbound traffic from these systems.

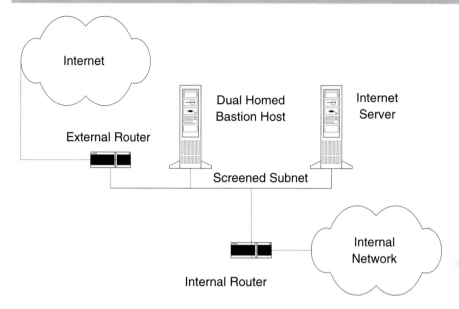

Figure 14.1 A typical Internet firewall

Network traffic is thus forced to selected destinations where it can be better controlled. [Arguably, the subnet shown in Figure 14.1 is not a "screened subnet." It would require another router to control access to its hosts to be officially regarded as a "screened subnet," but most people would regard the firewall as sufficient.]

Both routers not only limit traffic based upon the source and destination of the traffic, but also according to the *type* of the traffic based upon the TCP/IP source and destination ports. Incoming traffic is commonly limited to electronic mail, the Internet News service, the Domain Name System, and the Network Time Protocol services. All of these are directed to the Internet server where they are processed before being forwarded to any internal systems. The internal router ensures that only these services will be allowed and that they must have come through our bastion host. The bastion host may also offer a number of *proxy* Internet services, such as Telnet and FTP. It is common for HTTP services to be offered on a system outside of the firewall (if the firewall does not adequately support incoming HTTP traffic). As mentioned previously, proxy servers perform services on behalf of valid users and do not require that the user actually login to the gateway system.

The firewall architecture is a "belt and suspenders" approach to ensuring that the organization's "pants do not fall down" while providing access to Internet services for employees. If access is gained to the incoming host from the Internet, the internal router will stand in the way of access to the internal network. Similarly, the external router may block unauthorized conversations between the internal and external networks. In this architecture, the failure of one of the components of the firewall system will not result in the compromise of the entire system.

VIRTUAL PRIVATE NETWORKS

The use of encryption to protect traffic between firewalls has created a concept called the virtual private network (VPN). If two corporate networks need to be connected over an untrusted network such as the Internet, traffic between the two networks should be protected. If both networks are protected by firewalls, the firewalls area logical place to put an encryption mechanism since all traffic must pass through these points. There are a number of firewall vendors that provide VPN capability as part of their product offering.

ATTACKS ON FIREWALLS

For the past five years, the Internet community has been witness to an ever increasing number of attacks on its networking connections. These attacks have used a variety of techniques to compromise firewall systems and gain entry into the internal networks of organizations. Proper configuration of the routers and bastion hosts is critical.

A firewall router examining external packets, for example, must be able to prevent the entry of any IP packet that claims to be from the internal network. It should also never accept routing information from an outsider to its own internal network and should not allow the routing of return packets by a route given by an outsider. Any packets received across the network claiming to be from the loopback address should be rejected. You still want to be able to use the loopback interface. Configuration of the router is obviously a sensitive security issue and should be performed on the router console. The router must never accept either control or routing information from the Internet. It should never allow itself to be told by an outsider how to route packets to the internal network. It should also reveal as little as possible about the internal network it is attempting to protect.

Similarly, bastion hosts must reveal as little as possible about the internal network. The configuration of the Domain Name System, in particular, must be such that information about the internal network is not revealed to outsiders. Bastion hosts should have a small number of user accounts. If practical, direct login and FTP access should be limited to the system console. Each bastion host should be stripped to a bare minimum. Compilers, editors, debuggers, and any other nonessential tools that may provide assistance to an attacker should be disabled or removed. Unused networking services and features, such as UUCP and IP forwarding, must be removed or disabled. Software to monitor security controls, as seen in Chapter 12, should be deployed. Using integrity checking programs on a regular basis to detect any changes to the bastion hosts is strongly recommended. All relevant security-related patches should be applied in a timely manner.

To Build or Buy?

Constructing a firewall that can withstand repeated attacks from the Internet is simply not an activity you should leave to amateurs. We have personally witnessed attempts to access systems attached to the Internet within a half hour of their connection. There are individuals, equipped with autodiscovery network tools, who will see your firewall and attempt to access it. The simple truth is that building and securing a firewall for an organization is a complex task. It is also one that should not be approached with a "learn-as-you-go" attitude. Senior management in most organizations could lose its sense of humor should the firewall be breached.

We strongly recommend that unless your organization has strong technical expertise in this area, a vendor or third-party supplier should be employed to construct and implement the firewall. There are simply too many things to learn to entrust this responsibility to novices. But this does not abdicate you of responsibility in this area. Whether an organization purchases a firewall or has it constructed by a consultant, the organization should endeavor to learn as much as possible about this technology. The responsibility for the operation and security of the firewall will remain long after the vendor or consultant has left.

Finally, firewall technology is continuing to develop, and it is important that an organization stay abreast of all recent developments. It is to be expected that increasing client demands will lead to new security exposures. New firewall technologies will undoubtedly be introduced to counter exposures and address new requirements.

We will now move away from our discussion on the technology of the Internet and introduce the need for standards governing the use of the Internet by employees.

Internet Acceptable Use Policy

There are a number of questions that should be addressed concerning the appropriate use of the Internet by employees. Do employees understand their responsibilities concerning the use of the corporate Internet connection? Does the employee understand that electronic mail, if not encrypted, can be intercepted, tampered with, and forged? The spoofing of an email address is one way of using a social engineering attack to obtain unauthorized information. What if the employee uses the corporate Internet connection for personal business use, or makes statements to an Internet newsgroup using the corporate email address that are damaging or offending to the corporation? What is the corporate response to an employee who accesses racist or pornographic material?

Employees must understand that they appear to represent the organization to the public when they access the Internet using corporate resources. They are trusted to perform in an ethical manner, and the organization will not sanction an abuse of this trust. These are questions that management will need to address, preferably in advance of any situation. An effective way of addressing this need is with the implementation of an Internet acceptable use policy. This policy would address the acceptable behaviors and responsibilities of the employees when using the corporate resources to access the Internet.

CONCLUSIONS

With proper technology, employee education, and a clear policy endorsed by management, the use of the Internet can bring many benefits. Failure to develop such a policy can expose an organization to many problems. Expect a great deal of improvement in the security of Internet services in the years to come. Security is one of the biggest issues in computing today and is attracting a great deal of attention. Regardless of future develeopments, corporate use of the Internet must be carefully planned. Clear objectives should be defined concerning what benefits are expected and what facilities and services are required. But don't forget that after the technology issues are solved, the people issues will remain.

CHAPTER 15

CRYPTOGRAPHY

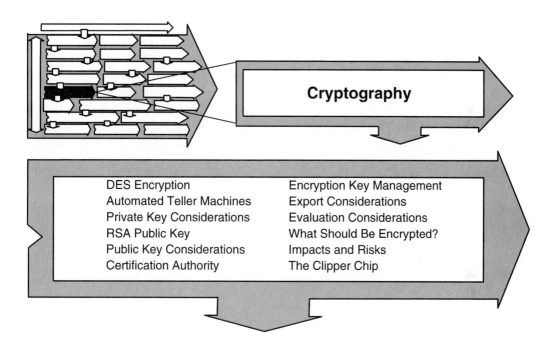

Cryptography

DES Encryption	Encryption Key Management
Automated Teller Machines	Export Considerations
Private Key Considerations	Evaluation Considerations
RSA Public Key	What Should Be Encrypted?
Public Key Considerations	Impacts and Risks
Certification Authority	The Clipper Chip

Ever since man started communicating with one another, there has been a need to keep secrets. Cryptography is defined as the principles, means, and methods for rendering information unintelligible, and for restoring the encrypted information back into intelligible form. In other words, cryptography is the science of writing in secret. Examples of cryptography have been discovered in the writings of Egyptians over 4,000 years ago. The ancient Greek, Chinese, and Roman civilizations used surprisingly advanced cryptography techniques. The use of cryptography, and the analysis of cryptography (cryptoanalysis), flourished in the Arab world during the Middle Ages. While lovers and theologians have long made use of secret messages, the overwhelming use of secret writing has historically been in diplomacy and the military.

239

A contributing factor in the intervention of the United States in World War I was the interception, and partial decryption, of a telegram by British military intelligence. The telegram, referred to as the Zimmerman telegram (Arthur Zimmerman was the German foreign secretary), revealed secret negotiations between Germany and Mexico. In return for naval bases in Mexico, Germany promised the return of American territory after the successful completion of the war.

World War II recorded an increased use of cryptographic and cryptoanalysis techniques. In the late 1930s, Polish military intelligence operatives reproduced a German cryptographic machine called the Enigma. After the outbreak of the war, the machine was passed on to Poland's French and British allies. The Enigma machine resembled a typewriter, and used a set of encrypting wheels called rotors. Advanced versions of the machine, using additional rotors, were thought to be unbreakable but British military intelligence was able to break the encryption scheme. From 1940 onward, an increasing amount of German naval and military intelligence was available to the Allies.

U.S. military intelligence played a significant role in the pivotal Battle of Midway in June 1942. Under a secret project called PURPLE, the decryption of Japanese communications (called MAGIC) forewarned the U.S. Navy of Japanese intentions to attack Midway Island. This knowledge allowed the U.S. Navy to surprise Admiral Yamamoto's fleet. The American victory was a turning point in World War II.

The encryption of data is generally considered to be the best method of providing confidentiality for data storage and transmission. Encryption is the transformation of data using an algorithm, from one form to another utilizing one or more encryption keys during the transformation process. The resulting encrypted data that is stored or transmitted is meaningless without using the correct key to decrypt the data. Encryption should be implemented whenever data that must be kept secret is sent over an untrusted network.

Encryption should be applied to data in two general cases. It should be used when secure storage and transmission of information that is considered secret or highly confidential is required. The encryption would be applied to a slice of the transaction message and not align on data field boundaries. On the one hand, the data needs to be protected; on the other, the transaction needs to be protected.

There are two leading approaches to encryption: private key and public key. The private key approach utilizes a shared secret or private key for both encryption and decryption. The public key approach uses a secret or private key for decryption and a different, mathematically paired public key for encryption. Each approach has benefits depending on the specific requirements and implementations.

PRIVATE KEY ENCRYPTION

Private key encryption utilizes a shared secret key between one or more parties. The possession of the key is used to authenticate one party to the other. A common use of private key technology is for the authentication of user passwords. An encrypted version of a user's password is stored on the computer. The user supplies a user ID and the associated password at login time. The password is encrypted, and if the password matches the stored key for that user ID, the user has been authenticated.

Private key technologies are also used to encrypt data. The key is stored in the encrypted file and must be provided to decrypt the data. The downside to private key encryption is that the key is shared among two parties, the user and the computer. Session keys, which are generated by a computing process, can be used for secure communications using encryption without the user's participation or knowledge. These can be stored in memory. The keys for the encryption of data that is stored in encrypted format are kept by the user and not by the computer system.

DES ENCRYPTION

The most common private key encryption standard that is used is the Data Encryption Standard (DES) developed by IBM in the early 1970s. It is the de facto industry standard for cryptography systems and is the world's most commonly used encryption mechanism. This private key system is widely deployed in financial networks including automated teller machines and point-of-sale networks. It was adopted as a Federal Information Processing Standard (FIPS PUB 46) in 1977 and as an American National Standard (ANSI X3.92) in 1981. Further clarification on the modes of use of the algorithm is contained in ANSI standard X3.106. The specific application of encryption for a personal identification number (PIN) is addressed in ANSI X9.8 and International Standards Organization (ISO) 9564. The DES algorithm uses a 56-bit private key (plus 8 bits for key integrity checking) and operates on 64-bit blocks of data.

Figure 15.1 illustrates the private key-based encryption process. The client uses a private key and an encryption algorithm to transform a message into something that is not intelligible. The server uses the same private key and the same encryption algorithm to reverse the process and recon-

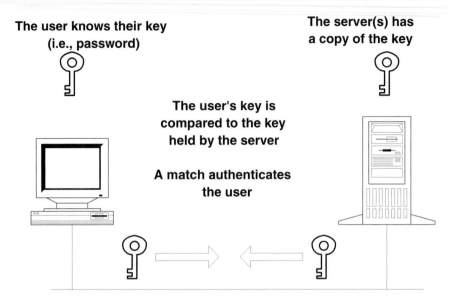

**The user knows their key
(i.e., password)**

**The server(s) has
a copy of the key**

**The user's key is
compared to the key
held by the server**

**A match authenticates
the user**

Figure 15.1 Private key encryption

struct the intelligible message. The security in this process depends on keeping the private key secret.

The encryption process can be executed using either a software or hardware process. Several vendors supply encryption products that can be operated on many different platforms. Specialized hardware is also available that is specifically designed to execute the encryption algorithm. A few products will supply the DES encryption capability contained on a Smart card or PCMCIA card. In this manner the algorithm and encryption keys remain on the card and can be transported from place to place. A hardware solution is attractive when speed is important or the required processing power for a software solution is not readily available.

The DES encryption algorithm has yet to be successfully broken, at least to our knowledge. The increase in available computing power, however, may provide the capability to break the algorithm in the future. It has been estimated that a computer capable of one DES encryption per second would take over 2,000 years to break one key. However, DES is showing its age. Theoretical studies have demonstrated that DES may be vulnerable. The ability to break the algorithm is based on the size of the encryption key. The utilization of Triple-DES, using the DES algorithm three times with two keys, will extend the life of the algorithm.

AUTOMATED TELLER MACHINES

The majority of automated teller machines (ATMs) that you use to obtain cash and perhaps deposit money into your bank account utilize the DES encryption algorithm to supply the required transaction confidentiality. Parts of the transaction are actually encrypted twice using two different keys, creating confidential information that has yet to be broken. The confidentiality of an ATM transaction becomes more interesting when it has to cross network boundaries. Figure 15.2 represents a typical ATM transaction.

There are two parts of a typical ATM transaction that are considered to be highly confidential. The first is the personal identification number (PIN) the user supplies while using the ATM; the other is the specifics of the transaction itself. The bank card that is inserted into the machine to initiate the transaction provides the required identification. The PIN number the user enters during the transaction provides the basis for authentication. The PIN is encrypted using a key specifically used for PIN, and is inserted into the transaction message.

Parts of this message are then encrypted using a key specifically used for secure transmission of the message. In this manner, the PIN is actually doubly encrypted. When the message reaches the host system, the message is decrypted using the transmission key. If the message has to cross network boundaries, it is decrypted with the originating network transmission key and encrypted with the target network transmission key. This process is generally executed using special function hardware to offload the host from this processing burden as well as providing a secure, tamperproof encryption capability. All of this processing takes place before you get your money from the ATM.

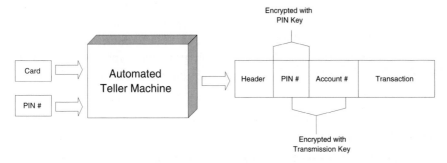

Figure 15.2 ATM transaction

Private Key Considerations

The use of the private key DES algorithm is well entrenched in the financial world. Virtually all of the automated teller machines use DES to protect the data that is transmitted from the machine to the processing centers. The same key is used for both encryption and decryption and must be kept safe from disclosure. A key that is discovered may create a large exposure among all of the locations that utilize the same key. The storage and use of the key must be done in a secure manner.

Key management is a concern with DES encryption because the encryption and decryption keys must be known to both ends of the process. A secure method of changing and storing the keys must be utilized. Computer power is required to execute the encryption process. The larger the amount of data that requires encryption or decryption, the larger the amount of processing power that will be required. The private key approach is well suited to situations where one location requires secure interaction with relatively few other applications or users. The management of the encryption keys can be accomplished in a secure manner and confidentiality of the keys maintained.

PUBLIC KEY ENCRYPTION

A significant event in the history of cryptography occurred in May 1975, with the discovery of public key techniques by Whitfield Diffie and Martin Hellman. Public key encryption, which is also known as asymmetric encryption, uses two separate but mathematically connected keys. Every user has a pair of keys, one of which is kept strictly confidential (the private key) and another that is shared among other users or computers (the public key). The two keys are mathematically related, and both are used in the cryptography process. A message encrypted with the public key can only be decrypted using the private key. The advantage of this method over secret key technology is that the private key is never shared with the other principals. Another benefit of public key technology is that it may be used for the creation of digital signatures. A digital signature is used to verify both the sender and contents of an electronic message.

RSA Public Key

RSA (from Ronald Rivest, Adi Shamir, and Leonard Adleman) is a public key algorithm, based on the algorithm originally developed by Diffie-Hellman. This system uses two related, complementary keys, one of which is kept secret for encryption with the other one publicly available and used for decryption. Only the private key is known for the encryption process and must be kept secret. The use of the RSA algorithm is rapidly growing, particularly in the area of electronic messaging and electronic mail. The downside to this process is that encryption with RSA takes significantly more computer power and is therefore slower than DES.

While the size of the DES encryption key has been fixed at 64 bits, the size of the RSA based key can be variable. The RSA algorithm can use a much longer key than DES (512 bits is common). Because of this, RSA is regarded as being stronger than DES. Even so, the 429 bit (RSA 129) key was broken in April 1994 by a team of hundreds of researchers using many hours of computing time.

The RSA technology can also be used to provide a digital signature for document authentication. A message digest is produced using a hashing function performed on the document which is then encrypted with the private key. This digest is known as the digital signature which is attached to the message. The decryption of the digital signature using the public key and processing with the same hashing function should produce the same result as the message digest. An alternate public key encryption system was proposed in 1985 by ElGamal which built upon the RSA system. This system is being used for authentication and forms the basis of the proposed U.S. Digital Signature Standard (DSS). Figure 15.3 describes the public key encryption process.

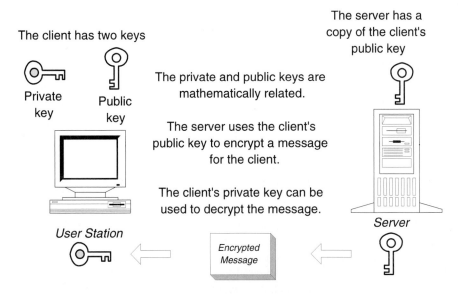

The client has two keys

Private key   Public key

The private and public keys are mathematically related.

The server uses the client's public key to encrypt a message for the client.

The client's private key can be used to decrypt the message.

The server has a copy of the client's public key

User Station

Server

Encrypted Message

Figure 15.3 Public key encryption

In the Figure 15.3 the client has two encryption keys, public and private. The public key is also known to the server. A message that is sent to the client is encrypted using the client's public key. The client then uses the private key to decrypt the message. Using this method, only the client with the private key can successfully decrypt this message.

Secure communications between two parties can be accomplished using an exchange of public keys. For example if Beth wants to send a secure message to Ted and make sure that only Ted can read it, she will encrypt the message using Ted's public key. Only Ted, using his private key, can decrypt the message. Ted can respond to Beth by encrypting the response with Beth's public key which Beth will then decrypt using her private key. If Beth wants anyone to read the message, she will encrypt it with her private key, and anyone who knows Beth's public key can decrypt the message. If Beth wants to prove that only she can have sent a message, she will use her own private key to create a digital signature for the message which will be decrypted by Ted, using Beth's public key. It can be a little confusing about whose key to use. Care must be taken to make sure the security is maintained in the proper direction.

CONSIDERATIONS OF PUBLIC KEY

The public key encryption algorithms are much more compute intensive than the private key algorithms. The amount of computing power required is based on the size of the encryption key utilized. The larger the key, the less likely it can be broken, but the more processing power is required for the encryption and decryption process. Key management will be an issue if a large number of users require individual keys. Each user location must maintain or have access to a directory of the public keys for the users or applications with which they interact. The public key approach is suited to situations where a user requires secure interaction with several other applications or users. This would be defined as a many to many relationship of users to applications. The public key algorithms generally include a digital signature capability that can be used for nonrepudiation.

The strength of most encryption mechanisms is based upon two factors—the integrity of the algorithm and the length of the key used. Most encryption mechanisms, such as RSA and DES, support different versions based upon the key length used in the particular implementation. RSA 129, for example, uses a 129-digit (or a 429-bit) key length. DES has an implementation, called weak DES, which has not been subject to standard U.S. export restrictions because it uses a shorter-length key.

CERTIFICATION AUTHORITY

The management of the public keys for hundreds of users can be a significant problem. How can every user know every other user or server with whom they might communicate with? One solution to this problem is the use of certificates managed by a certification authority. A certificate is a signed message specifying a name and a public key. A certification authority is a secure repository of these certificates. A certificate is a data record that typically contains the user's public key, the type of encryption algorithm used, the name of whose certificate it is, the period of time the certificate is valid, who issued the certificate, and a digital signature to verify the validity of the certificate.

If a user wants to send a message to another user or server using public key encryption and they do not know the public key of their intended destination, they can apply to the certification authority to obtain this key. The user must first know the public key of the certification authority and use it to recover the public key of the user served by that certification authority. The certificate authority can also be used to verify a user's authentication credentials and may be required to generate authentication certificates for use by the users for other network applications and services.

The certification authority is charged with the responsibility of protecting and managing the certificates including the creation, expiration, and revocation. The predominate standard for certificates and the certification authority process is Open System Interconnect (OSI) standard, X.509. The X.509 authentication framework is a widely accepted standard within the computing industry, not only OSI networks. This standard defines the structure of certificates, the protocol for managing the certificates, and the methods that can be used to provide authentication, including digital signatures.

One major question is: Who will provide the certification authority? Many certification authorities may exist, each covering a different collection of users. One certification authority may apply to another for certificates on behalf of a user. The Internet Request for Comment (RFC) 1422 contains a recommendation on the organization and hierarchy of certification authorities that should be followed. It would seem natural that banks, the post office, and even credit card processors will be vying for the opportunity to operate certification authorities. Telephone companies are starting to announce their positioning for providing network certification authority services.

ENCRYPTION ISSUES

The management of the keys required for the encryption algorithms is one of the complex issues to be addressed when selecting encryption technology. The use of a private key algorithm requires that the same key be secure-ly used and stored at all of the locations that require messages or data to be encrypted or decrypted. Any changes to the private key need to be imple-mented simultaneously and in a secure manner in all of these locations to maintain the required security of the data. The public key approach requires that individual key pairs be selected and implemented for all of the users of the system. This may result in the requirement for a large number of keys to be generated, assigned, and utilized. The basic problem with public key encryption is the proliferation of the keys. The primary problem with pri-vate key encryption is that knowledge of the private key is required.

ENCRYPTION KEY MANAGEMENT

The management of encryption keys requires that the several specific issues of key management be addressed. Key generation and registration is the ability to bind a key to its intended use. The problem is essentially how to associate the key to a user. Key distribution addresses the secure delivery of the encryption keys to all of the locations where encryption takes place. Key activation/deactivation is the ability to enable or disable keys. Keys may be changed in a specific interval- or time-dependent process. Specific keys may only be used for the secure distribution of changed encryption keys. Key update or replacement is the organized change from one encryp-tion key to another. Key revocation or termination is the ability to mark an encryption key as invalid. This may be required in the case of a suspected compromise of an existing key.

A standard has been defined under the American National Standards Institute (ANSI) to manage the key distribution process in the financial sec-tor. The Financial Institution Key Management (Wholesale) standard, ANSI X9.17, was defined in 1985. Multiple layers of keys are required to provide the secure change of encryption keys. The X9.17 standard defines a proto-col for establishing new keys and replacing existing ones.

Another key management issue becomes important when considering the requirement for key escrow. That is the requirement to hold an encryp-tion key in escrow in case it is needed for extraordinary purposes. This may be important in an instance when an employee, who has encrypted corpo-rate data, leaves, and takes the key. Access to this data will not be possible without access to the encryption key. A provision for holding a key in escrow may address this problem. On the other hand, a policy that requires the employee to keep encryption keys secret is also required. The strongest locked door is useless if the key is found hanging on a hook beside the door.

EXPORT CONSIDERATIONS

The encryption technology that is available from the United States is classified as munitions. It is restricted for export outside of North America unless a proper export license can be obtained. The granting of the license is generally dependent on what the encryption algorithm will be utilized for and against what type of data. If the encryption requirement is tied to specific data in a contained environment, the license may be easier to obtain than if the implementation will be available for generalized encryption over nonspecific data. The export license application can take several months from application submission to approval. There are some exemptions to the export restriction for financial institutions.

An export license may be easier to obtain if the application that will execute the encryption algorithm uses the algorithm for predefined functions against predefined data. The export license is much more difficult to obtain if generalized technology used to develop an encryption capability is exported instead of the application. Recent developments have indicated that there are copyright concerns over the distribution and use of some public key technologies. Users of contributed encryption mechanisms, as with any contributed software, should check for copyright or governmental restrictions on its use.

EVALUATION CONSIDERATIONS

There are differing performance impacts on computing resources depending on the encryption algorithms selected. The public key algorithms generally require more processing resources than private key algorithms. The utilization of resources is also dependent on the chosen size of the encryption keys for public key encryption. The larger the number of bits in the encryption key, the more secure the encrypted message is, but at an increasing resource utilization expense. The strength of the encryption algorithm is also important and must be considered along with the size of the encryption key.

Access to support for the encryption technology should be available. The ease of use for key generation and assignment will be a factor. The availability of the required key management processes will be another consideration. Key management must itself be able to be handled in a secure manner. The impact on integration of the encryption technology with existing applications and processes should be a consideration. A hardware approach to encryption would be more costly than a software approach in terms of capital expense but may avoid a performance problem. A hardware solution should only be contemplated if a solution is required that is completely outside of the application system.

WHAT SHOULD BE ENCRYPTED?

As mentioned previously, encryption should be applied for two different reasons. The first purpose of encryption is to provide confidentiality for the storage and transmission of authentication or authorization components such as passwords, personal identification numbers (PINs), and any message authentication tokens. The second purpose is for confidentiality of network transmissions.

The variation between a minimum or recommended implementation of encryption services will differ in the amount of information that is encrypted and not on the encryption technology. Encryption should always be used for the secure storage and transmission of logon passwords or other information used for authentication or authorization. It should be used for the secure storage and transmission of customer assigned information such as PINs. Any message authentication codes or digital signatures should be encrypted when included in a transmitted message.

Portions of messages transmitted on a network, especially an untrusted network, should be encrypted. The encrypted data should not be limited to transaction field boundaries and should include portions of fields that are subject to change on every message. This will make it very difficult to predict or replay values from the message. For example, bytes 11 through 27 of every message should be encrypted. This will prevent the ability to use a replay of an intercepted message. Any information that is classified as highly confidential should be encrypted when stored or transmitted.

IMPACT AND RISKS

The impact of the implementation of encryption will be most noticeable on the processing resources required to support the encryption algorithms. The algorithm will require CPU cycles to complete the encryption process. The larger the size or number of the data fields where encryption is required, the larger the impact on the CPU resources required to support the encryption. The larger the size of the public key will also increase the processing cycles consumed.

The major risk with the private key encryption approach is the potential for exposure of the encryption key. Secure storage of the encryption keys is required. The exposure can be limited if separate encryption keys are used for each user, but this compounds the key management problem. The impact of the management of the required encryption keys will depend on the number and the required location of the keys. Care must be taken to ensure that the correct encryption key is used.

An alternate approach to providing encryption that does not have an impact on system processing requirements is with the use of hardware encryption devices. The encryption will take place completely outside of the application by specific hardware devices. This approach will secure every transaction between a client and a server if the encryption devices are used in all of the locations. This, however, can introduce significant expense depending on the number of locations and the requirement for support and backup units.

THE CLIPPER CHIP

A great deal of controversy and debate has surrounded a proposal by the Clinton administration for a hardware encryption standard. The initiative, which proposes a standard for the digital encryption of messages, is based on an encryption computer chip design called Clipper and an encryption algorithm called Skipjack. The suggested uses of the Clipper chip include its incorporation in computer hardware and wireless digital communications.

Most of the controversy surrounding the chip involves a security backdoor to the chip, which would allow the U.S. government access to its secrets. The backdoor is called the LEAF (Law Enforcement Access Field), whose access requires a series of keys, which would be held by agencies of the U.S. government. The concerns surrounding the Clipper chip include the cost and performance of the chip, fears over invasion of privacy, acceptance of its use outside of the United States, and the subsequent impact on the U.S. computer manufacturing industry and the strength of the LEAF access control mechanism. Suspected weaknesses in the LEAF Escrowed Encryption Standard (EES) [NIST94] algorithm was described in a June 1994 abstract titled "Protocol Failure in the Escrowed Encryption Standard" by Dr. Matt Blaze of AT&T Bell Labs.

DIGITAL SIGNATURE

A digital signature is a method of attesting to the origin and contents of an electronic document. Digital signatures are based on the idea that if the entire contents of a document is used as input to an encryption algorithm, then even the smallest changes to the original document will cause significant changes to the encryption output and can be easily detected. The encryption mechanism used for documents is termed a hash algorithm, and the output is called the message digest. What if the hash algorithm also uses an encryption key known only to the sender? The result would be a document where the smallest change to the document is detectable and the originator can be uniquely identified.

The message digest is created with the sender's private key, which produces a unique digital signature for the original document. The recipient is given the sender's public key, which is used to verify the digital signature on the document in a process termed signature verification. Figure 15.4 illustrates the use of public key encryption to generate a message digest. This message digest is re-created by the recipient and compared to the digest attached to the message. If they both agreed, then the message came from the sender and has not been altered.

The creation of a message digest whose key is known only to the sender is termed a digital signature. An original copy of the message, along with the message digest, is sent to the recipient of the document. The recipient uses the original document and a similar hash algorithm to create a second message digest. The original message digest is compared to the re-created message digest, and even the smallest change to the signature or data can be detected. Digital signatures are said to provide irrevocable evidence as to the contents and originator of a message. Figure 15.4 outlines the process of protecting a message using a digital signature.

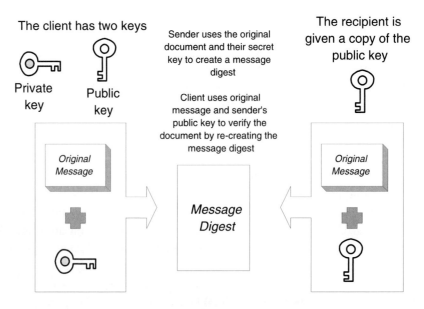

Figure 15.4 Digital signature process

If the original message must be kept private, then it may be encrypted with a secret key unique to the message. The secret key is then encrypted using the recipient's public key, and may be retrieved by the recipient using their private key. This method seems complex, so why not just encrypt and decrypt the entire message using the public key? The secret key method, such as DES encryption, is used because encrypting and decrypting the document using a public key is orders of magnitude slower than using a secret key.

Recently, the Department of Commerce's National Institute of Standards and Technology released FIPS Standard 186. This document proposed a new standard for digital signatures, called the Digital Signature Standard (DSS). The DSS uses a new hash algorithm, called the Digital Signature Algorithm (DSA).

The primary uses for digital signatures are for electronic mail, document submission, Electronic commerce over a public network, and electronic data interchange (EDI). Many other uses can be anticipated. Basically, we foresee the technique being used by any application that requires irrevocable authentication of information. This can happen as long as you trust the privacy of the private key. What does it take to convince a court of law?

SUMMARY

Encryption is one of the best ways to provide confidentiality in a computing system. It can also be used as another line of defense if unauthorized access is gained to computer systems and data. Little use of the data can be made if it is encrypted. Encryption is often specified as a requirement in a security solution, perhaps even before the requirements for confidentiality are clearly understood. A thorough understanding of your requirements is recommended before selecting a particular encryption technology. Both the private key and public key approach have their place in providing confidentiality. Public key technology has been recently receiving most of the attention since it provides the capability of supporting many-to-many relationships without adding significant management overhead. Remember that confidentiality is the requirement and encryption is the solution.

Encryption provides a further level of safeguarding corporate information assets beyond the operating system and network controls. With the increased availability of both commercial and contributed solutions, in particular public key technologies, the use of encryption to enhance security will increase. If the problem of key management can be more easily addressed, encryption technology should provide a strong weapon in the war for computing security.

CHAPTER 16

THE DCE ENVIRONMENT

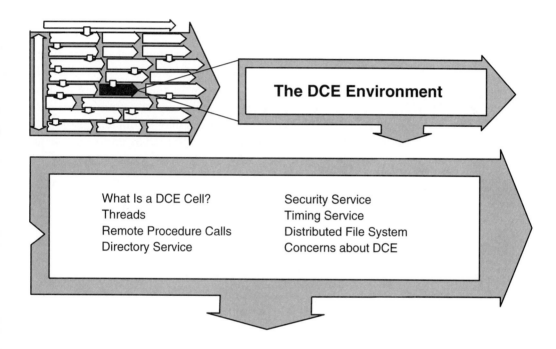

The DCE Environment

What Is a DCE Cell?	Security Service
Threads	Timing Service
Remote Procedure Calls	Distributed File System
Directory Service	Concerns about DCE

In previous chapters, we have discussed the key problems surrounding trust in the distributed environment. Passwords are sent over the LAN in cleartext, which may be intercepted and discovered. Authentication based upon network identity can be easily counterfeited, by changing a network address. There is little or no authentication of application servers to the client, which allows the impersonation of service providers. Encryption of data over a LAN is not provided as a standard feature by most operating systems. Most operating systems and applications have a host-centric approach to authentication, which forces users to remember multiple user IDs and passwords. Finally, it is difficult to segregate security from system administration duties.

WHAT IS DCE ?

These problems have been with us for a number of years. One interesting approach to solving these problems (and others) is the Distributed Computing Environment (DCE) from the Open Software Foundation (OSF). It provides the tools and framework to build secure, distributed applications in a multivendor environment. DCE is currently supported on a number of different hardware platforms, including Bull, SUN, DEC, HP, and IBM. A number of operating systems support DCE, including DOS/Windows, Windows/NT, OS/2, UNIX, VMS, and MVS.

The OSF/DCE environment is comprised of a number of interrelated, yet independent, components or services. The architecture is very flexible, allowing an application developer latitude in the implementation of OSF/DCE. The OSF/DCE environment includes security, timing, directory and distributed file services. Additional services may be implemented in the future. The architectural components of the OSF/DCE environment are shown in Figure 16.1.

OSF DCE provides an important framework of middleware services (between the network, operating system and the application) that bind clients to servers together in a secure manner. The individual components

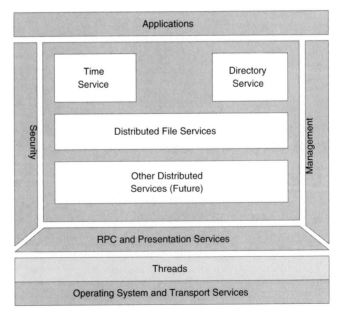

Figure 16.1 Architectural view of OSF/DCE

are all interrelated. For example, the timing service is authenticated to clients using the security service. The timing service provides the security service with a definition of time for the expiry dating of DCE credentials.

DCE services are provided within the confines of an administrative domain called a *DCE cell*. One point about DCE must be understood before we proceed. While it provides a set of interrelated services, not every service is required. For example, a DCE cell may opt not to use the distributed file service. It is all up to the designer of the cell, although use of the security service is considered mandatory. Each individual service may also be implemented in different ways. The point is that there is a great deal of flexibility, which leads to diverse customer DCE applications. There are no strict rules as to how a particular organization should implement DCE. Before we look at the individual DCE services, let's see what comprises a DCE cell.

What Is a DCE cell?

One of the more interesting customer discussions we've had concerned the makeup and composition of a DCE cell. What is a DCE cell? "Just about anything you want it to be" is a flippant answer to the question. A more definitive answer would be that a DCE cell is a group of networked hosts and services sharing a common namespace, security policy, and other aspects of a security domain. A functional DCE cell can be implemented, for demonstration purposes, on a single computer system. DCE cells may therefore be comprised of from one to hundreds of computer systems (or nodes). A typical DCE cell will have hundreds of clients and offer a multitude of services, as shown in Figure 16.2.

Cells are usually defined along organizational or corporate structures. One limitation on the size of a DCE cell is the ability of DCE system administrators to manage the cell. Another is that a DCE cell should be divided, if it crosses WAN links, for performance reasons. The number of nodes in a cell are usually limited by one, or both, of these factors. Limitations on the size of a DCE cell can be expected to lessen as WAN performance and DCE administration tools improve. We will now examine the individual components of DCE, beginning with ability to multitask using a component called threads.

Threads

Threads allow a DCE program to service multiple client requests simultaneously. A service request from a client may be awaiting the release of a resource. DCE threads allows additional requests to be serviced or routine server maintenance activity to occur in the interim.

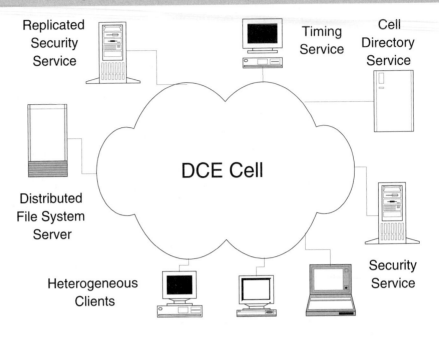

Figure 16.2 A typical DCE cell

A multithreaded program supports several execution contexts of the program. They exist within a single process and are executed until they are terminated. Not only may threads execute simultaneously, but they may also share memory address space, external data, and program variables. Because threads share information with other threads, each thread must be aware of the other threads and not do anything that will adversely affect them. For example, the removal of a thread must not result in the destruction of information used by other "live" threads. A set of library calls that protects the integrity of data used by threads is termed "thread safe."

The most common use of threads is to allow the server to answer a number of incoming requests from different clients simultaneously. The "threaded" approach allows the server to respond to an incoming client request by creating a thread. The client then communicates directly with the newly created thread. The server process returns to its job of listening for new client requests. The client's thread is removed when the client is finished with the request. This is similar to the traditional UNIX daemon that creates a new process in response to a request by a client. However, the creation of a thread is much faster than the creation of a new process.

REMOTE PROCEDURE CALLS

In OSF/DCE, the remote procedure call (RPC) mechanism is the "glue" that binds the environment together. A DCE RPC is essentially a procedure in which the server code is executed in an address space separate from the client's calling routine. While a DCE RPC may be executed solely within a single machine, it is most common for the RPC to occur between a client and server residing on separate machines connected by a network. For this to occur, information must be shared between the client and server. Common data items must be available to both the client and server, and in a multivendor environment, a common definition for data must be agreed upon. As well, networking requirements and unreliable network transport protocols must be dealt with.

The DCE RPC hides the complexities of the network and multivendor environments from the programmer. The DCE RPC runtime library shields the programmer from the following tasks:

- Locating an appropriate server for the client using a process called binding.
- Moving data to be shared on to the network in a process called marshalling.
- Unloading the data at the server in a process called unmarshalling. This process also converts the data to the appropriate server machine format.
- Executing the appropriate server code using a process called entry point vectoring.
- Answering the client request by marshalling the requested information from the server on to the network. The information is then unmarshalled on the client.

The DCE RPC runtime library facilitates these complex operations. The developer needs only to focus on a definition of the client-server interface. The RPC runtime will take care of the actual communication. In DCE terminology, an interface defines the data and operations used by a server. An application or service will typically have a number of interfaces, depending on the types of requests that will be answered.

The first step in creating an interface is to create a universal unique identifier (UUID). The UUID is a 32-character hex number generated using a special utility called *uuidgen*. The machine's LAN hardware address and current time are used to create the UUID, which should result in a unique

UUID for every DCE interface. All DCE interfaces, including those used by the timing and security services, have their own unique UUID.

The interface, common to both clients and their servers, is created using a special language called the Interface Definition Language (IDL). The IDL both contains the UUID number for the interface and defines the input and output data to be marshalled. Local data definitions (for specific client or server configurations) are also provided by a special feature called an attribute configuration file (ACF).

Directory Service

The purpose of the directory service is to assist clients in a DCE cell to find, and connect to, resources. Resources may include application servers, print services, or data files. Use of the directory service is not mandatory. Clients may be connected to the server without going to a directory service, but the alternatives reduce the ease at which a service may change its location without disadvantaging its clients.

The directory service has three major components: the global directory service (GDS), the cell directory service (CDS), and the global directory agent (GDA). Resolution of names outside the local cell is provided by either the GDS or the Internet Domain Name Service (DNS). Based on the X.500 Directory standard, the GDS can determine the location of resources outside of the current cell. The X.500 standard is specified by the CCITT X.500 and ISO 9594 standards. DNS is a widely used global name service, and is currently the de facto standard for locating computers on the Internet.

The CDS stores the names and attributes of resources located in a DCE cell and provides a central lookup facility for these resources. Clients not only use the CDS to find local application servers, but also to locate DCE servers such as the timing and security servers. The CDS facilitates the implementation of redundant services, when multiple copies of a service are required, by allowing each copy to register its location under a single name. Clients may request a service by name and other attributes. They will be directed by the GDS to an appropriate, functioning service provider.

The GDA provides an interface between the CDS and the two name resolution services, DNS and GDS. Figure 16.3 provides an overview of the cell directory service.

Client requests for directory services go to a local agent, called a CDS clerk, which runs on the client computer. The CDS clerk keeps a cache of lookup requests. If the requested information is contained in the cache, the request is fulfilled immediately. If not, the clerk will contact a CDS server.

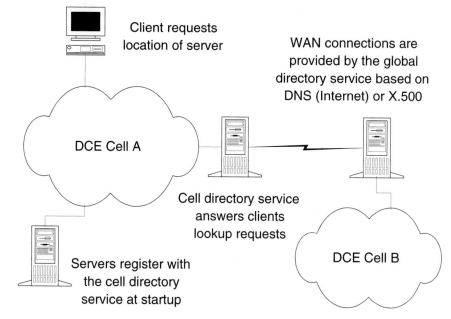

Client requests
location of server

WAN connections are
provided by the global
directory service based on
DNS (Internet) or X.500

DCE Cell A

DCE Cell B

Cell directory service
answers clients
lookup requests

Servers register with
the cell directory
service at startup

Figure 16.3 Overview of the DCE directory services

SECURITY SERVICE

The DCE security service provides an answer to many of the TCP/IP networking issues, such as protection of passwords and spoofing, presented in Chapter 7. DCE assumes that the network is insecure and that any information on it may be subject to unauthorized examination or modification. No trust is placed in the unauthenticated identity of either the client or server. DCE assumes that either the client or the server may be counterfeit.

Essentially, DCE security provides

- A single registry of clients and servers (registry service) per cell.
- The secure authentication of client and server using the Kerberos authentication model (authentication service).
- Message protection options which help ensure the integrity and privacy of data over an untrusted network.
- Access control lists which allow servers to authorize access to their resources.
- Security services and administration are segregated from other cell administration functions.

We will discuss the DCE security service in depth in the next chapter.

TIMING SERVICE

We require an accurate notion of time for many key functions in distributed computing. Computers use time for many critical functions, including the coordination of transactions and maintaining accurate audit trails. But what keeps better time—a $50,000 workstation or a $10 watch? That's correct, it's the $10 watch! The reason computers keep a poor notion of time is that they advance their clocks at irregular rates compared to true time, some faster and some slower. The deviation from true time is termed clock skew. If individual computers keep a poor notion of time, imagine the timing problems if a thousand computers are networked together.

The DCE distributed time service (DTS) provides a solution to this problem based on the ISO 8601 time standard. It allows individual computers to be provided with a common notion of time from DTS servers. Redundancy is built in by allowing the use of multiple DTS servers, which are polled to find a common time interval. The individual DTS servers constantly communicate with one another to synchronize their own clocks.

DTS does not provide each client with an absolute definition of time, but rather seeks to ensure that all clients will have clocks set within a predefined interval. Systems that are deemed to be too slow will have their clock speeded up to move to the norm. A clock too far ahead is never reversed, but rather the clock rate is slowed down until the clock approaches the predefined timing interval.

The definition of time may be from a coordinated universal time (UTC) provider, such as an atomic clock, government source, or a radio station. Alternatively, the Internet Network Time Protocol (NTP) may be used, or a single computer may be selected as the cell's true time. In this case, all computers will skew from true time at the same rate!

DTS authenticates itself to both the security service and the client systems. The reasoning for this is that the security credentials in DCE are time sensitive. If DCE were not required to authenticate itself, a counterfeit time provider could set the system clocks either forward or backward. This would allow them to present outdated credentials as valid or invalidate all existing security credentials.

DISTRIBUTED FILE SYSTEM

The distributed file system (DFS) provides the ability to access and manage data (i.e., files) in a distributed manner, see Figure 16.4. It provides transparent access to distributed files to a user regardless of where the user or requested resource is physically located. DFS is based on a global naming convention. A DFS file is accessed by a single name, using this convention, no matter where in the distributed system it is accessed from. For example, the *example.txt* file in the cell *Polaris* can be referred to as */usr/example.txt* by any DCE client within, or outside of, the *Polaris.canada.hp.com* cell.

DFS makes its service and data highly available by allowing DFS servers and resources to be replicated. Replication allows multiple copies of a file to exist on distributed servers. If the primary server is lost, clients may transparently access the alternate servers for the file. This type of replication is especially useful for files which change infrequently and are accessed by many users. Caching is also used for redundancy. It allows for copies of files to be stored on DFS clients, so that even if a client is temporarily disconnected from the server, it is possible for a user to access a copy of the file. Both the backup and relocation of DFS files can occur without making the files unavailable to users. DFS also has the ability to interact with other types of networked file systems. Hewlett-Packard provides support for the secure use of network file system (NFS) file systems through the secure DFS to NFS gateway.

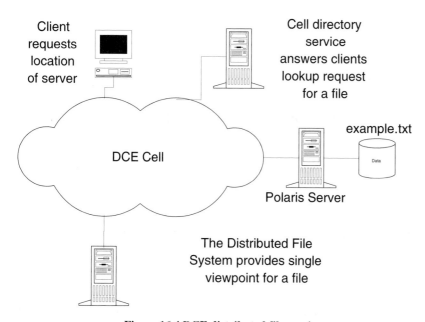

Figure 16.4 DCE distributed file service

CONCERNS ABOUT DCE

We believe that DCE presents a solution to many issues encountered when deploying distributed applications. Support for the DCE environment has increased in recent years, including recent product offerings by the major database vendors. However, the computing community has shown some reluctance to move to DCE computing. There are limitations in DCE which are preventing it from becoming the pervasive middleware technology. The reluctance is based on the following concerns:

- The environment is very complex to program in.
- Some networks may suffer in performance due to increased traffic.
- The current administration tools are command driven. They need to be incorporated with GUI-based network management tools.
- Support for OSF/DCE by the major application vendors is limited.
- The object-oriented standards committees are perceived to have limited support for OSF/DCE.
- There are fears that DCE is not going to gain momentum and become a pervasive technology.

However, while there are legimate concerns about the future of OSF/DCE, there are positive developments as well. Many of the world's largest financial organizations are now deploying applications which use this technology. Time will tell whether or not momentum will build for OSF/DCE and it will become a pervasive technology.

CONCLUSIONS

At the current time, it is impossible to predict the future for OSF/DCE. It is clear that more widespread commitment to DCE is required, particularly from the DOS/Windows and application solution areas. But if DCE is not the solution to the problems addressed, what is? At the current time, the alternative to DCE appears to be to attack the issues in piecemeal fashion, solving each problem with a different, unrelated technology. In the next chapter, we will review the security mechanisms of DCE in depth.

CHAPTER 17

DCE SECURITY CONCEPTS

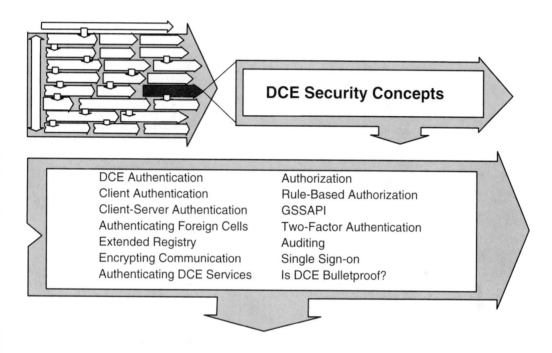

DCE Authentication	Authorization
Client Authentication	Rule-Based Authorization
Client-Server Authentication	GSSAPI
Authenticating Foreign Cells	Two-Factor Authentication
Extended Registry	Auditing
Encrypting Communication	Single Sign-on
Authenticating DCE Services	Is DCE Bulletproof?

One of the central issues in distributed computing today is what should be done with an "untrusted" network? How can we trust security mechanisms when clear-text passwords are transmitted over the LAN? What reliance can be placed in distributed authorization controls when these controls rely on network addresses which are easily counterfeited? The answer to these problems may be to get yourself a big, mean, ugly dog. Perhaps one with three heads!

The authentication mechanisms of DCE are based upon the Kerberos authentication model, which was developed at the Massachusetts Institute of Technology (MIT) in the late 1980s. Besides having a great name, Kerberos presupposes that the network cannot be trusted. Kerberos uses a combination of secret key techniques to allow the mutual authentication of both client and server.

> Kerberos, or Cerberus, if one is a student of Greek rather than Egyptian mythology, was the three-headed dog that guarded the gates of Hades. Cerberus was known to trick humans into Hades with assuming expressions and imaginative use of his tail and ears. Cerberus could be overcome. Hercules bested Kerberos in his 11th, and most difficult, trial.

In this chapter, we will examine the DCE implementation of the Kerberos model (it's an enhanced version) and explore other DCE security-related mechanisms such as access control lists. We have taken some liberties in our discussion of DCE security in order to make it easier for the first-time reader to understand its complexities. We will not be able to examine all of the mechanisms used by DCE in detail. Rather, the intent is to provide a good overview of the concepts DCE uses and to provide a basic level of understanding of how DCE security works.

DCE AUTHENTICATION

DCE authentication has been explicitly designed to provide secure authentication under the following assumptions:

- Network packets are subject to inspection if not encrypted. Packets containing clear-text passwords can be detected and the "secret password" discovered.
- Packets containing authentication information may be captured, examined and replayed in future attacks.
- No reliance can be placed on the network addresses (either the IP or the hardware address on the LAN card).
- Not only do clients require authentication, but servers also need to be authenticated.

The DCE authentication process uses a combination of packet encryption, time-based authentication credentials, and a "trusted third-party" to provide secure authentication. DCE enhances the Kerberos authentication model by incorporating authorization and other security controls not present in Kerberos. In DCE terminology, a principal is anything or anyone whose identity may be proven. A principal may be a user, application program, computer, DCE service, or DCE cell. An authentication credential is an electronic certificate, which when presented, proves the identity of a principal. Passwords and conversation keys are encrypted, but not the actual packet information, when sent over the network. A conversation (or session) key is a system generated random number, which is used to protect communication between parties. Once authenticated, users and servers are given a number of time-sensitive credentials, which are resistant to replay attacks. The DCE security is based upon the Kerberos model, but extends the model by supporting additional security attributes. This allows a service provider to not only check the identity of a client, but also to authorize access based on other attributes. These additional attributes include group identity and other arbitrary attributes. A trusted third-party, the DCE security service, is employed to perform the *mutual* authentication of both the client and server. Every user of the DCE security service, whether they be humans, computers or applications, are termed principals.

An explanation of the mutual authentication used by DCE is the "first date." If two people are interested in discovering more about one another, but are a little shy and apprehensive about how to start, they might arrange an outing with a mutual friend. It's not really a blind date, both people know a little about each other, but use a mutual friend to perform the preliminary introductions. Going to movie or having a dinner are common *venues* for such a meeting. If all goes well, the mutual friend will discretely leave, allowing the two new-found friends to communicate in private.

The DCE security service has three component services—the authentication, privilege, and registry services. It is the job of the authentication service to initially validate the identity of the principal. The authentication service provides a user, upon receipt of a valid password, a certificate called the Ticket Granting Ticket (TGT). The TGT enables the user to make additional requests for tickets from application servers. The privilege service encloses additional security attributes (or privileges) for a principal in an additional credential, called the Extended Privilege Attribute Certificates (EPACs). Applications can examine the EPACs presented by clients and can make decisions to authorize access based upon their contents. The registry service is a repository for information about the principals, groups, and accounts in the DCE cell. It also contains the security policy for the DCE cell. Figure 17.1 illustrates the organization of the DCE security process.

The DCE security service maintains a database of users, servers, and security policy for the entire DCE cell. This collection of security data and its associated interfaces are called the registry service. A key, generated from a user's secret password, is used to identify the user and is maintained by the registry service. Any DCE application, regardless of its location within the DCE cell, can authenticate the credentials of a client.

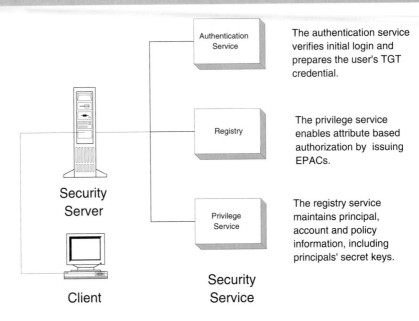

Figure 17.1 An overview of OSF/DCE security

CLIENT AUTHENTICATION

The client uses a DCE utility (most common is *dce_login*) or an operating system login utility that performs a DCE login, to obtain DCE credentials. The login program will contact the cell directory service (CDS) to determine the location of an available security server. Earlier versions of DCE used a (relatively) simpler key exchange mechanism to authenticate users. In OSF RFC 26.0, Joe Pato of Hewlett-Packard discussed a number of concerns about the ability of attackers to use password guessing techniques in the Kerberos model. The problem is that both Kerberos and DCE credentials could be intercepted on the LAN or stolen and subject to password cracking. Mr. Pato suggested techniques that would avoid sending any information encrypted by the user's secret key over the LAN. Called third-party preauthentication, the technique involves introducing a new session key stored on the client machine. The approach used prevents the successful guessing of a user's password from an encrypted credential. Third-party preauthentication has been incorporated in the OSF/DCE 1.1 release.

The client contacts the DCE security service (actually it's local DCE security libraries) on the local machine. The local machine has its own TGT (called the machine TGT) and session keys, obtained when the DCE security service was initiated. The user does not obtain a TGT directly, but rather the local security service will obtain a TGT on the user's behalf. Because the local security service and the security server share common keys, the user's password can be transformed into a secret key. The user password is not transmitted to the security server, but rather a secret key created from the password is exchanged. The local security service also generates conversation keys. These are forwarded to the DCE security service, along with its TGT, and are encrypted with the user's secret key. The entire package is protected by multiple levels of encryption. Because of its design, the traffic is protected from password sniffing or replay attacks.

Figure 17.2 provides an overview of the initial stages of the DCE authentication process.

The security server uses the machine secret key, which it knows, to obtain the additional conversations keys and decrypt the package. If the time stamp is within acceptable limits, the security server will create a TGT for the client. The TGT contains basic information about the client and is sealed (i.e., encrypted) by a key known only to the security server. The security server will also create a client conversation key, to be used by the client for future conversations with the security server. Both the sealed TGT and the client conversation key are placed in a package, which is subsequently

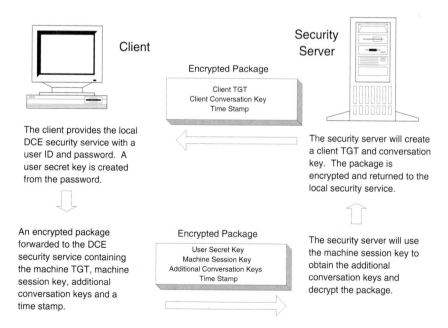

Figure 17.2 Initial authentication stages for the client

encrypted with a conversation key obtained from the local security service. The package, including the sealed client TGT and the conversation key, is then returned to the local machine. The local receives the encrypted package, decrypts it using the conversation key it provided, and stores the client's TGT and conversation key. The benefits of this approach are as follows:

- Only the local security service can unlock the client's TGT and conversation key, because they are encrypted with a conversation key initially provided by the local security services.
- Only a valid security service could provide the TGT package because it was encrypted by the local machine's session key which it obtained from the security service. The client and security server are thus mutually assured of each other's identity.
- The user's password and key need only remain in memory for a very brief instance. This deters attempts to discover passwords or keys on the client's system, by "poking" around in memory.

The TGT has a limited lifetime, configurable by the security administrator, set by default to ten hours. After the ten-hour period, the client must get a new set of credentials by reinitiating the login procedure. The PTGT is usually limited to two hours. While most clients will renew their base credentials by logging in after ten hours, there are methods to have the clients automatically renew these credentials. This technique is especially useful when a client runs long batch jobs.

Application and machine service tickets (as opposed to the client's TGT) are renewed automatically. No intervention is required by a human operator. The use of many conversation keys may seem overly complex, but it does have certain advantages:

- Conversation keys and credentials are relatively short-lived. Not only must a hacker discover the key, but he must do so in a very short period of time.
- There are multiple keys that must be discovered.

It should also be noted that the complexity of the key and credential authentication is handled by the DCE runtime layer, *not* by the application programmer.

The next step is for the client to obtain additional credentials, called the Extended Privilege Attribute Certificate. The EPAC contains more information about the client, such as group membership and site, specific security attributes for the client. The EPAC is an improvement to the original DCE Privilege Attribute Certificate (PAC) mechanism. It is very common in the distributed environment for one server to make a request to a second server on behalf of a client. However, there is a very basic concern which must be addressed to allow this to occur. How can the second server recognize that the request from the first server is on behalf of the client? Joe Pato of Hewlett-Packard's Chelmsford Labs proposed a model for practical extended delegation in OSF RFC 3.0. The proposed solution involved extending the Privilege Attribute Certificate of the server to incorporate the client credentials. The current ACL model was also redesigned to check for the extended PACs (termed EPACs). OSF/DCE incorporated the use of EPACs in the DCE 1.1 release.

The client first forwards a PTGT request to the privilege service. A Privileged Ticket Granting Ticket (PTGT) allows a client to request privilege service tickets from the privilege service. The process of obtaining the initial PTGT and EPAC is similar to the initial authentication request, in that the conversations are protected by an exchange of the client TGT and session keys.

The client does not directly communicate with the services, but obtains the necessary credentials through go-betweens. For an extensive description of the entire process, the reader is directed to the article "The DCE Security Service" by Frederic Gittler and Anne C. Hopkins [Gittler & Hopkins, 1995], published in the Hewlett-Packard Journal.

CLIENT TO SERVER AUTHENTICATION

When a client wishes to contact a server, the client will look up the server in the cell directory service. A new set of conversation keys will be introduced to perform a mutual authentication of the server and client. Before we explore how this works, it's important to understand three concepts.

First, an application server does not necessarily need to perform authenticated RPCs at all. It is up to the application designer to determine the appropriate level of authentication and security required. Second, the server *enforces* a certain minimum standard, but the client may request that stronger security be used. The server will reject the client only if the client fails to meet the minimum standard. The client is free, in essence, to negotiate a higher standard with the server. Third, clients who fail to meet the minimum standards are not automatically rejected. The application server must *explicitly* check the client's request and reject it if it fails to meet the minimum standard. The client must know the minimum requirements of the server in advance as they cannot be obtained directly from the server.

A request by the client begins by declaring the desired level of security. A request is made to the authentication service to obtain a ticket to the desired application. The original EPAC is forwarded to the security service, and it is reencrypted with the application's secret key. This will prove to the application server that the client's EPAC is valid. An exchange of conversation keys is used to protect the process. The complexities (as much as possible) are hidden from the application programmer and user. The application ticket is usually limited by the existing lifetime of the TGT and PTGT.

> There are many similarities between OSF/DCE authentication and international travel controls. The TGT and EPAC are similar to a passport. They are valid for a limited period of time. They employ technologies (the paper, stamp, and seal) which are difficult to forge. Servers may be compared to nations. Some may accept you without a passport (e.g., Canadians traveling to the United States and travel within the EEC). But most international travel requires you to have a valid passport. In addition, a country may require a visa. The visa is valid for a more restrictive period of time than the passport, and usually expires when the passport expires. Visas are comparable to the application tickets, which may be required as additional pieces of identification by an application server.

AUTHENTICATING FOREIGN CELLS

What if a user arrives from a foreign cell (i.e., a cell with a security service different from your own)? Should you treat the user as if they were authenticated by the local security service, or should you accept the credentials at face value because bad guys do not operate DCE cells? DCE essentially allows you to make the call by designating the user as authenticated but foreign. It is up to the application to determine the appropriate treatment of foreign users.

Joe Pato of Hewlett-Packard, in a request for comment (RFC) submitted to OSF (OSF RFC 7.0), also suggested a model for cross cell authentication. It allows a cell administrator to decide which foreign cells can be trusted and which will not. One might trust tickets generated from a cell within your organization, but no one else. These recommendations have been incorporated in the OSF/DCE 1.1 release.

EXTENDED REGISTRY

A criticism of DCE is that it is biased toward UNIX. In OSF RFC 6.0, Joe Pato suggested a more flexible design for the registry service. It allows the use of dynamic attributes, which are more appropriate for a wider range of operating systems and applications. The ideas from this RFC have been incorporated in a feature termed the extended registry attribute (ERA) facility. The ERA facility allows the introduction of new attributes. This makes DCE more attractive to non-UNIX environments and should increase the general acceptance of DCE.

SERVER AUTHENTICATION

In our discussion of how a client is authenticated, we implicitly assumed that the application server has been authenticated. The reason for this trust is that the mutual authentication performed between the client and security service also occurs between the application server and the security service. The authentication of the two parties follows the same method as a client to security service authentication, with important exceptions. Application servers are typically long running and cannot be taken down every eight hours to reinitiate the login process. The servers use alternative methods to renew their credentials and conversation keys prior to expiry time. The application cannot wait for the system administrator to key a password at bootup. The servers secret key password may be stored in a number of places, but it is typically kept in encrypted format in a special file called the *keytab*. The *keytab* file is protected by local file system resources.

ENCRYPTING CLIENT-SERVER COMMUNICATION

DCE supports a number of levels of encryption to protect communication between the client and server. As mentioned earlier, the client can negotiate the level of protection required, as long as it meets or exceeds the level enforced by the server. The protection levels available are shown in Table 17.1.

TABLE 17.1
PROTECTION FOR CLIENT-SERVER COMMUNICATION

Type of Protection	Description
Default	The default level of the DCE cell is used.
None	No protection is used, which defeats the need for Kerberos authentication.
Connect	The identity of the client and server are authenticated at initial connect time.
Call	Each RPC call is encrypted using a conversation key. Individual data packets are not encrypted.
Packet	An encrypted field is attached to each data packet.
Packet integrity	The individual packet has an encrypted checksum to protect against tampering.
Full encryption	Full encryption of all communication between client and server.

The bare minimum level of protection for even the most insecure applications will be the call level. The lower levels of protection are subject to packet tampering. Most applications with concerns about security will use either the packet integrity or full encryption levels. Full encryption is subject to the U.S. State Department restrictions on the export of encryption technologies (see Chapter 15, Cryptography, for further information on the topic). It should also be noted that the full encryption option only encrypts on the data portion of the packet on the LAN. The TCP/IP address and delivery information, including source and destination address, are not encrypted and may be viewed using packet-sniffing techniques. The actual data, however, is encrypted and cannot be understood. Once a level of protection for communication is determined, DCE handles the exchange of session keys, the encryption of data, and the decryption of data transparent to the client and server.

Authenticating DCE Services

An important feature of DCE is that individual DCE services, such as the timing service and cell directory service, are also authenticated by the security service. This makes it very difficult to impersonate any of the DCE service providers.

> However, non-DCE applications that provide services to a DCE cell are fair game. We have heard of a situation where a DCE cell, which used the Internet NTP time service, was subjected to an attack. The attacker set the time forward to the next century, thus invalidating all current credentials!

AUTHORIZATION

DCE uses a mechanism called access control lists (ACLs) to authorize the use of resources in a cell. The use of ACLs is very flexible—in fact, they are relatively unstructured and up to individual application to implement. ACLs may be used to restrict access to files, directories, hardware devices, or even the application server itself.

In early releases of DCE, the application developer was required to define, manage and enforce ACLs. The individual ACLs are typically stored in flat files, protected by the local file system on the server. But it is really up to the individual application to determine where the ACL is stored, and how it is applied. As of the DCE 1.1 release, programming libraries and tools are provided to administer ACLs.

TABLE 17.2
TYPICAL ACL ACCESS RIGHTS

Access Rights	Description
Read	The client may open and examine the contents of the resource, but is not allowed to modify the contents.
Write	Modifications may be made to the resource.
Control	The resource is controlled by the client.
Insert	A new resource may be created by the client. For example, a new file or directory can be created.
Delete	An existing resource can be deleted by the client.

ACLs are created in combination with access rights. While it is up to the individual application to define its own access rights, examples of access rights include those in Table 17.2.

An ACL is created by combining the class of client (e.g., "any other"), and an appropriate access right (e.g., "none"). ACLs may be applied to individual users, but are most commonly applied to a class or group of users. While definition of these classes is under the control of the application, standard classes of clients might include those in Table 17.3.

TABLE 17.3
TYPICAL ACL CLASSES OF CLIENTS

Class of Owner	Description
Owner	The client currently has ownership of the resource. There is only one owner.
Specific user	The client is authenticated and is specifically identified.
Foreign user	The client is specifically identified, but is a member of a foreign DCE cell.
Group	The client is a member of the group to which the resource belongs.
Specific group	The client is a member of the group specified. There may be multiple groups identified.
Other	The client is an authenticated user from the local DCE cell, but not a member of the above.
Foreign other	The client has been authenticated from another Cell.
Any other	A catch all class if none of the above classes match.

RULE-BASED AUTHORIZATIONS

One problem with ACLs is that their current management is very cumbersome. As mentioned previously, it is essentially up to the developer to manage ACLs. The management problem becomes a larger issue when you wish to use ACLs in combination. We might want to set up rules on how ACLs are to work, rather than simply access lists to files. For example, if you were a credit manager, you might be able to approve loans up to $500,000 for clients in your district. Management tools that allow for rule-based authorizations are expected to be available for the DCE environment in the near future.

GSSAPI

What if I have a client, for whom the full suite of DCE is impractical, but I wish them to be subjected to use DCE applications in a secure manner? This implies that these clients must be able to authenticate themselves to the DCE security service and obtain security credentials. The answer may be provided by the proposed Generic Security Service Application Programming Interface (GSSAPI). Not strictly a DCE solution, the GSSAPI allows a client or server to request security services using a common (or generic) method. The GSSAPI sits between the client and the security mechanism, allowing an application programmer to code requests for authentication and authorization in one way regardless of the security mechanism used. Support for the GSSAPI is increasing, and we have witnessed its use in a wide number of security applications and products. For example, the GSSAPI can support both OSF/DCE and the Kerberos V security mechanisms.

An initial discussion of the use of the GSSAPI was presented by J. Linn of Digital Equipment Corporation who submitted OSF RFC 5.0 to the OSF DCE Special Interest Group (SIG) in June 1992. This initial research has been recently expanded with the submission of RFC 1508 and 1509. The RFC has proposed that non-DCE clients be given a set of interfaces which would permit the authentication of the client using the DCE shared secret key (or other) mechanism. It would also protect the confidentiality of messages, using encryption and checksums.

The importance of the GSSAPI, from a DCE viewpoint, is that it will extend the strong security capabilities of DCE to the non-DCE world. It is expected that use of the GSSAPI will greatly increase the use of Kerberos and DCE. Use of the GSSAPI is supported in the OSF DCE 1.1 release.

TWO-FACTOR AUTHENTICATION AND SMART CARDS

In RFC 59.0, J. Kotanchik of Security Dynamics has suggested that the Kerberos V implementation be expanded to incorporate two-factor authentication. Two-factor authentication is based upon two pieces of identification, such as something you know (e.g., a password), something you have (e.g., an authentication device), or something you are (e.g., reading of biometrics). Mr. Kotanchik has described a possible implementation of DCE security with a combination of user-supplied passwords and a pseudo random number (PRN) generated by a hand-held device.

Two Australian researchers, Gary Gaskell of DSTC and Michael Warner of Telstra, prepared OSF RFC 71.0 which was released in February 1995. The RFC makes a strong case for incorporating the use of smart card technology to protect DCE secrets and perform cryptographic functions.

AUDITING

Early versions of DCE have not defined an audit trail, on a cellwide, application, or server basis. It has been left to the application design team to address auditing standards and the composition of the audit trail. Shyh-Wei Luan of VDG, Inc., and Robert Weisz, of IBM Canada's Laboratories, have proposed a standard audit trail mechanism. In RFC 28.1 and 29.1, they suggested a common auditing API and audit trail be defined that would address C2 security requirements. The proposed audit trail would allow the logical grouping of events into event classes. It would also allow the DCE administrator to selectively increase auditing on an individual, single event or class of event. The DCE 1.1 release provides support for an audit library and audit logs and adds audit administration capabilities.

SINGLE SIGN-ON

Single sign-on is a concept that would allow a user to log onto a network once and have that login accepted by all other networked systems and applications. The benefit is that the user will only need to remember one user ID and password for network access. Because of its support for a number of different hardware platforms and operating systems, OSF/DCE is a logical candidate to construct single sign-on solutions. The use of extended attributes, and support for the extended user registry, make incorporating single sign-on much easier.

IS DCE BULLETPROOF ?

We have witnessed a number of clients with the attitude, "Let's implement Kerberos and DCE and we won't have to worry about security!" That attitude is not justified. First, security is more than any particular technology.

You cannot address the issues without examining the entire picture—policy, procedures, education and awareness are all equally important factors in ensuring a secure environment. One cannot simply implement a single technology and have solved the issue of computer security. That being said, the security measures of DCE do go a long way in solving many of the key issues in implementing security in a distributed environment. But is it a bulletproof solution? The answer is no!

DCE does have a few Achilles heels. DCE relies on the client's operating system to protect a users' credentials. If the credentials can be stolen, counterfeit requests may be made. Similarly, DCE trusts the local file system controls on the server to protect the servers secret password. If the local system has weak controls, the DCE authentication programs may be replaced with Trojan horse programs which steal the users password. Also, DCE does not provide any additional file protection mechanisms other those used by the operating system. It does not provide a system administrator or user with the ability to encrypt files.

Simply because DCE has some weaknesses should we throw up our hands and do nothing? No! Deploying DCE is infinitely better than accepting the status quo! It may not be a silver bullet, but it's certainly better than being out of ammunition.

Products have been recently introduced to help overcome some of the above problems. Hewlett-Packard has recently announced the Odyssey product, which is capable of securely storing DCE credentials. Using the GemPlus smart card, Odyssey authenticates the user prior to releasing credentials. The DCE credentials are protected if the card is stolen, because the user must know the password on the card to unlock it.

CONCLUSIONS

It is clear that the status quo will also cease to be acceptable to the general computing community. The exposure of clear text passwords on the LAN, requirements to securely authenticate clients and servers, and the protection of communication dictate the need for change. As well, the need for redundancy, directory services and multivendor capabilities in a complex network environment will continue to grow.

There is no clear successor or replacement, based upon industry standards, to DCE on the market today. No technology currently provides the breadth of services DCE can provide. While we cannot predict the future for DCE, the need for this type of technology will remain. We simply will not be able to place trust in the current middleware technologies for much longer.

CHAPTER 18

DISTRIBUTED DATABASES

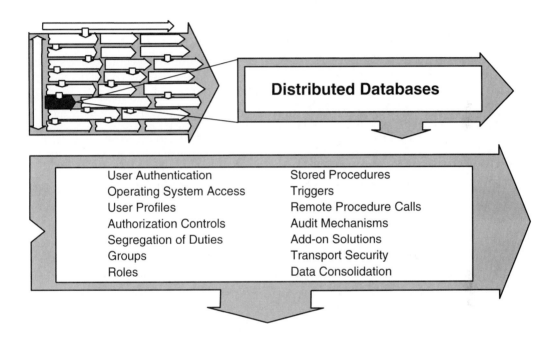

Distributed Databases

User Authentication	Stored Procedures
Operating System Access	Triggers
User Profiles	Remote Procedure Calls
Authorization Controls	Audit Mechanisms
Segregation of Duties	Add-on Solutions
Groups	Transport Security
Roles	Data Consolidation

In this chapter, we will examine the security features of distributed database solutions. Databases are the *wall safes* of distributed computing. They can protect our most valuable personal assets, even in the event an intruder gains access to our house. Databases offer several important advantages in terms of security, including strong data access controls and audit trails.

As with our previous studies of technologies, our focus will be on the security issues affecting distributed databases, how distributed databases work and what some of their enabling technologies are. There will not be a focus on any particular database implementation. Instead, we will review common features of three vendors of distributed database technology: Informix, Oracle, and Sybase. Having gained an understanding of the database environment, we will look at solutions to the problems that have been raised.

WHAT IS A RDBMS?

A relational data base management system (RDBMS) is a data storage and retrieval system based on the relational database model. This model uses the concept of a table as its basic structure. A table is a logical way of viewing related information. An employee table, for example, might contain such information as employee number, name, department, position and date of hire. Relational tables consist of multiple sets of rows and columns. Within a table, data is organized into vertical columns and intersecting rows, with only one data item per intersection. The rows can be loosely thought of as a data record, and the columns as data items within the record. For example, in an employee table, there might be one row per employee and one column for employee numbers, names, and the like. Information about database users, including passwords and user profiles, are also stored in tables.

An RDBMS is comprised of a number of tables, many of which are related to each other. They can be linked together using common data elements called keys. Indices can also be created for the fast lookup of keys. A *view* is a logical table that is not physically stored but allows access to a subset of information in a single table or collection of tables. For example, a manager may require limited access to the payroll table. The manager can have full read access to the salary information for those employees who are direct reports, but will be restricted from viewing the salary data of senior management. The information the manager is allowed to see, which might span many subsets of columns in the same row or different rows, is termed a "view."

Most relational databases support a common language for performing ad hoc queries, programming and administration. The Structured Query Language (SQL), defined by the American National Standards Institute (ANSI) and International Standards Organization (ISO), provides a standardized set of data definition and data manipulation statements which are used by all standard RDBMS implementations. An SQL database environment is actually composed of a number of standards, including the Embedded SQL (ESQL) standard for use of SQL statements in programming languages. It should be noted that efforts are also underway to standardize the application programming interfaces (APIs) used to call the server from a client program. For example, the SQL access group (SAG) provides a common API definition endorsed by most RDBMS vendors.

Interactive Structured Query Language (ISQL) is an utility used for both database administration and ad hoc queries. It permits the user direct access to data. Using standard SQL commands, a user can create customized reports and perform one-time queries against the database. Most RDBMS vendors support the use of standard SQL, but add extensions to the language and database environment for additional functionality. Unfortunately, vendor extensions have resulted in different approaches to solving the problem of security. Not every database implementation offers the same overall level of security.

DIFFERENT MODELS TO ENABLE APPLICATIONS

There are three different architectures used in enabling RDBMS applications. These are server centric, limited client/server, and full client/server. In the traditional server-centric model, both data and application logic exist on the database server. The local workstation is used as a smart terminal to access the application. All program logic is predefined and executed within the application on the server. The application data is kept within the confines of the database on the server. The limited client-server model uses a client workstation which acts as a smart interface to the RDBMS. It provides a sophisticated graphical user interface for the user, but almost all of the application data and logic exist on the server. In the full client-server model, data and application logic exist on both the client and server. The client maintains local tables of data, but also has the ability to make requests for additional data or processing from the database server. The database server may in turn become a client, on behalf of the original client, by making requests to other databases.

The client communication occurs over the network, using a number of different communication methods. These methods tend to vary from one vendor's product to another. For example, Oracle uses the SQL*NET as a basis for network communication, while Sybase employs the remote procedure call (RPC) mechanism.

Security controls are common features of an RDBMS. Figure 18.1 provides an overview of the security functions provided by an RDBMS.

RDBMS solutions (e.g., Oracle, Sybase or Informix) provide a number of security functions, although their individual availability on a particular database solution may vary from vendor to vendor. These include the ability to authenticate a user and assign them to a group structure. Based upon their user ID or group membership, a user can be allowed, or denied, access to tables, views, or individual data elements. An audit trail of user actions is a common feature of RDBMS solutions. Finally, advanced functions such as stored procedures and triggers may be available. We will review each of these

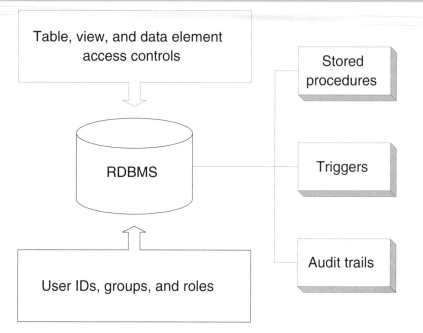

Figure 18.1 Overview of typical RDBMS security functions

security functions in following sections of this chapter. But, first, we will look at the relationship between operating system access and the database.

USER AUTHENTICATION

As with operating systems, the authentication of database access is performed through the use of user IDs and passwords. While unique database user IDs and passwords may be used, most RDBMS implementations allow them to be coordinated by the operating system. In Oracle 7.0, for example, the database can be configured to prevent a user from accessing the database using a nonstandard operating system user ID.

While clear-text passwords transmitted over the LAN has been the norm, RDBMS vendors are moving to solve this problem. Both Sybase and Oracle, for example, have the ability to optionally implement one-time password (i.e., challenge-response) authentication techniques. These techniques may also include the encryption of the entire authentication process.

OPERATING SYSTEM ACCESS

It is very common for database application designers, using the server-centric model, to prevent users from directly accessing the operating system.

The user will log on via the operating system, but is instantly placed into a database application menu. One advantage of this approach is that the user does not need to understand the operating system and its internal commands. It also allows the application designer to focus on the database.

Another technique we have seen employed (and is a current requirement for some transaction monitors) is to force all access to the database under a single user ID (i.e., the applications user ID). The advantages, and disadvantages, of this approach include the following:

- It is relatively easy to implement and administer.
- All access to data is forced to occur (as long as no one can counterfeit SQL requests) from within the application.
- The strong database access controls, such as table, view and data element security, are eliminated.
- The effectiveness of audit trails are reduced because all activity will appear as coming from one user ID (i.e., the application).

USER PROFILES

User profiles allow a database administrator to define characteristics about a user's session. While mostly used to provide configuration settings which limit the users access to database resources, a profile can also be used to automatically disconnect the user after a period of inactivity.

AUTHORIZATION CONTROLS

RDBMSs perform authorization using the concept of privileges. A privilege is a right to perform certain actions. Users are authorized to perform a given action on the database provided they have sufficient privileges. The user who initially creates the database is termed the DB owner and has full rights and privileges to the database. The DB owner grants privileges (i.e., rights to perform selected actions on the database) to other users. Such rights may include the ability for the user to also grant privileges to other users. In most RDBMS environments, the database owner is called the database administrator (DBA) and is granted a complete set of privileges.

The privileges that can be granted are broken down into two main types. System-level privileges provide privileges for the entire database, while table access privileges are used on a selected table or view.

Typical system-level privileges are shown in Table 18.1.

TABLE 18.1
TYPICAL SYSTEM-LEVEL PRIVILEGES

Privilege Name	Description
CONNECT	Can access the database; issue commands to manipulate data (including import and export); create views.
RESOURCE	Can change the structure of the database; create tables and indexes; create and assign users to groups and roles.
DBA	Full access to every table and all data; can grant and revoke access rights; create and administer user accounts; control the audit function.

Users with CONNECT and RESOURCE privileges can access the database and create new tables and indices. Users with only CONNECT privileges can access tables but not create new tables. A special authority is given to users who have created tables. These users are termed the *owner* of the object, and have full table access rights to the object they have created. Table access privileges may be assigned to other users by either the owner of the object or the DBA.

Typical table access privileges are included in Table 18.2.

Individual users or groups of users are given access privileges, by either the DB owner, the DBA, or the user that owns the resource. The privilege may be given on a table, view, or column (data item). A user may also

TABLE 18.2
TYPICAL TABLE ACCESS PRIVILEGES

Table Access Privilege	Description
SELECT	Can select an object and query it.
INSERT	Can create new records in a table or view.
UPDATE	Can change data items (records) in a table or view.
DELETE	Can delete a column or row.
ALTER	Can change the data type; can add or delete table columns.
INDEX	Indices may be created to facilitate table lookup.
REFERENCES	The user can create a special reference to the table, called a foreign key.

be allowed to grant privileges to other users, who may in turn pass this privilege on to others. Only the user from whom the privilege is granted can revoke it. An interesting side effect is that the original user may not be able to directly revoke individual privileges on their table. However, the database owner may revoke all table privileges and reissue them.

SEGREGATION OF DUTIES

Traditional RDBMS functions, such as backup and recovery, require DBA authority. Many of the database vendors have recognized this as a problem area and designed solutions into their product offerings. In Sybase 10.0, for example, a new set of system privileges have been defined. These system privileges include system security officer and operator. The system security officer privilege allows a user to maintain user IDs, passwords, auditing information, and the administration of privileges. The operator privilege permits the delegation of backup and recovery functions.

BATCH SQL STATEMENTS

A batch SQL job is a file containing a series of SQL statements. These statements are authenticated by providing a user ID and passwords. But batch jobs may be initiated at times when the actual person is not available. If a password is embedded within the SQL statements, anyone who can read the statements can easily read the password. Another problem is that the command line, containing the password, can be viewed by performance monitoring tools. Approaches to solving this problem include forcing the user to enter the password when the batch job is submitted.

GROUPS

Most RDBMS systems allow the creation of user groups. This allows access privileges to be granted to the group, rather than the individual user. The creation of groups is typically based on either an organizational structure, a job function, or a combination of the two. In comparison to uniquely identifying access rights for each individual user, the use of groups generally reduces and simplifies database administration. A special group, called PUBLIC, allows privileges to be assigned to every user of the database.

The group structure works well when access to data can be structured along departmental or job function lines, and the access privileges are fairly static. The use of groups tends to break down when users are granted different rights depending upon the type of function they are performing. In this case, group structures tend to be too rigid.

ROLES

A new feature offered by selected RDBMS implementations is role-based access privileges. Roles allow the assignment of privileges based upon a job function. Roles differ from groups in that they are intended to be mapped to the actual duties of a job, rather than on a departmental or organizational structure. For example, a role may be defined for personnel managers that would allow them access to all personal data.

Roles are less rigid than a group structure and may be combined with other roles to perform more complex functions. Roles may also be granted to other users, and combined with other roles to form new roles. They are also not specific to data and may be combined with database system privileges. For example, a role may allow a privileged user the ability to create a new view of a table even though they do not have the RESOURCE privilege.

In Oracle 7.0, use of roles can allow the creation of an OPERATOR role for backup and recovery without granting full DBA privileges. Roles can be customized to allow the segregation of DBA duties. As well, passwords can be optionally required for use with a specific role.

While roles are very flexible, standards and guidelines must be developed surrounding their use. Otherwise, their use can result in a confusing web of overlapping and contradictory security privileges.

STORED PROCEDURES

A stored procedure is a set of predefined SQL statements, which are preprocessed, compiled, and optimized. A single stored procedure call can execute multiple SQL statements. They are especially attractive to the client-server architectures, where they usually outperform other methods of issuing SQL statements. Stored procedures can be shared by multiple programs, thus permitting greater efficiency in programming. They may also be called by ordinary users issuing ISQL requests. While there is an effort to standardize their use, vendors have currently implemented them in different ways.

A stored procedure can be used to allow the temporary use of the privileges of its creator, assuming the user has authority to execute it. These privileges are temporary, and only in effect for as long as the stored procedure executes. If a stored procedure is created by the DBA, it can allow an ordinary user access to DBA privileges. The most common use of this practice is to allow segregation of duties, permitting users a limited access to DBA privileges for selected functions.

> Stored procedures can be manipulated by the database designer to greatly enhance security. By revoking access by ordinary users to selected tables or views and granting it to a stored procedure, the database designer can force all access to occur through that stored procedure. Not only does this reduce administration, but it can deny access to sensitive tables from users, programmers, and applications. It can also deny access to SQL Report Writers, as well as guarantee the consistency of an audit trail.

Passwords may be used to authorize the use of stored procedures. As with batch SQL statements, the problem is where to store the password. A commonly used approach, if the stored procedure is executed from a PC client, is to hide the password within a library on the personal computer.

TRIGGERS

A trigger is a stored procedure that is automatically executed after a predefined event takes place in order to maintain the referential integrity of the database. Triggers are normally initiated by data-related events, such as table inserts, updates, and deletes. From a security aspect, they are very useful in enforcing additional security controls.

We have seen many examples of the use of triggers to increase security and audit in the RDBMS environment. One implementation used triggers to selectively monitor access to sensitive records. In this case, all access to senior management payroll records are audited. A more subtle use of triggers can be employed as a backup to database security. A separate table of user access privileges is created and maintained separately from the normal database access privileges. This method is intended to detect any user who has compromised security and given themselves additional privileges. As with stored procedures, triggers have been implemented differently by the vendors.

REMOTE PROCEDURE CALLS

A remote procedure call (RPC) is a special type of stored procedure, designed to operate in a client-server environment. While normal stored procedures execute almost exclusively on the server (i.e., on the database engine), RPCs are initiated by the client and cause some form of execution on the server. This generally results in a response being sent back to the client. Different types of RPCs include the OSF DCE RPC, Sun's RPC, and the Sybase RPC mechanism.

As with all client-server communication, there are several security concerns involving the use of RPCs:

- If the RPC relies on data passed by the client (such as a user ID) for authentication purposes, how can we be assured that the client has not forged the information?
- If the client possesses knowledge of the RPC calls, how can we prevent the client from bypassing the authentication method entirely?
- Last, how can we prevent an interception or replay of an RPC?

The answer depends on the strength of the remote procedure call mechanism.

AUDIT MECHANISMS

There are two types of auditing mechanisms available in RDBMS solutions: transaction logging and audit trails. Transaction logging is used as a method of recovering the database after a system failure. These logs capture all changes to the database and allow the database to be re-created if problems occur. A transaction, in database terms, is defined as a sequence of actions required to perform a logical item. Transactions are usually explicitly defined in the application with a BEGIN WORK statement and can only end with a COMMIT or ROLLBACK statement. Databasewide transaction logging is also supported, for example, on the recent Informix release. This type of logging records all activity, allowing a database recovery regardless of whether an individual transaction has issued a BEGIN WORK statement. Transaction logs are generally stored external to the database.

The central function of transaction logging is to provide the ability to *rollback* incomplete transactions in the event of a database or transaction failure. The classic example for the use of rollback is with funds transfer in a banking application. When a transfer of money is made between a savings and checking account, a system failure should not leave the accounts out of balance. If a system failure occurs after a debit is made to checking and before the credit is applied to savings, the entire transaction should be *rolled back* to leave the two accounts in a consistent, balanced state. The transaction recovery mechanism ensures the transactions are *rolled back* in their proper sequence, resulting in a *consistent state* for the database.

The RDBMS environment also provides for audit trails. RDBMS audit trails provide a log of changes to the database. They differ from transaction logs in their purpose and structure. Transaction logs are used to recover implementation in case of a database failure, while audit trails are meant to trace events. While audit trails do track changes, the changes are selected and not necessarily comprehensive. They are also unsynchronized. If a database is reconstructed from an audit trail, it would almost certainly result in a corrupt and inconsistent state.

RDBMS auditing is useful as a security tool as well as a recovery mechanism. When auditing has been enabled, it can be used to track user actions in the event of a security incident. It can also be used to provide data to trigger alarms or provide alerts if specific security events are detected. This may include the failure by a user to gain access to a table or view, which might indicate the user is attempting to breach normal security mechanisms.

ISSUES SURROUNDING RDBMS

The database environment has a fairly robust security environment, and a moderate level of trust can be placed in its operation. Unfortunately, there are a number of problems, both inside and outside the database, that must be addressed before additional trust can be placed in the RDBMS environment.

While RDBMS authorization mechanisms are quite robust, the underlying authentication mechanisms are not strong enough. Some problems are

- If the operating system security on either the client or server is compromised, database security may be compromised as well.
- If users cannot access the operating system or database directly, how can they change their password on a regular basis?
- The authorization of batch applications, if performed by coding the clear-text password within the batch statements, is easily compromised.
- If the vendor provides for encryption of the authentication process, the solution is proprietary to the vendor and may not be able to be used by other RDBMS implementations.
- Authentication and authorization support for an RDBMS that calls another RDBMS on behalf of the user provides an area of concern. Essentially, the identity of the client is passed in clear-text (or not at all) to the second RDBMS.
- The ability to limit (or disable) ISQL access, based upon user and the type of access, is required.
- Management of a large number of remote RDBMS systems requires automated tools to synchronize user IDs, passwords, and user access rights.

Authorization mechanisms are only as strong as the accompanying authentication mechanisms. In most database environments, passwords are transmitted over the LAN in clear-text. These may be easily intercepted by monitoring LAN traffic. Operating system authentication may also be compromised in this manner.

If operating system controls are weak, any database may be compromised regardless of how strong its internal controls are. Client authentication programs (i.e., logon) can be replaced by a Trojan horse, which imitates the valid program but captures the user's password. If security is lax on a UNIX system, the device file on which the database resides may be examined using a debugging tool and the DBA password revealed.

> Database administrators should be aware of attacks against the UNIX raw disk device. Using a number of common debugging tools (such as the UNIX octal dump utility), you can very easily find a DBA password on some RDBMS versions. Even with strong RDBMS controls, security on the operating system really does count!

Problems can occur if the user contacts one database application, which in turn accesses a second database on behalf of the user. How can we apply access control at the second database, when all requests appear to be from one source (the initial database)?

What if clients are given permission to insert columns or rows in a database table through an application. The application can ensure that the database is modified in a consistent manner, but if ISQL is implemented, their access is uncontrolled.

Centralized management of database users and privileges, for multiple databases, is also a problem. RDBMS security management is generally provided on a database-centric basis by the database vendors, which does not allow for centralized management.

ADD-ON SOLUTIONS

There are a large number of solutions, provided by third parties, available for the RDBMS environments. They provide a number of security enhancements, including

- One-time challenge-response password solutions for authentication which prevents discovery of the password over the LAN.

- Password policy enforcement, such as minimum password length and expiration date.
- Centralized management of users, roles, and privileges.
- SQL access is forced through SQL access control mechanisms, which authorize each query.
- Providing time-of-day access controls.
- Audit trails of users actions and commands.
- Access control on use of stored procedures by users.

Database vendors are usually more than happy to provide catalogs of third-party solutions for their environment.

TRANSPORT SECURITY

Many of the database vendors have recognized that in the client-server world, there must be mechanisms to support the integrity of communication over untrusted networks. These mechanisms provide for the encryption of both the authentication process and subsequent communication between the client and server. This can include encryption of the data passed between the two.

An example of this type of mechanism is the Secure Network Services (SNS) product offered by the Oracle Corporation. SNS provides for encryption of the password before it leaves the client. It offers data integrity through support for both the RC4 algorithm from RSA Data Security, Inc., and the DES40 algorithm.

SYBASE has included the capability, under Version 10.0, to encrypt the storage of the user password. It also provides for the optional encryption of the password as it is passed from client to server.

Most RDBMS vendors, including Informix and Oracle, have announced products that integrate with the OSF/DCE environment. From a trust aspect, database users can be authenticated using the Kerberos authentication model supported by DCE. Tickets obtained from the DCE Security Service can be verified by the database server. As well, the six encryption levels defined by DCE are supported. This allows for multiple levels of security (i.e., encryption) to be used to protect calls from the client to the database server. The use of DCE security also provides a single sign-on capability, which may be used by other non-RDBMS applications. Some vendors also allow the DCE security service to manage and control database security privileges, such as the assignment of users to roles.

Unfortunately, comprehensive support for the full OSF/DCE environment is not offered by all vendors. While support for the naming service, for example, is offered by some, it is not provided in all vendor solutions.

DATA CONSOLIDATION

A common point of frustration in using databases has been the inability to access and make sense of the tremendous amount of data that has been accumulating. Information is required to make better decisions. But how can you benefit from the information if you cannot locate the data? Another problem is the performance problems that can occur if you provide an online query capability against the production databases. A proposed solution to these challenges is the establishment of a data warehouse.

WHAT IS A DATA WAREHOUSE?

A data warehouse is an organized collection of data generated and kept by the corporation. More formally, a data warehouse is a subject-oriented, integrated, time-variant, nonvolatile collection of data that is used primarily to support organizational decisions. It is used as a repository for collecting, standardizing, and summarizing the accumulation of the transactions that take place in the operational systems. The information within the warehouse is static in nature, being primarily used for decision support and management reporting. A data warehouse is as much an organizational concept as a technological one. When implemented properly, it provides a method for the organization to make better decisions. Data warehousing is used for

- A central distribution point for historical and summary data
- Organizing data by subject rather than by application
- Integrating data to meet the needs of the whole organization
- Providing historical information for modeling and trend analysis
- Providing standard definitions and representations of the information for the organization

To be effective the data warehouse must include a profile of the warehouse users, a list of who can put data into the warehouse, and a catalog of the data that is contained in the warehouse. Tools should be available to enable the user to access and arrange the data into meaningful reports. This might also include a subscription service if repeated reporting is required.

A data warehouse is generally used as a tool for analyis and decision support, it does not normally support business transaction processing. The data stored in the data warehouse is based on subjects, products, or employees, for example, rather on the transactions of the operational databases. The data in the data warehouse should be stored with an indication of when the data was captured. We need to know the time context of the data to make sense out any of the generated reports and put it into historical perspective. Data in the warehouse is generally read-only. It is not generated by the warehouse nor is it generally updated or deleted within the warehouse.

A data warehouse is not easy to define and implement. Care must be taken to identify the data that is housed in the warehouse, where it comes from, and how it is summarized or filtered for storage. A data warehouse that is implemented without a great deal of care in the analysis and planning stages will provide just another place for the storage of data that is difficult to access and use. Careful attention must be made to the extraction, transformation and loading processes from the source systems.

From a security and trust aspect, data warehouses provide the ability to centrally manage access to corporate data, no matter where it resides. The basic security problems faced by a single RDBMS will still be evident in a data warehouse. It is easier to solve these issues for a single, centralized database than for a number of distributed databases. A distributed data warehouse will suffer all of the security issues faced by a distributed database.

CONCLUSIONS

A database can act as a wall safe to store valuable information. Databases can protect the application data (to some degree, at least) even if a system has been compromised. They offer strong data access controls, including limiting a users view of data based upon a specified criteria. Databases also provide relatively robust audit trails, which can be protected (though not totally) from the local system administrator. These benefits make them a logical place to store and protect application data in a distributed environment.

CHAPTER 19

ON-LINE TRANSACTION PROCESSING

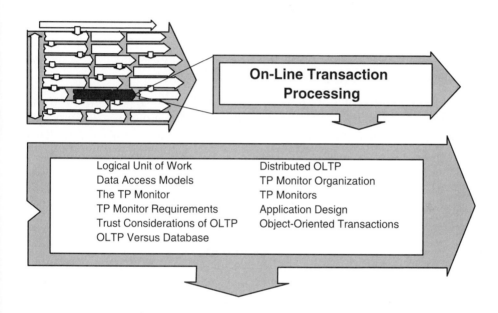

On-Line Transaction Processing

Logical Unit of Work	Distributed OLTP
Data Access Models	TP Monitor Organization
The TP Monitor	TP Monitors
TP Monitor Requirements	Application Design
Trust Considerations of OLTP	Object-Oriented Transactions
OLTP Versus Database	

How many of you use an automated teller machine (ATM) instead of a bank teller for most of your banking transactions? These days it doesn't much matter what type of ATM you use or which institution actually controls it. When you deposit or withdraw money using the ATM you will most likely be executing an on-line transaction. The concept of a transaction is actually an extension of batch processing where a computer program is executed, files are accessed and manipulated, and results are delivered based on the data that was entered. A computer terminal is used to enter the data and display results instead of using an input file and a printed report.

The banking and insurance institutions were early adopters of on-line transaction processing (OLTP). With an OLTP system, a bank teller is able to access accurate information and execute financial transactions while you are at the counter. These transactions have been completed and your accounts updated before you leave the counter. In this chapter we will review the components of a transaction and what sets it apart from other forms of processing. The management and security of these transactions become even more interesting when they are part of a distributed system.

Another illustration of the power and value of OLTP in its earliest form was the implementation of the airline reservation system. The use of an OLTP system allowed the airlines to fill the seats in their airplanes even when they didn't exactly know who would be in the seat or who actually sold the seat. A travel or airline agent can access a single database representing the flight to see if space is available and, if it is, allocate it to a customer. These OLTP systems have to process an enormous number of transactions in a short time frame and provide almost instant response to the agent. It is hard to imagine what air travel would be without the ability to manage the flights using on-line transaction processing.

The banking and airline reservation systems process transactions as they occur. The ATM, for example, follows a strict protocol for transaction execution and control. The bank wants to ensure that you always get your money when your account is debited or, if the machine malfunctions for some reason, your account is not debited for the amount that was not dispensed. The bank is also very interested in making sure that you cannot withdraw $200 on one machine and withdraw the same $200 on another machine or from another branch of the bank.

The trust concerns in a transaction system are somewhat different from those of the usual user-based system. Security is usually a split responsibility among the operating system, network systems, and the transaction system itself. In a transaction system, the actual user of the transaction, and even the location of the transaction initiation, may be transient. The authorization to execute a transaction is based on the authenticated identity of the user. The authorization to accept transactions is based on the authenticated identity of the transaction initiation location or network access. For example, authorization of a banking transaction at an ATM will rely on physical location and identity of the ATM along with the identity of the individual when they supply a card and a personal identification number (PIN). The challenge of resolving this authorization is especially difficult in distributed transaction processing systems.

WHAT IS A TRANSACTION?

In the past it was very easy to determine a transaction- from a nontransaction-driven system. If you used a terminal and pressed the enter key it was an on-line transaction system. So what do we define as a transaction? A transaction is a data-driven relationship between a user and an application or between two or more applications, that require real-time execution of a program based on supplied data and producing demonstrable results. A transaction has a definite start and end with processing in the form of program execution in the middle. The on-line unit of work is considered a transaction if it has what are called the ACID properties. The ACID properties are

- **Atomicity**—The transaction is considered to be either complete or not complete. Transactions cannot be partially completed and left in an uncertain state.
- **Consistency**—An update to data preserves the integrity of the data by mapping from one steady (consistent) state to another steady state.
- **Isolation**—The effect of a transaction on shared data is visible to other transactions only after the transaction is committed. Any information required by a transaction in progress is locked to prevent other transactions from changing it.
- **Durability**—The effects of the transaction are permanent and critical modifications to data will not be lost by subsequent system failures.

A transaction is a complete unit of work with on-line access to and update of shared data with integrity. The execution of the unit of work must adhere to the ACID properties to be considered a transaction.

DISTRIBUTED LOGICAL UNIT OF WORK

In Chapter 9 we covered the concept of a logical unit of work or LUW. We are now going to extend this concept to a distributed logical unit of work. The concept of logical unit of work remains the same, it just happens to be distributed over more than one processor. Figure 19.1 represents a process that contains one individual logical unit of work that is distributed over two servers. The action of reading and writing file X, reading file Z, and then requesting a process to be executed on server B which reads and updates file Y can be considered to be a single logical unit of work. The logical unit of work includes process A on server A and process B on server B. If any of the operations from the start of process A through to the update of file Z is not successful the updates to files X, Y, and Z are returned to the point before process A was started. Each logical unit of work represents the completion of a task.

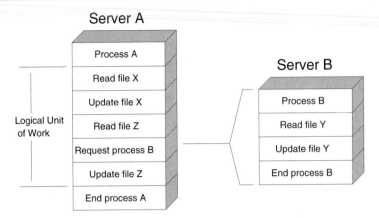

Figure 19.1 Distributed logical unit of work example

In the previous chapter we talked about the mechanisms to provide the rollback of work in order to keep the database in a consistent state. The concept of commit and rollback are very important in transaction processing. A commit is a point in the life of a transaction where all of the work completed to that point is to be permanently applied. If anything goes wrong during the transaction, a rollback will be invoked to set everything back to the point before the previous commit point or before the transaction began execution. The commit is generally invoked at the completion of a logical unit of work. A rollback, if required, is performed to reset the transaction back to the start of the logical unit of work.

DISTRIBUTED DATA ACCESS MODELS

An OLTP system collects and processes data about business transactions and posts changes to the organizations shared databases and files. One of the long-standing issues with accessing shared files or databases is who manages the access. Will the user have to manage the access or will that be taken care of by an automated process? In Figure 19.2 we see a couple of different models of executing programs and accessing shared data describing the requirements in client-server terms.

One way of accessing multiple files or databases during a process is to maintain all of the management and knowledge of what server process to access with the client. This puts a major burden on the client to understand where the database servers are located. A client-managed model is not widely used. Another way of looking at the problem is to make the server responsible for maintaining the knowledge and management of the files or database. Again coordination and update problems are present. A much bet-

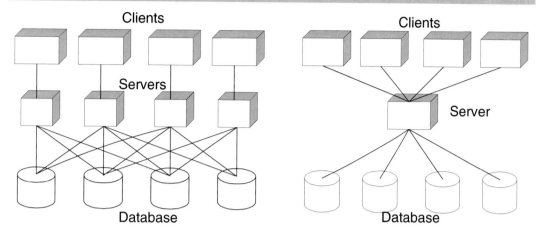

Figure 19.2 Transaction processing models

ter way of managing the database access is to centralize the execution of the programs and the access to the files or database. The burden of accessing and managing the files or database is placed with software and not with the user. The management is greatly simplified.

COMPONENTS OF A TRANSACTION PROCESSING SYSTEM

A mechanism is required to provide this central management of the execution of transactions and the management of access to the different databases. A transaction processing (TP) system utilizes a main program called the TP monitor to manage the execution of the transactions. The TP monitor functions as a minioperating system, including the scheduling of the execution of transactions and data access. The TP monitor also manages the ACID properties and provides the services that are required to ensure that these properties are maintained. The TP monitor manages the commit requests when execution is successful or completed and the rollback requirements if the execution is unsuccessful. The TP monitor plays an important role to maintain data integrity in the event processes fail.

Figure 19.3 indicates the various building blocks of an OLTP system. Over time some of these building blocks have been moved outside of the OLTP system to take advantage of database systems and the processing

power of the desktop systems. The screen manager provides the user interface mechanisms and is now usually provided by a local PC. The management of the resources required by the OLTP system is somewhat dependent
on the operating system under which the system is implemented. The transaction processing services manage the dispatch of the work to be done. The
resource managers provide organized access to the processor, memory, and
other resources. The management of data has mostly been delegated to separate database systems to which the OLTP system interfaces. The distribution
services component manages the access to, and sharing of, the data. There
may also be tools available to help build the transaction based applications.
The TP monitor itself operates as an application using the processing and
communication services of the operating system and network transport.

THE TP MONITOR

Transactions are, by their nature, unpredictable by their origin and in the
number that will be required to be processed within a given time. We can
guess at how many people might want to withdraw money from a bank
using a number of tellers or the ATMs, but we don't know for sure. We need
a way of managing the processing of these transactions in order to allocate
the required resources in a manner that will ensure that they are processed
accurately and as quickly as possible. The easiest way to come up with a
prediction is to assume that all of the ATMs and teller terminals will be used
equally. But this is not realistic, not all of the tellers or ATMs will be fully
utilized all the time. We need a mechanism to help us manage the peaks and
valleys. This transaction management mechanism is generally referred to as
a transaction processing monitor.

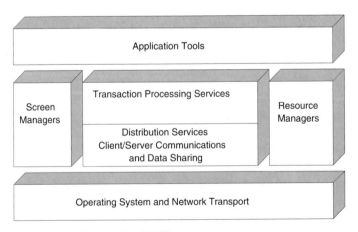

Figure 19.3 OLTP system components

The main purpose of an on-line transaction processing monitor is to manage the scheduling of transactions and the access to resources. The term resources is often used to describe anything that can be consumed or requires management. We will use the term "resources" to refer to processor memory, data files and database, processor cycles, and the communication system. The transaction monitor must manage the transactions as they arrive against the availability of the resources to ensure that the transactions are completed in as short a time as possible. The OLTP monitor must be able to dynamically manage a variable number of transactions since we will have trouble predicting when they arrive and how many there will be.

On-line transaction processing monitors are often used for distributing transactions within the corporation and between corporations. The OLTP monitor must be able to provide transaction services that can span individual OLTP and database systems. This includes the routing of the complete transaction or processing components of the transaction. When you use an ATM that is controlled by a bank that is not the same as the one where you keep your accounts, a transaction must be processed in at least two systems. One system is used to debit your account for the amount of the withdrawal and transfer money from your bank to the bank owning the ATM; another system is used to dispense the money, decrease the amount available at the ATM and accept money from your bank to cover your withdrawal.

TP MONITOR REQUIREMENTS

Previously we reviewed the ACID properties as a way of testing if a unit of work can be called a transaction. A TP monitor must also provide solutions to additional requirements in order to provide the service required by a transaction system. The resources required by the transaction are managed by the TP monitor. Therefore the monitor must contain properties and mechanisms normally found in an operating system or database system. Any comparison of commercial TP monitors should include a review of Table 19.1, which outlines the requirements and qualities that an OLTP system must provide.

TRUST CONSIDERATIONS OF OLTP

The OLTP system provides the availability and performance components of trust. TP monitor technology has been available for over 20 years and has been developed and tuned to deliver high transaction processing performance. This performance can be carried across distributed environments. The ACID properties have also been a feature of OLTP environments for quite some time. These properties have also been extended across multiple

TABLE 19.1
ON-LINE TRANSACTION PROCESSING MONITOR REQUIREMENTS

Requirement	TP Monitor
Priority management	Prioritize the execution of transactions by their prespecified priority or time of arrival.
Recovery	Preserve data updates in the event of system or application failures.
Application interface	Interface applications with the transaction monitor through standard APIs.
Data integrity	Preserve data integrity when managing concurrent updates and system failures.
Data access	Provide reliable real-time access to large database.
Performance	Process many transactions simultaneously without sacrificing performance to the users.
Security	Provide access to data only to authorized users and through authorized channels.

platforms in a heterogeneous environment. While the ACID properties are available on local databases, they are not generally extended across a distributed, heterogeneous environment. Almost all of the TP monitors contain security mechanisms that can manage access to the applications. Many of the OLTP implementations include support for DCE and the DCE security services. This support can provide strong authorization, authentication, and confidentiality across networked transactions.

OLTP Versus Database

The database products and the on-line transaction monitors are both trying to address similar problems but from somewhat different approaches. The choice between using an OLTP monitor or a database solution depends on the specific requirements defined by the problem. The choice, it seems, is also driven by almost religious beliefs in either of the approaches. There is likely no perfect choice for each transaction problem, but a few considerations should be taken into account. Table 19.2 contrasts a few of the considerations between using a TP monitor or a distributed database system for a transaction-based problem.

All of the database system vendors advertise the high rates of transactions per second or per minute that can be obtained with their technology. While very impressive scores can be obtained in a local environment, these

TABLE 19.2

TRANSACTION PROCESSING MONITOR VERSUS DISTRIBUTED DATABASE

Feature	TP Monitor	DDBMS
TP environment	Transactions and batch only, no ad hoc query	Transactions, batch, and ad hoc query
Client-server support	Calling services, conversations	Remote stored procedure calls
Distribution	Using application services or peer interaction	Using data or stored procedure access
Heterogeneous access	X/Open DTP interface	Proprietary gateways
Scope of resource management	Can commit resources across multiple resource manager	Cannot commit using remote resource managers
Scalability	Fewer resources are required to support the same work load	Require additional linear resources
Performance	Ablility to operate faster and handle higher volumes	Poor performance under heavy loads
Transaction management	X/OPEN DTP or proprietary	Proprietary
Number of users	Large number (> 100)	Small number (<100)
Data location	Stored in heterogeneous databases or file	Stored in homogeneous databases
Span of distribution	Any number of servers	Three servers or fewer
Security	Business function needs to be protected	Adequate data security

levels cannot normally be obtained if the transaction unit of work is distributed across a network. The main database transaction mechanism, the stored procedure, is used to initiate transactions in the database but normally cannot be used with other transaction units across the distributed environment. The database can only commit transaction resources that are managed by the vendors database. The database cannot synchronize or commit work that is managed by a foreign database of other resource manager.

The database solution is well suited to a local environment with a contained number of users. Applications can be quickly developed and implemented, and they are easier to set up and administer. A lot of development software exists for the development of applications using database technology. Packaged applications are also more readily available for database technology. A TP monitor can generally manage higher volumes of transaction invoked from any network locations or other applications. However, OLTP applications are generally more complex and difficult to develop.

DISTRIBUTED OLTP

The TP monitor keeps track of transactions that operate within a single server. In a distributed environment we also need to keep track of transactions that may be required to be executed across more than one server. To do this, we need to have additional mechanisms available in the TP monitor to manage the execution of a logical unit of work across multiple servers. This includes the commit and rollback requirements. In Chapter 9 we reviewed several models that are used for sharing work between client and servers. The same basic models are used for sharing work between TP systems. Some work has been accomplished to define a standard architecture that can be used by distributed transaction systems.

OSI TRANSACTION PROCESSING STANDARD

The International Standards Organization (ISO) has defined a layered network architecture standard called the Open System Interconnect (OSI) model. Definitions of the protocols and services, segmented into seven layers, are included in the architecture. The segmentation of the layers of the OSI model is used for many other network protocol and service definitions even if the specific protocols are not. The architecture model is used more often than the OSI protocols contained within it. The OSI architecture also contains two standards to help transaction processing systems interoperate. The OSI-TP (transaction processing) standard describes how the transaction identifiers should be defined and managed. Also included are mechanisms for coordinating the commit of logical units of work or rollback in the case of transaction failure. The OSI-CCR (commit, concurrence control, and recovery) defines the protocols for unit of work commitment used on a single session.

X/OPEN DISTRIBUTED TRANSACTION PROCESSING

X/OPEN is a not-for-profit international consortium of member corporations dedicated to the advancement of open systems. In X/OPEN terms, an open system is defined as a vendor-independent computer environment made up of commonly available products, implemented using accepted de jure and de facto standards. The distributed transaction processing (DTP) model of X/Open defines a set of application programming interfaces (APIs) and system-level interfaces that allow applications to interoperate with different transaction managers across multiple platforms while still forming a single logical transaction.

Figure 19.4 represents the X/OPEN distributed transaction processing model and the APIs between the resource managers. The DTP model is based on four software components.

- The application program (AP) defines the processes that make up the transaction and defines the transaction boundaries.
- The communication resource manager takes care of the coordinating transactions across applications.
- The resource manager (RM) provides access to shared resources.
- The transaction manager (TM) coordinates and manages the transactions including recovery if a failure occurs. The DTP standard uses the two-phase commit, as explained in Chapter 9.

The X/OPEN distributed transaction processing model defines APIs to service communication between the managers. The communication resource manager includes three interfaces that can be used to communicate with the application programs. The Common Programming Interface Communications (CPI-C) uses the SNA specification LU 6.2 for peer-to-peer communication. The transactional RPC (TxRPC) is the mechanism used by the Encina TP monitor. The XATMI specification is used by the Tuxedo OLTP system. The communication manager interacts with the transaction manager using the XA+ API. This API is used to inform the local transaction manager of the status of a distributed unit of work. The XA interface is used as the interface between the resource manager and the

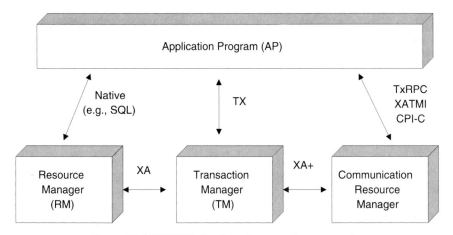

Figure 19.4 X/OPEN distributed transaction processing

transaction manager to synchronize resource changes. The TX interface is used between the transaction manager and the application program to define the beginning and the end of the unit of work. Transactions and TP monitors will be able to interoperate if they follow these API specifications.

TP MONITOR ORGANIZATION

We have just reviewed the DTP model from X/Open. That model defined the responsibilities and interfaces between the resource managers and the application to support distributed transactions. Let's use the DTP model as a base for describing a few of the services that are delivered by the component managers of a typical OLTP system. Figure 19.5 is an illustration of a model containing the required components to support distributed transaction processing. This is a logical model; some of these services may be provided by components outside of the specific OLTP system.

The communications manager is usually the first manager to receive the transaction from a user or from another connected system. The heart of the transaction processing system is the transaction manager. This manager is responsible for receiving the transaction requests and overseeing the transaction as it flows through the system. Transactions can be prioritized by type and a predefined class as well as by time of arrival. Those with a higher defined priority will be dispatched earlier than ones with less priori-

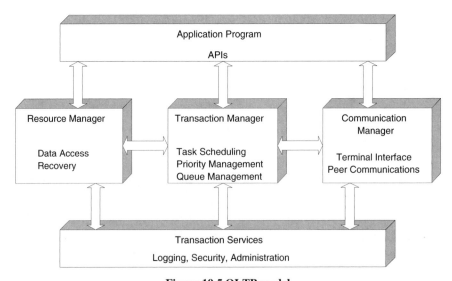

Figure 19.5 OLTP model

ty. The resource manager interacts with the files or the database to access and process the data required by the transaction. The applications interact with the managers through a standard API. A group of functions to provide transaction logging, administration, and security services supports the transaction processing system.

RESOURCE AND COMMUNICATION MANAGERS

The resource managers play a major part in the execution of the transactions. The communication manager dictates the interaction between the transaction processing system and the user or another connected system. Messages are assembled using the appropriate protocols and communication is established with the required user or system. The resource manager handles the requests for data from a file system or a database. The facilities required for a two-phase commit are managed in this area. The files and the database must be kept in a consistent state in the event of a transaction or system failure. This must extend across connected systems.

TRANSACTION SERVICES

Transaction administration functions are required to configure and manage the transaction and resource managers. The transaction must be identified as a collection of processes to be executed and have all the appropriate resources ready to allocate for the execution. Other transaction services include trace facilities that are invoked to keep track of a transaction that is in execution and aid in problem determination. A dump facility provides a snapshot of the status of an application and the associated resources to be used for problem analysis. Security services are required to be able to authenticate the user and determine if the user is authorized to execute the transaction.

TP MONITORS

The major developments in transaction systems tend to be in the area of distributed processing. The mainframe and highly specialized proprietary systems are being well served by their current processing capabilities. A lot of effort has been made to provide transaction processing on alternate platforms as well as providing distributed processing capabilities between the various platforms. The ability to distribute transaction work among various types and levels of platforms is a goal of a robust transaction processing system. There are several commercial transaction monitors available that address distributed transactions. The following sections outline a few of the more popular ones that include distributed transaction processing capabilities.

ENCINA

The Encina family of products from Transarc was developed to address the specific needs of the open, distributed OLTP requirements. The definition of open in this case refers mainly to the UNIX marketplace. Encina was developed to take advantage of the facilities provided by the Distributed Computing Environment from the OSF. Encina provides a fully featured TP monitor as well as many of the base services for the implementation of CICS from both IBM and Hewlett-Packard on a UNIX-based platform.

The architecture of Encina is based on two levels of technology in the architecture. Encina utilizes components from the OSF Distributed Computing Environment for some of the distributed services. The first level contains the services that extend the DCE environment to include distributed transaction support. The second level includes the services and resource managers to assemble and operate the distributed transactions.

The Encina monitor is the transaction processing engine that supports distributed transactions. The monitor is responsible for providing load balancing, cell management, and scheduling of the distributed transactions. Access to the transaction monitor by the clients is accomplished using terminals, PCs, or UNIX workstations. The monitor also uses the security services of DCE for authentication and authorization using access control lists (ACLs). The Encina monitor also provides the required administration functions for the configuration and support of the distributed transactions.

CICS

The Customer Information Control System (CICS) from IBM is the de facto standard for transaction processing applications with over 36,000 implementations worldwide. Almost all of the *Fortune* 100 companies operate a CICS environment to support a transaction processing system of some sort. The CICS system is also one of the more enduring transaction systems with the design originating in the late 1960s. The base architecture of CICS was developed to operate under an IBM mainframe operating system.

The CICS system manages the allocation of memory, scheduling of work (transactions) to be done by the processor, accessing of files, and delivering results to the user instead of the actual operating system. Management facilities are provided to assist with the configuration and operation of the CICS system. Transactions operating on a CICS systems are protected by internal CICS security mechanisms and by an external security monitor if available. The internal security mechanisms of CICS use a transaction-level and resource-level security. A user sign-on can be used to establish a user ID and a transaction and resource security level, although a sign-on is not required. A transaction security level (TSL) and a resource security level (RSL) key list is associated with a user definition. These lists are used to govern the ability to execute transactions and access resources. If the key of the transaction or resource matches a key in the RSL or TSL list of the user, the operation can proceed.

Both IBM and Hewlett-Packard offer a full-function CICS system operating under the UNIX operating system. The implementation of CICS on UNIX is actually a composite of several distributed computing facilities which provide complementary services. The CICS monitor runs on top of the services provided by Encina and replaces the Encina monitor. The distributed elements are provided by DCE, outside of the CICS region. The mainframe principles upon which the CICS design is based do not have the same impact or cause the same concern in a UNIX environment. The mainframe environment has been geared to batch program execution, while the UNIX environment is always available to execute commands from logged on users.

TUXEDO

The Tuxedo product is one of the more mature OLTP products targeted at a UNIX platform. It was introduced in 1983 by AT&T, owned for a time by Novell and now owned by BEA Systems, Inc. Tuxedo was one of the first products to provide a TP monitor for distributed systems. The product consists of three levels: the PC or workstation, the UNIX system, and the mainframe. Tuxedo provides interconnectivity with CICS, if additional mainframe software for Tuxedo is installed along with the CICS system. The communication between processes under Tuxedo is accomplished using software bridges which forward messages between processes that are not on the same machine. Tuxedo supports data-dependent routing which is the ability to route a message to the appropriate server node based on the contents of the message without the requirement of application coding. This routing criteria is defined and maintained in configuration tables.

TOP END

Top End is a transaction processing product developed by NCR and brought to the market in 1990. Top End supports multiple APIs, including one for CICS and another for Tuxedo. Top End has been ported to IBM, HP, and Sun platforms as well as the ones supported by AT&T. Top End is a message-passing product operating on a UNIX platform with DOS, Windows, OS/2, or Windows NT operating as clients. The product can also operate in a work load balancing capacity. The routing of a message can also be based on the contents of the message. Two types of application styles are supported: the standard application model and the managed server model. The standard application model specifies that the application is in full control of its own events with the application managing the entire transaction process. The managed server model operates like the Encina or CICS product, with the Top End system maintaining control on behalf of the applications. The main usage of the Top End product has been to support distributed decision support systems as much as typical distributed transaction processing systems.

APPLICATION DESIGN

The design of a transaction based application is somewhat different from that of a typical batch- or command-driven application. The application will be executed sharing resources with other transactions that also want to execute at about the same time. The transaction applications should be designed in a manner that requires them to hold on to resources for the shortest amount of time possible. We earlier discussed the logical unit of work. The transaction application should be designed to group the required functions into logical units of work. File or database updates will require an exclusive lock for a period of time. The shorter the period of time, the better to allow other transactions access. It is not considered good form if a transaction application reads a data record for update at the start of the transaction and does not release it until the end of the transaction. All of the other transactions must wait until the first transaction is complete. The transaction application must be viewed as a function to be completed in as quick a time as possible using the minimum of resources.

> Transaction processing is a lot like freeway traffic. When an accident occurs on the other side of a busy freeway, all traffic will be affected. When one car slows down to have a look, all of the others behind it must brake. In a very short period of time traffic can come to a dead stop miles from the accident.

OBJECT-ORIENTED TRANSACTIONS

The object-oriented paradigm is also being included in on-line transaction processing. Transaction processing is being combined with distributed objects. The Object Management Group (OMG) has adopted an interface called the Object Transaction Service (OTS) in the CORBA 2.0 specification to address distributed objects. The OTS enables objects that are distributed across multiple object request brokers to participate in an ACID transaction. This service provides for the interoperability of object transactions with procedural transactions if they adhere to the X/OPEN DTP standard. The OTS defines Interface Definition Language (IDL) interfaces for objects that make up a transactional unit. The marriage of objects and distributed transactions is a natural extension to object oriented processing.

THE TOP FIVE LIST

Distributed transactions can have many different approaches and use many different technologies to address the challenges. There are always issues and trade-offs to be taken into consideration when reviewing the potential solutions. We have constructed the following list of the top five issues or considerations, in terms of trust and security, facing organizations that are using or considering distributed transaction processing.

1. Authentication and Authorization. One of the main considerations in a distributed transaction processing environment is determining what the authorization and authentication requirements will be and where they need to be invoked. If a common security mechanism is used, such as that provided by DCE, the problem is mostly solved. If a common mechanism is not used, you have to determine where all of the places that authentication and authorization are required. Next you have to determine what is required for authentication and what will be used as identification for authorization. Will the authentication take place at the first point where the transaction is executed and making the transaction trusted after that? Will authentication be required at every distributed point the transaction is executed? Is the identification passed from one portion of the transaction processing system to another?

2. Resources. The resources (memory and processing power) that are consumed by a transaction system are difficult to estimate. The resources are dependent on how many transactions arrive to be processed by the system at any one time and the length of time it takes to complete the transaction. If you know precisely how many transactions will be executed in a given time frame and how many will be executed at any one time, then accurate resource planning is possible. There are three rules to use when planning the resources required by a transaction processing system.

- Rule 1—You never have enough resources.
- Rule 2—Your resource estimates are too low.
- Rule 3—See rule 1.

3. Rollback/Recovery/Restart. Any time work is distributed across multiple systems, consideration must be given to the implementation of mechanisms that provide rollback processes in the event of a transaction failure, and recovery and restart processes in the event of a system failure. These features should be built into the transaction monitors. Will the design of the transaction processing be influenced by the requirement for recovery and rollback? Perhaps you can break the transaction up into multiple logical units of work to make the recovery easier.

4. Transaction Tuning. Besides the wizardry involved in early transaction application programming, the next stop on the "Black Art" scale is transaction application tuning. A lot of attention must be paid to the performance and utilization information of the transaction that is available. An easy way to tune a transaction system is to throw more money at the problem by way of purchasing more resources. Tuning can be like those moving block puzzles where there are several square, movable pieces in a puzzle with one space open and the squares must be moved around to solve the puzzle. The real trick is to find the right open square so you can start moving the pieces. You need good detection and analysis tools to be able to determine what is happening in a transaction based system. This becomes a very complex problem when the transactions are spread over multiple systems. You have to know where to look.

5. Management. The management of a distributed transaction is one of the more challenging areas of system management. Specific tools to control and manage the environment should be obtained. Tools that span all of the systems in the distributed environment are required. Some action may have to be taken to respond to a congested system or when an unavailable resource is blocking transaction completion. Some thought should be given to monitors or platforms that have the ability to automatically balance the processing load over multiple executions of the transaction monitor. The management of the distributed processing system requires informed decisions. A monitoring tool operating in real time would be helpful in determining what is actually happening in the systems and what can be done if a problem is detected.

SUMMARY

The use of OLTP mechanisms can provide a strong, robust transaction environment in a distributed environment. This may be one of the only choices in a high-volume or heterogeneous environment. The advancement of object technology will again change the nature of transactions and transaction processing. On-line transaction processing on the mainframe utilizes mature, reliable products, while transaction processing systems for a distributed environment are the new kids on the block.

As this distributed environment matures, the transaction processing capabilities will also improve. The key is to use a standards based distributed processing infrastructure. Competition for OLTP systems comes from the more established database systems with transaction capabilities. At this point in time it is perhaps better to look at industry standards and the products that use them for a solution rather than at proprietary based products. The ability to connect and manage these systems will also mature. Now about those distributed object-oriented transactions ...

PART IV

SOLVING THE PROBLEM

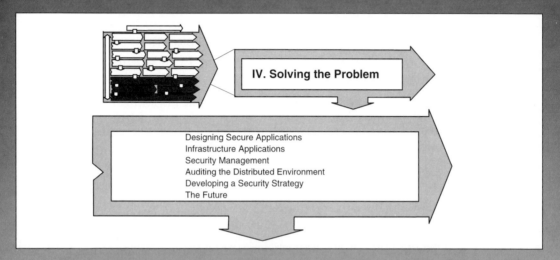

IV. Solving the Problem

Designing Secure Applications
Infrastructure Applications
Security Management
Auditing the Distributed Environment
Developing a Security Strategy
The Future

In previous chapters, we have described the challenge of security in the distributed computing environment. We have seen how large and complex the problem truly is. We have reviewed the need for constructing proper foundations in the form of policy, guidelines, and architecture. We have also examined many of the leading technologies in distributed computing. It was seen how technology not only provides solutions for, but may also contribute to, the problem of computing security. In the following chapters, we discuss actions that can be used to address the problem.

In Chapter 20, we will outline how security must be designed, from the very beginning, into applications. It is very difficult, if not impossible, to retrofit security into client-server applications once they have been developed for implementation. We will also examine the use of object-oriented technology and the many security issues that this technology introduces. In Chapter 21, we will examine how security can be deployed in infrastructure applications. In particular, we will review its use in electronic mail and workgroup computing.

Security management is the focus of Chapter 22. It will examine the role that centralized security technology can play, as well as review various aspects of the management of security. Many of us use electronic devices to add further protection to our homes. A common sales pitch presents the message that they offer us *peace of mind.* Why? What is it about the use of an electronic alarm system that allows us to trust that our house is safe? Some of the reasons behind our faith in electronic alarms are

- When triggered, they automatically sound an alarm, regardless of whether or not we are at home.
- Alerts of illicit entry can be detected from many entrances.
- They can summon others for assistance.
- Compared to the potential loss from a burglary, they are inexpensive.
- They are relatively easy to use and implement.

The same reasons behind the use of automated alarms in our homes are also valid in the distributed computing environment. An automated alert, which notifies us of illicit entry into our networks and computer systems, will increase the overall security of our computing environment. Once an alert is given, security personnel can get involved in dealing with the incident.

Chapter 23 will provide the reader with a methodology that we have used to address the overall problem of computing security. Termed a security strategy, it provides a method of analyzing those steps that will move to, or in some cases merely maintain, the appropriate level of security for an organization.

In Chapter 24, we will explore the important role of audit in ensuring that standards and guidelines are followed. Unfortunately, in many organizations there exists a confrontational attitude between the internal audit and information technology departments. We will examine the reasons behind this problem and suggest how an effective relationship can be implemented.

The final chapter presents a contradictory view of the future. There are many reasons to believe that the problem of computing security, as we currently know it, will be solved. Improved technologies, management commitment, the increased use of encryption, and many other factors will contribute to the overall solution. On the other hand, we also argue that the problem itself will continue to evolve and will become more complex and sinister in its nature.

SECURE APPLICATIONS

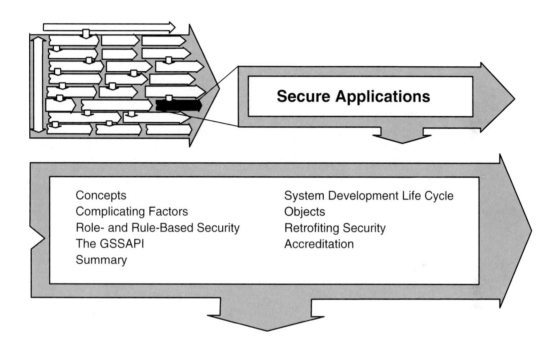

Secure Applications

Concepts	System Development Life Cycle
Complicating Factors	Objects
Role- and Rule-Based Security	Retrofiting Security
The GSSAPI	Accreditation
Summary	

Security must be an important consideration in the design and development of distributed computing applications. The mainframe environment, with its centralized security mechanisms, has allowed the application designer to concentrate on the security requirements of the application itself. With a distributed system, the question of application security becomes more complex. The developers of a distributed application not only have to address the specific security mechanisms for the application but also address security issues of the distributed environment. The advent of client-server computing has promoted the physical separation of the computing resources, and with it, created additional security risks.

The security of the network also poses some unique challenges to implementing a secure application. Security may be both difficult and costly to introduce into a distributed application after the design has been completed. In this chapter, we will see that it is imperative that security be an important consideration in every stage of the application development, from requirements definition, through development and deployment. We will begin our discussion on the design of secure applications by examining a few key concepts.

CONCEPTS

The term trusted computing base (TCB) is used to describe the sum of the security protection mechanisms within a computing system. It is an important concept for the design of distributed applications because it forces us to review the security of the computing environment, not just the application itself. The concept of a TCB forces a designer to question the security of nontraditional aspects of the application, such as the security of the operating system. In a sense, it expands the scope of an application design to include operating system and network components. The concept of a TCB is important in order to understand the overall security of the operating system and how to determine how much reliance an application can place on its function. For example, considerations for a UNIX application design might include additional security mechanisms to deter the use of Trojan horse programs, spoofing or the other types of attacks we saw in Chapter 11.

Another important concept in considering distributed applications is the security domain. A security domain is defined as the collection of information or applications to which a person or process has access and where common security policies are in force to govern that access. There may be one or several defined domains in a distributed processing system. It is important to determine or recognize these security domains during the design phase of the system. Interoperability between security domains is determined by the security technologies, policies, and standards that span the domains. We need to understand if separate security domains exist and what needs to be done to operate and secure the access between the domains.

SYSTEM DEVELOPMENT LIFE CYCLE

Many organizations have adopted a formal approach or methodology for the development of computing applications, called a system development life cycle (SDLC). This life cycle defines the processes and milestones that are required to guide a computing project from first concept to implementation, and ongoing operation of the application. This formalized process is sometimes formed by experience, adopted from published material or in some cases dependent on the development technologies. In any case, security considerations must be included in whatever life-cycle process is used.

There are many different approaches to the implementation of computer applications. The classic approach to application development has six broad phases: the initial requirements definition, analysis and design, the development of the application software, testing, implementation, and the ongoing operation and maintenance of the application.

Figure 20.1 provides an overview of the system development life-cycle process.

Other methodologies, such as rapid application development (RAD), attempt to shorten the time to deployment through the use of advanced software development and prototyping tools. RAD essentially seeks to shorten the development phases by allowing users active involvement in all phases of the project. The basic concepts of the SDLC are still valid, however, regardless of the methodology or technique used.

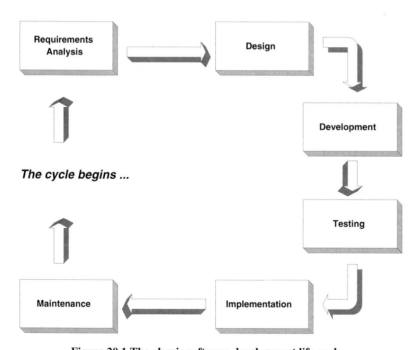

Figure 20.1 The classic software development life cycle

REQUIREMENTS PHASE

The objective of the requirements phase is to collect and document the business requirements that will be addressed by the application. These will include aligning the application requirements with the business objectives of the organization and determining the needs of user departments. Overall performance and cost objectives for the application may also be collected. We believe that the security objectives for the application must also be outlined. Many security objectives can be obtained from the corporate security principles and policies, as described in Chapters 4 and 6.

The active participation of the Security and Audit departments, especially on the development of large or mission-critical applications, is strongly recommended. Their role will be to ensure the application will meet corporate security and audit objectives. There are a number of advantages to involving Security and Audit as early as possible in the development of the application. First, both departments will ultimately pass judgment on the conformance to corporate policy and security procedures of the application. It is simply common sense to seek their input as soon as possible. Second, securing the application may impact both the timeline and cost of the application. It is best to determine these constraints as early as possible. Finally, failure to address security requirements early in the project merely delays the problem. We have witnessed many organizations scrambling to address security requirements after the development and even deployment of the application. Nine times out of ten this approach to the security of the application will diminish the alternatives available and subsequently increase the cost of addressing the problem. And we all recognize the truth that it is prudent to ask management once, and only once, for funding.

The overall security requirements may include requirements for determining the identity of users (authentication), safeguards to protect corporate or personal information from unauthorized disclosure (confidentiality), and the recording of user actions (audit trails). Corporate computing policy and principles, if they exist, are an excellent source for overall security requirements.

DESIGN AND ANALYSIS

In the design and analysis phase, the requirements of the application are analyzed against the constraints of cost and time. This process is essentially one of selecting the appropriate balance in which the application will meet the overall requirements and objectives for the least cost. It is more productive and cost effective to address the security requirements of an application during the design phase of a system. Security that is added after the fact is usually not as effective and is more costly to implement and maintain. This is where security principles, policies, and architecture comes in. We can use them as a reference blueprint to check off the security requirements. They will assist in making the decisions on what needs to be included and where the functions belong. The provision for audit information must also be considered during the design phase. Finally, the performance of the selected security mechanisms must be considered.

A preliminary activity for the design and analysis phase is an analysis of risk. The process seeks to balance the expected consequences of a security exposure against the likelihood that it will occur. This forces the application design team to focus on those security problems that have a higher probability of resulting in a significant incident causing material damage or loss to the organization. For example, if an application is intended to be accessed using dialin, what is the likelihood someone else could tap the line and discover passwords? What is the likelihood that someone may discover an employee's password, and if so, what are the consequences if the intruder can access the application?

After the analysis of risk is performed, the application design team can begin to address the security requirements defined in the previous phase. Again, the process is one of seeking an appropriate balance. For example, if confidential employee information is to be stored on a laptop computer, what controls should be used to protect the data? Should software to protect the laptop by providing access controls such as user ID and passwords be used? Is encryption of the data required, and if used, what type and strength are appropriate? Should a hardware device be used to protect the encryption algorithm and its keys? An analysis of risk will help to answer these questions. Constraints, such as performance and cost, will of course also heavily influence the design selection.

In client-server applications, designers must address the question of how comprehensive the security environment will be. Are controls required on personal computers to protect unauthorized access to the personal computer? Should encryption be used to protect data stored on the personal computer? If encryption is used on the personal computer, is additional hardware, such as a smart card, required to protect the encryption algorithm and keys? How trustworthy is the network between the client and server? Does network traffic need to be encrypted? Is it all traffic or only selected data fields? Are additional operating system or database controls required on the server? What audit trails are required and where will they be kept? Corporate computing policy and principles may provide the answers to some of these questions. The active involvement of both the Security and Audit departments is also recommended. We recognize that it is never possible to answer every possible security concern and exposure. The best approach is to balance the exposure using the resources available and have management decide whether additional resources are warranted.

APPLICATION DEVELOPMENT AND TESTING

Security controls should be rigorously tested prior to the deployment of an application. The testing should include active tests of the middleware, operating system, database, and network controls. Called a risk assessment, the objective of the tests should be to determine whether or not unauthorized access to the application, database, or operating system is permitted. If possible, those conducting the tests should not be members of the development team. A person not connected with the development will not make assumptions about the environment and is more likely to uncover any exposures missed by the development team. A sensitive application may also warrant a structured *walk-through* of the actual application code. A code walk-through can be used to detect fraudulent activity by the application programmers and designers.

The use of test data should also be reviewed. There should be a strict segregation of test and production environments. No possibility should exist for the test data to be moved to the production environment. Application programmers and developers should not have access, through the testing activity, to sensitive information to which they would not normally have access.

IMPLEMENTATION

The security considerations for application development fall into a few distinct categories. The first one concerns the protection of the application itself, another deals with the implementation of security features into the applications, a third addresses the test and production environment, and the last one is concerned with the ongoing maintenance of the application. The protection of the application is perhaps the most straightforward to address. Access to the applications should be limited only to those with a defined need.

In general, it is not a good idea to incorporate specific security functions into the applications if alternatives are available. Specific passwords or other authentication services should not be coded into the applications. The applications should not be allowed to operate in a privileged state. If errors or bugs are encountered, users should not be left in a privileged condition which gives unauthorized access to applications or facilities. The applications should operate under a principle of least privilege, by which only the privilege level that is absolutely required is given to the user.

The application testing and production environments should be isolated. Testing should be carried out without the fear of changing or impacting the production systems. In no case should live production data be used for application testing. Otherwise, the integrity of the production data could be at stake. Once the system has passed testing, a formalized change process should be invoked to implement the system into production. The segregation of the duties involved in application development, testing, implementation, and operation is an important principle and one that is not regularly addressed. Basically the principle states that no one person should have the ability to make changes to the applications, and then implement those changes into production. The duties should be clearly defined to limit the potential for unauthorized access or modification of production systems by any one individual.

Testing of the applications for errors that could have security impacts is also very important. A great deal of the security holes that hackers exploit are the result of software errors or bugs that can open a doorway into other parts of the system and even take command of the operating system. Testing the applications for unusual occurrences, what if I overload this string value for example, will reduce the risk of these type of security exposures.

MAINTENANCE

A recurring headache of a distributed application is the requirement for distributing and implementing changes. This headache seems to grow exponentially depending on the number and geographic location of the applications that must be changed. A formalized change management process is required to ensure that all of the required changes are implemented correctly and in a timely manner. This usually means that all changes must be implemented at the same time, or at least in a coordinated manner, in all locations. The change management process must also ensure that only authorized changes are implemented. Automation of the change process is a great help in this area.

The change management should be governed by a policy outlining the responsibilities for implementing change and the processes for making the change happen. The security of the change management process should ideally be considered during the design phase of the system. An attacker should not be able to use the change management system to distribute unauthorized software such as Trojan horse programs. An application change should only be required for alterations to the processing logic. The applications themselves should not require a change when the authorization tables are updated or the security rules are changed. It is also a good idea to choose security standards that will allow interoperability or incorporation of other security mechanisms into the system.

ACCREDITATION

The accreditation of a system is a formal recognition that the system meets a defined standard for security as measured by an official process. The outcome of an accreditation program is an official acceptance of risk. An accreditation program is much like a quality control process used to verify that security standards will be met. Every system and application should be subject to an accreditation process before they are moved into production. This process reviews the security components of the system to see if the design requirements and standards are followed, as well as checking to make sure they are the correct solution for the problem. The accreditation process should also be undertaken on a periodic basis, particularly after substantive changes have been made to the system.

The components of a formal accreditation process include assurance testing and certification. Assurance testing exercises the controls to gauge whether they are technically correct and effective. A certification process is a formal way of testing the security mechanisms to see if they still meet the specified standards when implemented. The more critical or higher the risk to the system, the more formal the certification process should be. This process should be undertaken by an authority that was not involved in designing or building the system. Planning for assurance should be included in the system development life cycle.

THE GSSAPI

There is help available for the need to integrate security services into applications. A standard has been proposed that provides the link between the application program and the required security functions. The Generic Security Service Application Programming Interface (GSSAPI) is a proposed standard of the Network Working Group of the Internet Engineering Task Force, described by the request for comment (RFC) 1508. The GSS-API provides a generic interface to the security functions for client-server applications. A variety of security mechanisms can be used with the GSS-API using a number of API calls from the application. The responsibility for managing specific security mechanisms can be removed from the application. The GSSAPI is security mechanism independent and protocol independent. It is intended to allow source level portability of the applications between different environments.

An implementation of an application using the GSSAPI would be to interface the application with the security functions supplied by the Distributed Computing Environment (DCE). The application can communicate with the DCE security server using the GSSAPI instead of the application being required to become a DCE node of its own. The GSSAPI on the client platform is used to request and manage the required security credentials between the DCE security server and the target applications. The GSS-API can be used to provide privacy for the communications, data origin authentication, and data integrity in the distributed system. Work is also continuing on expanding the use of the GSSAPI to provide security for World Wide Web (WWW) applications.

OBJECTS

We have talked a bit about distributed objects in Chapter 9 and outlined a few of the considerations for security. One of the biggest challenges in a distributed object-oriented application is to make sure the required protection follows the objects. One of the main characteristics of an object-oriented system is its ability to delegate function from client object to target object. The execution path may not always be predictable, a target object can itself become a client object. The objects that are potentially distributed around various platforms do not normally carry the concept of a user. In order to protect the objects from unauthorized access, we need a way to provide a credential from one object to another.

We generally use a user ID or some other way of assigning a unique identity to the person or program requesting the application service. We also need a list of the privileges associated with this identification. In Chapter 9 we looked at the need for an object request broker to referee the access to the distributed objects. The ORB must also include responsibilities for managing the relationships between the objects in order to preserve the required level of protection. We need to ensure that the access to the objects is authorized no matter how the object was invoked. The privileges that are established when the user or system is authenticated need to be delegated to all of the objects that may be executed.

The standards and technologies dealing with the security of distributed object computing are not yet as mature as other distributed technologies. When considering distributed object processing, the object framework that provides the richest level of security functions and provides the greatest flexibility should be considered. The growth in the use of public key technology and the use of certificates and certification authorities will help define the required functions and qualities of the object framework. The ORB should be able to take advantage of differing security technologies while hiding the differences from the applications.

The concept of objects can challenge the identification, authentication, and authorization processes that we normally associate with users. Objects do not generally have a concept of a user. This situation is further complicated if the objects are distributed across multiple locations or platforms. The database systems generally do a very good job of protecting the database with their own security systems. This becomes less evident when the database is accessed by a transaction or object-oriented system. Due to the security complications when using object technology, it is strongly recommended that the Security and Audit departments be involved in the entire application design process.

ROLE- AND RULE-BASED SECURITY

Authorization is usually performed using the identity of the individual or process requesting authorization. This means that the mechanisms used for authorization must access a list defining these identities and the privileges associated with them. This can lead to a large amount of administration time and effort to maintain the identification and privileges lists. Additions or changes to these lists because of employment or responsibility changes may require significant attention.

Another way of allowing authorized access is by using defined roles instead of an individual identity. A role is defined by the job responsibility and not by the user, and as such are group oriented rather than user oriented. Authorized access is granted by membership in a role group instead of by individual identity. This can reduce the overall administration requirements as well as moving the responsibility for defining the required security from the system administrator to the defined security policies and guidelines. Instead of maintaining privileges by individual, they are defined by role. A change in a person's responsibility will simply reflect a different role rather than change to all of the locations where authorization lists may be maintained.

An extension of role-based security is the ability of providing authorization based on business rules instead of an identity. The usual authorization decision is based on determining if the individual can access the protected resource or not. There may be a requirement to allow access to the protected resource by the type or characteristic of the request rather than only the request. For example, one individual may be allowed to process transactions for dollar amounts up to $1,000 while another is allowed to process the same transaction for amounts up to $10,000. Many applications have provided this function by including a specific program code to handle the required access rules. This can be very cumbersome if the rules have to be included and maintained in all of the locations the authorization process is required.

A more appropriate response in a distributed system would be to have a centralized authorization service grant access based on the business rules applied to the identity or role of the request. These rules can be incorporated into the authorization process. Hewlett-Packard, for example, provides a centralized authorization service that has the ability to grant authorization from distributed requests, based on defined business rules. This removes the requirement for an application code to apply the rules. These rules can be changed without altering the application code. Temporary changes in the authorizations can be accommodated without elaborate additional authorizations or overrides. Security can be implemented at a finer level of granularity without incurring significant extra effort.

RETROFITTING SECURITY

Throughout this chapter, we have stated that security must be designed into an application from the start. If this has not occurred, it is possible to retrofit security into a production application environment. The trick will be to introduce security in a manner that is least disruptive to the production environment. For example, one approach to network security concerns would be to introduce hardware encrypting devices between the client and server. These *black boxes* would be used to encrypt data flowing between the client and server. There would be no need for any modification of either the client or server code. An alternative approach to the problem of introducing secure network traffic on a LAN-based network, would be to intercept traffic between the LAN card and the application. The software solution rests between the application and the network and can be used to seamlessly intercept and decrypt application traffic between a client and server.

Retrofitting security to an application system should never be a preferred approach. While technical solutions do exist, as with most problems it is always best to address the issue of security as early as possible. Failure to plan and act early will limit the choices available to solve the problem and most likely increase the overall cost.

SUMMARY

In today's client-server environment, it is neither a simple task nor inexpensive to retrofit security into a system. Unlike the mainframe environment, comprehensive controls cannot usually be independently layered on top of applications. Security must be addressed early in application design or included as a core component of the application development process.

The security considerations for computer applications include the secure development and management of the applications as well as the security facilities required by the applications. The security considerations don't end when the system has been implemented. Security must be considered at the design phase of any computer system with specific requirements included during the development phase. As there is an amazing array of security approaches and technologies available, the challenge is to integrate the right ones into the application. In the next chapter, we will examine how security is being put to work in a number of distributed applications.

CHAPTER 21

IMPLEMENTATION EXAMPLES

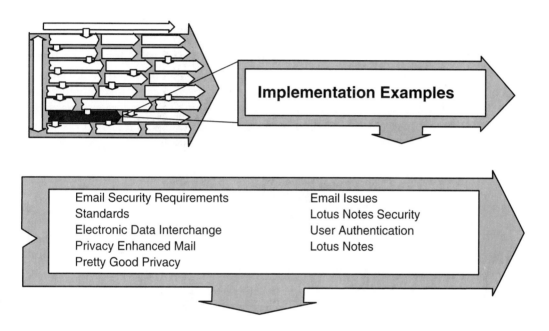

Implementation Examples

Email Security Requirements
Standards
Electronic Data Interchange
Privacy Enhanced Mail
Pretty Good Privacy

Email Issues
Lotus Notes Security
User Authentication
Lotus Notes

Okay, now let's get down to business. We have spent a good deal of energy outlining the issues and complexities of operating in a distributed secure environment. Now it's time to put this environment to work. One common application that is well on the way to operating in a secure, distributed manner is an electronic mail system. Extensions to mail systems, which are having a great impact, are the groupware products operating as distributed knowledge support systems. In this chapter we will examine the trust issues involved in distributed electronic mail systems, and see how emerging technologies and standards are addressing them. We will also look at how the trust issues are addressed by one of the leading groupware products, Lotus Notes.

We will define infrastructure applications as those that utilize a framework of technology and standards to execute their functions within a distributed processing environment. In other words, these applications communicate and coordinate between systems to complete their tasks. To do this requires either a common interface, or an interface capable of communicating with all of the various platforms and mail applications.

ELECTRONIC MAIL

Electronic mail or messaging systems have been around for quite a while. They have matured from simple messaging store and forward systems to fully functional distributed applications. The very early mail implementations provided a central mail box repository to deposit messages and a method for storing and retrieving them. Each user was assigned his or her own mail box. The mailing of a message was as easy as storing the message in another mail box. The user formatted, mailed, and retrieved the mail messages using the central mail application. This worked well as long as everyone could use the same mail system.

Simple messaging applications also migrated to the PC/LAN environment. These applications served a local population of users as a departmental mail box system. Next came the challenge of connecting these departmental systems to other mail systems and potentially other organizations. This problem was relatively easy to solve if the mail products that were being used came from the same vendor and followed the same standards. The solutions were less clear when different products were involved. Some of the more popular products provided translation gateways to move mail between their products to solve some of the problems.

Providing electronic mail system security is a major challenge when dealing with the interconnection of mail systems. Sending confidential messages across a network requires that the transmission be secure and protected from eavesdropping. The message sender should be authenticated to prove who sent it and prohibit spoofing of the sender's identity. The message should also be sent in such a manner to protect its integrity and detect any changes. The message system should also provide proof of delivery to ensure the message was delivered and read by the intended recipient.

There are two standard electronic mail (email) architectures used for providing email services directly to users and for interconnecting proprietary email systems. The first architecture, which defines a vendor independent mail standard, is commonly known as the X.400 standard. This standard includes a comprehensive set of security mechanism specifications. The second is known as the Internet mail architecture. The security features of this architecture are not as mature as those in X.400. The Privacy Enhanced Mail (PEM) option of the Internet mail architecture became operational in 1993 and also provides security features. Pretty Good Privacy (PGP) is a public key encryption tool, which has found widespread popularity in its application to Internet mail. We will look at these security components in a little more detail later.

EMAIL SECURITY REQUIREMENTS

Today's electronic mail systems are used to communicate both within and between organizations. To support this external communication requirement, a secure method of sending messages between mail systems is required. Table 21.1 outlines some of the requirements needed to support this secure message interchange. All of these requirements should be addressed before confidence can be placed in a mail system.

TABLE 21.1
ELECTRONIC MAIL SECURITY REQUIREMENTS

Requirement	Explanation
Proof of submission	Verification that the message was accepted by the mail system.
Proof of delivery	Verification that the message was delivered to the mail addressee.
Confidentiality	Verification that the contents of the message is kept private and the fact that a message was sent may also be kept private.
Proof of origin	Ability to prove the identity of the sender of a message.
Anonymity	Ability to send a message so that the recipient cannot discover the identity of the sender.
Audit	Ability of the system to record security related events for later analysis.
Self-destruction	Ability for the message sender to specify that the message should be destroyed after it is received and read by the recipient.
Nonrepudiation	Ability to prevent the denial that the sender sent a message or that the recipient received the message.
Message integrity	Reassurance that a message or a set of messages arrive in the order they are transmitted, without any loss of data.
Key management	The ability to coordinate security keys among the mail system participants without compromising the security of the keys.

STANDARDS

As in almost every other area of distributed computing, there are several standards that are involved in distributed electronic mail services. Some of these standards are complementary, some of them are competing. The standards are constantly changing as the distributed technologies mature and our focus on electronic mail technologies shifts. We will outline a few of the standards currently involved in distributed mail services.

X.400 MAIL SERVICES

The X.400 standard, as defined jointly by the International Standards Organization (ISO) and the International Telecommunications Union (ITU), defines a vendor-independent mail standard. This standard is used by network applications to store and forward messages for transfer between applications such as email. Compliance to the X.400 specification is now a standard requirement for most public service or military messaging applications. Most email vendors support the X.400 standard or market X.400 compliant products. The standard provides for support of binary large objects (BLOBs) to exchange image, fax, or other binary files that can be attached to mail messages. The X.400 specifications include directory services as defined by the X.500 standard. Security for X.400 is specified in part by the X.509 standard. The X.509 standard, previously mentioned in Chapter 15, specifies the mechanisms for password identification, encryption, digital signatures, and audit.

X.400 SECURITY

The security features of the X.400 standard are comprehensive and are in fact used as a model for other open system applications. The X.400 architecture includes a logical level called the user agents (UA) and a lower level called the message transfer system (MTS). The MTS is comprised of a number of message transfer agents (MTA). The UA performs all of the message services that are in contact with the user. The MTA provides the message store and forward services to carry the messages from one UA to the appropriate destination UA. Additions have been made to the X.400 standards to support the transfer of electronic data interchange (EDI) transactions defined as the X.435 standards.

The X.400 secure messaging features comprise 19 elements of service that can be grouped into five areas: basic end-to-end services, message path services, MTS corroborative services, nonrepudiation services, and security management services. There is currently no encryption algorithm identified in the standard and either a private key or public key encryption mechanism can be used. The X.400 standards provide a wide range of security options that are available for implementation. The options include message origin authentication, proof of delivery, content integrity, content confidentiality, peer entity authentication, and several nonrepudiation services.

X.500 DIRECTORY SERVICES

One of most basic problems is finding out where things are. The X.500 Directory can be utilized to join and organize information from different sources in a way that is useful to both users and applications. This capability is defined by a set of standards published jointly by the International Standards Organization (ISO) and the Consultative Committee for International Telephony and Telegraphy (CCITT). The X.500 Directory is defined by a schema, very similar to an object-oriented schema, that provides a map of the overall logical structure. The base structure of the X.500 directory is a tree structure which holds global or general information near the top and more detailed information about the objects farther down the tree. The objects in the tree inherit attributes from the objects found along the path down to the root. When implemented, the X.500 Directory can appear as a single directory while maybe actually using several directories that are distributed across multiple platforms and locations.

VENDOR-INDEPENDENT MESSAGING

Vendor-independent messaging (VIM) is a message interface that is supported by several software vendors including Lotus, Apple, IBM, Borland, Oracle, WordPerfect, and Novell. VIM was designed to provide a cross-platform message interface. It is a specification for directly addressing the mail engines from the various client environments instead of providing a gateway. The message layer is actually a part of the various email engines. The individual vendors provide support for VIM on their traditional platforms. VIM consists of 55 API calls to support simple mail, message store, and directory services. While the name implies that VIM is a vendor-independent standard, the reality is that it represents a rather small group of message system vendors.

MESSAGING APPLICATION PROGRAMMING INTERFACE

Messaging Application Programming Interface (MAPI) is Microsoft's answer to the electronic mail standard. It is a Windows-based data link library (DLL) that performs client services and interfaces with other mail processing engines through the service provider interface (SPI). The basic functions, which are called simple MAPI, include a series of 12 API calls that invoke common services to mail, store, and provide directory services. For additional functionality, advanced features called extended MAPI, give an additional set of API calls. These 100+ API calls provide support for more complex messages and functions as well as additional mail services. The inclusion of the MAPI client functions in the operating system, such as Windows for Workgroups, provides free mail access but may limit the cross-platform choices in a distributed environment since MAPI is specific to the Windows environment.

COMMON MAIL CALLS

Common Mail Calls (CMC) was defined by the X.400 API Association (XAPIA) as a way of providing support for both VIM and MAPI. The CMC interface defines common messaging calls between these messaging services and the mail-enabled applications. Both Microsoft and Lotus provide libraries that application developers can use to avoid maintaining separate versions of mail products for either VIM or MAPI. The CMC specification provides for ten API calls for simple mail functions. The use of an interface standard like CMC reduces the available functions to a common subset and does not support many of the extended message functions that both VIM and MAPI do.

SIMPLE MAIL TRANSPORT PROTOCOL

The Simple Mail Transport Protocol (SMTP) is supported mainly in the UNIX domain and is the main transport specification used for mail on the Internet. The use of this protocol has also been one of the biggest opportunities for hackers. The mail programs that use SMTP have been the victim of several attacks that have exploited the security exposures provided by the debugging capabilities of the mailer. These exposures have included using the UNIX mailer to forward copies of the password file, using flaws in the debug process to obtain superuser privileges, and saving files with high-level privileges.

MULTIPURPOSE MAIL EXTENSIONS

Multipurpose Mail Extensions (MIME) is an Internet standard to define how message types, other than ASCII text, can be passed using an Internet mail message. The types of content definitions include text, multipart, message, application, image, audio and video as defined in the Internet Request For Comment (RFC) 1521, Part I for text, and RFC 1552, Part II for non-ASCII text. The Hypertext Transfer Protocol uses MIME to describe the content of documents. The basic MIME specification does not include specific security protection.

The Internet RFC 1847, Security Multiparts for MIME, defines the interface to the security services which may be applied to the parts of the

MIME message. The RFC defined two new types of the parts of a MIME message: multipart signed and multipart encrypted. The multipart signed type specifies how authentication and integrity is supported by using a digital signature. The multipart encrypted specifies how a message part is kept confidential by using encryption. The RFC does not actually specify security standards but describes a framework of how MIME can interface with other existing security protocols.

And yet another Internet RFC (1848), MIME Object Security Services (MOSS), defines the security protocols that can be applied to the multipart framework defined by RFC 1847. MOSS is in fact based in large part on the Privacy Enhanced Mail standard defined by RFC 1421. The MOSS services is based on public cryptography. The originator of a message will use a private key to apply a digital signature to the message and use the recipient's public key to encrypt the message for confidentiality. The receiver of the message decrypts the message with their private key and checks the digital signature using the sender's public key. The use of MIME security will enable different message content types or body parts to be protected or not, as well as allowing the components of the message to be protected with different security services.

ELECTRONIC DATA INTERCHANGE

One of the innovations actually spurred on by changing economic factors, has been the use of electronic data interchange (EDI). EDI can be described as the movement of commerce documents, in electronic form, to support a business relationship. The change to just-in-time inventory systems by many manufacturers is aided by the support of electronic interchange of the purchase orders and confirmations. In some cases the requirement for parts or materials, for example, to manufacture automobiles, is measured in hours. EDI is a specific business implementation of a network message system designed to support this quick order and ship requirement. One business sends a purchase order message to the parts supplier which is in turn confirmed to the requester with a returned shipping notice. The invoice can be returned by the same route.

Various standards for EDI exist, usually based on specific industry implementations. The standards generally fall into three main groups. The United Nations/Technical Document Interchange is used mostly to support European EDI. The ANSI X.12 standard is the EDI standard ratified by the American National Standards Institute (ANSI). The Electronic Data Interchange for Administration, Trade and Commerce (EDIFACT) is the emerging international standard. The X.435 standard, EDI messaging service enhancement to X.400, allows for both mail and EDI transactions to share the same mail backbone. X.435 is essentially the envelope into which the EDI transaction messages are placed. The extended security capabilities provided by X.435 include proof and nonrepudiation of transaction notification, proof of content received, and nonrepudiation of content origin or received. When you are using an electronic system to advise you on how many parts should be produced, you will want to confirm that the order and its contents are genuine.

PRIVACY ENHANCED MAIL

Privacy Enhanced Mail (PEM) is a draft Internet standard that defines message encryption and authentication procedures to provide secure mail services on the Internet. The standard specification is contained in a four part set of Internet Request for Comment (RFC 1421) documents. These documents include, Part 1: Message Encryption and Authentication Procedures; Part 2: Certificate-Based Key Management; Part 3: Algorithms, Modes, and Identifiers; and Part 4: Key Certification and Related Services. PEM is designed to work with existing email systems, but is primarily directed at mail systems using the Simple Mail Transfer Protocol (SMTP). Internet mail is built upon an underlying text-string transport system rather than a transparent binary transport system as with X.400. This makes it necessary for PEM to include some extra processing steps beyond the usual cryptographic functions.

PEM is designed to work with existing electronic mail systems by providing security with three types of messages. A PEM message is basically a normal mail message protected by PEM. A simple message integrity check (MIC) message provides integrity and authentication checks but no confidentiality. Another type of PEM MIC message provides the same services as the simple MIC message but includes an additional encoding step that allows the message to pass through various mail gateways. This type of message will ensure the integrity and signature information remains intact. The final type of message adds confidentiality to the integrity and authentication components. Various private and public key encryption mechanisms can be used for integrity and authentication. The message type that uses encryption currently uses only the DES encryption algorithm.

PRETTY GOOD PRIVACY

This is an interesting technology with an odd name and an odder pedigree. A computer programmer by the name of Phil Zimmerman developed an encryption program that he intended to be used as shareware. Mr. Zimmerman's intention was to provide the capability of strong encryption to the computing public. Unfortunately the early versions of PGP utilized the

RSA encryption algorithm which violated the patent held by RSA. A copy of this program found it's way onto the Internet. Since the program was readily available, it quickly became an informal standard for security using encryption although it was technically illegal. Legal and supported versions of the program now exist but they may still be subject to U.S. export restrictions.

Pretty Good Privacy (PGP) is a general encryption program which uses public key cryptography to provide privacy and authentication. PGP is becoming very popular because of its flexibility and relatively low cost. PGP provides confidentiality, data origin authentication, message integrity, and nonrepudiation of origin services for electronic mail. It is designed to work within an existing electronic mail system, primarily those used on the Internet. The International Data Encryption Algorithm (IDEA) is used for data encryption, the RSA algorithm for encryption key management, and either MD5 (Message Digest 5) or RSA for the message integrity checks and digital signatures. The IDEA encryption algorithm is a relatively new one that was developed in Switzerland and is based on a 128-bit key.

PGP has been under a cloud of controversy regarding alleged patent violations and export restrictions. Early versions of PGP were subject to potential patent violations. PGP version 2.6.1 uses the RSAREF toolkit for public key cryptography and is legal to use for noncommercial purposes although export may be restricted. A version of PGP, called 2.6ui (unofficial international), exists outside of the United States and violates the RSA patent. A commercial version, PGP 2.4, is available and is fully licensed for commercial use. Although PGP has had a somewhat shaky start, it is being widely used to secure Internet mail.

EMAIL ISSUES

A lot of progress has been made to solve the challenges presented by distributed mail systems, but unfortunately many issues still remain. The following are some of the items that should be considered when investigating distributed mail security.

- PEM is not compatible with X.400 secure messaging. The two sets of end-to-end security features cannot internetwork. The Internet mail protocols are different from the X.400 mail protocols but share the same underlying architectural model. A specification for internetworking between X.400 and Internet mail environments has been developed.
- PEM is based on the concept of hierarchical organization while PGP is based on a distributed network of individuals. PEM is more

suited to companies and organizations while PGP is more useful to individuals who use the Internet for mail.

- Encryption key certification and distribution is a concern for any encryption mechanism used to provide security. How will this service be provided and by whom?
- Care must be taken if using different mail text applications. The alignment or insertion of spacing, for example, may violate message integrity checks.
- Data encryption mechanisms may not be compatible with data compression algorithms.
- Attention must be made to any export restrictions that may be in place for the encryption algorithms. Care must also be made for potential patent violations such as using earlier versions of PGP.
- Private key encryption using the DES algorithm uses less processing power than public key encryption algorithms such as RSA or PGP.

LOTUS NOTES

In Chapter 9 we introduced groupware into the discussion of distributed systems. Lotus Notes is a very sophisticated groupware product that acts more like a computer conferencing product than a mail system or distributed transaction processor. The product was developed by Iris Associates under contract to Lotus in the late 1980s. Lotus Notes consists of a document database server, an email server, a server infrastructure to route mail and documents, a client GUI environment, security services, distribution services, and an application development environment. The base concept of Lotus Notes is to have the ability to cooperatively share documents among a defined group of people in an organized manner.

The definitions of documents and database may need to be slightly modified when dealing with Lotus Notes. At the base of Notes is the concept of a document capable of combining multimedia components (data fields, text, graphics, audio, and video) into a single defined unit. A collection of these related documents are stored in a database. The documents can be retrieved using any identified property or content of the document. The database of the documents can be represented to the user with an identifying icon and a title, and include help panels and explanation data. A collection of the databases make up the document storage on the Notes servers.

The Notes databases are shared between the Notes servers and Notes clients using replication, keeping the databases the same at regular intervals. There is no definition of a master database in Notes. The replication mechanism operates in a bi-direction mode among the database replicas to make sure that all of the replicated databases are synchronized. The replication can take place on a selected frequency, operate in a background process, operate unattended, and by full or selected documents. The replicated databases can be synchronized in two ways. A server-based replication is usually a scheduled event using the unattended feature. A client-based replication usually happens at the user's request. Mobile users can store replicated databases on their notebooks and log on every so often to synchronize documents. Different updated versions of the documents are tagged as responses to the main document to get around the concurrent update problem. The latest response in fact may not be the most up to date.

Lotus Notes Security

The security of Lotus Notes is provided in three ways. Security mechanisms are provided to protect access to the documents stored under Notes, the authentication and authorization of the users of the Notes documents, and the confidentiality of the contents of the Notes documents. These data security mechanisms include document read access lists, data field encryption and the use of access control lists (ACLs).

Figure 21.1 illustrates the hierarchy to which the security mechanisms are applied. The first point of entry for either a user or another Notes server is at the server level. Access to the server requires a certificate that is accepted by the server being accessed. The database level access is granted if the server or user is authorized to use the database ACL.

Table 21.2 outlines the access rights granted by the different ACL levels. The database ACL is useful only when the database is accessed through Lotus Notes. The database may still be copied outside of the Notes environ-

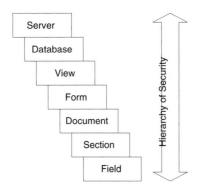

Figure 21.1 Notes hierarchy of security

TABLE 21.2
ACCESS CONTROL LIST LEVELS

No access	Users may not access this database; servers may not replicate it.
Depositor	Users may submit documents to the database but cannot read them; servers cannot replicate the database.
Reader	Users can only read documents; servers can only receive changes to documents.
Author	Users can read all documents and edit or delete documents they created; servers can receive documents and replicate changes or deletions if the database owns the documents.
Editor	Users can read and edit all documents in the database; servers can replicate new documents, replicate changes, and perform deletions if allowed.
Designer	Users can change database structures and edit all documents; servers can perform all functions except replicate access control changes.
Manager	Designer access plus control of access control lists, replication priority and deletion of the database. Servers can replicate all changes, including access control lists.

ment. The database ACL level is used to manage the access to lower components of the hierarchy. The user must also have the appropriate encryption key if a data field is encrypted.

Access control lists are used to determine whether a user or server has access to the database, what the user or server can do to the database if they have access, and what database role or security level the user has. The ACL is unique to each database. A replicated database can have a different ACL than the original. An entry in an ACL can be a user name, a server name, or a collection of user and/or server names in the form of a group name.

USER AUTHENTICATION

Access controls, as we have seen before, are dependent on the identity of the user. The authentication and confidentiality provisions are accomplished using both public key encryption and private key encryption. Public key encryption is used for user authentication and private key encryption is used for confidentiality. Lotus Notes was an early user of the RSA public key encryption technology. Because of U.S. export restrictions, however, there are two versions of Lotus Notes depending if it is being used within or outside of North America. A different encryption algorithm using shorter keys is used with the international version. As a result of these two versions, each user has two public key pairs, a long key of about 512 bits, and a short one of about 400 bits.

The authentication process utilizes a challenge-response protocol between the user and the server or between two servers to prove they are who they claim to be. When a user attempts to establish a session with a Notes server, they initially send their identification (ID), which also includes their public key and a list of certificates. The certificate is used to validate the user's name with his or her public key assuming that the server trusts the authority granting the certificate. The server than sends a challenge number to the user who encrypts it with her own private key and sends it back to the server. The server decrypts this number with the user's public key, and if the numbers match, the user is authenticated. The process is then repeated in the other direction to authenticate the server to the user.

Confidentiality of a Notes document can be invoked at the document level or by specific fields using encryption. The keys used for document encryption can be generated by a user and added to their ID. The access level defined as designer or manager must enable the document fields to be encrypted. The user must distribute the encryption key to other users who may require access to the document. This can be done using the email facility of Notes or using a specific dialog. Digital signatures can be attached to the field level in the documents.

Lotus Notes Mail

Lotus Notes provides email facilities that are treated as just another database containing mail documents. All of the Notes facilities can be used to manage the mail documents. Notes can be used as the backend message storage using a VIM-based front end. Gateways to many other mail systems are also supplied. The users in a Notes database can use X.500 compliant naming to be able to interoperate with other X.500-based systems. All mail can be encrypted for mailing or storage using the RSA public key mechanisms. The sender uses the receiver's public key to encrypt the message, and the receiver will use his or her private key to decrypt the message. In this manner, only the recipient can decrypt the message. Electronic signatures can also be used to sign the document. Notes uses the electronic signature to verify the identity of the sender when the user opens the document.

WHAT'S NEXT

Next on the horizon are the document facilities of the Internet and the World Wide Web services. The availability of Hypertext Transport Protocol (HTTP) servers and Hypertext Markup Language (HTML) browsers will provide some of the same look and feel type of document services as Notes, although not on the same scale or capability. The document navigation capabilities using the Hypertext documents provide an easy-to-use and highly effective way of dealing with widely distributed documents. The ability to access HTML documents is available on many platforms for relatively little cost. The development and security of HTML documents is, however, not on the same level as Notes.

The next versions of Notes will provide the capability of on-the-fly conversion of HTML to Notes, HTTP navigation, and support for Java. This means that Notes documents can be accessed by Web browsers as well as by the usual Web client software. This also means that a Notes client can be used as a Web browser. If a Notes document contains a reference to a Web document via a URL link, Notes can fetch the Web page.

Other distributed applications which rely on a well-defined infrastructure include calendaring and workflow technology. A scheduling or calendaring facility has been part of groupware technology for quite some time. Calendaring is also subject to several standards efforts. The Vendor Independent Calendaring (VIC) API is being supported by Lotus and IBM. Microsoft is including calendaring and scheduling facilities in their extended MAPI, and XAPIA is concentrating on calendaring exchanges. When scheduling and calendaring technology is coupled with workflow facilities, much more automation can be implemented in the office. Whether this will increase the efficiency of the corporation or will be perceived as losing more control of our lives to the computer is a matter of opinion.

SUMMARY

Electronic mail systems were one of the first implementations of a distributed system. Many of the technologies and standards pioneered for mail have allowed other distributed systems to mature. Lotus Notes is a good example of a mature groupware product with a focus on distributed documents that are accessible and useable by groups of individuals no matter where they are located. An effective workgoup can be scattered around the building or around the world. The Internet will continue to have a large influence on how the technologies and standards develop and mature. In the past couple of chapters, we have started to put the distributed processing environment to work. In the next few chapters we will see what it takes to make sure it is effective.

CHAPTER 22

SECURITY MANAGEMENT

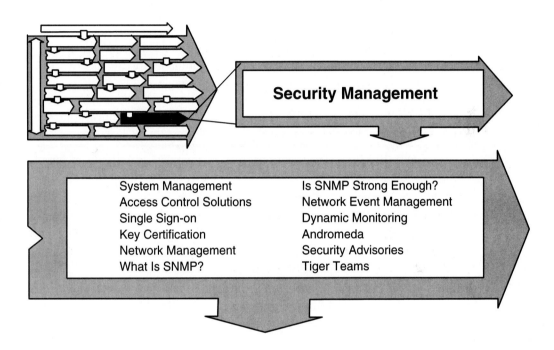

Security Management

System Management	Is SNMP Strong Enough?
Access Control Solutions	Network Event Management
Single Sign-on	Dynamic Monitoring
Key Certification	Andromeda
Network Management	Security Advisories
What Is SNMP?	Tiger Teams

Management is an important consideration in the deployment of any security solution. A solution that is unmanageable will be less effective and more likely to be compromised. The timely removal of access privileges is a very common problem in distributed environments where privileges are extended on a system-by-system basis. In the absence of centralized management control, former employees may retain their access rights after they leave the organization. It is up to the local administrator to revoke them.

Another problem is that there may be a great deal of inconsistency in local system administration duties. System administrators have different education, experience, and work loads. While some are devoted full time to administration, others operate part time and are involved only when required. These factors contribute to different levels of security on the systems for which each individual system administrator is responsible.

343

Because intruders seek weak systems to use as a base for their activities, it is important to raise the general level of security of the entire computing community. In the absence of a centralized management tool to enforce a minimum of security standards, how is the problem of inconsistent system administration addressed? Does it make sense to rely on the expertise of local administrators to catch an intruder? Or is this the type of activity that lends itself to a centralized approach?

Although the cost of distributed system and security administration is usually hidden, it is an area of concern for most organizations. Having the problem of security addressed by a select group of highly trained individuals, rather than delegating the task to local administrators, does have merit. Most organizations simply cannot afford to educate and train every system administrator in every aspect of computing security. While some education on security issues is desirable, it is more cost effective to concentrate security expertise with a few individuals.

Centralized security functions also have appeal with the user community. No one likes having to remember multiple user IDs and passwords. Centralized solutions can utilize single sign-on technologies, whose authentication mechanisms can be used by a number of systems and applications. The overall requirement for local administration can also be reduced through the use of centralized system administration solutions. This has the added benefit of reducing the number of people that require high-level privileges, such as UNIX *root* access, on the local system.

Centralization of audit functions is also a desirable direction, which permits the tracking of user actions across many systems, rather than relying on individual audit trails on different systems. Centralized alerting mechanisms can provide faster detection of illicit activity than do systems which rely upon an individual system administrator to detect intruders.

Are common mechanisms and the central administration of security functions necessarily a good thing? One point of view is that diversity, not commonality, is an ideal characteristic for security controls. A single control, it is argued, can be overcome no matter how strong it is. But it is much more difficult to overcome multiple levels of controls. Diversity in nature, the argument goes, prevents a single disease from destroying the entire species. Centralization of security is therefore bad news, because it implies a common approach to security. This is a very interesting argument and not without some merit. Compensating controls are certainly stronger than a single control. The answer to the centralized versus decentralized argument may be to employ a balanced approach that uses a combination of both local and centralized controls.

There are a number of reasons for looking at a common, centralized solution for security. First of all, a centralized solution can enforce standards for the community, thus increasing the overall level of security. They can also be expected to reduce the overall cost of security and system administration by centralizing its function within a few highly trained and trusted individuals. For the individual user, they can provide single sign-on capabilities, eliminating the need for multiple user IDs and passwords. Centralized security management also limits the overall number of users who require high-level access privileges to information. Alerts and detection of illicit activities are more efficient when such activities can be directed to individuals given the responsibility to investigate them. Finally, centralized auditing is supported which provides a consolidated trail of a user's activities across multiple platforms.

In this chapter, we'll look at solutions that can be used to centrally manage security in the distributed environment. These solutions can be loosely grouped under the following headings:

- System management
- Access control
- Single sign-on
- Key management
- Network management
- Event management

As with previous chapters, our intent is not to provide a review of an individual product's features and benefits, but to give an overall indication of how the solution may be achieved. We will look at the problems addressed and examine the general approach used, by each type of solution.

SYSTEM MANAGEMENT

Centralized system administration products perform a wide variety of tasks including the maintenance of user accounts, data backup, and print spooling services. Products of this class include CA UNICENTER from Computer Associates, Inc., the system management suite of OpenView products from Hewlett-Packard, and the management tools offered by Tivoli Systems, Inc. They provide the ability to centrally administer a large number of systems. Typically, they also provide support for a number of different platforms, ranging from individual workstations to mainframes. Different operating environments, including UNIX and Novell Netware, are also commonly supported by this class of tools. They reduce, if not eliminate, the need for local expertise and support by centralizing the administration role.

> It's very common to find systems today which are administered and supported by administrators located miles away. Our local UNIX server is supported by a team 2,500 miles away. The only local administration function is to replace backup tapes every evening. No one in our local office knows the superuser password to the system.

An easy-to-use interface, common to all platforms, also reduces the expertise required to perform common security tasks. This has the advantage of allowing the more mundane security administrative tasks, such as user maintenance, to be delegated to a central authority.

System management products provide a number of security functions, including

- Central management of authentication, including maintenance of user IDs and enforcement of password policy.
- Application of security control mechanisms, such as time-of-day access restrictions.
- Mapping of user access rights to resources.
- Monitoring for weakness or gaps in the application of controls.
- Centralized audit trails, including the monitoring of failed access attempts.

Central control of user IDs, and related user ID numbers, solves a number of problems. First of all, access rights to resources are granted based upon user IDs. If two users are given identical user IDs, each may have access to the others resources. A central management solution supports the consistent assignment of user IDs and user ID numbers.

The most common complaint about security from ordinary users is the need to remember multiple user IDs and passwords. Most of the systems management solutions also offer single sign-on capabilities. For example, Tivoli provides management support for the Kerberos authentication model. This allows the user to be authenticated once, and only once, by a central authority provided with the solution. Unfortunately, single sign-on tools are rarely able to support every platform, operating system, or application.

Another problem resolved by system management solutions is the control of user access rights. In the distributed computing environment, a single user may have access to many systems and resources. Without a common user ID, identification of these resources and access privileges on diverse systems can be quite a chore. Centralized system management will allow resources, to which the individual has access, to be easily identified and revoked when an individual leaves the organization.

Because authentication is centrally managed, it is possible to not only dictate, but also enforce, security policy. The solutions, for example, require users to change their passwords every 30 days. In the absence of a central system, policy is left to the individual system administrator to enforce. Another area addressed, at least partially by system management solutions, is centralization of the audit trail. Because authentication is performed centrally, and common user IDs can be enforced, it is possible to track users centrally. The central audit trails are not usually comprehensive, and rely on local audit trails for the bulk of their data. This means that much of the audit of user activity will occur using a local, rather than a central, audit trail.

Will centralized system management solutions be the right answer for every situation? In a word, No! First of all, some of the solutions allow central management of the security function but *enforce* the functions locally. By this, we mean that the local access controls are used to control security. Systems that are managed centrally are still subject to all of the security problems and limitations we have discussed in previous chapters. An exposure, such as clear-text passwords over the LAN, is magnified in centralized solutions. A single password discovered on the LAN can give an intruder access to many systems and applications.

Most significantly, security management is only one of the areas addressed by this class of tools. The other functions included in the system management solution, such as centralized data backup and print spooling, may not be required. Should the vendor not be willing to separate the security component from the total solutions management product, you will have invested in a rather expensive solution. Finally, not all of the computing platforms used by an organization may be supported by a particular systems management solution.

For organizations that wish to solve the problem of security as part of the overall system administration problem, system administration tools may provide a solution. Before you adopt a system administration solution, a review of your security requirements in comparison with the capabilities of the tool is strongly recommended.

ACCESS CONTROL SOLUTIONS

Access control solutions provide additional controls for an operating system. These types of solutions exist for many computing environments, including DOS, Windows, OS/2, and UNIX. Access control solutions allow the enforcement of password policy, provide controls over access to system resources and keep audit trails of user activity. Protection of the authentication process is also a standard feature. Many of the solutions prevent the discovery of passwords over the network and many provide support for alternative password technologies. For example, some access control vendors allow for the integration of one-time passwords and digital password generators. The passwords cannot be captured and replayed.

Controls provided by these solutions may include the ability to specify access on a host-to-host basis, time of day, and access method (login, telnet, FTP, and others). The products may also support user profiling, including the implementation of least privilege policies for system administrators. Centralized audit and logging mechanisms of user actions is a common function, as is the reporting of weaknesses in the controls.

A consideration for all centralized security mechanisms is the protection around their internal communications. Many centralized solutions communicate using untrusted mechanisms, such as unencrypted remote procedure calls, for communcation.

SINGLE SIGN-ON

Single sign-on is a concept that a single user ID and password should suffice to validate the users to every computer and application available to them. It is very popular with users who are currently forced to remember one user ID and password for LAN Services, a second for UNIX, a third for mainframe access, and so on. When the requirement for password aging is added, and is not synchronized among the servers to which the user has access, many users show an understandable frustration. When forced to remember a large number of ever changing passwords, they quite naturally respond by recording the required passwords. This is most commonly done on sticky notes which are kept in plain view for easy access and can be read by others.

> We once performed a study of how easy it would be to discover user passwords by examining work areas. We looked at sticky notes pasted on terminals, looked under keyboards, and at desk calendars. We were able to uncover passwords in over 50% of the work areas that were examined!

The frustration of an ordinary user is intensified by computer support personnel, who typically require access to a large number of systems. Single sign-on solutions attempt to solve the problem of multiple user IDs and passwords by centralizing the authentication function. The obvious caveat to a single sign-on solution is that it must be performed securely. If an intruder can illicitly discover a user's password or otherwise breach security, they will have access to every account, on every system, to which the user has access.

There are currently three approaches to the single sign-on problem. The first is to use the system management tools and access control solutions we have just reviewed. These tools typically extend user administration to all of the platforms they manage. This provides system management tools with a basis to also extend single sign-on capabilities. Unfortunately, many of these solutions have rather weak authentication capabilities. They typically send passwords in clear text over the LAN. But probably the single most limiting aspect of their use as a single sign-on solution is that they rarely are able to address all of the computing environments required by an organization.

A second approach to single sign-on uses a method called scripting. Scripting (sometimes called screen scraping) essentially captures a user's keystrokes which can be replayed at a later date. Using this method, the user ID and password are captured for all of the different systems and applications to which a user has access. The scripting application stores these commands and acts as a smart front end. The captured commands and keystrokes can then be replayed by issuing a command or clicking on an icon. The advantage to this approach is that it can be adapted for use with a wide variety of operating systems or applications. A major drawback to scripting is that commands that are captured must be securely held by the scripting application. If they can be uncovered by an intruder, they will reveal user IDs and passwords.

A second drawback becomes evident in client-server applications. In such applications, the user may not be given an actual session on the host system. They communicate with the server using methods such as remote procedure calls. In these cases, it is desirable for the login process to provide the user with some proof or evidence that they have actually performed the login. The use of certificates or access tokens is commonplace. The Kerberos model, used by OSF/DCE, provides a good example of this approach. For most organizations, however, an investment in Kerberos or similar technologies for every application and computing system is simply unrealistic due to their complexity.

In recent months, we have seen three separate, unrelated customers in Canada and the United States analyze single sign-on technology. In these three cases, the customers concluded that no single supplier could meet their requirements for single sign-on. The good news is that current suppliers will continue to add improvements to, and widen the support for, their products. As well, many new players are expected to enter the marketplace. The winning solution will likely be the one that can address the issues of security, ease-of-use, and support for a wide variety of platforms and applications.

KEY CERTIFICATION

Another aspect of the centralization of security management functions is the control of encryption keys. As discussed in Chapter 15, the protection and distribution of encryption keys is better served by a centralized function. The use of a central security group, with no direct access to computing systems or applications, to distribute and maintain encryption keys is generally the desired direction for most organizations. This approach both segregates the security functions from those that support the application and permits a strongly secured central site to be used.

NETWORK MANAGEMENT

Network management tools, such as HP's OpenView Network Node Manager, provide network administrators with the ability to manage complex, enterprisewide networks. This type of software can produce a single, simplified view of diverse networking components, including routers, bridges, hubs, printers, and computers. The software can

- Provide a central view of the network and its devices.
- Permit the central management of network devices, such as hubs, bridges and routers.
- Monitor network traffic flows.
- Autodiscover any new devices attached to the network.

The traffic filtering capabilities that these tools provide can also be applied to security. One of the most common methods to increase network security is to divide the network into trusted subnetworks. The methods used to implement trusted subnetworks include segregating the network, limiting access to the network and filtering traffic by source address, by destination address, or by the type of traffic (e.g., TCP/IP port number).

SEGREGATE THE NETWORK

Routers and bridges may be used to segregate the local subnetwork from the corporate internetwork. This can create *trusted* subnetworks, accessible only by members of the local workgroup and trusted outsiders. Unless specifically destined for the local subnetwork, traffic is prevented by a network device (e.g., a router) from entering. Similarly, internal traffic is limited to the trusted side of the local subnetwork. This prevents local traffic from being monitored by those outside of the local subnetwork.

FILTER TRAFFIC

It's obvious that *some* traffic must be permitted between the trusted subnetwork and the internal network. Otherwise, why have a connection to the internetwork? Filtering tables on a router can be used to explicitly define the incoming connections. For example, if the only valid communication originating from the outside are from the IP addresses in the range 15.37.xxx.xxx, filtering tables can be constructed to reject all connections outside of this range of IP addresses.

Bridges and routers can also limit traffic to the internetwork from inside the subnetwork. For example, an application development area may wish to limit its access to the internetwork to a single software distribution station. Only traffic originating from this station would be allowed to enter the internetwork. The bridge or router can also be used to limit traffic to specific addresses. Not only can traffic be limited by its source and destination addresses, it may also be filtered by the type of traffic. For example, traffic into the development subnetwork may be limited to the FTP service.

ACCESS TO THE NETWORK

Depending on the type of network, LAN devices called hubs are used to connect local devices to the LAN backbone. Access to the local network, and hence the internetwork, may be restricted by the hub. Most hubs have the ability to disable unused ports. This would prevent an individual from using a personal computer to plug into an unused port and monitor LAN traffic. An optional approach is to provide an alert if an unused port becomes active, but not to restrict use of the port.

Hubs can also detect changes to network addresses, and forward an alert if a new LAN card is used on a port. In the event that an intruder unplugs an existing station on the LAN and uses their own device, an alert can be forwarded to the centralized network management system.

Network management tools provide the ability to manage the segregation of the network centrally. The configuration of network devices can be continually checked to ensure that controls have been implemented and are still functioning. The management of hubs and bridges is also provided by this class of tool.

What Is SNMP?

The Simple Network Management Protocol (SNMP) is a de facto industry standard for managing network devices and computers on the network. Local programs, called agents, are used to communicate with the network management software. The communication can be based upon a predefined standard, or they can be customized to meet a particular requirement. Agents that can be customized are termed *extensible*.

A database containing information on various types of network objects is called a Management Information Base (MIB). MIBs are used for a variety of purposes. A MIB entry may provide, for example, information about the protocols used on a specific vendor's router. MIBs are ideal for the management of many networking devices because they can be implemented with relatively little overhead.

The current use of SNMP to manage networked devices can be extended to provide security solutions. Extensible SNMP agents, capable of detecting weakness in controls or violations, could be implemented to forward alerts to the network management system. MIBs could be interrogated to monitor the continued functioning of router filtering controls, for example.

Is SNMP Strong Enough ?

The current version of SNMP does not address authentication. Any client capable of formulating SNMP requests are given a response. SNMPv1 simply provides no effective way to prevent a third party from observing the traffic between a manager and an agent. Worse than this, no effective way exists to prevent unauthorized access to the SNMP manager. In answer to this shortcoming, a new version, SNMPv2, has been proposed.

An SMNPv2 request is provided with two security features—an authenticator to identify the originator of a message and a privacy protocol to protect the SNMPv2 request from disclosure. Data integrity is protected by using message digests, which are described in Chapter 15. The recipient of the request uses the message digest technique to verify the requester. Further information on SNMPv2 may be obtained from the Internet RFCs 1445, 1446, and 1447. Unfortunately, as of the writing of this book, it appears that the initial release of SNMPv2 will not address security.

NETWORK EVENT MANAGEMENT

A network event management system, such as HP's IT OpenView Operations, is capable of collecting information from throughout the corporate internetwork. The information, consisting of both messages and alerts, can be prepared, consolidated, and presented at a central event management station. Based upon the type of alert or message, either manual or automated responses can be initiated. Logs of alerts and subsequent actions are generally maintained for auditing purposes.

While primarily used for network and system management, event management solutions can be expanded to include security. Alerts of various kinds can be forwarded to the event management system. For example, an extensible agent could be developed to look for accounts without passwords. A message to the event management system could be forwarded if one is found. The types of messages and events that can be monitored are almost limitless, but constant monitoring and messaging will place demands on network and system performance.

Messages can be generated in a number of ways:

- Agents on the local system can monitor the local system and communicate directly with the event management system.
- A message can be written to a log file which can, in turn, be accessed by the event management system.
- SNMP alerts, generated by networking devices, can be trapped and processed.

As mentioned previously, SNMP-based agents can be built which would provide alerts based on a variety of conditions, including file and directory permissions or the existence of a local security program. If the local agent detects a problem, an alert may be forwarded to the central event management system. The security-related activity which could be monitored might include repeated attempts to login to a system. Other security-related events might include a stoppage of the audit program or modifications to a login program. Messages could be segregated and grouped by a variety of characteristics, including

- Type (e.g., security)
- Severity (e.g., critical)
- Originating node

Operators may be given different capabilities for different groups of messages, including restrictions of their response to messages. They may also be prevented from viewing messages of selected groups. It's usually recommended that the security functions of the network event management system be segregated from normal operations. Only security personnel or their designates should have access to security-related alerts.

Based upon the type and severity of the message received, a number of actions may take place. Responses to messages can include

- Requiring the security operator to acknowledge the message
- Preventing access by the offending device to the network by automatically disabling the appropriate port on the hub
- Paging a security officer

If the local system has an agent to communicate with the event management system, automated responses could be developed. These might include

- The disabling of an account that has had a number of failed logins
- Removal of unauthorized files or directories
- The initiation of a special auditing process to track all the keystrokes of a particular user

Logs of all activity, including operator actions and automated responses, are kept in an audit trail. The messages themselves are usually stored within a RDBMS, which can be customized to include additional security controls and reporting capabilities.

Later in the chapter, we'll look at a special use of network event management capabilities. It will be used to build a detection tool for hackers that try to attack the entire network. We've called this tool Andromeda.

DYNAMIC MONITORING

Dynamic monitoring products can be used to provide immediate alerts to security personnel. These products can monitor target systems in real time, looking for violations. Obviously, not all resources can be monitored in this manner. There are, however, a number of significant security-related events that are logical candidates for monitoring. If a violation is detected, alerts could be forwarded to an event management system.

The dynamic monitoring of systems is performed through three key facilities: a local agent, network management software, and centralized alert management software. Local agents, provided as part of the event management solution, run on the monitored system and may be developed to detect a number of security-related events. These events may include changes to the system security programs. Three failed login attempts in the last 24 hours might also signify a security event. Changes to the access controls of key authentication and authorization mechanisms, including the login program and password files, might also constitute a security event. As well, the detection of unauthorized changes to authorization controls, such as permissions on system files and directories, may indicate problems. A further security check might involve checking the characteristics of key operating system programs.

Digital signatures can be employed to ensure that operating system programs are valid. Digital signatures produce numeric values based on the internal characteristics of a program or data file. Even a small change to the program will result in a significant change to the digital signature. A digital signature could be taken of key programs, such as the login program, and the resulting value compared against a known digital signature value. A deviation could provide an indication of tampering. Figure 22.1 provides an overview of the use of remote detection technologies.

Commercial products also provide local agents capable of dynamically monitoring a number of security controls or events. These solutions can

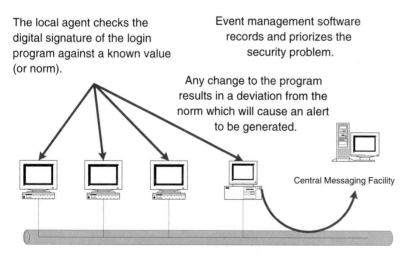

The local agent checks the digital signature of the login program against a known value (or norm).

Event management software records and priorizes the security problem.

Any change to the program results in a deviation from the norm which will cause an alert to be generated.

Central Messaging Facility

Figure 22.1 Remote detection of security issues

monitor a number of target systems and forward auditing information to event management solutions. They can also continuously check file and directory permissions and produce alerts in near real time if unauthorized changes are detected. The existence and proper execution of local control mechanisms, such as the C2 shadow password file, can also be monitored. Even running programs can be monitored. The local agent, for example, can itself be monitored. Missing or counterfeit agents can be detected.

The Computer Misuse Detection System (CMDS) from Science Applications International Corporation (SAIC) provides the real time detection of security incidents. Using a combination of local audit data and user profiles, CMDS can detect suspicious activity and provide a centralized alert.

ANDROMEDA

If an intruder gains access to your internal network, there is a reasonably good chance the intruder will use tools that will sweep the network looking for weak points. These tools use wildcarding techniques (e.g., 15.37.*.*) to contact every available network address. Starting with the first possible address, and incrementing through each possible address, the attacker will look for weaknesses in the network services. The network services likely to be tested include the FTP, TFTP, Berkeley, and network file system services.

What if systems were deployed on the network under the authority of a security group, for which *any access* is considered unauthorized? The purpose of these systems would be to detect network sweeps by an intruder and forward alerts to security personnel. Such systems would be constructed on the premise that any attempt to communicate with them would be an attempt to breach the security of the corporate internetwork.

Older personal computers, running a version of UNIX for which source code is provided, are ideal for this task. Software for trapping all network access attempts could be easily developed by "shelling" the UNIX portmapper and network daemons. By modifying the source code, *any* network access to these services would be recorded. Information about the access request could be forwarded to an event management system such as HP IT/Operations. In turn, HP IT/Operations could forward an alert to security personnel about the possible network attack. Figure 22.2 demonstrates such an approach to detecting network sweeps.

This idea has been around for some time, and we do not want to appear to take credit for it. Contributed software tools, such as *Courtney* and *Gabriel,* have been developed in response to network probes. Our solu-

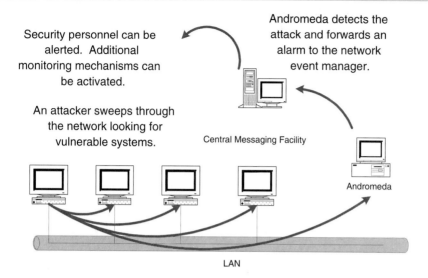

Figure 22.2 Andromeda

tion, which we like to call Andromeda, uses the same ideas but is implemented as a stand-alone solution rather than using local operating system log files.

Cassiopeia, wife of King Cepheus of Ethiopia, was said to have angered the sea-nymphs by her vanity. In their anger, the sea-nymphs unleashed a sea monster to devastate the coasts of Ethiopia. On the advice of an oracle, King Cepheus ordered his daughter, Andromeda, to be sacrificed. Chained to a rock, she was rescued from certain death by Perseus who slew the approaching sea monster.

Here are some recommendations for building Andromeda:

- Use older, outdated UNIX systems. There is no need to use new hardware, as the only job of the machine will be to listen to network traffic and forward alerts if any are detected.
- The only user on the system should be root. If possible, access by root should be restricted to the system console (using */etc/securetty*).
- The machines should be physically secured.
- All current network daemons should be replaced with a surrogate version, which will trap the traffic and create the alert.

- The surrogate network daemon should also capture as much information about the probe as possible and forward the alert information to the event management software. The security group should be automatically notified of the alert.
- Change the location of the Andromeda machines on the network on a regular basis.

The alerts can be sent to the network event manager in two ways. An SNMP-based alert could be generated and forwarded to the event manager. But we've found it easiest and safest to format the alerts and place them in local files, which are in turn accessed by event management agents.

We've had discussions with clients over whether or not to tell internal employees about Andromeda machines. We are of the opinion that rumors of their existence will occur anyway which is not necessarily a bad thing. If the rumor discourages an employee from unauthorized testing of the network using a tool such as SATAN, so much the better.

SECURITY ADVISORIES

Many vendors routinely publish advisory warnings when they become aware of problems involving security and their products. The intent is to allow their customers to address the problem as quickly as possible and not leave them vulnerable to attack. Rather than waiting for an operating system or application upgrade, it is a very good idea for organizations to obtain and apply these vendor advisories. Since the vulnerability is generally uncovered as a result of illicit activity, and may already be known to a wide number of individuals, the advisories should be applied as soon as possible. Most vendors also provide digital signatures to ensure that their advisories are complete and correct. Each advisory can be validated using the digital signature and forgeries easily detected. Having a central point within an organization for the collection and distribution of security advisories is recommended.

TIGER TEAMS

When an incident involving security occurs, many organizations find themselves unprepared to effectively deal with it. In our experience, such incidents tend to occur very quickly. The situation can be quite confusing and is difficult for even the most experienced system administrators to respond to an incident. From our experience, it is recommended that a team be created in advance to respond to attacks on the computing environment. The team should be comprised of highly qualified individuals whose capabilities will allow an effective response to a breach of security. Commonly referred to as a Tiger Team, the team should be composed not only of technical experts in various fields (database, networking, and operating systems), but also of security officers and management. The Tiger Team should maintain contact with other Tiger teams, including vendors, law enforcement officers, communication providers, and the Internet Computer Emergency Response Team (CERT) organization. From our experience, the Tiger Team must have access to both computerized tools and a wide range of system and network information in order to analyze the situation and make an effective response. Preparation, training, proper tools, and knowing where to get information in advance are critical. In the midst of a critical security situation is no place to discover this truth.

CONCLUSIONS

The ability to centrally manage security in distributed systems increases their effectiveness. Centralized security management solutions will allow enforcement of standards throughout the computing community. Other benefits include a reduced overall administration effort and the ability to concentrate expertise. But centralized security solutions do not necessarily imply a *big brother* approach to security. They can be viewed as providing support to local system administrators. Local security solutions, used to detect intruders who use broadcast techniques, is simply not cost effective if implemented on every system. Centralization allows more sophisticated approaches to be used, and for the required level of expertise to be concentrated in a few individuals.

In the next chapter, we will review a methodology that has been successfully used by organizations to create a corporate strategy to address the problem of computing security.

CHAPTER 23

DEVELOPING A SECURITY STRATEGY

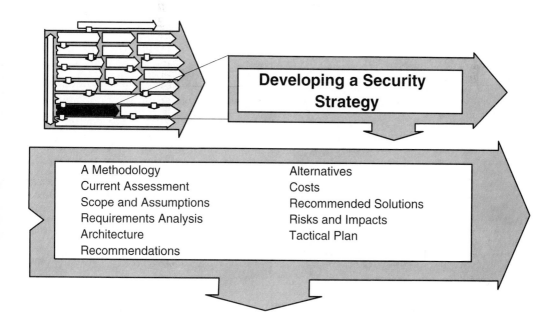

Developing a Security Strategy

A Methodology	Alternatives
Current Assessment	Costs
Scope and Assumptions	Recommended Solutions
Requirements Analysis	Risks and Impacts
Architecture	Tactical Plan
Recommendations	

The problem of computing security for an enterprise is a complex one. As we have discovered in previous chapters, there are many different aspects to the problem. For example, we have seen the need to implement strong, robust security controls, to monitor the controls, and to educate the user community. The problem cannot be solved by technical solutions alone. In fact, uncoordinated expenditures on diverse technical solutions actually contribute to the problem.

When you stop and think about it, there are a number of analogies we can draw between computer and home security. We lock our doors at home as a basic preventive measure. It does not make a breakin to our home impossible, but it certainly makes it more difficult. As with home security, locking the doors to computing assets is simply common sense.

A balance must exist in our approach to both home and computing security. There is no point in spending money on a superb lock on the front door if the back of the house isn't built. Neither does it make much sense to only lock one of the doors. We should focus on the most likely security exposures. Thieves do not usually carry ladders. Money should therefore be first spent on barring the lower-level windows.

Many organizations have invested heavily in individual, uncoordinated security technologies. These investments have failed to address the overall security requirements of the enterprise. A common approach would allow for stronger, comprehensive solutions to be implemented, while reducing administration and training costs. Individual, uncoordinated solutions combine to form a "dogs breakfast" of controls that are neither cost effective, comprehensive, nor unobtrusive to users. While they may address individual security issues, they usually will not meet the overall objectives of the organization. The best technology will be of no use if people are unaware of their responsibilities. If your children leave the door unlocked when you are away, whether or not you've used the strongest lock in the world is immaterial.

A final point about security is that it must reflect our organization and IT architecture. There is little point in designing solutions based on a centralized architecture if the organization is going to implement distributed computing. Security cannot be viewed in isolation from the environment. The safety of our homes is directly related to the security of our neighborhoods. You cannot fully address one without addressing the other.

A SECURITY STRATEGY

Computing security is an issue that affects the entire corporation. In this sense, computing security is a business problem rather than simply an issue of technology or computing. Solving a business problem requires an organization to take a strategic view of the problem. Many organizations have created strategies, using a methodology we will discuss later, to address the problem of computing security.

A security strategy is a series of specific steps that an organization can take to raise the existing level of security to a higher one. The methodology takes an organization through an assessment process to determine where they are currently positioned in terms of the overall security of their computing environment, defining where they want to be and planning the steps required to get them there.

Using a defined methodology ensures that all the windows and doors have been locked. The new addition to the house will also include secure doors and windows while it is being built. It has been successfully used to address the problem of computing security in a number of diverse organizations. A security strategy ensures the overall objectives are going to be met. It is a plan that moves an organization from today into the future. The strategy is developed with a recognition of the current environment and promotes a common solution to the problem of security. It should also be recognized that the ideal environment probably cannot be reached immediately, but will evolve over a course of years. Figure 23.1 demonstrates a sample security strategy, which is implemented over an extended period of time.

For most organizations, the reason the problem of computing security is not being solved is rarely due to a of lack of security technology. In fact, most organizations suffer from the problem of too much computing security technology. They have invested in technology to solve individual issues and

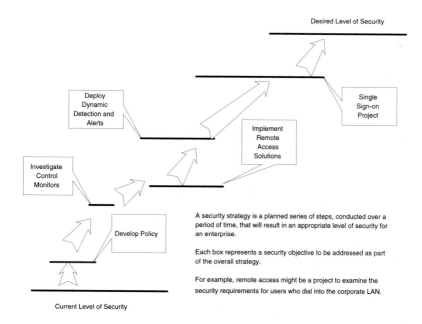

Figure 23.1 A sample security strategy

problems, without regard to the global picture. The problem is how to best employ technology for the common good of the organization, rather than focus on piecemeal security problems. Technical solutions are certainly part of an overall strategy, but the strategy should encompass more than just technology. It must also address organizational and business issues.

Many organizations have adopted the divisional business model. This model separates the organization into semiautonomous business entities. Diverse business entities, each with its own culture and business goals, can complicate the problem of developing an overall strategy for security. The strategy should recognize the differences in the corporate cultures and business entities, but give a common direction and set of actions that can be followed by all. The security strategy must also have a view of the future, and recognize as best as is possible, new requirements and directions for the organization.

A METHODOLOGY

We have developed security strategies for a wide variety of clients, as diverse as the government of Mexico and a Canadian energy-based utility. The strategies have unique goals and objectives, reflecting the differences in the organizations. In one case, the strategy involved moving the organization toward a common technology base for security. In others, the strategy defines steps to strengthen the overall security of the computing environment. In a recent request for proposal, one of our clients summarized its need for a security strategy in the following way:

> The objective of this project is to define a security strategy for our information technology environment. This strategy will provide the framework for the implementation of security solutions as required to adequately secure and maintain controls in a highly decentralized, mission-critical, and complex environment.

In the course of developing security strategies, we have developed a methodology to help us through the process. The security methodology has five major phases:

- Phase 1—Understand where you are now.
- Phase 2—Define the environment that you would like to have.
- Phase 3—Assess the alternatives in getting where you'd like to go.
- Phase 4—Recognize the best path to take.
- Phase 5—Get started.

Phase 1 of the security strategy starts with a current assessment level of security for the organization. It reviews the technologies used by the organization, its policies and procedures, and its management directives. A risk assessment is performed using techniques and tools that test the current strength of controls. The boundaries of the study, and critical assumptions made during the study, are also compiled. For example, if the study is to exclude a selected area, such as the security of microwave transmissions, we state this limitation. If it is assumed that the future direction of the organization is toward a particular suite of technologies, we state this assumption. We also attempt to understand the major issues facing the organization and detail each of them.

In phase 2, the overall objectives are defined. A requirements analysis is compiled and a security architecture is developed. Based upon the requirements analysis and the architecture, a set of overall recommendations is made. A sample recommendation might be for the organization to increase its ability to detect unauthorized activity in a timely manner.

The activity in phase 3 focuses on an assessment of the alternative solutions that may be employed to meet the requirements. Each recommendation is examined, and the alternative solutions that can be employed to meet the recommendation are studied.

In phase 4, recommendations on particular solutions and courses of action are made. Estimated costs, risks, and impacts are analyzed, and a tactical plan can be developed. The security strategy has at this point been created, and the major task of its implementation can begin.

The final step, phase 5, proceeds with the execution of the plan and implements the recommended technological and procedural solutions. In absence of a security strategy, many organizations have inadvertently moved to the final stage of the strategy and deployed technical solutions in an uncoordinated manner. However, such an approach is rarely effective.

A few concepts about the security strategy should be understood before we describe the process of building one. While each strategy will be unique to an individual organization, there are some common themes. There are four points to understand about the development of a security strategy:

- First, the objective of the strategy is to provide a direction for the future, *not* to find an immediate solution to every security concern. The strategy may recommend an interim solution to address a current problem, but the idea is to focus on the *big picture.*

- Second, you will not be able to meet every individual security objective put forward by every entity in the organization. The strategy must balance the common objectives of the organization with individual objectives.
- Third, not all objectives can be realized immediately. Many of the recommended solutions will be deployed in the future. But it may be wise to take small steps now, to facilitate these future solutions.
- Fourth, the strategy will change and evolve. Changes to the business objectives and directions of the organization will cause the security strategy to evolve. The strategy should be reviewed on a regular basis and modifications made if required.

THE SECURITY STRATEGY ROADMAP

We've developed a roadmap to describe our route through the various steps and phases of the security strategy. In developing a strategy, you always learn new things about the organization, its technologies, its problems, and its issues. The construction techniques used in building the strategy must be able to address these new issues. So we always try to be flexible in the use of our methodology. Figure 23.2 is the roadmap diagram we use to represent the development of a security strategy.

Let's take a look at the steps involved in creating a security strategy, starting with the current assessment.

CURRENT ASSESSMENT

In order to understand how to best get to a destination, it's important to understand where we are starting from. A current assessment is intended to provide this starting point for the security strategy. It involves five major steps:

1. A review of current policy, procedures, and best practices.
2. Interviews with a number of people, including IT technologists and management.
3. An examination of the technology currently employed.
4. A risk assessment to learn new things about the environment.
5. A review of future applications and directions.

The first step of a current assessment is to try to get a sense of the corporate culture. For example, does the corporate culture abide by the trusted

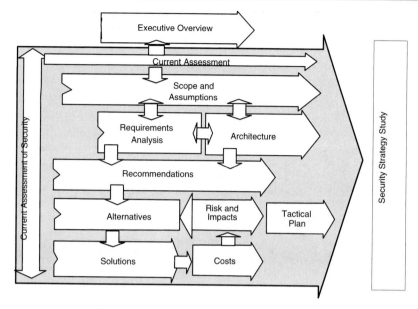

Figure 23.2 The security strategy roadmap

employee philosophy? This philosophy assumes that all employees are inherently trusted, and should have access to corporate information unless there are good reasons why they shouldn't. The reverse philosophy assumes that all employees must be specifically authorized for access to all information. The security strategy will *not* normally be a mechanism to change corporate culture (there are bigger forces at work here). The security strategy should understand and complement the corporate culture.

A review of existing policy and procedures will give an indication of corporate culture. Keep in mind that the modification of existing policy and procedures can become a recommendation, if they are found to be inadequate. The subject of computing policy was examined in previous chapters. But let's review the major points concerning the development of computing policy:

- Policies should not reflect a particular technology. They should reflect issues of concern to all platforms. The implementation of a policy on a particular platform is a procedure.
- A policy should reflect the culture of the organization. A computing policy that is contrary to corporate culture is not likely to be followed.

- The policies of the organization should be understood by employees. If most employees are unaware of their existence, they won't be effective.

After a review of corporate culture, the next step is to interview a number of people within the organization. An open discussion with different levels of staff and management is absolutely the best way to get a sense of the current problems, issues, and directions. The purpose of the meeting is to gain an understanding of the issues and problems people are facing, and to get their views on what the future should be like. It is always a good idea to send a sample questionnaire in advance, but the meeting itself is usually informal and unstructured.

> We always let the people we interview know that our activity is not part of an audit. The intent is never to cast blame on any individual or group; rather, it is to get their thoughts and ideas on future directions. We have found, after hundreds of interviews, that the vast majority of people will be very open in discussing security issues and solutions.

It's preferable to interview a wide number of individuals, including the members of the user community, IT technologists, audit, and management. The actual users of applications can provide excellent (and usually quite emphatic) information on how security should function. The audit department can provide information on the strength of controls and their feelings of the overall security environment. From the technologists, you can learn a lot about the current problems and issues. Management cannot usually comment on technical details, they can provide future directions. Management may have knowledge, for example, of plans to implement a key new technology in an upcoming project.

> We have found that three people is the maximum number to interview at one time. If more than three people are in the room, one person will tend to dominate the discussion. It's funny, but we've seen that individual participation will decrease as the number of people increases. Most important, people are generally more open to sharing their thoughts and ideas in smaller groups. As a courtesy, we also review our interview notes with the interviewees and make any changes that are requested. If the interviewee agrees, the interview notes are included in the final report. When the interviewee expresses concern about the notes, we either modify the interview notes or reschedule the interview.

The interview process is also a good place to understand and record the current technology used by the organization. It was a surprise to discover that this section of the strategy was of general interest to many groups in the organization. Many organizations publish IT business plans, both for corporate IT and business units. They are also a good starting point to see what's going on within an organization.

After the interviews are finished, a matrix is created showing the major concerns and issues found. The matrix lists problem areas that have been identified as a result of the individual interviews. For example, if an interviewee feels that the policies and procedures of the organization are inadequate, a star is placed in the appropriate row and column. This helps to focus on the major issues and concerns.

A sample issues and requirements matrix is shown in Figure 23.3.

A final note: Be nonjudgmental in the interviews. Listen to all concerns, issues, and suggestions equally. Try to learn, not sell!

The interview process gives a good idea of the problems and issues known to the organization. The next step, a limited risk assessment of the computing environment, is meant to discover problems of which the organization

Issues and Requirements	Dave	Karen	Fred	Andy	John	Carol	Kim	Mike
Policies and procedures	✓			✓		✓		
Digital signatures		✓			✓		✓	
Audit Trails				✓				
Network controls			✓			✓		✓
Application controls	✓	✓						
Database synchronization						✓		
Centralized controls, monitors, and automated alerts	✓		✓	✓	✓			✓
System accreditation						✓		
Database access controls			✓				✓	
Segregation of duties	✓			✓				
Protection and distribution of software	✓		✓		✓		✓	
Physical security						✓		
Remote dialup access		✓	✓					
Security education and awareness				✓	✓			✓
Password and authentication standards		✓		✓			✓	
Audit				✓				✓
Digital signatures	✓					✓		

Figure 23.3 Sample issues and requirements matrix by interviewee

is unaware. This involves an active test of network, operating system, and application controls. The limited risk assessment is used to measure the overall exposure of the organization to abuse. It should be noted that an overall assessment of computing risk comprises much more than a review of controls. It includes a review of technical controls, but also reviews issues such as physical security, organizational procedures, and the likelihood an attack can occur.

We have used a variety of tools, including many of the assessment tools discussed in Chapters 22 and 24, to get an idea of the overall strength of controls. Reports from the audit department, if available, may also provide useful information. But we've always found that it's best to conduct your own assessment.

Upon completion of the interviews, reviews and assessments, the results are compiled into a section called the current assessment. This summary is essentially the statement of understanding of where the organization is at the current time, including the issues it must face and its view of the future.

Scope and Assumptions

While constructing the strategy, it's a good idea for those developing the strategy to list what the strategy is intended to accomplish. It is equally important to describe areas that the strategy is not intended to address. For example, if the report is not going to address the physical security of buildings, mention this in the scope area. If the strategy excludes certain computing resources, such as the mainframe, record this as well. An assumption is a decision made on behalf of the client in the absence of an actual decision. For example, we may assume that a particular project is critical to an organization, but we do not really know if it will be implemented. Recording assumptions about the strategy will help readers understand why decisions and recommendations are made. The recording of both scope and assumptions can start after the current assessment is complete, but they are usually modified and changed all the way through the process.

Requirements Analysis

The requirements analysis is really a checklist of issues we have discovered as part of the current assessment. Using the findings of the current and risk assessments, we can construct a set of overall requirements, for example,

- To have a common authentication mechanism, which authenticates a user at initial access and is usable by multiple applications and environments.

- To segregate the management of security from system administration functions, wherever possible.
- To provide controls over the use of remote and mobile users.
- To facilitate the commercial use of the Internet.

Usually, we have found that a limited number of statements (20 to 30 statements are common) will address the overall requirements for an enterprise.

ARCHITECTURE

In Chapter 3, an architecture for the security environment was presented. The architecture is used to present a model of how security will function in a particular environment. One question that always comes up in the security strategy is

Can the security strategy develop an architecture in absence of a corporate systems and network management architecture?

Ideally, the security strategy is created after the development of a corporate architecture for network and systems management. But this is rarely the case. Usually, because of demands made by new projects and applications, a strategy for security is required in advance of the development of a corporate architecture initiative. It is very common for the development of the security strategy to proceed, or coincide, with the creation of an overall architecture for the distributed environment.

In the absence of an overall architecture, one approach is to define your own architecture as part of the strategy based on assumptions of what the future architecture might be. You should include any assumptions in the scope and assumptions area of the strategy.

RECOMMENDATIONS

After the overall requirements have been defined, and an architecture developed, a set of recommendations can be developed. The recommendations provide the future strategic direction for the organization, in terms of security. Essentially, you want to define those areas that require further investigation, require a decision to be made, or initiate a separate project. Sample recommendations are

- Develop a policy for endorsement by senior management governing the use of the computing environment, including distributed systems and applications.

- Develop an accreditation process for all systems seeking access to the corporate internetwork, based upon the class of system.
- Implement a robust authentication mechanism that will provide a single sign-on solution for applications and systems.
- Use security monitors to review the existing controls in the distributed computing environment.
- Implement trusted sub-networks, which limit network access on a least privileged basis, to reduce the exposure of critical subnetworks.
- Implement the capability of dynamically detecting security incidents. The solution should record the incident, and based on the type of alert, notify security personnel and allow subsequent action to be taken.

It is highly recommended that each point be endorsed by management prior to proceeding with the individual recommendation. As each recommendation will be investigated in depth for the best possible solution, time will be saved if only those recommendations which management can support are reviewed. You do not want to waste time investigating solutions to recommendations that will not be followed.

ALTERNATIVES

After the recommendations have been agreed upon, a search for potential solutions can be conducted. A substantial portion of the overall effort of developing a security strategy is spent on this activity. It involves an analysis of the alternative solutions available to meet the recommendations made in the previous section. The solutions, which may or may not involve technologies, should be weighed for their ability to address the requirement, their applicability to the proposed architecture, and the associated costs and impacts on the organization. The alternatives section can also be used to provide an education in security technologies, a discussion of the strengths and weaknesses of the alternatives, and details about the candidate technologies.

COSTS

In addition to considering the risk and impact of adopting the recommendations that were developed, a balance should be struck between the benefit of the recommendation and its cost. The estimated costs for each alternative including purchase, maintenance, training, and support, should be detailed. Wherever possible, the costs should be expressed in terms of both one-time and annual charges. To simplify the task of determining costs we suggest that budgetary pricing be used. But it must be stressed that these costs are provided only for guidance, as the actual cost of any particular solution is usually a matter of negotiation between the client and vendor.

RECOMMENDED SOLUTIONS

The courses of action, both technical and nontechnical, to implement the recommendations previously defined are developed during this phase of the project. These recommendations can range from the acquisition of specific hardware or software products through to the commissioning of studies in such areas as policy development. In some cases, the recommendations may be simply the continuation of initiatives already underway, for example,

- Develop an accreditation process for all systems based upon system and data classification. The accreditation process should, as a minimum, define and enforce standards for authentication, access control, monitoring, and audit.
- Purchase and deploy personal computer access control solutions.
- Implement a centralized access solution, using hand-held one-time password generators for remote and mobile users.
- Use the current network management facilities to capture security alerts. The proposed solution would record all security violations. Any alert deemed to be severe would result in the immediate notification of security personnel.
- Launch a pilot project to investigate and understand the implications of using OSF/DCE in a mission critical application.

RISK AND IMPACTS

Each recommended solution and course of action will have an impact on the organization. The impact may be felt in terms of changes to current procedures, education, increased staffing, and so on. As well, each has risks associated with the decision to proceed, or not to proceed. The potential impacts and risks for each recommendation should be reviewed and documented as part of the development of the strategy.

The main reason we do this is to help formulate a tactical plan. Those activities which require little effort on behalf of the organization and have a low cost and a low risk of failure are good candidates to start with. These are the activities that will provide immediate results. Those recommendations that have a major impact on the organization will generally require more time to implement and may require additional planning.

TACTICAL PLAN

There are simply not enough hours in the day to implement every recommendation immediately. It is recommended that a tactical implementation plan be developed for the security strategy. To facilitate the development of the plan, each of the recommended solutions and courses of actions needs to be prioritized. This is accomplished by categorizing the recommended solutions by impact, risk, and implementation time. Having completed the priority ranking of the recommended solutions, a tactical plan can be developed for the implementation of the security strategy. The solutions may be grouped into projects as appropriate and arranged in the plan according to their constraints and prerequisites.

CONCLUSIONS

The single largest problem, in terms of trust and security, in the distributed computing environment today is not a lack of technology. It is, rather, a failure to have a strategic plan to address the problem. By having a vision of the future and planning the right steps, corporate objectives in the area of computing security can be realized. If you fail to align the computing security architecture with the computing architecture, you'll end up with a breakfast a dog will love! Taking a strategic view of security and deploying centralized security mechanisms are large steps to solving the problem of computing security. An equally important step is to conduct an independent review of computing security and its related activities. We will review the role of audit in distributed computing in the next chapter.

AUDITING

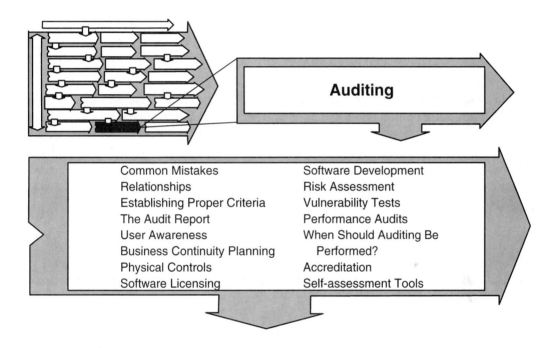

Auditing

Common Mistakes	Software Development
Relationships	Risk Assessment
Establishing Proper Criteria	Vulnerability Tests
The Audit Report	Performance Audits
User Awareness	When Should Auditing Be
Business Continuity Planning	Performed?
Physical Controls	Accreditation
Software Licensing	Self-assessment Tools

We have reviewed the need for policy and guidelines, and have seen how to create the proper foundation for security. How can we ensure that the policies and guidelines, such as the need to protect against unauthorized access and the illegal copying of software by users, are being followed? We know that controls, such as password management and access authorizations, can be used to enforce conformance. But how do we know that the necessary controls have been implemented and are still working? Even the best door lock is useless if the door is left unlocked.

The obvious answer to these questions is that we need to routinely review the conformance to policy and established security guidelines. In most organizations, this *policing* of the computing environment is performed by the Internal Audit Department.

In many cases the systems professionals have an excellent rapport with their counterparts in the Audit Department. We have witnessed the productive collaboration of system administrators and audit personnel in many organizations. While they would never describe the audit of computer systems as "fun," the necessary work is accomplished in a minimum amount of time with the least possible disruption to those involved.

In other organizations, we have detected a great deal of antagonism between the two parties. The audit process was very much a confrontational experience, which unnecessarily resulted in a longer completion time with diminished results. We believe that the root of the problem was a lack of mutual understanding of the purpose, goals, and methodologies of computer auditing.

In this chapter, we will study the role of Audit in the distributed computing environment. After understanding the purpose behind auditing, we will review the interrelationships of the Audit Department with other departments. Next, auditing tools and methodologies will be examined. Finally, different types of audits, which focus on areas outside of the traditional review of computing controls, will be explored.

WHAT IS AN AUDIT ?

There is a good deal of confusion as to what an audit actually is. If you were to ask a group of IS professionals what the term "auditing" means to them, you would likely get a variety of answers. To some, auditing implies the process of collecting data on the activities and resources of a computer system. Others might view auditing as a review of the existing controls or the detection of fraudulent activity. To others, they are the corporate embodiment of the Grim Reaper!

An audit has been defined as "a process by which an independent individual accumulates and evaluates evidence ... for the purpose of reporting between quantifiable information and established criteria."[1] The essence of an audit is to perform an independent review of a given subject, and to report on the conformance of the findings to acceptable standards. Throughout this chapter, we will refer to the process of reviewing compliance to acceptable standards as an *audit* or *auditing*. The department charged with the responsibility of conducting independent reviews of computing security will be referred to as the Audit Department.

For example, a financial audit involves the formal review of the financial statements. Investors and shareholders are not usually willing to rely solely upon management's interpretation of their financial performance. They require an independent report on the fairness of the accounting practices and financial statements to ensure they give an accurate reflection of the organization's economic performance.

The role of an audit is not to reconstruct the financial reports. Rather, to undertake an audit is to review whether or not the financial reports were prepared in accordance with established accounting practices. The financial statements are considered to be fair and accurate if they are produced in conformance with accepted accounting practices. Any significant deviance, which might result in a misinterpretation of the financial statements, is reported. If many deviations are found, and the auditor believes the financial statements are misleading, the auditors must clearly state their misgivings in the audit report.

The primary purpose of an audit, in the computing environment, is to independently review the conformance of an application, system, or network under review to established policies, guidelines, and standards. Failure by the application designer, system, or network administrator to conform to acceptable standards is reported to management. The responsible party is induced to take preventive actions and implement proper security controls. This should result in a higher overall level of security for the enterprise.

However, if the auditing function is performed in isolation, without the participation and interaction of other groups, it will not have the desired effect. Instead, it can result in needless antagonism between the Audit Department and the department under review. We will examine how the relationship between the Audit and other entities should work a little later. First, let's examine who should conduct an audit.

WHO SHOULD PERFORM AN AUDIT?

There are three qualities required of individuals to conduct an audit:

- Knowledge
- Independence and
- Trustworthiness

A computer audit will involve an active review of controls, an analysis of audit trail data, and recommendations on changes to computing proce-

---

[1] Alvan A. Arens, and James K. Loebbecke, Auditing—An Integrated Approach (Englewood Cliffs, NJ: Prentice Hall, 1994).

dures. These activities obviously require some understanding of the technologies involved. But objectivity is also required. Although some of the toughest audits we have witnessed are by their peers, members of the organization's computing community do not usually make effective auditors.

Auditors in essence perform an independent review of the security related activities of the computer department. Computer professionals may be reticent to pass judgment or make unpopular recommendations on their colleagues' activities. They may also focus entirely on the technical issues, losing sight of the overall purpose for the audit. As an audit will involve the review of controls, its activities and findings must be kept confidential. Those conducting an audit must possess a high degree of trustworthiness. For this reason, most organizations are reluctant to allow third parties they do not fully trust (especially ex-hackers) to conduct audits.

> As a professional accountant and auditor, I take great exception to those who joke that the auditors are people who show up after the battle and shoot the wounded. It is well known that we are only allowed to carry knives.

The ideal computer auditor is a hybrid, who possesses both auditing experience and a strong computer background. If an individual possessing these "hybrid" skills is not available, an effective computer Audit team could be created made up of both IS and Audit professionals. Let's now look at some common mistakes Audit Departments make in their approach to auditing the distributed computing environment.

COMMON MISTAKES

Over the years, we have had the opportunity to observe the Audit Departments of many organizations at work. Unfortunately, the interaction between the Auditing Department, the Security Department, and the user computing community at many organizations is either nonexistent or confrontational. In almost all of these cases, the poor relationship has contributed to either a weak security environment or an inefficient use of time and resources.

The problem has occurred because of the following critical mistakes:

- The Audit Department failed to be involved with efforts to solve the problem of computing security.
- The role of audit was misunderstood by the computing community.

- The user departments, including the Security Department, had a poor relationship with the Audit Department.
- The criteria used to perform the actual systems audit was inappropriate.
- The final audit reports were unnecessarily critical of the computing environment they have examined.

WHY IS AN AUDIT OF COMPUTING IMPORTANT?

Most enterprises have a formal Audit Department and extend the mandate of this department to include the computing area. Computer auditing involves the independent review of computer controls, and the delivery of a formal report detailing its findings against acceptable standards. The objective of the review is to produce recommendations which will enhance the security of the computing environment. This is important because

- Computer systems represent a significant investment to most organizations. An independent review of their custodian's (i.e., the system administrator's) ability to safeguard these investments from misuse is simply a good business practice.
- It will give an indication of the overall level of security in the enterprise.
- It promotes conformance and instills a disciplined approach to security. The saying, "You may not do what I expect, but you will do what I inspect," might be a theme for audit activity.
- It gives an overall indication of the degree to which trust may be placed in critical systems and applications.

Many Audit Departments have either ignored or given only a token effort to the audit of the distributed environment. The reasons for the lack of involvement in this area include insufficient knowledge by the Audit Department and labor constraints. We have also witnessed a lack of interest based on the premise that the effort should be focused on more *important* mainframe systems and applications. The problem with this attitude is that it does not recognize that organizations have witnessed compromises of the mainframe environment and applications because of weak controls in the distributed environment. It will also forestall the organization's ability to adopt distributed and client-server architectures and technology because of a failure to implant a disciplined approach to security and audit. It is extremely important that the issue of security be addressed as early as possible in the deployment of these technologies. The best advice we can provide to an Auditing Department is to get involved in auditing the distributed environment as soon as possible. It is easier to establish proper standards and guidelines early in the game, rather than to retrofit them later.

WHAT ROLE SHOULD AN AUDIT PLAY ?

The roles and responsibilities of the Audit and Security Departments, and their relationship with the user community, will vary from organization to organization. In many organizations, both systems auditing and the security functions are part of the IT department. Whether or not they are structurally independent departments, the Audit and Security Departments should be functionally independent from those that operate and manage the organization's computing resources. Figure 24.1 demonstrates, in general terms, the roles performed by system administrators, the Security Department, and the Audit Department.

As mentioned previously, the role of the Audit Department in computing is to perform an independent review of the security of the computing environment and produce a report detailing their findings. The essence of the audit report is an analysis of how the current computing environment measures up against an acceptable set of standards.

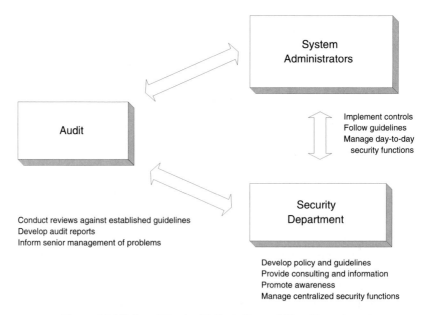

Figure 24.1 Roles of the Audit, Security, and User Departments

Standards and guidelines are normally published by the Security Department. While this department may have many different names, we will generically refer to those who have responsibility for security policy and guidelines as the Security Department. We will examine how standards and guidelines should be established in the next section. The Security Department is also responsible for user education in, and awareness of the security issues. It is also typical for the Security Department to perform centralized security management functions, such as user ID maintenance. Implementing corporate standards and guidelines on systems is normally the duty of a system administrator. They will also typically have the responsibility of managing day-to-day security functions.

RELATIONSHIPS

Ask a member of a police force what they believe is the most important characteristic of their being successful, and they will tell you it is based on the relationship between the police force and the community it serves. They rely on the community to report criminal behavior and provide information. Without the participation of witnesses, the prosecution of criminals can be very difficult. A police force simply cannot be effective without the support of the community it serves.

The same is true for the Audit Department's relationship with the computing community. Like a police force, an Audit Department must rely on the goodwill of the user community to meet its objectives. It's important that the Audit Department make the user community aware of its goals. The Audit Department must also work with the user community and the Security Department to improve the audit process. This working relationship is most important in the establishment of effective auditing criteria.

ESTABLISHING PROPER CRITERIA

Audits are performed by comparing the current environment to an *established criteria.* In a previous chapter, we discussed the establishment of security principles, policy and guidelines. Policy and guidelines, though usually initially created by the Security Department, must be reviewed by the Audit Department. A problem we have seen all to often is a reluctance by some Audit departments to recognize criteria put forward by the Security Department. They feel that by publishing standards the effectiveness of the review is diminished. In fact, the reverse is usually true! The Audit Department must work with the Security and User Departments to establish an effective set of guidelines that all can endorse and follow.

It is imperative that the criteria used reflect the environments that are being audited. There is no point in auditing a UNIX server in the same way as if it were a mainframe computer. Many of the guidelines simply cannot be implemented on a UNIX system or fail to address real exposures. Both the Security and Audit Departments, with input from User Departments, must work together to establish a realistic set of guidelines. It will then be the responsibility of the individual User Departments and system administrators to implement them.

SAMPLE CRITERIA FOR A UNIX AUDIT

The following list provides a limited (it's by no means a complete list) sample of audit criteria for a UNIX system:

- Each account should have a password or have login capability disabled.
- Knowledge of the superuser account should be limited.
- TCP/IP services should be disabled if not required.
- The users should have their last login date displayed upon login.
- Users should have a message concerning authorized use displayed upon login.
- A "." should not appear in a PATH variable.
- The user's $HOME directory and files should not be writable by others.
- The sticky bit should be on the directories */tmp* and */usr/tmp*.
- Write access to system files and directories must be limited.
- The system should be physically secured.
- Host equivalency should be disabled.
- Security advisories from vendors should be applied on a timely basis.

Audit criteria are created using a combination of computing policy and guidelines. They are typically compiled into a list of items called an audit checklist. An audit checklist will generally cover many different topics, including password management, access controls to system resources, and networking services.

THE AUDIT REPORT

How angry would you be if your child received an "F" on an exam after answering 98 out of 100 questions correctly? Most of us would be incensed! How motivated would most children be to continue to work hard? Some auditing departments operate under the assumption that any deviation from their criteria should result in a poor audit report. They fail to recognize that, due to application or networking requirements, not every guideline can be met under every circumstance. There is little point in failing a User Department over operating system features that they are powerless to correct.

In one case of which we are aware, a particular audit criteria was not met on a departmental server, but the actual security exposure was diminished by a complementary control. The Audit Department reported an unacceptable failure in controls to senior management, which resulted in an unfavorable performance review for the unfortunate system administrator. The administrator subsequently displayed an understandable reluctance to continue efforts to address security issues. A far better approach is to prepare the final report according to the overall level of security. If the overall level is poor, then a poor report should result. But failure to address a small number of security issues should not result in an "F." It is more important that the report reflect fairly the overall level of security. This is not accomplished by producing a report which fails system administrators over a minor transgression to an audit guideline.

Now that we've examined the overall purpose of an audit, let's look at the types of things an audit should review.

THE BASICS OF COMPUTER AUDITING

Traditional audits of computer systems have tended to focus on three main areas: conformance to policy, review of the control structures, and an examination of the audit trail. It's important to note that the focus of many corporate policies originated in the mainframe computing environment and may be biased to that environment. A primary focus in the audit of computing is the conformance to policy and standards. Unfortunately, the policy used by many organizations has tended to be developed solely for the mainframe. This policy is of questionable use in the distributed environment. Our view is that policy should be generic in nature and independent of a particular computing platform. Standards are the application of policy and need to be developed specifically for distributed computing platforms.

A key focus of a computer audit is the review of the control structures of the system, application or network being audited. This activity will typically include a review of authentication requirements, such as the use of passwords and unique user IDs. Password management functions, including requiring the use of strong passwords and password aging, are also examined. Access controls, such as those that deny unauthorized access to confidential information, are also reviewed. Reviews are also conducted of high-level access privileges, such as the use of the UNIX superuser privileges.

A computer audit trail is a collection of data, generated from activity on the computer system. The audit trail provides information on the actions of users and processes, and can be used to trace illicit actions. The purposes of audit trails include

- Detecting unauthorized activity, such as attempts to guess a password, through repeated failed access attempts.
- Determining how unauthorized access occurred through recording login and changes in access rights.
- Tracking access to system resources.
- Providing the capability to recover from abuse.

Auditors will sometimes review audit trails looking for evidence of unauthorized activity. But usually an auditor will just want assurances that the audit trail is sufficient to track user activity in the event unauthorized activity occurs.

EXPANDING THE FOCUS

Traditional auditing techniques and methods were developed for the mainframe environment. They have focused on the well-known controls surrounding a single computer system. But the traditional review of control mechanisms is only one aspect of a much bigger picture, and should be expanded to incorporate other issues introduced by distributed computing. Such issues include the proper segregation of duties, user awareness, business resumption planning, physical controls, software licensing, and application development. Figure 24.2 shows the new activities that expand the focus of auditing in the distributed computing environment.

We will now examine these new areas that an audit should address.

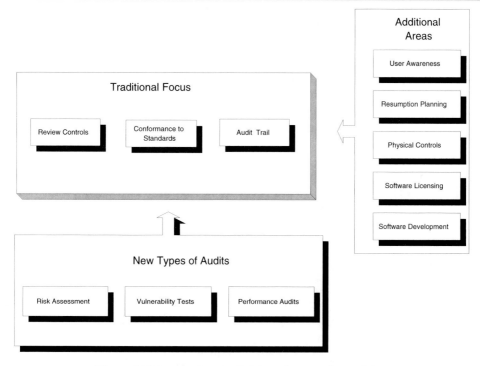

Figure 24.2 Proposed expanded focus for security auditing

USER AWARENESS

Users must be aware of their responsibilities in regards to computer security. Without knowledge of their responsibilities, users can hardly be expected to maintain and exercise proper security procedures. It should be the responsibility of all levels of management to instill awareness of the issues in security within the user community. Awareness programs start with the communication of security issues and procedures to new employees. Employees should formally acknowledge their understanding of their responsibilities in this area. Audits of distributed computing should include examinations of the existence and content of user awareness programs.

BUSINESS CONTINUITY PLANNING

Business continuity planning (BCP) provides a plan and methodology which allow the organization to recover from a disaster affecting its computing services. This is a very complex subject, but it has at its core a properly implemented backup schedule and a disaster recovery plan. Audit of distributed computing should review not only backup procedures, but also examine the ability of the application or system to recover from a disaster.

PHYSICAL CONTROLS

If physical access can be gained to a computer or network device, a wide variety of techniques may be employed to gain unauthorized access to the device. An audit of distributed computing should address the susceptibility of target systems and network devices to physical attacks. Recommendations should be made to address deficiencies in physical controls, such as the placement of critical systems in secured facilities.

SOFTWARE LICENSING

Copyright laws protect the right of software manufacturers to create and distribute their software. Commercial software packages, and some contributed software packages, place restrictions on the use of software included in vendors' licensing agreements. Most manufacturers allow users to copy the software as a backup or working copy. However, licensing agreements typically specify that software may be only installed on one machine at a time. If copies of software are desired for other machines, users must obtain additional licenses or possess a site licensing agreement.

Practices which involve copying of software for purposes other than those outlined in licensing agreements are illegal. An audit of distributed computing must review software licensing to ensure strict compliance of the licensing regulation and copyright law.

SOFTWARE DEVELOPMENT

Test and production facilities are generally segregated. The reason for separating the two is just common sense—one does not want the activities in testing to affect a production machine. However, controls over the movement of software from "test" to "production" may not be adequate. We have witnessed situations where software "patches" and application versions are "hot loaded" into production without adequate testing. Another area of concern involves the use of production data in the test environment. Issues here may include the exposure of classified data (e.g., personnel data) to developers and the possible contamination of "production" data if test data is mistakenly loaded into the "production" environment. In general, the isolation of test environments from production is desirable.

OTHER TYPES OF AUDITS

Other types of audits may be employed to help understand the degree of trust that may be placed in the environment. These audits include risk assessment, vulnerability testing, self-assessments, and performance audits.

RISK ASSESSMENT

Although in many cases it is the responsibility of the IT Department, a risk assessment can be an effective tool in the audit of computer systems. A risk assessment is a study which attempts to quantify potential losses from an incident or event against the likelihood that the event will occur. Risk assessments may be performed for applications, systems, or networks, which are called subjects. For each control in the subject, the potential damage is estimated if the control is compromised. A risk coefficient or factor, which is essentially the percentage likelihood the event could occur, is then applied to the expected damages. The results from the multiplication yield an expected loss figure. The intent is to focus on those areas that have the highest expected loss, and would therefore cause the most harm to the organization.

> It is also common to use the term "risk assessment" to describe the active testing of controls on a computer system. These tests, which are usually called vulnerability tests by auditors, seek to identify potential threats by discovering weak areas in the existing controls. Once identified, the controls can be tightened and the potential threat averted.

The primary deliverable of a risk assessment is a report that details controls and associated weaknesses, and then quantifies the potential loss should the weakness be exploited. From an audit perspective, the use of a risk assessment will

- Allow audit activity to focus in the areas of highest expected loss.
- Inform management of the risks and potential losses associated with a computing environment.
- Alert developers and system administrators to potential problem areas.

There are limitations to the use of risk assessments. Without access to data from other sources, it is very difficult to determine an appropriate risk factor. When determining potential losses, it is important to include indirect losses from all the systems and applications that may be compromised. For example, the compromise of a test system may not have a significant financial impact. But if the compromise of this system allows an intruder later access to the personnel system, significant losses may result.

VULNERABILITY TESTS

Risk assessments are termed passive in that they perform no direct actions on the controls of the environment under review. Vulnerability tests, on the other hand, actually test the environment for suspected weaknesses. They imitate and utilize the tools a hacker would use to gain unauthorized access to systems. Typical checks include

- Weak or nonexistent passwords
- Attempts to acquire the password file
- Unprotected system binaries and files
- Attempts to access classified data
- Exploitation of known bugs
- Inadequate implementation of controls

The objective of vulnerability testing is to highlight weaknesses, using the methods an intruder would use. With knowledge gained in the test, an appropriate control or countermeasure can be used to eliminate the weakness. The scope of the test may be a single system or application or may include a large number of networked systems. Network tests are recommended as an initial activity because of their comprehensive approach. They are good at discovering potentially weak systems, and for obtaining an overall indication of security. Comprehensive testing of critical systems is usually performed following network testing.

Extreme care must be taken to ensure that the tools and information gained by vulnerability testing are not available to unauthorized individuals. The reports and tools should be removed from the candidate systems when testing is completed. Examples of vulnerability testing software for the UNIX and TCP/IP environments include the contributed COPS and SATAN utilities. COPS monitors UNIX system controls while SATAN provides the ability to probe a TCP/IP network testing for vulnerabilities.

SELF-ASSESSMENTS

Self-assessment audits allow system administrators to review their system or systems against established auditing criteria. The intent is to allow system administrators to meet, or exceed, security standards in advance of an audit. If used on a regular basis, rather than merely in anticipation of a visit by the Audit Department, they can be very effective in raising the overall level of security in an organization. We will review the use of self-assessment tools later in this chapter.

PERFORMANCE AUDITS

A special type of audit, called a performance audit, measures the efficiency and effectiveness of both computer systems and applications. The usual focus of this type of audit is on applications. The goals of a performance audit are

- To measure whether a system meets the business objectives for which it was implemented.
- To review the cost-effectiveness of the new system.
- To measure whether the new system meets its design objectives in terms of performance.

Because of the relatively high costs associated with the delivery of a performance audit, they are usually restricted to large, complex systems and applications.

WHEN SHOULD AUDITING BE PERFORMED?

Audits of the financial statements primarily occur in a three- to six-month period following the fiscal year end. While some preliminary investigation is done before, most of the work occurs after year end. Computer system audits have tended to follow the same cycle and occur on an annual basis. But we believe a more timely approach is recommended. While activities such as software licensing checks can occur on an annual basis, it is recommended that control monitoring and vulnerability checks be performed year round as part of normal system administration duties.

ACCREDITATION

Accreditation is the process of fairly applying security criteria to different classes of systems. Many organizations recognize the need to audit systems differently based upon their operating system. They have developed an accreditation process, which defines a set of standards for authentication, access control, monitoring, and audit based upon the type of system and its use. This does not imply a lessening of standards, but rather that the full suite of security controls available on a particular platform are used.

It's easy to see the need to treat different operating systems differently because the control structures are different. But many organizations also accredit systems based upon a functional classification and apply different standards based upon the nature of the system. For example, application development machines will usually have a lower set of standards than a production machine running a payroll application. But the application development environment may be denied certain privileges, such as direct access to the corporate internetwork, as a result of the lower accreditation.

Typical classifications of systems for accreditation by function include

- Not classified
- Personal workstation
- Demonstration
- Production
- Network management
- Application development
- Security and audit

Table 24.1 lists suggested networking limitations, based upon the accreditation classification.

The primary motivation for accreditation is to raise the overall security of the entire environment. Those systems that cannot meet accreditation standards are denied privileges, such as full connection to the internetwork. The accreditation process forces the weakest systems to become stronger, if they wish to have an extended set of privileges.

SELF-ASSESSMENT TOOLS

There are a number of automated software tools available today that monitor the security of the computing environment. They are generally known as control monitors by security personnel, but are termed self-assessment tools by auditors. Their use is usually specific to a selected platform. Examples of self-assessment tools include the LT Auditor from Blue Lance and the Kane Security Analyst from Intrusion Detection for Novell networks. For UNIX, examples of self-assessment tools include the contributed COPS software, SecurityAudit/UX from VeSoft, and the security monitoring features of the OmniGuard family from Axent Technologies.

Recognizing that most Audit Departments in today's organizations live under financial and work force constraints, the use of existing control monitoring software to assess security is recommended. In general, Audit should simply use existing security tools whenever they exist. The best approach is for Audit to promote the use of a common tool for monitoring security, and to check that it is run by the system administrators on a regular basis.

TABLE 24.1
ACCREDITATION REQUIREMENTS

Accreditation Class	Requirements	Limitations
Not classified	None	System must be isolated and may not be directly connected to the corporate internetwork.
Personal workstation	Access controls Virus checking	System is a single-user workstation.
Demonstration	Access controls	System is reloaded from vendor-supplied materials. There is no access to the network unless accredited as per production systems.
Production	Access controls Physical controls Network controls Auditing	An accredited system may access the internetwork.
Development	User Controls	The system cannot be connected directly to the internetwork, but must use proxy services on an accredited system.
Operational support	As per production	The system provides support for the continued operation of the infrastructure, such as software distribution and networking.
Security	Physical controls Access controls Auditing Network controls	The system provides security-related functions.

It is strongly recommended that Audit promote and endorse the use of self-assessment tools (control monitors). They can provide a common link between the criteria Audit wishes to establish and the controls enacted by the system administrator. Unless detection of fraud is a concern, Audit and system administrators should share common security tools. The tools should be used on a regular basis by the system administrator to detect security exposures. They will be used only periodically by Audit. Audit should not rely totally on the use of control monitors and complement their use with audit checklists and interviews of key personnel.

CONCLUSIONS

The audit of computer systems is an important component in achieving a solution to the problem of computing security. Auditing promotes conformance to established policy and guidelines, thus raising the overall level of computing security in the enterprise.

The focus, scope, and timing of computer Audit activity must change from the traditional annual review performed with a mainframe focus. The traditional audit of the controls environment should be expanded to include other areas, such as licensing provisions and conformance to policy. As well as expanding on traditional audit activities, different types of audits should be performed to include vulnerability tests and risk assessments. Most important, however, is that the Audit Department must build an effective working relationship with the computing community it serves.

CHAPTER 25

THE FUTURE

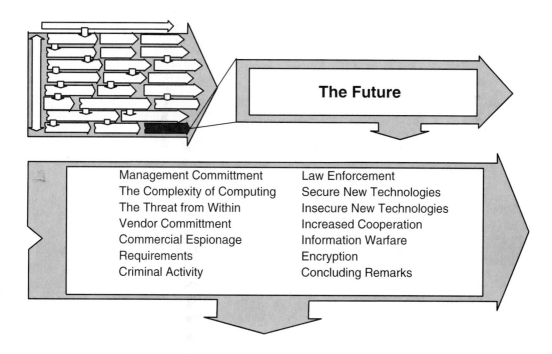

The Future

Management Committment	Law Enforcement
The Complexity of Computing	Secure New Technologies
The Threat from Within	Insecure New Technologies
Vendor Committment	Increased Cooperation
Commercial Espionage	Information Warfare
Requirements	Encryption
Criminal Activity	Concluding Remarks

Can we solve the problem of computing security? With an optimistic view, the problem of computing security will be solved. New technologies are, or will be available, to address the problem. These technologies will feature single, secure sign-on; strong access controls; and the dynamic detection of security incidents. An increasing awareness and commitment by the management of most corporations will result in the deployment of these advanced technologies. We have seen the need to implement strong, robust security controls, to monitor the controls, and to educate the user community.

To a pessimist, the problem of computing security will not be solved in the future. New technologies, such as wireless LANs, will introduce a new set of security issues to be addressed. Fraud and other illegal activities will likely continue to be of interest to organized crime. Armed with sophisticated tools and using their knowledge of fraud and other white-collar crime, organized crime might be in a position to unleash a new wave of computer-based crime. The fact they could potentially do so in relative safety, using international borders to shield them, would be especially attractive. Finally, a logical target of a future war may be the enemies' computing resources. The ability of most organizations to defend themselves against a sophisticated attack by a foreign military against their computing resources should be at least somewhat questionable.

It is very difficult to answer the question of whether or not the challenge of computing security will be met. Figure 25.1 shows the conflicting reasons behind why computing security will, or will not, be solved.

It is very difficult to predict whether or not the problem of computing security will be solved. We will now examine reasons for, and arguments against, the solution of the problem.

MANAGEMENT COMMITMENT

In the past, there was little recognition of the importance of computing security by senior management. In many of the organizations we have visited in recent years, this has changed. Senior management has recognized that the security of the organization's computing resources is an important business problem. They are committed to addressing the problem and have demonstrated this commitment in a number of ways. In the past, it was very

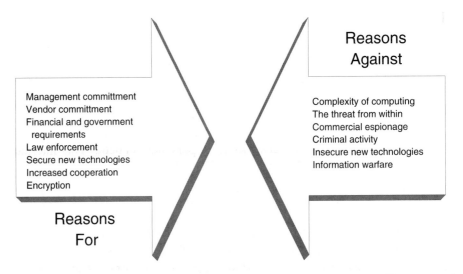

Reasons
Against

Management committment
Vendor committment
Financial and government
  requirements
Law enforcement
Secure new technologies
Increased cooperation
Encryption

Complexity of computing
The threat from within
Commercial espionage
Criminal activity
Insecure new technologies
Information warfare

Reasons
For

Figure 25.1 Will the challenge of computing security be answered?

difficult to gain an audience with senior management on the issue of computing security. Based upon our personal experience, this is no longer true. Many of the security initiatives we have participated in have had the direct involvement of senior management. They were keenly interested in the progress and results of our activity. In many organizations, the position of information security officer has risen from an information services position to one that reports directly to a vice president. The strongest indication of senior management's commitment has been their financial support for computing security activities. In many organizations, management's commitment has extended beyond a recognition of the problem to applying financial support to solve the problem. The commitment by senior management to finding solutions to the problem of computing security is vital to the success of corporate security activities.

THE COMPLEXITY OF COMPUTING

The new client-server technolgies, although easy to use, are very complex compared to other computing environments. When both data and application logic are distributed the complexity of the environment increases. When networking considerations are added, the result is a complex computing environment involving many different facets. From a general security viewpoint, complexity is bad. It increases the likelihood of bugs and other security exposures that may be exploited by an intruder. Advanced software is becoming available that provides easier implementation of distributed services, but this also increases the complexity of the resulting solution.

THE THREAT FROM WITHIN

Corporations today are undergoing tremendous changes. The massive corporate layoffs and downsizing have arguably produced a working force with less loyalty to the corporation than was previously held by employees. It is likely that incidents involving disgruntled employees, or those that see an opportunity for personal gain, will continue. Most organizations are most vulnerable to attacks from employees who have the ability to use their access rights to systems or networks for a personal vendetta. This internal threat has been by far the largest cause of loss due to breach of security.

VENDOR COMMITMENT

In the past, the security of a vendor's product was never high on the list of desirable attributes. Today, this situation has changed and strong security in a product is viewed as a competitive advantage. Similarly, many vendors have developed solutions for their specific customers security concerns.

Never have so many security products been available on the market. This adds confusion to the attempt to solve the distributed security problem. These varied solutions are also many times accompanied by an attempt to get the solution recognized as an industry or de facto standard. Not only do we have competing solutions but we also have competing standards.

COMMERCIAL ESPIONAGE

The competitive pressures on business today have never been greater. Due to global competition, most businesses are faced with ever-increasing demands for quality improvement, cost reduction, and reduced time to market. Information is a critical factor in addressing these demands, and is arguably the most critical resource a major corporation can possess. Most corporate secrets are held today in computer systems. Given the pressures of the marketplace, it is probably inevitable that at least a few organizations will seek to gain an advantage on its competitors by attempting to discover their secrets.

Industrial secrets are not only of interest to a competitor, but are increasingly of interest to foreign governments. Especially in the area of new and emerging technologies, it is simply more cost effective to gain access to another nation's research than to develop it on your own. It is suspected that most nations indulge in industrial espionage in one form or another. Using international communication links, such as the Internet, to perform industrial espionage from within the safety of one's own borders, this type of activity is likely to increase. With the resources of a national government behind them, the security agencies of a foreign government can be expected to utilize the most sophisticated methods and technologies to gain competitive knowledge.

FINANCIAL INDUSTRY AND GOVERNMENT REQUIREMENTS

Government and the financial industry are likely to be more demanding with their requirements in the area of security. It can be expected that the demand for security from these two powerful market segments will have to be addressed by vendors. The buying power of these market forces is simply too strong to ignore. This should result in stronger and more sophisticated security solutions being available for the entire computing community. These industries also have a large influence on the development and deployment of standards.

CRIMINAL ACTIVITY

Until now, most computer hacking has rarely been motivated by money. Theft of computing and telecommunication services has become quite common but not usually for monetary gain. Aside from a few sensational cases, criminal activity, including fraud and electronic theft, has been a relatively rare occurrence. It is perhaps inevitable that a marriage will occur between hacking expertise and a criminal's knowledge. When this happens, criminal attacks against commercial computing systems may become more prevalent. Criminal elements may be able to provide their accomplices with funding for elaborate equipment and computing devices.

A troubling aspect of this activity is that it does not necessarily need to be close to the victim. The criminal who launches an attack over the Internet, from a country with limited relations with that of his victim, may be for all intents immune from prosecution. While international organizations are cooperating in many ways to solve this problem, there are still many countries from which the extradition and subsequent prosecution of a computer criminal would very difficult. The criminals in these countries would for all practical purposes be immune from international prosecution. Fraudulent activity on the Internet might be very difficult to prosecute. Tricksters use a variety a methods to make people part with their money; it's probably only inevitable that these methods surface on the Internet. For an excellent reference text on this important topic, the reader is directed to *Computer Crime in Canada* [Davis & Hutchinson, 1994].

LAW ENFORCEMENT

In *The Cuckoo's Egg,* Clifford Stoll [1989], relates a fascinating true story of computer espionage in which he discovered an intruder who was abusing a large number of computer networks. One of the early frustrations in attempting to uncover the intruder was the lack of cooperation by local, state, and federal police forces. Even after the intruder was suspected of intruding on a Central Intelligence Agency computer, the official reaction was lukewarm. This type of reaction by law enforcement agencies in most jurisdictions would be different today. The awareness of the general public, including law enforcement agencies, about computer crime has risen. Jurisdictional disputes, as well as the question of actual loss, complicate prosecution in many cases. There appears to be a much greater willingness in the law enforcement communities of North America and Europe to participate in the investigation of computer crime. Many police forces in North America have special teams dedicated to the investigation of information technology crime.

SECURE NEW TECHNOLOGIES

New emerging technologies, such as Kerberos, allow for the development of strong, secure applications. New applications, such as Lotus Notes, using public encryption and other advanced security technology are being introduced to the marketplace. A host of new vendors are also offering security solutions. The Windows NT operating system was developed with security as a requirement. We are seeing the marketplace demand, and the vendors respond with new technologies that have been designed to meet their security demands. Advancements in new security technologies and product offerings are being made daily. The deployment of new technologies will make it more difficult for an intruder to compromise the computing security of an organization.

INSECURE NEW TECHNOLOGIES

New technologies are almost assuredly going to bring new security issues along with them. Wireless LANs, using the airwaves rather than a physical wire to communicate, will introduce new issues. Transmissions on a wireless LAN, based upon radio frequency, could have its signals intercepted by individuals using appropriate scanning technology. By using equipment ranging from a simple scanner to a sophisticated spectrum analyzer, an intruder could monitor the airwaves surrounding a corporate installation. Actually making sense of the transmission is quite another matter. Depending on the skill of the attackers and the sophistication of their tools, analysis of the wireless data streams may be possible. Diagnostic tools for wireless LANs are likely to allow for the isolation of selected nodes for troubleshooting. Similar tools would likely be used by an attacker. Again, depending on the sophistication of the equipment used, the attacker may not need to be inside the organization's physical grounds to conduct the attack. The encryption of sensitive data may be required by many organizations when using wireless technology.

INCREASED COOPERATION

There is an increased cooperation between government, vendors, and the computing community to see a resolution to the problem of computing security. The large number of Internet Requests for Comments (RFCs) in the area of security arguably attests to the willingness of people and organizations to share their thoughts and ideas on the topic. Numerous committees and working groups from the various standards committees also demonstrate a shared commitment to resolve the problem. The work of the Computer Emergency Response Team (CERT) at Carnegie Mellon University and the Computer Incident Advisory Capability (CIAC) of the U.S. Department of Energy to inform the computing public of serious security exposures has also been invaluable.

INFORMATION WARFARE

The feature story of the August 21, 1995 *Time* magazine was titled "Cyber War—The U.S. rushes to turn computers into tomorrow's weapons of destruction. But how vulnerable is the home front?" The story describes how attacks on a nation's computing resources will likely be an objective in any future war. The attacks, unlike most criminal activity, will not focus on monetary gain but rather on the disruption of computer-based services. They would logically, if war can ever be called logical, be extended beyond military sites to commercial and governmental computing systems. The ability of most commercial organizations to defeat a concentrated, military attack on its computing-based resources must be, at least somewhat, suspect. These attacks might also focus on industrial utilities by attempting to disable control systems for gas and electric utilities, local and state government, and law enforcement. Essentially, any target whose disruption of service would demoralize or disrupt the civilian population could be considered a target. The disruption of the networks themselves will cause great harm.

ENCRYPTION

Encryption provides a further level of safeguarding corporate information assets beyond operating system and network controls. With the increased availability of both commercial and contributed solutions, in particular public key technologies, the public use of encryption promises to increase. If the problem of key management can be addressed, encryption technology should provide a strong weapon in the war for computing security. It will not, of itself, preclude the need for strong network and operating system controls. A computer whose operating system controls are weak, even when data encryption is used, can still be successfully attacked by a masquerading Trojan horse program that steals a user's encryption keys.

CONCLUDING REMARKS

If the problem of computing security is to be solved, it will be as a result of organizations recognizing it as a business, not a computing, issue. New technologies are certainly going to contribute to solving the problem, but they are only part of the answer. Policies, management commitment, and a strategic view of the problem will also be required.

Organizations are going to have to get serious about computing security. Management commitment, evidenced by the allocation of both workers and financial resources, will be required. Unfortunately, this commitment may all too often only be gained after a serious security incident has occurred. But an allocation of resources is not the only requirement. An organization will also require a strategy for security to ensure the effective use of resources. The strategy will identify those actions, including the acquisition of appropriate technology, that will be required to address the problem. But most important, the strategy will align security requirements with business goals and directions. A program for increased user education and awareness in the area of security will likely be identified as an important recommendation of the corporate strategy. Because of the wide variety of goals, however, a strategy for security may take years to execute. In addition, the problem of computing security is likely to evolve, making its solution evasive. Thus, a long-term commitment to its solution is required. A humorous history of the English[1] has provided a fitting quotation to describe the long-term nature of the problem:

> Gladstone invented the education rate... and spent his declining years trying to guess the answer to the Irish Question; unfortunately, whenever he was getting warm, the Irish secretly changed the Question.

The question of computing security is simply going to take a few years, and a great deal of commitment, to be answered.

---

[1] W. C. Sellar and R. J. Yeatman, 1066 and All That, (London: Meuthen & Company, 1930).

APPENDIX A

STRONG AUTHENTICATION

As we have seen, the use of "secret" passwords to authenticate users does present certain problems. First of all, the secret passwords might be guessed or revealed by using a dictionary attack. Passwords may also be written down by users and subsequently discovered. Possibly a more significant problem is that the password is usually transmitted in clear-text over a network. Even if the password is encrypted, it might be possible to capture and replay it.

To counter these vulnerabilities we may need to implement stronger authentication methods. We briefly reviewed the various forms that can be used to authenticate someone: something you know such as a password, something you have such as a special card or token, and something personal such as a handprint or eye retina scan. The greater the need to be sure of an identity, the stronger the required authentication mechanism. We will review a few of the methods used for strong authentication in this appendix.

ONE-TIME PASSWORDS

A one-time password is a unique password generated at a particular instance in time and valid only for a limited period. These unique passwords are generated from one or more factors, such as the time of day, or an event such as passing an input string through an algorithm. Because the input factors used to create the password are unique, the password can't be reused or regenerated. A password that is captured from a network cannot be reused for subsequent unauthorized access.

The implementation of one-time passwords uses the current date and time which are entered into an algorithm to create a unique numerical string. A simple implementation of this process would be the generation of a list of predefined passwords, based on the date and time of day. A user will consult the generated list to find the appropriate password that is valid for the current time. The target system will also use this same generated list. For this specific time the password on the list will match the password expected by the system.

TOKEN-BASED AUTHENTICATION

Two solutions using the *something you have* approach, involve the use of a token or card and one-time passwords or challenge-response authentication. In a one-time password solution, a hand-held authentication device or internal hardware card is used to generate a valid password every 60 seconds. The device itself may be protected by an internally held password which the user must present to the token before obtaining the generated password. The server has the ability to generate the identical password for the user for that specific period in time. The password generated by the client device will match the password generated by the server. However, one drawback to time-based authentication is the need to coordinate and maintain clocks between the authentication device and the server.

This type of authentication is much stronger than a single password since the capture of the password cannot be reused to gain entry. However, as the password is usually valid for up to 60 seconds, it may be intercepted and reused by an attacker within this time period. An example of a two-factor authentication, based on the time of day, is shown in Figure A.1.

A challenge-response solution does not rely upon a time-based password but on the processing of a challenge value to produce a response value. In these solutions, the user will initiate a request for authentication to the server which then responds by returning a numeric code to the user. In the meantime, the server will use its copy of an encrypting algorithm to generate a one-time password using this same numeric code. The user, using either an authentication token or software, will enter the code on their local system. The local token or software will generate a one-time password using the numeric code as a key and executing the same encryption algorithm as the server. This response is then sent back to the server. If this value agrees with the value generated by the server, the user is authenticated. Once the user has been authenticated, the password is invalid and will never be reused. Figure A.2 illustrates the challenge-response technique.

The benefit to the challenge-response method is that the password is truly a one-time password and cannot be intercepted and replayed. On the downside, many users complain about having to key two sequences: the initial login request and the response to the challenge. Event-based one-time

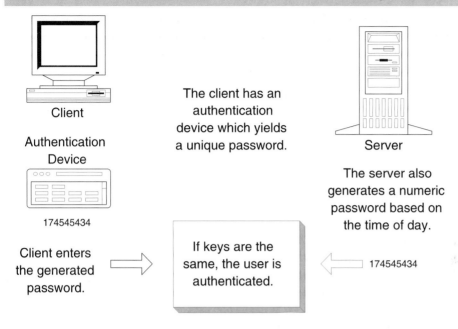

Client

**Authentication
Device**

174545434

Client enters
the generated
password.

The client has an
authentication
device which yields
a unique password.

If keys are the
same, the user is
authenticated.

Server

The server also
generates a numeric
password based on
the time of day.

174545434

Figure A.1 Time-based one-time passwords

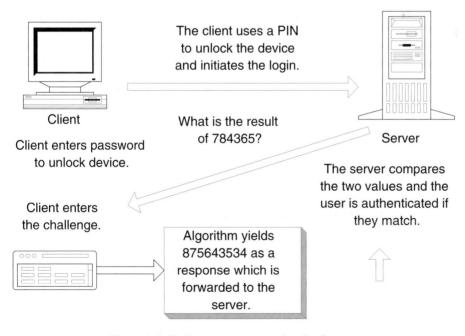

Client

Client enters password
to unlock device.

Client enters
the challenge.

The client uses a PIN
to unlock the device
and initiates the login.

What is the result
of 784365?

Algorithm yields
875643534 as a
response which is
forwarded to the
server.

Server

The server compares
the two values and the
user is authenticated if
they match.

Figure A.2 Challenge-response authentication

passwords are not always popular with users due to the fact that they require the user to key both a password to unlock a device and submit a response to the servers' request.

The use of a smart card can further enhance and strengthen authentication methods. Some implementations of smart cards contain personal identification number (PIN) information, encryption algorithms, and the encryption keys on tamperproof, protected storage on the card itself. The processing power contained on the microchip embedded in the smart card is used to perform the required encryption. In this manner the client system does not have to be concerned about the secure storage of encryption keys or algorithms.

The use of an authentication device, protected by a password, is superior to a single password in the strength of authentication, since the loss of one of the authentication factors will not yield entry. The likelihood of losing both factors is also quite remote. It also provides a way of providing strong authentication that can be portable.

BIOMETRIC-BASED AUTHENTICATION

A more stringent from of authentication can be based on a physical characteristic or personal traits. Authentication based on such biometric information—something you are—is called third-factor authentication. Many different types of biometric factors can be used for authentication, such as a thumbprint, hand geometry, voiceprint, or eye retina scans. Minute measurements such as the timing of a pattern of keystrokes can also be used to differentiate between people. A handwritten signature is another obvious way of providing authentication, although it is difficult to capture in its graphic form.

A more interesting way of authenticating a written signature is to measure the accelerations and movement of the pen used to write the name rather than the resulting signature. The way the name is written tends to be better at providing authentication than the actual written signature.

Since biometric data is captured by sensors or scanning, there is always a chance of obtaining incomplete or incorrect results. The performance of biometric methods is based on the percentage of false rejections and false acceptance. A false rejection occurs when a valid individual is rejected by the process. A false acceptance happens when an invalid individual is accepted by the authentication process. Biometric authentication over a network can still be subject to capture and replay if additional encryption is not used for the biometric data.

LOCATION-BASED AUTHENTICATION

Another interesting function that is being explored is the use of geodetic location-based authentication. The ability to accurately determine the specific location of a user when compared to the expected location can be used as an additional authentication method. A specific location signature can be generated using the information provided by the satellites of the Global Positioning System (GPS). This is compared to the computed expected location of the client system. The location signature changes with the orbital motion of the satellites thus preventing a replay attack. Continuous authentication is also possible. Mutual authentication can be accomplished by authenticating the specific location of the server to the client. If a user's identification device is stolen, the subsequent use of it will enable the authorities to pinpoint the thief's exact location.

ADVANCED AUTHENTICATION STANDARDS

The Federal Information Processing Standards Publication 190 (FIPS 190) provides guidelines for the use of advanced authentication technology alternatives. This document is issued by the U. S. National Institute of Standards and Technology (NIST) as a guide to federal departments and agencies in designing, acquiring and implementing authentication systems. The guide provides a good overview of approaches to authentication from passwords to biometric implementations. Also included is an overview of encryption considerations in authentication as well as implementation guidelines.

APPENDIX B

SMART CARDS

A smart card is generally considered to be a card the size and shape of a credit card with a microchip embedded in it. The microchip can provide read-only and updatable storage and even include a processor complete with an operating system and the ability to execute stored programs. The microchip on the card can be accessed with a special card reader using exposed contacts on the card. Other smart cards do not require contacts and can communicate by electromagnetic induction if the card is held in close proximity to the reader. Still other smart card implementations utilize a radio frequency that can read and update the smart card at a distance. This type of smart card has been used for vehicles traveling on toll roads or bridges. The information on the card can be read while the vehicle is moving.

The simplest type of smart card is the storage card where the microchip embedded on the card has a specific data storage capacity. One of the first widespread implementations of this type of card was with the French public telephone system. Instead of coins, a smart card is used to store a specific purchased dollar value. For eample, the card could contain $25.00 worth of credit. To place a call from a public telephone, the card is inserted into a reader on the phone and the call is placed. When the call is finished, the telephone calculates the amount of money the call costs and deducts that value from the amount stored on the card. This card can be used until the value on the card has been depleted and a new card with a new value is required.

A variation of the storage card is the multiple or personal storage card. The data storage that is available on the card can be divided into several separate areas. Access to these areas can be protected by an individual password or personal identification numbers (PINs). This type of card can be used to store multiple values for different uses or protect different specific data with passwords or PINs. An even more advanced type of smart card includes a processor on the card, complete with an operating system. This processor can be used to execute programs on the card itself which has the ability to implement very sophisticated applications. These types of cards have been used to store and execute an encryption algorithm on the card. The encryption algorithm and keys can be used on the card itself and carried from location to location. This will reduce the complexity of the management function while providing robust security in certain implementations.

In addition to the processor-based card, additional models exist that include a small keyboard and display. These type of cards, also known as tokens, can be used without a card reader. They are sometimes used to provide security credentials and one-time passwords or in a challenge-response capacity. The keyboard on the card is used to input a PIN to prove that the user is the actual owner of the card and thus unlocks the card functions.

USES OF THE CARD

Smart cards can be used for many different functions related to security. The most common use of a smart card is to provide second- and third-function authentication. Second-function authentication is something you have in your possession (i.e., the smart card) and a third function positively identifies you (e.g., a thumbprint or eye scan). To support second-function authentication, the card is sometimes used to generate a secret that can only be accessed by the user. For example, a PIN is entered to unlock the card, and then the secure storage area is accessed to execute a program contained on the card. The following are some of the implementations where a smart card can be used to support security requirements:

- *Challenge-response*—The target processor generates a challenge in the form of a random number. This number is processed by the card and a response is generated using some encryption algorithm and a secret key. The response is compared to a calculated response provided by the processor. If the response from the card agrees with the calculated response, then the card and the user of the card are authenticated. A PIN is used to first unlock the card functions.

- *Encryption*—The encryption algorithm can be stored and executed on the card itself. A set of characters to be encrypted is sent to the card and the encrypted set of characters is returned. The secret encryption keys are not exposed and never leave the card. In this manner, a PIN can be internally verified without sending the PIN across the network. The card can also be used to generate electronic signatures to attach to messages.

- *Stored photograph*—The card can be used to store a digitized photograph which can be used to authenticate the user.
- *One time password*—A password generation mechanism on the card is executed in sync with one on the target processor. The card generates a unique password each time that it is used and compared to the same generation function on the target processor. This password is unique and changes on a short time interval. If the passwords agree, the user is authenticated.
- *Bometric data*—A digitized thumbprint or eye retina scan or other personal unique information is stored on the card. This information is used to compare with the actual characteristics of the user.
- *Secure storage of credentials*—The card can be used to securely store credentials or session keys. The card can also be used to securely store distributed encryption keys.
- *Single sign-on*—The card can be used to store a collection of identifications and passwords that are themselves protected by a encrypted PIN number or password. This secured storage can be accessed and the identification and passwords used to logon to the various applications or systems. This is one way to securely address the requirement for multiple identification's and passwords without causing the user to write them down or forgetting them.

STANDARDS

The current standard for smart cards is defined by the International Standards Organization (ISO) 7816 set of standards. These standards define the physical characteristics of the card and the dimensions and location of the microchip contacts on the card. The standards also address the electronic signals and transmission protocols, and the interindustry commands used for interchange. The imbedded microchip is accessed using eight standard contacts at a specific location on the card. The ISO is working on extending the 7816 standard set into the areas of registration for applications and common data elements. The current ISO specifications include

- ISO 7816-1: Identification Cards—integrated circuit(s) cards with contacts; Part 1; Physical Characteristics, 1987
- ISO 7816-2: Identification Cards—integrated circuit(s) cards with contacts; Part 2; Dimensions and Location of Contacts, 1988

- ISO 7816-3: Identification Cards—integrated circuit(s) cards with contacts; Part 3; Electronic Signals and Transmission Protocols, 1989
- ISO 7816-4.2: Information Technology (Identification Cards)—integrated circuit(s) cards with contacts; Part 4; Inter-Industry Commands for Interchange, 1993

The Distributed Computing Environment (DCE) is looking at smart card technology to augment its current security capability. The introduction and specifications for smart cards with DCE are contained in two request for comment (RFC) documents from the Open Software Foundation: OSF DCE RFC 57.0, *Smart Card Introduction,* and OSF DCE RFC 57.1 DCE, *Smart Card Integration.* The introduction document explains the smart card concepts and the general approach to using them with DCE. The integration document explains how the smart card would be used for a two-factor authentication process with DCE. The proposed standard calls for the smart card to store the user's long-term DCE key. To access the key and log in to DCE, the user must possess the card and must know the password required to access the key file on the card.

PCMCIA Cards

Another technology that is used to implement smart card systems is the PCMCIA card. The Personal Computer Memory Card Interface Association (PCMCIA) was formed to develop a standard for the creditcard-sized plug-in adapters for PCs. The PCMCIA card is about the same dimensions as a credit card but is much thicker. There are in fact three types of cards defined in the PCMCIA standards, each of a different card thickness. The PCMCIA card provides expanded capabilities for data storage and processing power. They are a popular way of providing modems and LAN adapters for laptop and notebook computers. They provide additional storage (either RAM memory or even hard disks) and can be used for communication devices in the way of modems and LAN connections. The fact that many PC manufacturers are including PCMCIA capabilities into their machines ensure the long-term viability of this standard.

Smart Card Issues

One of the main liabilities with the use of a smart card is the fact that the card itself may contain valuable information or security access features. If the card becomes inoperative or is lost, another recourse may not be easily available. The standards concerning smart cards are continuing to evolve. The ISO standards address the physical characteristic of the card, but standardized use of the card has not evolved to the same level. The cost of the smart card readers can be high if readers are required at all of the system access points. The chip card may be losing ground to the PCMCIA card in some respects due to the fact that PCMCIA capability is being included with many notebook and laptop PCs as standard items. The smart card provides enhanced capabilities in security implementations, but it is not itself a solution.

Despite these issues, the use of smart cards is likely to grow. They represent a valuable tool in the fight for computing security by providing a safe storage mechanism for authentication keys, encryption algorithms, and other security mechanisms.

APPENDIX C

PERSONAL COMPUTER SECURITY

Personal computers, using the DOS, OS/2, and Windows environment, present unique security challenges. A personal computer using one of these operating systems has very few security controls, and the controls that do exist can be easily circumvented. These controls are usually limited to screen lockouts and bootup passwords. Screen lockout controls lock the screen after a period of inactivity and require the user to enter a password before resuming their activity. There are many different implementations of screen lockouts, but most can be defeated by recycling power and rebooting the system.

Some personal computers allow passwords to protect the bootup sequence. Again, these controls can usually be circumvented by simply booting from a floppy disk. Screen lockout passwords that are stored on the personal computer may be a special source of concern. For example, a screen saver might store the screen lockout password in an encrypted form in the file control.ini. If the file is copied, the encrypted password string may be subjected to the same password-cracking techniques we discussed in Chapter 12. The risk is not to the personal computer and its data since the attacker already has full access to everything on the PC. The user may have used this password elsewhere and create a larger security exposure. By discovering the screen lockout password, the attacker might be able to access to either the network or other more sensitive computing systems.

Some personal computer software, including databases, word processors, and spreadsheets provide optional encryption. Unfortunately, the encryption used is generally weak and can be easily broken. Tools to break the encryption schemes used by many popular PC software products is easily available on the Internet.

413

Another problem with DOS or DOS/Windows-based systems is that they are not designed to be multiuser. Anyone who gains access to the system has full access to all files and directories. WINDOWS 95 provides limited multiuser capability, but unfortunately it is not secure. WINDOWS 95 offers a logon screen, protected by a user ID and password. However, the default setting can be easily defeated by pressing the Cancel or Escape key. This will leave you in a default user setting, from which you can access the same system files and directories as if you had used a valid password! Security can be enhanced by limiting the resources that are granted to the default user, but this takes some in depth knowledge of WINDOWS 95 to configure. It is not likely that an ordinary user will bother to implement these controls.

Before we discuss security solutions for personal computers, let's examine the most annoying security and productivity problem associated with this computing environment—viruses.

VIRUSES

One of the most common reasons for the loss of productivity at the desktop has been due to the impact of computer viruses. The loss is due to the interruption caused by the virus, the destructive nature of some of the viruses, and the work involved in correcting a stricken machine. The virus is a very apt name for this problem. It is usually inflicted upon an unsuspecting individual without warning and spreads if not treated. Some are relatively harmless pranks, while others cause malicious destruction. All of them exact a toll on productivity.

A relatively new form of virus has been attacking word processing systems. It was previously thought that a virus consisting of a data file could not exist. This concept has been modified somewhat when viruses have been found in macros that accompany word processing data files. These macros can be executed when the document is opened or saved by the word processing software. Now viruses can be mailed to you.

The most common response to a virus infection is to use a virus scanner to find and neutralize any viruses that are found. The scanner is usually a software program that actively scans all memory and disk storage looking for specific patterns of data that indicate known viruses. When they are found they can be neutralized. The reconstruction of data that has been the victim of a destructive virus can often consume a great deal of time and effort.

The use of an antivirus program to rid the infected device is actually your last line of defense against a virus, not your first. A virus management program should be implemented that includes an available and regular virus scanning capability. A specific virus security policy should be implemented to outline the responsibilities for keeping the possibility of an infection low. The policy should restrict the use of personal software on corporate computers. All diskettes that originate outside of the corporate office should be scanned for viruses before being used in a corporate computer. A defined process for reporting and dealing with a virus should be available if one is found. Viruses can and will be a serious drain on the corporate resources if care is not taken to keep them out.

PERSONAL COMPUTER ACCESS CONTROLS

Aside from moving to an operating system with comprehensive security controls, such as UNIX or Windows NT, a solution to security on desktop computers is to implement access control software. Using a software package such as PC DACS from Mergent or Protec from IPE, security can be introduced to the personal computer. These solutions typically protect the personal computer by requiring user ID and passwords at login. The bootup process is also protected by a password. Once logged on, users can be restricted to selected directories, files, and programs.

Most access control solutions permit the optional encryption of files or directories, which protects confidential data from discovery even if the user access controls are circumvented. The encryption used is usually based on the industry standard DES or RSA algorithms. It is considerably more robust that the encryption schemes, mentioned previously, that are available with many popular PC products. Audit trails of user activity are also a common feature

LAPTOPS

The use of laptop computers poses a special concern in terms of security. They are frequently used by mobile employees from remote locations or to work from home. The primary users of laptops are management, sales, and other white-collar professionals. They are very portable and expensive, which makes them more likely to be lost or stolen than other types of personal computers. Any confidential information stored on these units could be subject to review by whoever is in possession of the unit. Many organizations have mandated the use of PC access control software and the encryption of sensitive data directories on laptops. This will prevent the discovery of corporate information should the laptop be lost or stolen. Employees are also warned, when receiving a laptop, of its attraction to thieves. They should never leave a laptop unattended and visible in an automobile. Extra care should be taken when transporting a laptop, and whenever possible, it should be left in safe storage in a hotel. Employees should also be aware of the risk when leaving laptops in office buildings, as thefts have been known to occur during working hours. In one case of which we are aware, thieves dressed in suits and carrying briefcases entered an office complex and quickly removed three laptops—it took less than 30 seconds and they were seen, but not questioned, by over 20 employees.

DATA SECURITY

A number of incidents have been reported recently where sensitive data, including medical records and other information, has been inadvertently distributed to the public. In a few cases, older computers were sent to public auction for disposal. While care had been taken to delete all files and directories, it came as a shock when those responsible learned that confidential files could be, and were, *undeleted.* The DOS operating system erases files by deleting their entry in the file allocation table (FAT). The actual data is still available on the disk until it is overwritten by other data. The undelete process rebuilds the file allocation table and establishes the pointer to the actual data that still remains of the disk.

In similar cases, confidential information has been released through improperly erased floppy disks. Many organizations require floppies and hard disks to be erased, using commercial or government file deletion utilities. These utilities force the erasure of the file by overwriting the data areas a number of times. Specialized services, using very sophisticated tools, are available that can even recover data from a disk that has been erased and rewritten. Great care should be taken when disposing of disks used to store highly confidential information.

HOW FAR SHOULD SECURITY BE EXTENDED?

An important security consideration in the design of a computing application or overall environment is whether or not security should be implemented only at the server. Should network traffic be encrypted to prevent password sniffing or replay attacks? If network security is implemented, are additional security controls required on the personal computer? If the personal computer is used to house confidential data, then access controls should be mandatory. However, even if sensitive information is not stored on the personal computer, they may be subject to Trojan horse attacks. This type of attack replaces PC programs, such as a network login utility, with a bogus program that captures user passwords.

CONCLUSIONS

Security efforts have concentrated, in the past, on the security of the server (e.g., mainframe security). Recently, attention has arguably been shifted to the network. The ultimate in client-server security is an environment that extends security from the users' keyboard or mouse to the server. Seamless security would be integrated in all three major components of the client-server model—the client, the server, and the network.

APPENDIX D

REMOTE ACCESS

There is an increasing demand by employees to access applications, systems, and networks from outside an organization's physical premises. Common reasons for this demand include employees who are working from home, vendor, or corporate support personnel and mobile road warriors. The solution for most organizations is to provide either a direct dialup access over serial phone lines or indirect access using a public network (i.e., the Internet). Because either type of solution can be accessed by outsiders, an organization is exposed to serious security risks if its systems are not properly secured. We have examined the many security issues related to the use of the Internet in Chapter 14. Serial phone links may also be compromised. Using a tool called a *war dialer,* which accesses every phone number in a given range looking for a computer to communicate with, a hacker can easily discover phone numbers used for remote access. Fortunately, solutions for secure remote access are readily available on the market.

However, these solutions must be balanced with the need by users for connectivity, performance, and ease of use. Users typically require access to the same applications and services which are available on their desktop at the office. This usually means access to mainframe and LAN-based systems. As with most security mechanisms, an ineffective solution can force the user community to implement their own solutions. Using inexpensive remote access software, a personal computer, and a modem, a user can easily implement a solution which provides remote access to a corporate network.

CENTRALIZED SOLUTIONS

Most organizations seek to meet the needs of remote users through a centralized system. Not only is the overall solution less expensive than user implemented solutions, but centralized solutions permit the introduction of standardized security controls such as audit trails and strong authentication. A centralized remote access solution that is cumbersome or doesn't supply access to required systems or networks, however, may tempt the user community to implement access solutions on its own. User-implemented solutions are usually less secure than centralized ones and may pose a serious security risk to an organization.

The most common type of remote access controls include the use of user IDs, passwords and dialback security. Passwords on serial lines are considered a minimum level of protection. Hackers can use password-guessing attacks to gain illicit entry. Many organizations also require the use a dialback mechanism, which drops the telephone line and calls the user back at a predefined location after the user ID and associated password are given. This is a good solution for remote, but static, users. It is not acceptable for mobile users who constantly change the telephone locations from which they are calling. There is also a fear that a hacker may be able to circumvent the dialback solution by keeping the phone line active. For this reason, many organizations require strong authentication through tokens, or smart cards, as discussed in Appendices A and B.

ENCRYPTION

Even when strong authentication is used, the transmission of sensitive data over an untrusted medium such as a public phone line or the Internet may require the encryption. Many remote access solutions provide for either the on-demand or complete encryption of the communication. The solutions also provide audit trails of user access, including the time of access, its length, and network access. It is less common, however, for the remote access solution to provide a complete audit trail of the user's activity. While the initial access to a server may be recorded, the recording of network access to additional systems or servers is less common.

REMOTE SUPPORT

Many vendors provide remote troubleshooting support over serial telephone lines. Unless a very close relationship exists between the support team and client, most organizations are reluctant to provide their authentication devices or passwords to the vendors. The access to systems and corporate networks by support personnel is usually granted on a as-needed basis. Very few organizations are comfortable with extending access widespread to vendors.

Probably the most common solution to this problem is to have support modems either powered off or placed on an inactive port system. When access is required by a vendor, local system support personnel will power on the modem or activate the port. The connection is protected by a password, that is provided to the vendor support personnel over the phone. The password is changed after entry to a system or the network is gained.

CONCLUSIONS

The problem of extending access to corporate systems and networks can be solved. Centralized remote access solutions are available which offer strong authentication using two-factor authentication devices and centralized audit trails. Encryption may be employed to protect communication once the user is authenticated. The solution, however, must balance the ability to connect and performance requirements of users with security considerations. Failure to reach a proper balance will result in the user community implementing solutions on their own.

GLOSSARY

Access Control An access mechanism that allows limits to be placed on who or what can utilize a computing resource.

Access Control List (ACL) A listing of users and their associated access rights, that is examined when determining whether or not access to a resource should be granted.

ACID Atomicity, consistency, isolation, durability. A transaction has "atomicity" if the operations that make up the transaction are either all executed to completion, or the transaction is returned to the state before the operations began. A transaction has "consistency" when it successfully transforms the system and the database from one valid state to another. A transaction has "isolation" if it is processed concurrently with other transactions but only has visibility to other transactions when it is complete. A transaction has "durability" if all the changes that it makes to the database become permanent when the transaction is committed.

Accountability The ability to reconstruct events on a computer system or network. It allows a system or network administrator to follow the actual steps that occurred in a security incident and detect the individuals responsible.

Accreditation The evaluation of security controls against a predefined set of specified security requirements.

Administrator Account A default account on a Windows NT system that has high-level privileges.

Analysis of Risk See Risk Analysis.

Anonymous FTP A special FTP implementation that permits users to login under the user ID "anonymous". The email address of the user is used as a password. Files are protected via the chroot environment.

API Application programming interface.

APPC An abbreviation for Application Program-to-Program Communication. This is an IBM defined protocol used in the IBM System Network Architecture to support communication between application programs which operate under separate operating environments.

Application Gateway A type of firewall that bases access decisions on the nature of the application's communication.

APPN An abbreviation for Advanced Peer-to-Peer Networking protocol. This is an IBM defined protocol used in the IBM System Network Architecture to support communication between computing systems.

ASCII An abbreviation for American Standard Code for Information Exchange. A standard coding scheme that assigns numeric values to letters, numbers, punctuation and control characters to enable compatibility between differing computing platforms.

Audit The review of a computer system or network by an independent, knowledgeable individual. The result of a security audit is typically a formal report on the conformance of the computing environment under examination to acceptable standards.

Audit ID An ID, used in constructing an audit trail, that is associated with each user.

Audit Trail A set of records that list in chronological order selected events on a computing system or network device.

Authentication The process of establishing the identity of either an individual or program.

Authorization The decision whether or not to grant access to a resource.

Availability The amount that a computing system is available for use to the user.

Awareness In security terms, awareness refers to the general knowledge of the user community about the importance of computing security, security measures and security related actions required of the user community.

B1 Security A security level for operating systems, defined by TCSEC, that requires a number of security measures, including mandatory access controls.

Bastion Host A computer system that interacts directly with an untrusted network. They should have strong security controls.

Berkeley Services Also called the 'r' services (rlogin, remote shell and remote copy), these services extend host equivalency to other trusted systems.

Biometric Based Authentication Authentication that is based on a specific personal trait such as a fingerprint or eye retina scan.

Boot or Bootup The sequence of steps involved in the initialization of a computer system.

Business Code of Conduct A formal set of regulations, usually endorsed by senior management, covering the business activities of employees.

C2 Security A security level for operating systems, defined by TCSEC, that dictates a number of security measures including protection of encrypted password strings.

CERT The computer emergency response team, which is dedicated to tracking computer security incidents.

Certificate A unique collection of information, transformed into unforgeable form, used for the authentication.

Certification Authority An authority that is trusted by one or more users to create and assign authentication certificates.

Change Management A defined process for the orderly management of change from one defined state to another.

Challenge-Response A process where a unique value or identification is generated and presented as a challenge which is then subjected to a defined algorithmic process to produce a response. If the response is equal to the expected one, the user is authenticated.

Chroot A UNIX system call that allows the system administrator to change a particular directory to the root directory for a user. This action effectively limits the users ability to traverse the UNIX file system.

Criteria In security terms, a basis or standard against which security controls can be measured.

Cryptanalysis The operations involved in converting encrypted text to plain text using the encryption algorithm without the aid of the encryption key used for the encryption process.

Cryptography The science of rendering information unintelligible and restoring the information into intelligible form using a specialized coding system and a coding key.

CICS The abbreviation for Customer Information Control System, an IBM developed program product to support the execution of transactions.

Client/Server Computing A type of computing where one computer system (the client) communicates with a resource provider (the server) over a network. A single computer may perform both roles.

Clipper Chip A hardware implementation of the Skipjack encryption algorithm.

COFC Commercially orientated functionality class. The European Computer Manufacturers Association has produced a security criteria for the commercial use of computing environments.

Command Interpreter A computer program that interprets key strokes as commands and performs actions based upon their content.

Comment Lines A comment line, in most UNIX files, is any line that begins with a "#". Comment lines are ignored by the operating system.

Commitment The level of desire by management and the user community to address the problem of computing security.

Compliance Monitoring The act of actively examining that security controls are both in existence and functioning properly.

Confidentiality The means by which information is protected from unauthorized disclosure.

Consistency A process is thought to be consistent if identical inputs will yield the same results on a regular basis.

Cooperative Processing   Refers to the ability to split application processing and logic between a client and server. Each participant in the execution of the business logic of the application.

Credential   A security token, used by security environments such as OSF/DCE, and Kerberos to store security information.

Cron   A process scheduler which is a standard feature on UNIX operating systems.

Daemon   A UNIX program that runs in the background and waits for requests to perform a task.

Data Classification   The labeling of information according to its sensitivity. Data classification is used to ensure that appropriate controls are implemented to protect sensitive information.

Data Custodian   A trustee who has been given responsibility for the protection of a corporate information resource.

Data Encryption   A method for protecting information, in which the actual data is scrambled and can only be understood with the use of a special key.

Data Guardian   The individual responsible for the protection of a corporate information resource.

Data Owner   The individual who has created or been given ownership of an informational resource.

Data Warehouse   A subject-oriented, integrated, time-variant, nonvolatile collection of data used primarily to support organizational decisions.

DB Groups   Groups are collections of users who have the same set of privileges for database access.

DCE   Distributed computing environment. A comprehensive middleware environment, based on remote procedure calls, that allows the development of secure, client-server applications.

DCE Cell   An administrative domain of DCE clients and servers.

Debit Card   A card used for identification to aid the direct access and manipulation of financial transactions, usually money transfers.

Delegation of Authority   The act of transferring, for a limited time or function, high-level privileges.

Denial of Service   An attack that attempts to deny corporate computing resources to legitimate users.

DES   Data encryption standard. A private key encryption methodology developed by IBM.

Detection   The ability of a computer system, application or organization to discover unauthorized use of its resources.

Device File   A special type of UNIX file which describes a physical device, including disk drives, tape or system memory.

Diagnostic Attack   A hacking technique that uses network diagnostic tools and utilities to gain illicit access.

Dialback   An authentication technique for modem users that disconnects the line and dials the user back at a pre-determined telephone number.

Digital Signature　A block of data that is appended to a message such that the recipient of the message can verify the contents and verify the originator of the message.

Directory　A special type of file that contains the names and locations of other files or directories. It provides a convenient means of organizing information.

Directory Service　A DCE service used to locate resources.

Distributed Database　A database whose data and logic is split amongst various computer systems. The systems are inter-connected by a network.

Distributed Computing　Computing whose controls, logic and processing occur over a large number of separate computers, inter-connected by a network.

Distributed File Service　A service used by DCE to manage distributed files.

Distributed Systems　Computer systems and applications that communicate and share resources and processing over a network.

DNS　Domain name system.　A network utility used to resolve system names and IP addresses.

DSS　Digital signature standard　A standard for digital signatures proposed by the U.S. government.

Dual Homed Bastion Host　A bastion host is equipped with two LAN cards and is used to filter network traffic. One LAN card is connected to an untrusted network and one to a trusted network.

Durability　The ability of a system perform its functions for a long time without any negative effects on its performance.

EUID　Effective user ID　The user ID under whose authority a user is currently operating. The UNIX user ID (UID) is the user ID used at login.

Electronic Data Interchange　A standard for communicating business transactions between organizations.

Electronic Commerce　The interchange of business documents via an electronic medium, such as the Internet.

Encapsulation　A technique where data and the procedures for operations on the data are packaged together to form a single identifiable entity.　This is used mainly in object-oriented processing.

Encryption　The principles, means and methods of rendering information unintelligible through an algorithmic process and a form of secret key, and for restoring encrypted information back into intelligible form.

Encryption Algorithm　The algorithm used to convert information into unintelligible form using a key.

file access permissions　A set of flags that are used to determine whether or not to grant access to a file or directory.

File system　The organization of files and directories on a computer disk, CD ROM or tape.

Filtering Router　A router capable of performing packet filtering.

Firewall　A computer system or network device that limits traffic between a trusted and untrusted network.

FTP File transfer protocol. A TCP/IP service that permits the transfer of files between systems.

Gecos A field in the UNIX password file used to store user information.

GUEST Account An account on NOS systems used by casual users. GUEST accounts typically have no password.

Group A logical association of users whose access rights will be determined based upon their membership in the group.

Groupware A general term used to describe software that is used to support the shared information needs of a department or organization.

GUI Graphical user interface.

GSSAPI Generic security service application programming interface. A standard programming interface for security.

Guidelines Recommendations on best security practices for a computing environment.

Heterogeneous In computer terms, a heterogeneous environment has a mixture of different technologies.

High Level Privileges Are rights bestowed to only the most trusted users of the system, such as the system or database administrator.

Home Directory The default directory into which a user is placed after login.

Host Equivalency A relationship that occurs when one system trusts another system and does not require users of programs to authenticate themselves before gaining access to resources.

HTML Hypertext markup language. A language used to describe the components of a document used mainly on the world wide web.

HTTP Hypertext transfer protocol. The standard communications protocol used between clients and servers on the world wide web.

ICMP Internet control message protocol. An IP protocol used for the monitoring and control of an IP network.

Identification A method of determining the identity of a computer user of program (e.g., user ID). It is generally the result of an authentication process.

Information Warfare A form of warfare whose aims are to nullify or destroy the computing resources of the opponent.

Integrity The ability to prevent the unauthorized modification of the computing environment.

Integrity Checks A utility or task that reviews a computing environment for unauthorized modifications.

IPv6 A proposed version of the Internet Protocol which will feature major security improvements.

IP Forwarding Attack A hacking technique used to attempt to pass TCP/IP packets to a protected network.

ISQL Interactive SQL. A utility that allows a user to directly query a relational database using standard SQL commands.

IPv6 A proposed version of the Internet Protocol which will feature major security improvements.

JAVA A platform independent programming language developed by Sun Microsystems.

LAN Local area network.

LEAF Access The law enforcement access field (LEAF) is a special component of the Clipper Chip encryption system to provide access to encrypted data by law enforcement bodies if authorized.

Leakage Occurs when a corporate firewall or router inadvertently releases information about a trusted network to an untrusted network.

LSA Local security authority. A security subsystem that runs on a Windows NT system.

Location Based Authentication Authentication that is based on an expected exact location of the device used for requesting authentication.

Login The process of gaining direct access to a computing system or network.

Mandatory Access Controls A type of security controls, such as sensitivity labeling, which cannot be turned off or deleted by a user.

Message Digest An algorithmic representation of a message that is encrypted and appended to a message to be used for integrity checking.

Middleware A software layer that provides a common interface and translation between the application, the data and the operating system.

Mount In UNIX, the process of obtaining access to a remote or local file system.

Mutual Authentication A form of authentication where both parties are authenticated to one another, usually through a trusted third party.

NIS Network information service. A UNIX network service, developed by Sun Microsystems, Inc., that permits the synchronization of key UNIX administration files between systems.

NOS Network operating system. A generic term for network environments that offer disk, directory and print sharing services to LAN users.

NFS Network file system. A utility, developed by Sun Microsystems, Inc., used by UNIX and DOS systems to share disk resources.

Nonrepudiation The ability to authenticate the sender of a message and contents of information.

NT Domain A grouping of Windows NT systems under a common administration function.

NTFS NT file system, The native file system used by Windows NT systems.

OLTP On line transaction processing. A system or action used for the processing of transactions as they occur.

One Time Password A password, generated by a special algorithm, that is never re-used.

OMG Object Management Group. A consortium of over 100 vendors used as a standards body to address interoperability and portability issues for object-oriented environments.

Orange Book See TCSEC.

OSF/DCE Open Software Foundation's Distributed Computing Environment.

Owner The owner of a resource is usually the creator of that resource.

Packet Filtering The limiting of TCP/IP traffic, based upon the type of traffic, source and destination IP addresses, ports or other information.

Packet Monitoring The active monitoring of traffic on a network. It is used by hackers to discover passwords and other sensitive information.

Password A secret word, phrase, alphanumeric string or combination of key-strokes that is used for authentication.

Password Aging A mechanism used to enforce user password changes.

Password Cracking A method which seeks to discover passwords by passing a dictionary of terms through a password algorithm and compares the output to the encrypted password string. A match indicates the password has been discovered.

Password Generator A computing device or software program which constructs unique and supposedly uncrackable, password strings.

Password Guessing A technique used to gain unauthorized access to a computer or network device by supplying a wide range of passwords for a user account.

Password Policy A policy dealing with the composition of a password, aging and other aspects of a user's password.

PATH Variable A variable that tells an operating system which directories to search through when a command is issued.

PEM Privacy enhanced mail. A draft Internet standard that defines message encryption and authentication processes to provide secure mail functions on the Internet.

PGP Pretty good privacy. An encryption scheme, developed by Philip Zimmerman, based on the RSA encryption algorithm.

Performance The ability of a computing environment to perform its required operations in a timely manner.

Physical Access The ability to interact directly with a computer system (i.e., having direct access to the system console, disk drives, CPU, etc.).

PIN Personal Identification Number. An individual numeric number used as part of an authentication process.

Principal In DCE terminology, a principal is any entity whose importance may warrant authentication. A principal may be a person, a computer, a DCE cell or an application.

Principles Statements of values, belief or philosophy that provide a fundamental base for the operation of the organization.

Private Key Encryption Also called shared secret key, it refers to an encryption method in which one or more identities (usually a user and computing system) share a password (i.e., a private key). The method is primarily used for authentication, although private key encryption is also widely used to protect sensitive data.

Procedure In terms of computing security policy, a procedure is the actual method used to enact computing policy for a particular computing or network environment.

Process The environment in which a program executes.

Proxy Service An Internet service that can perform tasks on behalf of users. Proxy services are generally more secure than giving users direct access to the Internet.

PUBLIC Account An account on NOS systems which can be accessed by any user on the network. They typically do not have a password.

Public Key Encryption An encryption method in which two mathematically linked keys are generated. One key is private and known only to the user. The second key is public and may be shared amongst trusted users or the public. The keys may be used to encrypt and decrypt information and prove identities.

Reboot The process of taking a computer system from a running state, down to a stopped state, and back to a running state.

Remote Access Usually refers to the ability to communicate with a computer or network over telephone lines using a modem.

RAS Remote access service. A Windows NT service that facilitates the communication of users over a modem. It has both user authentication and dial back facilities.

Remote Execution Facility A TCP/IP network service that permits the remote execution of commands without requiring the user to login.

Remote Procedure Call A method of communication between a client and server.

Risk In terms of computing security, a risk refers to a security exposure. It may also refer to, depending on the context, the likelihood that a security exposure will occur.

Risk Analysis In conventional terms, a risk analysis is the art of balancing the likelihood of an exposure (i.e. risk) with the probability it will occur. Security professionals and auditors may also use risk analysis to refer to the active testing of security controls.

Risk Assessment Also called a risk analysis, a risk assessment involves the analysis of controls, in terms of their appropriateness and effectiveness.

Role A feature of many databases that permit access to be assigned by job function.

Role Based Security A collection of security attributes that are given to defined roles or positions in an organization or entity.

Root A default user with high level privileges on a UNIX system. Root is also used to refer to the highest-level directory (root directory or /).

Routing Attack A hacking technique that uses the IP source routing option to route packets to a destination where they can be manipulated.

Rule Based Security A collection of security attributes <Glen>

SATAN Security administrators tool for auditing networks. A contributed security monitor, developed by Dan Farmer, which detects weaknesses in TCP/IP network services.

SDLC Synchronous data link control. A communications protocol used for the IBM System Network Architecture.

S-HTTP Secure hypertext transfer protocol. An extension to the HTTP protocol to provide encryption and authentication facilities.

Screened Subnet A network protected by a filtering router or other network device.

Secure RPC A RPC based communication method, developed by SUN Microsystems, Inc., which has secure authentication and data protection mechanisms.

SSL Secure sockets layer. A protocol used for authentication and encryption between a client and a server.

Security Access Mechanism (SAM) The central security authority for a Windows NT domain.

SDLC System Development Life Cycle. A methodology, comprised of six phases, used to develop computing applications.

Security Advisories Security information, usually distributed via electronic mail bulletins, which alert the computing community to security problems and their associated fixes. Advisories are available from CERT or directly from many vendors.

Security Criteria The security criteria refers to a recognized collection of required security attributes that form a standard used for the measurement or analysis of security functionality.

Security Descriptor Every resource on a Windows NT system has a security descriptor, which contain both information about the owner and Access control lists.

Security Policy A formal set of directives, endorsed by management, that provide an overall direction to an organization on various aspects of computing security.

Security Service Provides security services, including authentication and password management, to a DCE cell.

Security Strategy A strategic plan to move an organization to an appropriate level of security.

Security Token A device or file, usually protected by encryption, which contains security information.

Self Assessment An audit performed by a system administrator, user department or any nonindependant entity. Self assessments are commonly performed in anticipation of an actual audit.

Sensitive Information Any information whose unauthorized disclosure would result in a significant financial loss, embarrassment or have other negative effects.

Sensitivity Labels A method of applying data classification titles, such as confidential and top secret, to files, directories, and other computing resources.

Server A computing system which performs services when requested by another system, the client.

SET Secure electronic transaction. A message standard used for the secure communication and execution of electronic commerce transactions.

Set User ID Bit An executable UNIX file (or program) which will execute under the authority of the owner of the file rather than the user that invokes it.

Sequencing Attack A hacking technique (also called hijacking) that uses knowledge of TCP/IP sequence numbers to intercept and insert bogus traffic in an established TCP/IP communication.

Single Sign-on The ability of a user to perform the authentication process required to access all required network and computing resources once and only once.

Single-User Mode A special UNIX operating system level, used primarily for diagnostic purposes. In many versions of UNIX, it's use will allow unrestricted access to the system.

Smart Card A card that contains an embedded microchip used to store data or execute program code.

SMTP Simple mail transport protocol. A protocol for electronic mail applications, popular on systems using a UNIX operating system.

SNA System network architecture. A networking architecture developed by IBM.

SNMP Simple network management protocol. A standard protocol used to manage network devices and computing systems.

Socket The combination of an IP address and port number.

Spoof A program that masquerades as a legitimate program, but performs illicit actions. Also called a Trojan horse.

Spoofing A hacking technique which uses a counterfeit network address to gain illicit access to a network or system.

SQL Structured query language. A standardized set of commands to manage and report database information and structure.

Stored Procedure A set of pre-defined SQL statements.

Subnet A LAN segment.

Superuser The UNIX system administrator. This user, whose real or effective user ID is 0, and has high-level access privileges.

SUPERVISOR A special account on NOS systems which provides a comprehensive set of privileges.

System The term system is used to refer to a single computer.

System Classification The act of labeling a system in terms of the sensitivity to the organization of the information processed or stored by the system. A payroll system might be classified as both critical and confidential.

TCP Transport control protocol. A higher level IP protocol which features sequencing and other transmission integrity controls.

TCP/IP A generic name commonly used to address a family of networking protocols and services based on the Internet Protocol (IP).

TCSEC Trusted computer system evaluation criteria. A method developed by the U.S. Department of Defense to evaluate computing security in operating systems. It is also known as the *Orange Book*. Other books in the series include *Tan* for Audit and *Green* for password management.

Technology Envy The desire to be on the leading edge of technology .

TELNET A standard Internet service that allows a user terminal access to a remote computer over a network.

TFTP trivial file transfer protocol. A file-transfer program provided for downloading information.

Tiger Team A term used to describe a group of individuals tasked with responding to security incidents.

Timing Service A DCE service used to synchronize clocks among distributed systems.

Token Based Authentication Authentication that is provided by the possession of a unique physical card or device that supplies one component of the authentication process.

TP Monitor A software program that controls and executes transactions as they are presented to the program.

Transaction A collection of operations which comprise a complete unit of work. The execution of this unit of work must adhere to the ACID transaction properties.

Trigger A database stored procedure which is set off by a predefined event.

Tripwire A contributed software utility, developed by Gene Kim and Gene Spafford, which checks for the unauthorized modification of operating system and application data files and programs.

Trojan horse A computer program, which appears to function normally, but performs unauthorized actions.

Trust The composite of security, availability and performance. The ability to execute processes with integrity, keep confidential information private and perform the required functions on a continual basis.

Two-Phase Commit An update to the database is committed when all the required processes have completed successfully.

UDP User datagram protocol. A higher level IP protocol which has only limited integrity checking.

URL Uniform resource locator. A unique address that identifies a document, image or other resource stored for access on the world wide web.

User ID An assigned name or acronym used to identify computer users.

User Profile A file containing login and security information about a user.

UUCP UNIX to UNIX copy. A UNIX networking service that permits communication between UNIX systems.

Virus A type of Trojan horse program that infects a computer, causing the operating system to lose integrity in various ways.

VPN Virtual private network. A technique that encrypts and protects traffic between two trusted networks.

VTAM Virtual telecommunication access method. An IBM program product used to control networks.

Vulnerability Test An active test of security controls, performed to discover security weaknesses and exposures.

Web Browser A software product used to access documents stored for access on the world wide web.

X.400 A standard maintained by the International Standards Organization (ISO) used for the store and forwarding of messages.

X.509 Certificate A certificate that conforms to the X.509 authentication framework standard.

XBSS X/Open baseline security services. A set of security requirements defined by the X/Open organization.

X/Windows A windowing system used by UNIX systems.

REFERENCES

[Anderson, 1991] R.J. Anderson, *The External Audit,* Copp Clark Pittman, New Jersey,1994.

[Arens & Loebbecke, 1994] Arens & Loebbecke, *Auditing—An Integrated Approach,* McGraw-Hill, New York, 1992.

[Arnold, 1992] N. Derek Arnold, *UNIX Security—A Practical Tutorial,* McGraw-Hill, New York, 1992.

[Berson & Anderson, 1995] Alex Berson and George Anderson, *SYBASE and Client-Server Computing,* McGraw-Hill, New York, 1995.

[Blaze, 1994] Matt Blaze, *Protocol Failure in the Escrowed Encryption Standard,* AT&T Bell Laboratories, New Jersey, June 1994.

[Bonnefoy, 1991] Yves Bonnefoy, *Greek and Egyptian Mythologies,* University of Chicago Press, Chicago, 1991.

[Bulfinch, 1962] Thomas Bulfinch, *Mythology of Greece and Rome,* Collier Books, New York, 1962.

[Caswell, 1995] Deborah Caswell, "An Evolution of DCE Authorization Services," *Hewlett-Packard Journal,* Palo Alto, Ca., December 1995.

[Cerutti & Pierson,1993] Daniel Cerutti, and Donna Pierson, *Distributed Computing Environments,* McGraw-Hill, New York, 1993.

[Chapman and Zwicky, 1995] D. Brent Chapman and Elizabeth D. Zwicky, *Building Internet Firewalls,* O'Reilly & Associates, Sebastopol, Ca., 1995.

[Cheswick & Bellovin, 1994] William Cheswick and Steven Bellovin, *Firewalls and Internet Security,* Addison-Wesley, Reading, Mass., 1994.

[Citibank, 1994] Citibank, N.A., Coopers & Lybrand, The Institute of Internal Auditors and Microsoft Corporation, *Window NT 3.5 Guidelines for Security, Audit, and Control,* Microsoft Press, Redmond, Wash., 1994.

[Comer, 1991] Douglas E. Comer, *Internetworking with TCP/IP,* Volume I, Prentice Hall, Englewood Cliffs, N.J., 1991.

[Curry, 1990] David A. Curry, *Improving the Security of Your UNIX System,* SRI International, Reference ITSTD-721-FR-90-21, Menlo Park, Ca., 1990.

[Davis, 1994] Peter T. Davis, *Complete LAN Security and Control,* McGraw-Hill, New York, 1994.

[Davis & Hutchinson, 1996] R.W. Davis and S. Hutchinson, *Computer Crime in Canada,* Carswell, Thomson, Toronto, Canada, 1996.

[Dilley, 1994] John Dilley, *Experiences with the OSF Distributed Computing Environment,* Hewlett-Packard, Document NSA-94-035, Palo Alto, Ca., 1994.

[Fahn, 1993] Paul Fahn, *Frequently Asked Questions About Today's Cryptography,* RSA Laboratories, Redwood City, Ca., September 1993.

[Farmer & Spafford, 1991] Dan Farmer and Eugene H. Spafford, *The COPS Security Checker System,* Purdue University Technical Report CSD-TR-993, West Lafayette, Ind., 1991.

[Farrow, 1991] Rik Farrow, *UNIX Systems Security,* Addison-Wesley, Reading, Mass., 1991.

[Garfinkel & Spafford, 1991] Simson Garfinkel and Gene Spafford, *Practical UNIX Security,* O'Reilly & Associates, Sebastopol, Ca., 1991.

[Gittler & Hopkins, 1995] Frederic Gittler and Anne C. Hopkins, "The DCE Security Service," *Hewlett-Packard Journal,* Palo Alto, Ca., December 1995.

[Goodman, 1994] Kevin J. Goodman, *Windows NT: A Developer's Guide,* M&T Books, New York, 1994.

[Grottola, 1993] Michael G. Grottola, *The UNIX Audit—Using UNIX to Audit UNIX,* McGraw-Hill, New York, 1993.

[Hewlett-Packard, 1992] *HP-UX System Security,* Hewlett-Packard, Reference B2355-90045, Palo Alto, Ca., 1992.

[Hewlett-Packard, 1994] Hewlett-Packard, *AllBase SQL Reference Manual,* Part # 36217-900001, Palo Alto, Ca., 1994.

[Hu, 1995] Wei Hu, *DCE SECURITY Programming,* O'Reilly & Associates, Sebastopol, Ca., 1992.

[Huitema, 1996] Christian Huitema, *IPv6—The New Internet Protocol,* Prentice Hall, Englewood Cliffs, N. J., 1996.

[IBM, 1991] IBM, *Elements of AIX Security R3.1,* Document Number GG24-3622-01, New York, 1991.

[Icove, Seger & Von Storch, 1995] David Icove, Karl Seger, and William Von Storch, *Computer Crime—A Crimefighter's Handbook,* O'Reilly & Associates, Sebastopol, Ca., August 1995.

[Kahn, 1967] David Kahn, *The Code-Breakers,* New American Library, New York,1967.

[Keegan, 1989] John Keegan, *The Second World War,* Viking Press, New York, 1989

[Kipp, 1995] Cathy Kipp, *Programming Informix SQL/4GL,* Prentice Hall, Englewood Cliffs, N. J., 1995.

[Klein, 1991] Daniel V. Klein, *Foiling the Cracker,* Carnegie Mellon University, Pittsburgh, Pa., 1991.

[Kong & Truong, 1995] Michael M. Kong and David Truong, "DCE Directory Services", *Hewlett-Packard Journal,* Palo Alto, Ca., December 1995.

[Kong, 1995] Michael M. Kong, "DCE: An Environment for Secure Client/Server Computing," *Hewlett-Packard Journal,* Palo Alto, Ca., December 1995.

[Liu & Albitz, 1992] Cricket Liu and Paul Albitz, *DNS & Bind,* O'Reilly & Associates, Sebastopol, Ca., 1992.

[Liu, Peek, Jones, Buus & Nye, 1994] Cricket Liu, Jerry Peek, Russ Jones, Bryan Buus and Adrian Nye, *Managing Internet Information Services,* O'Reilly & Associates, Sebastopol, Ca., 1994.

[Lloyd & Horowitz, 1995] Paul Lloyd and Samuel D. Horowitz, "Adopting DCE Technology for Developing Client/Server Applications," *Hewlett-Packard Journal,* Palo Alto, Ca., December 1995.

[Lockhart, 1994] Harold W. Lockhart, *OSF DCE Guide to Developing Distributed Applications,* McGraw-Hill, New York, 1994.

[Loney, 1994] Kevin Loney, *Oracle DBA Handbook,* Osborne McGraw-Hill, Berkeley, Ca., 1994.

[Mailman, 1993] Statement to the Computer Systems Security and Privacy Advisory Board, U.S. Export Controls on Products Containing Cryptography, "Statement by Fred Mailman, Export Manager," Hewlett-Packard Company, Palo Alto, Ca., June 3, 1993, 1993.

[Marcus, Kumar & Rose, 1995] Jane B. Marcus, Naveenet Kumar, and Lawrence J. Rose, "HP Integrated Login", *Hewlett-Packard Journal,* Palo Alto, Ca., December 1995.

[Microsoft, 1995] *Microsoft Windows NT 3.5/3.52: Remote Access Server,* Microsoft Corporation, Redmond Wash., 1995.

[Microsoft, 1995] *The Microsoft Strategy for Distributed Computing and DCE Services,* Microsoft Corporation, Redmond Wash., February 1995.

[Microsoft, 1995] *Microsoft Windows NT 3.5/3.52: TCP/IP Implementation Details,* Microsoft Corporation, Redmond Wash., September, 1995.

[Miller, 1993] Mark A. Miller, *Managing Internetworks with SNMP,* M&T Books, New York, 1993.

[Morris, 1985] Robert T. Morris, *A Weakness in the 4.2BSD Unix TCP/IP Software,* AT&T Bell Laboratories, New Jersey,1985.

[Open Software Foundation, 1993a] Open Software Foundation, *OSF DCE Application Development Reference,* Prentice Hall, Englewood Cliffs, N. J., 1993.

[Open Software Foundation, 1993b] Open Software Foundation, *OSF DCE Administration Reference,* Prentice Hall, Englewood Cliffs, N. J., 1993.

[Open Software Foundation, 1993c] Open Software Foundation, *OSF DCE Administration Guide—Extended Services,* Prentice Hall, Englewood Cliffs, N. J.,1993.

[Open Software Foundation, 1993] Open Software Foundation, *OSF DCE Application Development Guide,* Prentice Hall, Englewood Cliffs, N. J., 1993.

[Orfali, Harkey & Edwards, 1994] Robert Orfali, Dan Harkey, and Jeri Edwards, *The Essential Client/Sever Survival Guide,* John Wiley, New York, 1994

[Orfali, Harkey & Edwards, 1996] Robert Orfali, Dan Harkey, and Jeri Edwards, *The Essential Distributed Objects Survival Guide,* John Wiley, New York, 1996

[OSF DCE SIG, RFC 3.0, Joe Pato] *Extending the DCE Authorization Model to Support Practical Delegation,* Open Software Foundation, Cambridge, Mass., June 1992.

[OSF DCE SIG, RFC 5.2, J. Wray] GSS-API, *Extentions for DCE,* Open Software Foundation, Cambridge, Mass., March 1994.

[OSF DCE SIG, RFC 6.0, Joe Pato] *A Generic Interface for Extended Registry Attributes,* Open Software Foundation, Cambridge, Mass., June 1992.

[OSF DCE SIG, RFC 7.0, Joe Pato] *Hierarchical Trust Relationships for Inter-cell Authentication,* Open Software Foundation, Cambridge, Mass., July 1992.

[OSF DCE SIG, RFC 29.1, S. Luan & R. Weisz] *Design of an Audit Subsystem for DCE—Implementation Specification,* Open Software Foundation, Cambridge, Mass., November 1993.

[OSF DCE SIG, RFC 28.1, S. Luan & R. Weisz] *DCE Server Auditable-Event Identification and A Proposed Audit Logging API,* Open Software Foundation, Cambridge, Mass., November 1993.

[OSF DCE SIG, RFC 26.0, Joe Pato], *Using Pre-Authentication to Avoid Password Guessing Attacks,* Open Software Foundation, Cambridge, Mass., June 1993.

[OSF DCE SIG, RFC 59.0, J. Kotanchik], *Kerberos and Two Factor Authentication,* Open Software Foundation, Cambridge, Mass., March 1994.

[OSF DCE SIG, RFC 71.0, G. Gaskell & M. Warner], *Improved Security for Smart Card Use in DCE,* Open Software Foundation, Cambridge, Mass., February 1995.

[Perlman, 1994] Radia Perlman, *Interconnections,* Addison-Wesley, Reading, Mass., 1994.

[RCMP, 1994] Royal Canadian Mounted Police IT Security Branch, *Information Technology Security Bulletin,* Ottawa, Canada, June 1994.

[Rosenberry, Kenney, & Fisher, 1992] Ward Rosenberry, David Kenney, and Gerry Fisher, *Understanding DCE,* O'Reilly & Associates, Sebastopol, Ca., 1992.

[Russell & Gangemi, 1991] Deborah Russell and G.T. Gangemi, *Computer Security Basics,* O'Reilly & Associates, Sebastopol, Ca., , 1991.

[Salemi, 1994] Joe Salemi, *Client/Server Computing with Sybase SQL Server,* ZD Press, Emeryville, Ca.,1994.

[Shirley, 1992] John Shirley, *Guide to Writing DCE Applications,* O'Reilly & Associates, Sebastopol, Ca., 1992.

[Spencer, 1996] Kenneth L. Spencer, *NT Server: Management and Control,* Prentice Hall, Englewood Cliffs, N. J., 1996.

[Stang & Moon, 1993] David J. Stang and Sylvia Moon, *Network Security Secrets,* IDG Books, San Mateo, Ca., 1993.

[Stevens, 1994] W. Richard Stevens, *TCP/IP Illustrated,* Volume I, Addison Wesley, Reading, Mass., 1994.

[Stoll, 1989] Cliff Stoll, *The Cuckoo's Egg,* Simon & Schuster, New York, 1989.

[Taylor, 1966] A. P. J. Taylor, *The First World War,* Penguin Books, Middlesex, U.K., 1966

[*Time* Magazine, 1995a] Douglas Waller, "Onward Cyber Soldiers," Time, Inc., August 21, 1995.

[*Time* Magazine, 1995b] Mark Thompson, "If War Comes Home," Time, Inc., August 21, 1995.

[Varadhan, 1992] Karinan Varadhan, *OaRnet Security Procedures,* OaRnet Engineering Group , Columbus, Ohio, 1992.

[Waterson,1995] Karen Watterson, *Client/Server Technology for Managers,* Addison-Wesley, Reading, Mass., 1995.

[White House, 1993] Office of the Press Secretary, Statement by the Press Secretary of April 16, 1993, 1993.

A

Acceptable use policy, for Internet, 237-38
Access control, 52, 348
  physical access, 28
  remote access, 25-26
  standards, 69
  See also Authorization
Access control lists (ACLs), 52, 210, 274-75, 308, 339-40
  access rights, 275
  classes of clients, 275
  UNIX, 155-56
    problems with, 156
    superuser access, 156-57
  Windows NT, 215-16
Access tokens, 211-12
Accreditation, 324, 389-90, 391
  requirements, 391
  standards, 69
ACID properties, 297
Add-on solutions, RDBMS, 290-91
Address Resolution Protocol (ARP), 103
Administration, systems, 80
Advanced Peer-to-Peer Networking (APPN), 100
  High Performance Routing (HPR), 100
  security, 101-2
Advanced Research Projects Agency (ARPA), 220
American National Standards Institute (ANSI), 241, 248, 280, 335

Andromeda, 354, 356-58
  building, 357-58
Anonymous FTP, 175-76
API, *See* Application programming interface (API)
APPC, *See* Application Program-to-Program Communication (APPC)
Applets, Java, 229
Application development policy, 83
Application gateways, 234
Application programming interface (API), 136, 206, 217, 280, 304
Application Program-to-Program Communication (APPC), 102, 133, 137-38
APPN, *See* Advanced Peer-to-Peer Networking (APPN)
Architecture, 45-57, 59-70
  Common ORB Architecture (CORBA), 140
  critical success factors, definition of, 47
  definition of, 46
  security, 46-47
  Systems Network Architecture (SNA), 96-102, 114
ARCHIVE (NOS access permission), 121
Armor (Los Altos Technologies, Inc.), 199
ARPA, 102, 169
Assurance testing, 324
Asynchronous Transfer Mode (ATM), 100
Attribute configuration file (ACF), 260
Auditing, 277, 375-92
  accreditation, 389-90, 391

443

auditor requirements, 377-78
audit trails, 38, 55, 56-57, 384
basics of, 382-83
business continuity planning (BCP), 385
common mistakes in, 378-79
definition of, 376-77
importance of, 379-80
network operating systems (NOS), 122
performance audits, 389
physical controls, 386
risk assessment, 387
role played by, 380-82
    establishing proper criteria, 381-82
    relationships, 381
self-assessment, 388
    tools, 390
software development, 386
software licensing, 386
standards, 69
UNIX audit, sample criteria for, 382-83
user awareness, 385
vulnerability tests, 388
when to perform audits, 389
Audit mechanisms, RDBMS, 288-89
AuditorPlus, 199
Audit trails, 38, 55, 56-57, 288, 384
definition of, 38
Authentication, 35, 52-53
and network operating systems (NOS), 118-20
policy, 75
standards, 69
UNIX, 149-51, 189-90
weak, 27
See also Strong authentication
Authentication header, 228
Authorization, 36
access control lists (ACLs), 274-75
access rights, 275
auditing, 277
definition of, 51
Generic Security Service Application
    Programming Interface (GSSAPI), 276
network operating systems (NOS), 120-21
policy, 75
rule-based authorizations, 276
single sign-on, 277
two-factor authentication/smart card, 277
See also Access control
Authorization controls, RDBMS, 283-85
Automated teller machines (ATMs), 10, 243, 295, 296
Availability, 53-54
and trust, 41-42
Awareness and education program, 87-88

B

Bastion hosts, 232
Batch SQL statements, RDBMS, 285
Berkeley Services, 169, 171-72
Binding, 259
Biometric-based authentication, 35, 404, 409
BoKs (Dynamic Software AB), 199
BOOTP, 103
Bridges, 351
Business community planning (BCP), 385
Business continuity, systems, 81
Business drivers, 10-14
    business environment, 11-12
    customer/public perception, 13
    ease of distributed computing, 12-13
    networking technology, 11
    technology envy, 13-14

C

C2 UNIX systems, 190-91
Cassiopeia, 357
CA Unicenter (Computer Associates), 200, 345
Cell directory services (CDS), 260, 268
Centralized security functions, 344
Cepheus, king of Ethiopia, 357
Certification authority, 227, 247
Challenge Handshake Authentication Protocol
    (CHAP), PPP, 216
Challenge-response method, 402-4, 408
Change management process, 55, 56, 323
CHANGE (NOS access permission), 121
CHANGE PERMISSION access right, 213
Checksums, 195
CICS, 308-9
Circuit relay, 233-34
Classification:
    data, policy for, 76
    systems, 80-81
Client authentication, DCE, 268-71
Client/server, 8-10, 129-34
    logical unit of work (LUW), 131-32
        cooperative processing, 133-34
        security considerations, 134
        two-phase commit, 132-33
    things to watch out for, 142-43
    See also Middleware
Client-server communication, encrypting, 273-74
Client to server authentication, DCE, 271-72
Clipper, 251
Clock skew, 262
Code walk-through, 322
Commercially Oriented Functionality Class (COFC), 66
Common Mail Calls (CMC), 334

Common Object Model (COM)/OLE, 140-41
Common ORB Architecture (CORBA), 140
Common Programming Interface for
    Communications (CPI-C), 99
Communication managers, and TP monitor, 307
Compliance monitoring, policies for, 80
Computer auditing:
    basics of, 382-83
    See also Auditing
Computer Crime in Canada (Davis/Hutchinson), 397
Computer Emergency Response Team (CERT), 21,
    164, 226
Computer Incident Advisory Capability (CIAC),
    201, 398
Computer Misuse Detection System (CMDS), 356
Computer Oracle and Password System (COPS), *See*
    COPS utility
Computers Emergency Response Team (CERT),
    201, 226, 398
Computer viruses, 23, 83, 125-26, 414-15
Computing security:
    basics of, 33-44
    as a business issue, 3-17
    commercial espionage, 396
    and computer complexity, 395
    criminal activity, 396-97
    distributed security, challenges of, 19-29
    encryption, 399
    financial industry requirements, 396
    future of, 393-400
    government requirements, 396
    information warfare, 399
    insecure new technologies, 398
    and law enforcement, 397
    and management commitment, 394-95
    networking, 93-115
    network operating systems (NOS), 117-27
    secure new technologies, 397-98
    security architecture, 45-57
        foundation, 59-70
    security policy, 71-89
    shared commitment to, 398
    UNIX security, 145-204
    vendor commitment to, 395-96
    Windows NT security, 205-18
    and workforce loyalty, 395
Condor, 226
Confidentiality, 36-37, 52
    standards, 69
Consistency, and availability, 53
Continuity, and availability, 53
COPS utility, 198, 388, 390
Copyright policy, 82-83
Corporate commitment, to security, 15-16
Cost, of security solutions, 15

Counterfeit addressing, and TCP/IP, 109
CPI-C, *See* Common Programming Interface for
    Communications (CPI-C)
CrackLib, 189
CREATE (NOS access permission), 121
Cryptography, 239-53
    definition of, 239
    digital signatures, 251-53
    encryption, 36-37, 240-51
Cuckoo's Egg, The (Stoll), 20, 397
Customer Commission Control System (CICS), 308-9

D

Database administrator (DBA), 283
Data consolidation, RDBMS, 292
Data custodian, 77
Data Encryption Standard (DES), *See* DES encryp-
    tion
Data guardian, 77
Data integrity, 76-77
    See also Integrity checks
Data policies, 76-77
    classification, 76
    data custodian, 77
    data guardian, 77
    integrity of data, 77
Data warehouse, 292-93
DCE authentication, 266-74
    client authentication, 268-71
    client-server communication, encrypting, 273-74
    client to server authentication, 271-72
    of DCE services, 274
    extended registry, 272-73
    of foreign cells, 272
    server authentication, 273
DCE cell, 257, 266
DCE Privilege Attribute Certificate (PAC), 271
DCE Security Service, 261-62, 291
"DCE Security Service, The" (Gittler/Hopkins), 271
DCE services, authentication of, 274
Defense Advanced Research Project Agency
    (DARPA), 102
Defined security architecture, 47
Definitions, standards, 68
DELEGATED PRIVILEGES, NOS, 120
DELETE access right, 213
DELETE (NOS access permission), 121
Delivery, repudiation of, 53
Denial of service attacks, TCP/IP, 110
DES encryption, 101, 241-42
    key management and, 244
    size of key, 245
    Triple-DES, 242
    weak DES, 246

Device file security, 164
Diagnostic attacks, TCP/IP, 110-11
Digital Signature Algorithm (DSA), 253
Digital signatures, 53, 195-96, 227, 244, 251-53, 355
  definition of, 251
  Digital Signature Algorithm (DSA), 253
  Digital Signature Standard (SS), 253
  message digest, 251-52
  primary uses for, 253
  process, 252
Digital Signature Standard (SS), 253
Distributed computing, 5-8
  business drivers, 10-14
    business environment, 11-12
    customer/public perception, 13
    ease of distributed computing, 12-13
    networking technology, 11
    technology envy, 13-14
  business issues, 14-16
    choices offered by technology, 16
    corporate commitment, 15-16
    cost vs. risk, 15
    security as religion, 14
  definition of, 7-8
  ease of, 12-13
  top five issues, 311-12
    authentication/authorization, 311
    management, 312
    resources, 311
    rollback/recovery/restart, 312
    transaction tuning, 312
Distributed Computing Environment (DCE), 52, 127, 255-64, 410
  concerns about, 264
  DCE cell, 257, 266
  definition of, 256-57
  directory service, 260-61
  distributed file system (DFS), 262-63
  remote procedure calls (RPCs), 259-60
  security concepts, 265-78
    authentication, 266-74
    authorization, 274-77
  security service, 261-62
  threads, 257-58
  timing service, 262
  weaknesses in, 278
  See also DCE authentication
Distributed databases, 279-93
  full client/server architecture, 281
  limited client/server architecture, 281
  relational data base management systems (RDBMS), 280-92
  server centric architecture, 281
  See also RDBMS
Distributed objects, 139-42

COM/OLE, 140-41
  object request broker (ORB), 140
  OMG CORBA, 139-40
  security considerations, 142
  SOM and OpenDoc, 141
Distributed systems vs. mainframe systems, 5-6
Domain name system (DNS), 107, 184, 222, 235, 260
Drawbridge (software), 194
Drawbridge software (Texas A&M University), 194
Dual homed host, 232-33
Durability, and availability, 53
Dynamic Host Configuration Program (DHCP), 205
Dynamic monitoring, 354-56

E

80/20 rule, 112
Electronic Data Interchange for Administration, Trade and Commerce (EDIFACT), 335
Electronic data interchange (EDI), 225, 253, 332, 335-36
Electronic mail (email), 330-38
  electronic data interchange (EDI), 335-36
  encryption of, 238
  Pretty Good Privacy (PGP), 336-37
  Privacy Enhanced Mail (PEM), 336
  security considerations, 337-38
  security requirements, 331
Electronic mail (email) standards, 332-35
  Common Mail Calls (CMC), 334
  Message Application Programming Interface (MAPI), 333-34
  Multipurpose Mail Extensions (MIME), 334-35
  Simple Mail Transport Protocol (SMTP), 334
  vendor-independent messaging (VIM), 333
  X.400 mail services, 332
  X.400 security, 332-33
  X.500 Directory services, 333
Electronic password generator, 35
email address, spoofing, 238
Embedded SQL (ESQL), 280
Encapsulating security payload (ESP) protocol, 228
Encina monitor, 308
Encryption, 36-37, 227, 240-51, 338, 399, 408-9, 420
  application, reasons for, 250
  of client-server communication, 273-74
  Clipper chip, 251
  and confidentiality, 52
  definition of, 36
  of electronic mail (email), 238
  evaluation consideration, 249
  export considerations, 249
  implementation, impact of, 250-51

key management, 248
minimum vs. recommended, 250
private key, 240, 241-44
public key, 240-41, 244-47
risks of implementation of, 250-51
strength of mechanism, 246
when to apply, 240
See also Cryptography; DES encryption; Private
key encryption; Public key encryption
Entry point vectoring, 259
EXECUTE access right, 213
EXECUTE (NOS access permission), 121
Extended MAPI, 333-34
Extended Privilege Attribute Certificates (EPACs),
267, 270-72
Extended registry, 272-73
Extended registry attribute (ERA) facility, 273
External network access, policy for, 81
External processing policy, 83

F

Farmer, Dan, 196, 198
FAX policy, 84
Federal Information Processing Standards, 241
Publication 190, 405
File Transfer Protocol (FTP), *See* FTP (File Transfer
Protocol)
Filtering router, 231
Financial Institution Key Management (Wholesale)
Standard, 248
Fingerprint, 35
Firewalls, 227, 230-38
architecture for, 234-36
attacks on, 236-37
components of, 230-31
application gateway, 234
bastion host, 232, 236
circuit relay, 233-34
dual homed host, 232-33
filtering router, 231, 236
proxy service, 233
screened subnet, 232
constructing, 237
growth of technology, 237
purchasing, 237
virtual private networks (VPNs), 236
"First date," 267
Footprints in the snow, 91-92, 159, 165, 172, 194,
197
Foreign cells, DCE authentication of, 272
Forum of Incident Response and Security Teams
(FIRST), 226
Foundation, security architecture, 48-50, 59-70
Commercially Oriented Functionality Class, 64

criteria/standards, 50
education, 50
guidelines, 70
Orange Book security criteria specifications, 64-
66
policies, 49
principles, 49-50, 60-62
security criteria, 64-70
security policy framework, 62-63
standards, 67-69
access control, 69
accreditation, 69
audit, 69
authentication, 69
confidentiality, 69
definitions, 68
Generally Accepted System Security
Principles (GSSP), 67
monitoring/detection, 68
nonrepudiation, 69
policies/procedures, 67-68
security management, 68
X/Open baseline security services (XBSS), 66-67
Frame Relay, 100
Frye Utilities for Netware, 122-23
FTP (File Transfer Protocol), 174, 222, 224
Anonymous FTP, 175-76
Trivial FTP (TFTP), 175
FULL OWNERSHIP access right, 213

G

Gaskell, Gary, 277
GemPlus smart card, 278
Generally Accepted System Security Principles
(GSSP), 67
Generic Security Service Application Programming
Interface (GSSAPI), 276, 324-25
Gittler, Frederic, 271
Global directory agent (GDA), 260
Global directory service (GDS), 260
Global positioning satellite (GPS) systems, 35
Global Positioning System (GPS), 405
Green Book, 67
Groups, RDBMS, 285
Groupware, 126
GUEST accounts, 158, 208, 218
GUEST privilege, NOS, 120
Guidelines for Computer Security Certification and
Accreditation, 69

H

Hewlett-Packard:
centralized authorization service, 327

Hewlett-Packard *(Cont.):*
   IT OpenView Operations, 353, 356
   OpenView Network Node Manager, 350
   Openview Systems Management, 200, 345
   password control, support for, 188
   Security Bulletins, 202
   System Adminstration Manager (SAM), 192
High Performance Routing (HPR), 100
HoneyDanBer (HDB), 177
Hopkins, Anne C., 271
Host equivalency, 171
HP Security Bulletins, 202
HTML, *See* Hypertext Markup Language (HTML)
HTTP, *See* Hypertext Transfer Protocol (HTTP)
Hubs, configuring for unauthorized access, 111
Hypertext Markup Language (HTML), 221, 342
Hypertext Transfer Protocol (HTTP), 221-22
   secure HTTP (S-HTTP), 228

I

IBM:
   LAN Server, 118, 127
   MQSeries, 139
   Open Blueprint, 96, 100-101
   Resource Access Control Facility (RACF), 101
   SystemView, 200
IDEA, *See* International Data Encryption Algorithm
   (IDEA)
Ideal computer system, 4
Identification, 34
   policy, 75
Illegal software, 21-22
Implementation, 329-42
   electronic mail (email), 330-38
   Lotus Notes, 338-41
Information integrity, policy, 76
Information systems, policies for use of, 78
Informix, 279, 281, 288, 291
Integrity checks, 37
   policy, 76
   and UNIX security, 194-96
Integrity protection mechanism, 51
Interactive Structured Query Language (ISQL), 280-
   81
International Data Encryption Algorithm (IDEA),
   337
International Standards Organization (ISO), 84, 241,
   280, 304, 409
Internet, 219-38
   acceptable use policy, 237-38
   advantages of, 222-23
   business use of, 223-25
   commerce on, 225
   corporate use of, 222-25

corporate information, 223
   corporation to corporation, 224-25
   corporation to new customers, 223-24
   customer support, 224
   internal company "Intranet," 225
   definition of, 220-21
   domain name system (DNS), 184, 222, 235, 260
   firewall, 230-38
   Internet PC, 229-30
   Java, 228-29
   Network Time Protocol (NTP), 184, 262
   and security, 28
   security problems with, 226
   security requirements, 226-27
   services of, 221-22
   standards/technology, 227-28
   See also Firewalls
Internet Control Message Protocol (ICMP), 104
Internet PC, 229-30
Internet Protocol (IP), 103, 180
Internet Protocol Security group (IPSEC), 113
Internet Request for Comment (RFC), 247, 336
InterNIC, 107
Intranet, 225
Intruder Alert, 199
IPng (IP Next Generation), 113
IPv6, 228
ISO/IEC 7498-2, 68
ISO/IEC 9594-8 (Directory Authentication
   Framework), 69
ISO/IEC 10164-7 (Security Alarm Reporting
   Function), 68
ISO/IEC 10164-8 (Security Audit Trail Function), 69
ISO/IEC 10181-2 (Authentication Framework), 69
ISO/IEC 10181-3 (Access Control), 69
ISO/IEC 10181-4 (Nonrepudiation Framework), 69
ISO/IEC 10181-5 (Confidentiality Framework), 69
IT OpenView Operations (Hewlett Packard), 353
ITU-T Recommendation X.800, 68

J

Java, 228-29
   applets, 229

K

Kane Security Analyst, 218, 390
Kerberos authentication model, 108, 134, 191, 261,
   265-66, 268, 291, 346, 349, 397
Kerberos V implementation, 276-77
Key certification, 350
Key management, 248
   and DES encryption, 244
Key replacement/update, 248

Key revocation/termination, 248
keytab, 273
Kim, Gene, 196
Klein, Daniel V., 161
Kotanchik, J., 276-77

L

LAN card, 107, 110, 164
LAN Manager (Microsoft), 118, 120, 122, 125
LAN Server (IBM), 118, 127
LEAF Escrowed Encryption Standard (EES), 251
LEAF (Law Enforcement Access Field), 251
Leakage, and TCP/IP, 108
Link-level address, 107
Linn, J., 276
Local security authority (LSA), 211-12
Location-based authentication, 405
Loopback address, 111
Lotus Notes, 338-41, 397-98
    definition of, 338
    email facilities, 341
    security, 339-40
    user authentication, 340-41
LT Auditor, 390
Luan, Shyh-Wei, 277

M

Machine TGT, 268
Magic Cookie (MIT), 168
Management Information Base (MIB), 352
Management responsibilities, policies for, 78-79
Management tools, 27, 54, 55-56
Marshalling, 259
MD5 checksum, 196
Measurement facilities, 54, 56
Menu Works (PC Dynamics, Inc.), 123
Message digest, 252
Message integrity check (MIC) message, 336
Message queue interface (MQI), 139
Message queue manager (MQM), 139
Message transfer agents (MTA), 332
Message transfer system (MTS), 332
Messaging Application Programming Interface
    (MAPI), 333-34
    extended MAPI, 333-34
    simple MAPI, 333
Middleware, 134-43
    definition of, 134
    enabling technology, 137-39
        Application Program-to-Program
            Communication (APPC), 102, 133, 137-38
        IBM MQSeries, 139
        remote procedure call, 138

sockets, 138-39
models, 136-37
need for, 135
services, 135-36
    application programming interface (API), 136
    directory, 135
    management, 136
    security, 135
    time, 136
things to watch out for, 142-43
MIME, *See* Multipurpose Mail Extensions (MIME)
MIME Object Security Services (MOSS), 335
MIT Magic Cookie, 168
Mitnick, Kevin ("Condor"), 226
Monitoring/detection, 54, 56
    standards, 68
Morris, Robert T., 20
MQSeries (IBM), 139
Multipurpose Mail Extensions (MIME), 334-35

N

National Communication Security Construction
    5100A, 68
National Institute of Standards and Technology, 253
Net/Assure (Centel Federal System, Inc.), 123
NetSqueeze+Encryption NLM (LAN Support
    Group), 121
Netware Loadable Modules, 121
Netware (Novell), 110, 117, 119, 124-25
    advanced features for enterprise computing, 124
    authentication scheme, 119
    Frye Utilities for, 122-23
    LOGIN authentication, 110
Network access, 54, 55
Network accessible unit (NAU), 98-99
Network connections, 26-27
Network File System (NFS), 84, 103, 109, 170, 178-80
    questions surrounding use of, 178-79
Network Information Service (NIS), 107, 138, 180-84
    local lookup service, 182
    maps, 181, 183
    master server, 181, 183
    netgroups, 182-83
    slave servers, 181, 183
    standard services, 182
Networking:
    Systems Network Architecture (SNA):
        Advanced Peer-to-Peer Networking (APPN),
            100, 102
        network accessible unit (NAU), 98-99
        network control program (NCP), 98
        nodes, 97
        and Open Blueprint (IBM), 100-101
        security, 101-2

Networking *(Cont.)*:
    sessions, 96
    Synchronous Data Link Control (SDLC) pro-
        tocol, 97
    TCP/IP, 102-14
        Address Resolution Protocol (ARP), 103
        basic structure of, 104-5
        counterfeit addressing, 109
        definition of, 102-3
        denial of service attacks, 110
        diagnostic attacks, 110-11
        future developments, 113
        how TCP/IP works, 105-8
        increasing security, 111-13
        Internet Protocol (IP), 103
        and leakage, 108
        and packet monitoring, 108
        routing attacks, 110
        sequencing attacks, 109-10
        SNA vs. TCP/IP security, 114
        Transport Control Protocol (TCP), 103
        User Datagram Protocol (UDP), 103
Network management, 350-59
    accessing the network, 351-52
    Andromeda, 356-58
    dynamic monitoring, 354-56
    filtering traffic, 351
    network event management, 353-54
    security advisories, 358
    segregating the network, 351
    Simple Network Management Protocol (SNMP),
        352
    Tiger Teams, 358-59
Network operating systems (NOS), 117-27
    access permissions, 121
    audit trails, 122
    authentication, 118-20
    authorization controls, 120-21
    implementation issues, 123-27
        consistency of administration, 124-25
        future developments, 127
        guest accounts, 125
        LOGIN scripts, 124
        password attacks, 124
        physical access, 123
        Trojan horses, 123
        virus protection, 125-26
        workgroup computing, 126
    privileges, 120
    security solutions, 122-23
Network packets, 266
Network policies, 81-82
    external network access, 81
    privacy of communication, 82
    remote network access, 81

Networks, 93-115
    Systems Network Architecture (SNA), 96-102
    trusted, 94-96
Network Time Protocol (NTP), 184, 262
NIC, 107
Nonrepudiation, 37-38, 53
    definition of, 37
    standards, 69
Nonrepudiationa, 227
Norton Utilities, 123
NT File System (NTFS), 214-16

O

Object Management Group (OMG), 139-40, 224
Object request broker (ORB), 140, 325
Object Transaction Service (OTS), 310
OLTP, 295-313
    database vs., 302-4
    distributed data access models, 298-99
    distributed database vs., 303
    distributed logical unit of work (LUW), 297-98
    distributed OLTP, 304-6
        OSI transaction processing standards, 304
        X/OPEN distributed transaction processing,
            304-6
    TP monitor, 299-311
        CICS, 308-9
        Encina monitor, 308
        organization, 305-7
        requirements, 301-2
        Top End, 309-10
        Tuxedo monitor, 309
    transaction processing (TP) systems:
        application design, 310
        components of, 299-311
        object-oriented transactions, 310-11
    transactions, defined, 296-97
    trust considerations of, 301-2
OmniGuard, 199, 390
Omni-Guard ESM, 200
One-time passwords, 217, 401-2, 409
On-line transaction processing (OLTP), *See* OLTP
Open Blueprint (IBM), 96, 100-101
OpenDoc, 141
Open Software Foundation (OSF), 127, 256
Open System Interconnect (OSI), 84, 247
Openview Systems Management (Hewlett-Packard),
    200
Operating system access, RDBMS, 282-83
OPERATOR privilege, NOS, 120
Oracle, 279, 281, 291
    and SQL*NET, 281
    user authentication, 282
Orange Book, 64-66, 67, 190-91, 217

ORB, *See* Object request broker (ORB)
Origin, repudiation of, 53
OSF/DCE authentication, compared to international travel controls, 272
OSF/DCE environment, 256-57, 271, 287
OSI-CCR, 304
OSI-TP, 304

P

Packet filtering, 231
Packet monitoring, and TCP/IP, 108
Password Authentication Protocol (PAP), PPP, 216
Password Management Guide (Green Book), 67
Passwords, 27, 35, 39, 255, 287, 348, 384, 401
   aging, 119-20
   characteristics/motives, 189
   issues/solutions, 192
   one-time, 401-2
   password cracking, 190-91
   password-cracking tools, 161
   password guessing, 159, 190-91
   policy, 75-76
   in user work areas, 348
Password theft, 21
Pato, Joe, 268, 271, 272-73
PC-DACS (Mergent International, Inc.), 123
PCMCIA Personal Computer Memory Card Interface Association) cards, 242, 410
Performance, 54
   and trust, 42
Personal computer security, 413-17
   access controls, 415-16
      data security, 416
      laptops, 415-16
   need for, 416-17
   viruses, 414-15
Personal use policies, 78
Physical access, 28, 54, 55
Physical security policy, 84
PIN (personal identification number), 243, 296, 404, 407-8
Point-to-Point Protocol (PPP), 216
Policies, standards, 67-68
Policy statement, 74
Port numbers, 170
PowerBrokers, 192
Pretty Good Privacy (PGP), 336-37
Privacy of communication policy, 82
Privacy Enhanced Mail (PEM), 336, 337-38
Privacy policies, 78
Private key encryption, 240, 241-44, 338
   automated teller machines (ATMs), 243
   computer power required for, 244
   DES encryption, 241-42

storage and use of, 244
   See also Encryption; Public key encryption
Privileged group, UNIX, 157
Privilege Ticket Granting Ticker (PTGT), 271
Procedures, standards, 67-68
Proxy service, 233
PUBLIC group, RDBMS, 285
Public key encryption, 240-41, 244-47
   certification authority, 247
   encryption algorithms, 246
   key management, 246
   RSA public key, 244-46
   See also Encryption; Private key encryption
PURPLE project, 240

R

Rapid application development (RAD), 319
Rapid Transport Protocol (RTP), 100
RARP, 103
RDBMS, 280-92
   add-on solutions, 290-91
   audit mechanisms, 288-89
   authorization controls, 283-85
   batch SQL statements, 285
   data consolidation, 292
   groups, 285
   issues surrounding, 289-92
   operating system access, 282-83
   remote procedure calls (RPCs), 287-88
   roles, 285
   segregation of duties, 285
   stored procedures, 286-87
   system-level privileges, 283-84
   table access privileges, 284-85
   transport security, 291-92
   triggers, 287
   user authentication, 282
   user profiles, 283
READ access right, 213
READ (NOS access permission), 121
Records management, policies for, 79
Recovery, and availability, 53
Red Book, 64, 67
Registry service, 267
Remote access, 25-26, 419-21
   centralized solutions to, 419-20
   encryption, 420
   remote troubleshooting support, 420-21
Remote Execution Facility (REX), 173
Remote network access, policy for, 81
Remote procedure calls (RPCs), 171, 185, 281
   RDBMS, 287-88
Replication, 263
Repudiation of delivery, 53

Repudiation of origin, 53
Resource Access Control Facility (RACF) (IBM), 101
Resource manager, and TP monitor, 307
Retina scan, 35
REX, *See* Remote Execution Facility (REX)
RFC 1351/1352/1353, 68
Risk assessment, 79-80, 322, 387
Role-/rule-based security, 362-63
Roles, RDBMS, 285
Rollback, 288
Routers, 351
Routing attacks, TCP/IP, 110
RSA Data Security Inc., 196, 291
RSA public key, 244-46
    and digital signature for document authentication, 245
    size of, 245
Rule-based authorizations, 276

S

SATAN (Security Administrators Tool for Auditing Networking) utility, 196, 388
Science Applications International Corporation (SAIC), 356
Screened subnet, 232
Screen scraping, 349
Scripting, 349
Secure applications, 317-28
    concepts of, 318
    system development life cycle (SDLC), 318-27
    trusted computing base (TCB), 318
Secure electronic transaction (SET) protocol, 228
Secure HTTP (S-HTTP), 228
SecureID, 217
Secure IP (IPv6), 228
Secure Network Services (SNS), 291
Secure sockets layer (SSL), 228
Security, 51-53
    access control, 52
    audit/audit trails, 38
    authentication, 35, 52-53
    authorization, 36
    balance in, 27
    basics of, 33-44
    centralization of, 344
    challenges of, 19-29
    computing, growth of, 22
    confidentiality, 36-37, 52
    data classification, 24
    definition of, 34
    detection problems, 25
    and diverse technologies, 28
    educating the organization, 29
    failing to plan for, 29
    goal of, 46
    identification, 34
    and inappropriate policies/procedures, 28-29
    integrity, 37
    integrity protection mechanism, 51
    and the Internet, 28
    and management tools, 27
    network connections, 26-27
    nonrepudiation, 37-38, 53
    and physical access, 28
    policies, 71-89
    problem recognition, 22-23
    process, 39
    and quality, 10
    remote access, 25-26
    retrofitting, 327
    risk analysis, 23-24
    single sign-on, 24
    source of, 26
    standards, 10, 68
    stories, 20-22
    top ten list, 27-29
    and weak authentication, 27
    and weakest point on the network, 28
Security Account Manager (SAM), and user accounts, 208, 212
Security administration, 79
Security architecture, 46-47
    building blocks, 47-48
    control, 54-57
        audit, 55, 56-57
        change management, 55, 56
        management, 54, 55-56
        measurement, 54, 56
        monitoring/detection, 54, 56
        network access, 54, 55
        physical access, 54, 55
    foundation, 48-50
        criteria/standards, 50
        education, 50
        policies, 49
        principles, 49-50
    model (illustration), 47-48
    need for, 47
    trust, 50-54
        availability, 53-54
        security, 51-53
SecurityAudit/UX, 390
Security domains, 318
Security management, 343-60
    access control, 348
    key certification, 350
    network management, 350-59
    product functions, 346

single sign-on, 348-50
standards, 68
system management, 345-50
See also Network management; *specific functions*
Security management policies:
  compliance monitoring, 80
  deviation to policy, 80
  management responsibilities, 78-79
  records management, 79
  risk assessment, 79-80
  security administration, 79
  segregated of duties, 79
Security for Open Systems (SeOS), Memeo
  Software Inc., 192-93
Security for Open Systems (SeOS), 192-93
Security policies, 71-89
  application development, 83
  authentication, 75
  authorization, 75
  basics of, 74
  compliance with policy, 74
  construction of, 73-74
  creation process, 86-88
    awareness and education program, 87-88
    policy process implementation, 88
    responsibilities, 86-87
    security policy manual, 87
  data policies, 76-78
    classification, 76
    data custodian, 77
    data guardian, 77
    integrity of data, 77
  example of, 84-86
  external processing, 83
  FAX, 84
  framework for, 73-84
  identification, 75
  information integrity, 76
  need for, 72-73
  network policies, 81-82
    external network access, 81
    privacy of communication, 82
    remote network access, 81
  passwords, 75-76
  penalties/consequences of noncompliance, 74
  personal use policies, 78
  physical security, 84
  policy statement, 74
  purpose of, 74
  scope of, 74
  security management policies, 78-80
    compliance monitoring, 80
    deviation to policy, 80
    management responsibilities, 78-79
    records management, 79

    risk assessment, 79-80
    security administration, 79
    segregated of duties, 79
  software policies, 82-83
    copyright, 82-83
    virus protection, 83
  standards, use of, 84
  systems policies, 80-81
    administration, 80
    business continuity, 81
    classification, 80-81
  user policies, 82
  voicemail, 84
Security policy manual, 87
Security reference monitor (SRM), 212
Security strategy development, 361-74
  alternatives, 372
  architecture, 371
  costs, 372-73
  current assessment, 366-70
  methodology, 364-66
  recommendations, 371-72
  recommended solutions, 373
  requirements analysis, 370-71
  risks/impacts, 373-74
  scope/assumptions, 370
  security strategy, defined, 362-64
  tactical plan, 374
Security token, 35
Segregated of duties, 79
Segregation of duties, RDBMS, 285
Sendmail program, UNIX, 176
Sequencing attacks, TCP/IP, 109-10
Serial Line Internet Protocol (SLIP), 216
Set user ID (SUID) programs, 163-64, 180, 198
Shimomura, Tsutomu, 226
Simple Mail Transport Protocol (SMTP), 334,
  336
Simple MAPI, 333
Simple Network Management Protocol (SNMP),
  104, 352
Single sign-on, 277, 348-50, 409
Sir George Williams University (Montreal), comput-
  er complex attack, 20
Skipjack, 251
Smart cards, 277, 407-11
  definition of, 407
  issues concerning, 410-11
  multiple (personal) storage card, 407-8
  PCMCIA cards, 410
  standards for, 409-10
  storage card, 407
  types of, 407-8
  uses of, 408-9
SNAP, 103

SNMP, *See* Simple Network Management Protocol
   (SNMP)
SOCKS (circuit relay services), 233
Software policies, 82-83
   copyright, 82-83
   virus protection, 83
Spafford, Eugene H., 196, 198
Spoofing, 158-59, 227
SQL*NET, 281
SQL access group (SAG), 280
Stoll, Clifford, 20, 397
Stored procedures, RDBMS, 286-87
Strong authentication, 401-5
   advanced standards, 405
   biometric-based authentication, 404
   location-based authentication, 405
   one-time passwords, 401-2
   token-based authentication, 402-4
Structured Query Language (SQL), 280
Sun Microsystems, Inc., 228, 287
SUPERVISOR privilege, NOS, 120, 122
Sybase, 279, 281, 287
   user authentication, 282
Synchronous Data Link Control (SDLC) protocol,
   97
System Administration Manager (SAM), 192
System components, 130-31
System development life cycle (SDLC), 318-27
   accreditation, 324
   application development/testing, 322
   design/analysis, 320-22
   GSSAPI, 324-25
   implementation, 322-23
   maintenance, 323
   objects, 325-26
   requirements phase, 320
   retrofitting security, 327
   role-/rule-based security, 362-63
System-level privileges, RDBMS, 283-84
System management, 345-50
System Object Model (SOM), 141
Systems Network Architecture (SNA), 96-102, 114
   Advanced Peer-to-Peer Networking (APPN),
      100, 102
   application program-to-program communication, 99
   network accessible unit (NAU), 98-99
   network control program (NCP), 98
   nodes, 97-98
   and Open Blueprint (IBM), 100-101
   security, 101-2
   sessions, 96
   Synchronous Data Link Control (SDLC) proto-
      col, 97
Systems policies, 80-81
   administration, 80

business continuity, 81
classification, 80-81
SystemView, 200

T

Table access privileges, RDBMS, 284-85
TAKE OWNERSHIP access right, 213
TAMU Tiger security toolset, 199
TCP/IP, 102-14, 220-21, 227, 388
   Address Resolution Protocol (ARP), 103
   basic structure of, 104-5
   counterfeit addressing, 109
   definition of, 102-3
   denial of service attacks, 110
   diagnostic attacks, 110-11
   future developments, 113
   how TCP/IP works, 105-8
   increasing security, 111-13
   Internet Control Message Protocol (ICMP), 104
   Internet Protocol (IP), 103
   leakage, 108
   and leakage, 108
   packet monitoring, 108
   routing attacks, 110
   sequencing attacks, 109-10
   Simple Network Management Protocol (SNMP),
      104
   SNA vs. TCP/IP security, 114
   Transport Control Protocol (TCP), 103
   User Datagram Protocol (UDP), 103
Technology envy, 13-14
Telnet services, 174
Tempest standard, 68
Theft of information, 21
Third-factor authentication, 35, 404
Third-party preauthentication, 268
Thumbprint, 35
Ticket Granting Ticket (TGT), 267, 270
Tiger Teams, 358-59
Tivoli Management Environment, 200
Tivoli Systems, Inc., 345
Token-based authentication, 402-4
Top End, 309-10
Transaction logging, 288
Transaction services, and TP monitor, 307
Transmission Control Protocol/Internet Protocol
   (TCP/IP), *See* TCP/IP
Transport Control Protocol (TCP), 103
Transport security, RDBMS, 291-92
Triggers, RDBMS, 287
Triple-DES, 242
Tripwire (software), 196
Trivial FTP (TFTP), 175
Trojan horses, 123, 194, 211

in Windows NT, 218
Trust, 40-43, 50-54
 and availability, 41-42
 availability, 53-54
 boundaries of, 42-43
 definition of, 40
 need for, 43
 and performance, 42
 security, 51-53
Trusted Computer System Evaluation Criteria (U.S.
 Department of Defense), 50
 Orange Book, 64-66
Trusted computing base (TCB), 194, 318
Trusted Network Interpretation (TNI) Red Book, 64,
 67
Tuxedo monitor, 309
Two-factor authentication, 277

U

United Nations/Technical Document Interchange,
 335
Universal unique identifier (UUID), 259-60
UNIX, 145-46, 346, 356, 388
 audit, sample criteria for, 382-83
 audit trails, 201
UNIX network services, 169-84
 Anonymous FTP, 175-76
 Berkeley Services, 171-72
 domain name system (DNS), 184
 FTP (File Transfer Protocol), 174
 informational services, 177
 intruder's toolset, 184-86
 network file system (NFS), 177-80
 network information service (NIS), 180-84
 Network Time Protocol (NTP), 184
 Remote Execution Facility (REX), 173
 remote procedure calls (RPCs), 171
 sendmail program, 176
 standard services, how they work, 170
 telnet services, 174
 trivial FTP (TFTP), 175
 UUCP (UNIX-to-UNIX Copy) services, 177
UNIX security, 145-204
 access control lists, 155-56
  problems with, 156
  superuser access, 156-57
 access controls, 153-54
 authentication, 149-51
  weaknesses in, 152-53
 authorization, limitations in, 154-55
 back door key, 148
 control monitors, 197-202
  audit trail, 200-201
  commercial access control solutions, 199-200

commercial control monitors, 199
contributed control monitors, 198-99
dynamic alerts, 201
security alerts, 201-2
system management, 200
vendor-supplied products, 199
delegation of authority, 157
effective user ID (EUID), 157
flaws in, 146-47
group controls, 151-52
history of, 147
illicit bootup, 148-49
intruder's toolset, 184-86
network services, 169-84
 See also UNIX network services
physical security, 148-49
privileged group, 157
single-user mode, 148
solutions, 187-204
 access control, 193-94
 authentication, 189-90
 C2 security, 190-91
 delegation of authority, 192-93
 integrity checks, 194-96
 network analysis of vulnerabilities, 196
 network design, 189
 password cracking, 159-61, 191-92
 physical controls, 188
 policy/guidelines, 188
typical abuses, 158-65
 backups, 165
 delegation of authority through set user ID
  program, 163-64
 device file security, 164
 guest accounts, 158
 HOME environments, 161-62
 password cracking, 159-61
 password guessing, 159
 spoofs, 158-59
 startup files, 163
 trojan horses in system directories/files, 162-
  63
 UNIX schedulers, 165
user's HOME environment, 151
X-Windows, 168-69
Unmarshalling, 259
U.S. Digital Signature Standard (DSS), 245
User authentication:
 Lotus Notes, 340-41
 RDBMS, 282
User Datagram Protocol (UDP), 103
User ID, 39, 75
User policies, 82
USER privilege, NOS, 120
User profiles, RDBMS, 283

U.S. National Institute of Standards and Technology (NIST), 405
U.S. National Science Foundation (NSF), 220
UUCP (UNIX-to-UNIX Copy Protocol) services, 169, 177

V

Vendor Independent Calendaring (VIC), 342
Vendor-independent messaging (VIM), 333-34
Venema, Weitse, 196
Vines (Banyan), 117, 118
Virtual private networks (VPNs), 236
Virtual Telecommunications Access Method (VTAM), 97
Viruses, 23, 83, 125-26, 414-15
Virus protection policy, 83
Voicemail:
    password guessing, 159
    policy, 84
Voice print, 35

W

Warner, Michael, 277
Weak authentication, 27
Weak DES, 246
Weisz, Robert, 277
Wietze Venema, 194
Windows NT security, 108, 199, 205-18, 398
    administrator account, 209
    domains, 206-8
    features of, 205
    groups, 209-10

networking, 216-18
    auditing/alerts, 217-18
    remote access, 216-17
    TCP/IP services, 216-18
and password guessing, 218
password guessing, 159
privileges, 208-9
security controls, 210-16
    access control lists (ACLs), 215-16
    NT File System (NTFS), 214-16
    user profiles/logon scripts, 212-13
security descriptors, 210
and Trojan horse attacks, 218
user accounts, 208
World Wide Web (WWW), 221-26, 325
    availability for providing information, 222
    See also Internet
WRITE access right, 213
WRITE (NOS access permission), 121

X

X.400 mail services, 332
X.400 security, 332-33
X.400 standard, 330-31
X.500 Directory services, 333
X-OPEN, definition of information technology security, 34
X/Open baseline security services (XBSS), 66-67
X-Windows, 111, 168-69, 189

Z

Zimmerman, Phil, 336
Zimmerman telegram, 240